UNIVERSITY OF CAMBRIDGE
DEPARTMENT OF APPLIED ECONOMICS

MONOGRAPHS

10

THE ECONOMICS OF CAPITAL UTILISATION

UNIVERSITY OF CAMBRIDGE
DEPARTMENT OF APPLIED ECONOMICS

MONOGRAPHS

This series consists of investigations conducted by members of the Department's staff and others working in direct collaboration with the Department.

The Department of Applied Economics assumes no responsibility for the views expressed in the Monographs published under its auspices.

1. The Measurement of Production Movements
By C. F. CARTER, W. B. REDDAWAY *and* RICHARD STONE

2. Social Accounts and the Business Enterprise Sector of the National Economy
By F. SEWELL BRAY

3. The Role of Measurement in Economics
By RICHARD STONE

4. The Analysis of Family Budgets
By S. J. PRAIS *and* H. S. HOUTHAKKER

5. The Lognormal Distribution
By J. AITCHISON *and* J. A. C. BROWN

6. Productivity and Technical Change
By W. E. G. SALTER

7. The Ownership of Major Consumer Durables
By J. S. CRAMER

8. British Economic Growth, 1688–1959
By PHYLLIS DEANE *and* W. A. COLE

9. Experiments with Input–Output Models
By A. GHOSH

10. The Economics of Capital Utilisation
By R. MARRIS

THE ECONOMICS OF CAPITAL UTILISATION

A Report on Multiple-shift Work

BY

ROBIN MARRIS

ASSISTED BY

IAN MACLEAN AND SIMON BERNAU

CAMBRIDGE

AT THE UNIVERSITY PRESS

1964

PUBLISHED BY
THE SYNDICS OF THE CAMBRIDGE UNIVERSITY PRESS

Bentley House, 200 Euston Road, London, N.W. 1
American Branch: 32 East 57th Street, New York 22, N.Y.
West African Office: P.O. Box 33, Ibadan, Nigeria

Printed in Great Britain at the University Printing House, Cambridge
(Brooke Crutchley, University Printer)

TO JANE

CONTENTS

PART I. THEORY

CHAPTER 1. CAPITAL UTILISATION AND ECONOMIC GROWTH

CHAPTER 2. OPTIMUM UTILISATION IN A SINGLE PROCESS

Chapter 3. Many Processes

Chapter 4. The Effect of Output Restraints

PART II. TESTS AND APPLICATIONS

Chapter 5. Summary of the Theory and its Predictions

Chapter 6. Survey of Empirical Material

Chapter 10. Implications for Policy

Statistical Appendix to Part II

LIST OF TEXT TABLES

LIST OF FIGURES

INTRODUCTION AND ACKNOWLEDGEMENTS

This study was undertaken by the Cambridge University Industrial Research Group with the aid of a grant made available by the Ministry of Labour under the Conditional Aid Scheme for the use of Counterpart Funds derived from United States Economic Aid. The agreement covering the project was signed late in 1954, with the intention that the work should be completed in three years. The main author is entirely to blame for the subsequent delay, which was due to his experiencing unusual difficulty in crystallising his interpretation of the material collected.

The project was directed throughout by Mr Marris. The work was divided as follows. Mr MacLean, who was employed full time from 1955 to 1958, conducted the majority of the industrial interviews and arranged for the inquiries described in Chapter 8. He also contributed ideas, administration and assistance in analysis of statistics. Although the theoretical approach now followed is considerably different from that of the rather incomplete model lying behind the initial investigations, it has been found that Mr MacLean, in conducting the industrial interviews, intuitively anticipated many of the points which subsequently gained importance; his notes were a particularly fruitful source of inductions. He also provided drafts of one or two sections of the report, but the final result (including industrial case studies and statistical and theoretical analyses) is entirely the work of the main author, and Mr MacLean cannot, therefore, be held responsible for any mistakes. Mr Bernau's association with the project was short but significant. A graduate student of mathematics, he was employed in the summer of 1960 to assist in computation. It soon became obvious, however, that he could make an important theoretical contribution as well. Much of the theory which is now expounded in Chapters 2–4 had been developed by non-rigorous or only quasi-mathematical types of argument. Mr Bernau was able not only to find rigorous proofs of all the important theorems but also to suggest extensions. In effect, after being given the definitions and assumptions of the problem he succeeded in consolidating the theory and thus enabled us to argue with greater confidence. This is much to his credit, considering that he had had no previous training in economics. The project is thus deeply indebted to both its assistants.†

The economic advantages of multiple-shift work have long been regarded as self evident. So much so, in fact, that attention has largely been concentrated on the social consequences—on, in effect, the social disadvantages—considered especially from the point of view of

† Mr Bernau is the author of the Appendix to Part I, and is responsible for any mistakes therein. He is not responsible for mistakes made in the use of his work elsewhere.

employees and personnel managers.† It has tacitly been assumed that in the absence of social resistances, only ignorance or inertia would permit management to fail to exploit an otherwise costless reduction in the quantity of capital required to support a given annual rate of output; and it has been assumed that in the absence of social 'disutility', high rates of capital utilisation achieved through shift-work must be unambiguously beneficial. The present study is not so much aimed at questioning these earlier premises, although they are considered in passing, as at considering the problem more generally and more analytically. Is it true, for example, that in a mature, fully employed industrial economy, an increase in the average intensity of capital utilisation will necessarily accelerate growth or raise the standard of living at a given point in time? Is it true that 'resistance' from employees—taking the form of prohibitions or demands for financial compensation—is the main deterrent to management's use of shift-systems? Is it true that changes in technical conditions in one process may influence the relative profitability of shift-work in another? Can intensive capital utilisation be discouraged by small markets?

In order to undertake an investigation of this kind it is necessary first to construct a theory, then to test the theory against such facts as are available or as can be collected. Scientific theories, however, are not woven from air, they arise from existing empirical 'clues'—the bases of induction. Therefore programmes of theoretical and empirical investigation must, ideally, proceed together: by induction one builds a theory; one collects facts designed to test this theory; one modifies or reconstructs the theory; one devises a revised testing programme; and so on. Rarely do the data first collected prove suitable for testing the final formulation. Unfortunately, for reasons which are fairly well known (they are discussed in relation to the present project in Chapter 6), the conditions characteristically surrounding empirical research in social science badly hinder the proper procedure. These factors were, in fact, a contributory cause of the delay referred to above. However, the main author is now confident that for all the defects it may contain, the account of the problem which follows is reasonably correct, and the theory sound. Had this report been completed earlier, on the basis of our then state of knowledge and understanding, the results would at best have represented half-truths.

The plan of the work is based on the objectives. In Part I we investigate the theoretical ramifications of the whole problem; first, in Chapter 1, from the point of view of the economic system as a whole and then, in Chapters 2–4, from the point of view of business management. Although much of the reasoning throughout this Part has necessarily a strong *a priori* flavour, most of the basic ideas were in fact suggested by

† See, for example, the report of a companion inquiry, 'Some Effects of Shift Work on Social and Domestic Life', by Hilda G. Brown, *Yorkshire Bulletin*, Occasional Paper, no. 2, published by the Departments of Economics of the Universities of Hull, Leeds and Sheffield (for information apply to the Secretary, Department of Economics, The University, Hull, England), March 1959.

statistical results, industrial interviews or other similar material. In Chapter 2 we begin by considering management motives and then apply a specific motivational assumption to a highly simplified problem in which a single commodity is produced at a fixed price for an unlimited market in a single manufacturing establishment. In Chapter 3 we complicate things by taking account of the fact that real commodities are produced by numerous interlocking processes. In Chapter 4 we take account of market limitations, and other restraints on the output of the individual plant, and consider also the effect of demand fluctuations. Finally, Mr Bernau's proofs are presented in a mathematical appendix. *At the end of Chapter 4 there is a glossary of definitions of the various analytical concepts developed in Part I and a recapitulation of the main conclusions of Chapters 2–4.*

Part II summarises the theoretical conclusions of Part I, assesses its 'predictions', surveys the empirical material, describes the results of the 1951 Census of Production (when a special question was asked about shift-work), analyses their implications in relation to the predictions and discusses the Ministry of Labour survey of 1954. Part II also analyses the results of special inquiries addressed to Employment Exchanges, Bus Companies and Trade Unions, as well as presenting a selection of industrial case studies. The Appendix to Part II contains the main statistical tables, essentially the results of special tabulations of the Census of Production. Economic policy conclusions are discussed in Chapter 10.

We owe acknowledgements to many persons and organisations who helped us with time, labour and ideas: a list of names is given at the end of this Introduction, and apology is due to any who may accidentally have been omitted. Among organisations, we must especially mention the Census-of-Production-Office of the Board of Trade for their major work of tabulation, the head office of the Ministry of Labour for both moral support and financial and administrative sponsorship, as well as the officers of the Ministries of Transport and of Labour for their work in connection with the inquiries described in Chapter 8.

Professional acknowledgements are due to a group of economists in Cambridge who from time to time criticised theoretical trials, in particular to Mr R. C. O. Matthews for a pregnant remark which generated much of Chapter 1, and to Mr Aubrey Silberston† for authoritative advice on the treatment of economies of scale. The theoretical apparatus employed in Part I is manifestly derived from methods widely employed by contemporary analysts of problems of growth and capital formation. Since no one 'model' has been used, but rather the recipes of several have been adapted for the purposes of our particular problem, confusion, rather than clarification, would be caused by attempting to indicate the detailed origins of the various flavours. One point, however, must be made. The author has been a student in, or a member of, the

† Mr Silberston is the author of another Industrial Research Group report, *The British Motor Industry* (London, 1958).

Faculty of Economics at Cambridge almost continuously since the age of seventeen. It would be arrogant to claim that any merits of the work must be attributed to the Cambridge background. What can be said is that local colleagues and traditions have had a great influence on both the theoretical and statistical methods adopted. In particular we should note the influence of Mrs Joan Robinson, whose work has sometimes been criticised (by the author, among others) for lack of sufficient empirical content. As this research progressed, however, the value of the analytical conceptions developed in Mrs Robinson's recent economic thinking became increasingly appreciated, and their empirical applicability increasingly apparent.

Finally it should be noted that the Industrial Research Group operated largely within the infra-structure in the Cambridge University Department of Applied Economics and that the assistance rendered by the typists, chartists and computors, by the administrative secretary, Mr Robert Davies, by the Deputy Director, Mr John Utting, and by the Director, Mr W. B. Reddaway, was all invaluable. Very special thanks are due to the Director in particular; he read the whole of Part I of the manuscript, made a large number of valuable suggestions and discovered a substantial number of errors. He is not, however, responsible for any errors which may remain.

The full-time research staff of the Department have developed an organisation ideally suited to the testing of hypotheses. Not only have they been among the pioneers in the use of computers for statistical analysis, but they have developed a stock of intellectual capital which is always readily available, and freely offered, for application to the many kinds of economic problems which may arise in this type of research. It may be said without qualification that the Department's support was vital to us.

Mrs Barbara Young not only most efficiently and speedily typed the whole original manuscript but also prepared the final draft for the printer. Mrs Patricia Hutchinson and Miss Marion Clarke provided invaluable assistance with the proofs, and the latter were also read by Mr A. K. Bagchi who corrected a number of significant errors.

R. M.

DEPARTMENT OF APPLIED ECONOMICS
CAMBRIDGE

March 1963

LIST OF PARTICIPATING ORGANISATIONS

Government Departments

The Ministry of Labour; the Board of Trade; the Ministry of Transport.

Firms and Trade Associations

A.E.C., Ltd.; the Agricultural Engineers' Association; Alston's (Long Melford), Ltd.; the Association of British Manufacturers of Printers' Machinery; the Association of Chemical and Allied Employers; Baker Perkins, Ltd.; the Ball and Roller Bearing Manufacturers' Association; the Birmingham Railway Carriage and Wagon Co.; the Brewers' Society; the British Bata Shoe Co., Ltd.; the British Brush Co., Ltd.; the British Brush Manufacturers' Association; the British Electrical and Allied Manufacturers' Association; the British Federation of Master Printers; the British Man-Made Fibres Federation; the British Paper Bag Federation; the British Plastics Federation; the British Pottery Manufacturers' Federation; the British Radio Equipment Manufacturers' Association; the British Shoe Manufacturers' Association: British Timken, Ltd.; the British Transport Vehicle Manufacturing Association; the Cable Makers Association; Cadbury Bros., Ltd.; Caird (Dundee), Ltd.; the Carpet Manufacturing Co., Ltd.; Century Glass Works; the Cocoa, Chocolate and Confectionery Alliance; Constructors, Ltd.; the Council of Ironfoundry Associations; Dartmouth Autocastings, Ltd.; the Distillers Co., Ltd.; Eastwoods, Ltd.; the Electric Lamp Manufacturers' Association; the Employers' Federation of Papermakers and Boardmakers; the Engineering and Allied Employers' National Federation; the Esso Petroleum Co., Ltd.; the Farmers' Manure Co.; the Federation of British Carpet Manufacturers; the Federation of British Rubber Manufacturers' Association; the Federation of House Timbers Association; the Federation of Manufacturers of Contracts Plant; the Federation of Master Cotton Spinners' Association; the Fertiliser Manufacturers' Association; Fine Spinners and Doublers, Ltd.; the Firestone Tyre and Rubber Co., Ltd.; Fisher and Ludlow, Ltd.; Fisons Ltd.; Fison's Milk Products, Ltd.; the Food Machinery Associated and British Chemical Plant Manufacturers' Association; the Food Manufacturers' Federation; the General Electric Co., Ltd.; Glass Bulbs, Ltd.; the Glass Manufacturers' Association; Guest, Keen and Nettlefolds, Ltd.; Harland and Wolff's Shipyard; Hayeshaw Ltd.; Howley Paper Works; Hunt Partners, Ltd.; the Imperial Chemical Industries, Ltd.; the Incorporated National Associations of British and Irish Millers; The Institute of British Launderers, Ltd.; James Mackie, Ltd.; Jos. Powell and Sons (Whitefriars), Ltd.; Laporte Chemicals, Ltd.; Laurence Scott and Electromotors, Ltd.; Lebus (Harris), Ltd.; the Linoleum and Felt Base Employers' Federation; the Linoleum Manufacturing Co., Ltd.; the Locomotive Manufacturers' Association of Great Britain; the Machine Tool Trades Association; Mars, Ltd.; May and Baker, Ltd.; the Mechanical Handling Engineers' Association; the Metropolitan Vickers Electrical Co., Ltd.; Michael Nairn and Co., Ltd.; Mitchell Engineering, Ltd.; Monkhouse and Glasscock, Ltd.; the National Employers' Association of Rayon Yarn Spinners; the National Federation of Clay Industries; the National Hosiery Manufacturers' Federation; the National Paint Federation; Nestle Co., Ltd.; the Newall Engineering Co., Ltd.; the Norvic Shoe Factory; the Office Appliances and Business Equipment Trades Association; Park Royal Brewery; Parripan Paints, Ltd.; Peak, Frean and Co., Ltd.; Pilkington Bros. Ltd.; Quaker Oats, Ltd.; the Radio Communication and Electrical Engineering Association; The Railway Carriage and Wagon Building Association; Rotary Hoes, Ltd.; Ruston and Hornsby, Ltd.; the Shipbuilding Employers' Federation; the Shirley Institute; the Skefco Ballbearing Co.; Smith, Anderson and Co., Ltd.;

Standard Telephone and Cables, Ltd.; the Stanton Ironworks Co., Ltd.; Stevenson and Son, Ltd.; A. F. Stoddard and Co., Ltd.; Tate and Lyle, Ltd.; the Thames Plywood Manufacturers' Ltd.; Thomas Hedley and Co., Ltd.; Unilever, Ltd.; Van den Bergh and Jergens, Ltd.; Vauxhall Motors, Ltd.; the Vulcan Foundry, Ltd.; Wade (Ulster) Ltd.; Watney Combe Reid and Co., Ltd.; Wedgwood and Sons, Ltd.; the Wholesale Clothing Manufacturers' Federation of Great Britain; Wickman, Ltd.; William Ewart and Son, Ltd.; W. T. Henley's Telegraph Works Co., Ltd.

Trade Unions

The Amalgamated Engineering Union; Amalgamated Weavers; the National Union of Foundry Workers; the Associated Society of Moulders and Foundry Workers; the Electrical Trades Union; the National Association of Carpet Trade Unions; the National Amalgamated Association of Nut and Bolt Makers; the National Society of Coppersmiths, Braziers and Metal Workers; the National Society of Brushmakers; the National Society of Pottery Workers; the National Union of Boot and Shoe Operatives; the National Union of General and Municipal Workers; the National Union of Hosiery Workers; the National Union of Sheet Metal Workers' and Braziers; the National Union of Stove, Grate and General Metal Workers; the National Union of Vehicle Builders; the Power Loom Weavers and Textile Workers' Association; the Scottish Carpet Trade and Factory Workers Union; the Transport and General Workers Union; the Union of Jute, Flax and Kindred Textile Operators; the United Rubber Workers of Great Britain; the United Society of Boilermakers and Iron and Steel Shipbuilders.

PART I

THEORY

CHAPTER I

CAPITAL UTILISATION AND ECONOMIC GROWTH

1.1. The Economic Significance of Shift-Work

Multiple-shift systems allow machines to work longer hours than their human attendants. Humans require periodic rest. Machines, by and large, are as efficient whether their working life is concentrated into five years or spread over ten: indeed, intensive utilisation may even actually reduce wear. Shift-work attracts attention, and is widely practised, because it in many cases reduces prime costs, and in all cases saves capital. The working year of equipment is freed from human constraints and the number of hours it is operated annually becomes an instrumental variable of business or economic policy.

We call the annual operating hours of an item of equipment the *rate of utilisation*; for example, the rate of utilisation of a machine operated on single shifts, 5 days a week, 8 hours a day, 50 weeks a year, is *2000*; on double shifts this becomes *4000*, on treble shifts, *6000*, and the maximum possible on earth, representing continuous operation through all 24 hours every day in the year, is *8760*. In effect, then, to study the economics of shift work is to study the economics of capital utilisation.

The subject has been surprisingly neglected in economic theory. When the problems involved are considered at all, analysts have thought mainly of situations in which a single firm or economic system happens to possess a given stock of capital equipment which for some reason is already operated at a particular rate of utilisation, and have then asked whether the rate could not with advantage be increased. They rarely ask how a stock of capital designed to produce this particular output at this particular utilisation rate came to exist. Similarly, in business inquiries, one of the commonest reasons given for working shifts or not (as the case may be) relates to demand: business men can rarely explain why, if output was to be restricted by demand, they chose to invest in a plant designed to work on single shifts when it might have been more profitable to meet the same demand with a plant half the size designed to work on double shifts.

The significance of this becomes apparent as we recognise that in an economy as a whole, with given capital, average utilisation cannot be increased unless previously unemployed workers are available to man additional shifts. Once capital sufficient to employ the whole working population at a particular (average) rate of utilisation has been built up, increased utilisation is impossible. If, therefore, an increase in utilisation *is* possible, the capital stock, given the current rate of utilisation, must be inadequate for full employment. In other words, this must be an economy which would normally be described as 'under-developed'. In a developed economy, under 'full-employment' conditions, the rate of capital utilisation is no more than an expression of the relationship between the size and character of the capital stock which has already been accumulated and the size of the employed population. The questions to ask in such cases, therefore, are how and why, in the course of previous development, the average rate of utilisation has been settled in such a way as to require a stock of this size to employ this population? Thus in both developed and under-developed countries, the problem must be seen as an aspect of the whole process of economic growth.

A corresponding proposition holds at the level of the individual firm. In business, although top management rarely sees shift-work primarily as a feature of long-run investment planning, an analysis based on the point of view of a firm contemplating a new investment to meet a given (estimated) demand is usually much more revealing, ultimately, than an analysis based on the situation of a firm whose capital stock is already decided by actions taken in the past.† For this reason, although we recognise that many readers may find the approach unfamiliar, we shall base our inquiry, almost throughout, on the question of whether, when planning to meet a given demand, one should build a plant designed to produce the required output at a low or moderate rate of utilisation, or build a smaller plant designed to produce the same output at a higher rate of utilisation. By analysing this basic case we shall find we can easily, and more fundamentally, deal with other cases.

Contemporary theories of economic growth depend much on the concept of a 'capital coefficient' or 'capital–output ratio'—measures of the quantity of capital required to produce one unit of output. Alternatively, they postulate the existence of a definite technical relationship, known as a 'production function', between the quantities of labour and capital employed in production and the resulting quantity of output. All such relationships must be considerably affected by the rate of utilisation. As compared with a one-shift system, a two-shift system may halve the quantity of fixed capital required to produce a given output while leaving the corresponding quantity of labour unchanged. On an extreme view, the capital–output ratio of an economic system is no more than a reflection of the system's average rate of capital utilisation. Or perhaps we could say that the rate of utilisation adds another dimension to the production function.

This function represents a technical relationship between quantities of capital, labour and output. An industrialist faces a production function when he has a choice of techniques for manufacturing a given commodity; on the one hand, perhaps, a highly mechanised or capital-intensive technique, on the other a labour-intensive technique, together,

† This is not to say that the short-run problem does not raise questions of intrinsic intellectual interest. See, for example, the elegant paper by K. Alexander and J. Spraos, in the *Quarterly Journal of Economics*, 1956, p. 603.

usually, with a range of intermediate possibilities. The economic characteristics of the whole array constitute a statement of the function. The statement is usually made in the form of an equation in which the dependent variable, output, depends mainly on two determining variables only: the quantity of labour measured in aggregate man-hours per annum and the quantity of capital measured at cost. If the quantity of capital is held constant, while the quantity of labour is increased, it is usually expected that total output will increase less than in proportion to the increase in labour, in accordance with the classical law of diminishing returns (which states that when the ratio of one factor of production to another varies, the relative productivities of the factors change in the opposite direction). Only if the quantity of capital is also increased, and in the same proportion as labour, can we expect output to increase in proportion to input, a condition described as 'constant returns to scale'.

The usual approach, however, rarely considers utilisation. Variations in utilisation do not properly fall either into the category of variations in scale or of variations in a single factor. They have effects which are similar to those of changes in scale, yet, if labour is measured in aggregate man-hours per annum, they certainly alter the ratio of capital to labour. We can see the position more clearly by noting that aggregate man-hours per annum may be expressed as the product of two components, the average number of workers employed at an instant of operation, which we call 'instantaneous employment', and the annual operating hours, i.e. the rate of utilisation. We may therefore restate the production function by saying that annual output now depends on three variables in place of two: instantaneous employment, quantity of capital and the rate of utilisation. But this restatement involves a major change in the character of the relationship. A given proportionate increase in instantaneous employment will by no means yield the same proportionate increase in output as will a corresponding increase in utilisation rate. The former variation will be subject to classical diminishing productivity while the latter will behave much like an increase in scale.

Suppose a man is working a lathe of given design. His hourly output may be considerably improved by the addition of a helper who fetches materials and refreshments, carries away product and occasionally adds a pair of hands. A second helper, however, would as likely as not be useless, if not worse than useless. Therefore, if for any reason it is desired to economise capital further it will be necessary to invest in a different, more labour-intensive, type of machinery, in which case, although the consequential decline in labour productivity will be smaller, it will nevertheless remain significant. By contrast, if a balanced team of two workers is added to the total number of users of the original machinery by means of a night shift, so the teams no longer get in each other's way, the results will be entirely different. As a first approximation we can suppose that they will be the same as if the number of machines as well as total employment had been doubled, because there is no particular reason to suppose that night workers will use the machinery less efficiently than day workers, while the technical characteristics of the machinery, measured by the hourly rate of output for given instantaneous employment remain, of course, unchanged.† This difference in effect is widely recognised and explains the business man's interest in shift-work.

Labour's attitude to shift-work is necessarily more ambiguous. Increases in utilisation raise the productivity of capital, but not the productivity of labour, and the means by which the benefits of increased utilisation may be shared between labour and capital are inherently indirect. We investigate these questions further below. Since profit and accumulation are centrally involved our answers will be expressed mainly in terms of effects on economic growth.

It is known that rates of utilisation vary considerably between countries, between industries and between periods of history. Some variations are cyclical and to that extent their causes have been investigated in theories of the trade cycle. Others are definitely not of cyclical origin, and it is these which theory has ignored. Even at the height of a boom no nation employs all its capital at the maximum practicable rate of utilisation, because in all nations the greater part of industrial capital is idle at night. It might be that the normal rate of utilisation can be explained separately from the factors which determine economic growth and is therefore itself qualified to rank as an independent member of those factors. This will not be our conclusion. We shall find that while the rate of utilisation obviously influences growth, some of

† A convenient mathematical form of the production function which takes account of utilisation would be

$$O = \lambda H^h E^e C^c \quad 0 \leqslant H \leqslant 8760; \quad E > 0 < C,$$

$$h = 1 = e + c,$$

where O is annual output, H utilisation measured in operating hours per annum, E instantaneous employment measured in number of workers of given quality, C capital measured at cost and λ is a constant. The exponents e and c represent the proportionate increase in output to be expected from a unit proportionate increase in employment and capital respectively; they are classical marginal productivities expressed in elasticity form. The condition that they sum to unity represents constant returns to scale. The elasticity with respect to utilisation is unity because this factor is assumed to behave like a scale factor. Diminishing returns to scale might be manifested in a less-than-unity utilisation elasticity, or in the elasticities with respect to labour and capital summing to less than unity or, most likely, in both forms together. (Diminishing returns to scale are usually attributed to difficulties of management in large enterprises and the result will depend on whether these relate mainly to the management of labour, of capital, of sales or of all three. Shift work, we shall see, may bring special managerial problems. Where these are serious the utilisation elasticity will be less than unity or the labour elasticity may have to be written as a function of the utilisation rate.)

A conventional production function is frequently written

$$O = \alpha L^e C^c,$$

where L represents aggregate man-hours per annum and α is an undefined constant. This presentation implicitly assumes that utilisation is constant and that L, therefore, varies through instantaneous employment only. The constant, α, subsumes the (fixed) rate of utilisation, but this is rarely explained.

the fundamental factors which also influence growth themselves influence utilisation, for example, as follows:

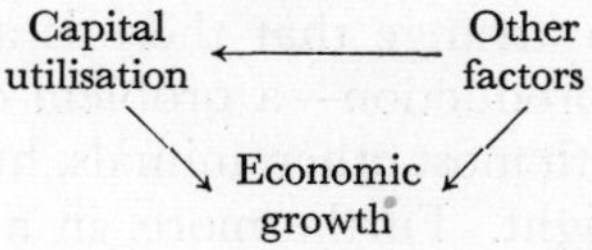

The relationships will be found to be reinforcing, variations tending to enhance growth also encouraging utilisation, which in turn further stimulates growth. One would therefore expect to find a positive correlation between growth rates and utilisation rates, but this does not mean that a high rate of utilisation can be described as a 'cause' of fast growth; nor that fast growth is a cause of intense utilisation. Unfortunately the data necessary for the intertemporal and international comparisons required to test the 'prediction' of a correlation between growth and utilisation do not exist. Instead, in the chapters which follow, we deploy other empirical evidence in support of the theory from which it arises.

1.2. Utilisation as a Business Decision

When an industrial plant is constructed, the management must be presumed to have some intention or 'plan' as to the rate of utilisation. If not, they could not decide how much equipment to order against the expected demand for the product. In practice, for reasons we shall discuss later, they may well intend that utilisation should fluctuate within a range according to circumstances. For the time being, therefore, we shall define the *planned utilisation* of an asset as the middle, in some sense or other, of the range of rates within which it is expected to operate. We can then distinguish between planned utilisation and actual utilisation. Several primary factors may cause the two to differ: demand for the final product may differ from what was expected, similarly the supply of labour or raw materials. The supply of labour may vary in two ways: either labour may become generally scarcer, or the length of the conventional working day may be reduced. Finally, the relation between the cost of labour hired within conventional hours and the cost of labour hired for other times—as represented by overtime and shift-work premiums—may also change. *This study is mainly concerned with the long-run problem, that is with the determination of planned, rather than unplanned, utilisation.* However, some of the factors which may cause unplanned variations are also relevant to planned variation, and the two areas of inquiry overlap when the expectation of fluctuating conditions in the labour and product markets is found to affect the planning decision.

If a machine is idle, it continues to incur capital charges which are no less real as a business expense than as a cost to the community. Idle machinery is wasted capital. At first sight the difficulty may appear trivial; why should not a battery of machines be set to work continuously while the operators come and go as they choose? Management, it could be argued, has only to arrange that there is always sufficient labour available to maintain production—a problem of administration. But, unfortunately, along with most other animals, humans prefer to work in the day and sleep at night. Furthermore, in most industrial activities the operator is involved in complex relationships with his peers, superiors, and subordinates, relationships which are as important to productive efficiency as his relationship with the machinery itself. Factory work is team work, and the problem of phasing becomes a problem in the rotation of teams, i.e. the familiar problem of organising multiple shifts. In the past, therefore, it has been regarded as primarily a problem in personnel management.

Alternatively, the question of multiple shifts versus single shifts has been treated as a rather narrow problem in costing. Typically, the argument runs as follows. The greater the rate of capital utilisation, the lower in general are likely to be capital costs per unit of output. Capital costs are divided into two classes, those which arise solely from the passage of time, and are totally unaffected by the amount of use made of the equipment, and those which do vary in some degree with annual output, that is with utilisation. In the first class fall interest charges, 'normal profit' and depreciation due to obsolescence; in the second class falls depreciation due to wear and tear. But obsolescence is sometimes ignored, all profits, normal or otherwise, omitted from cost and a calculation made as shown in Table 1.1. This example compares two methods of working the same type of equipment—case A with an index of utilisation† of 25 and case B with an index of 50. Case A assumes perhaps a day shift only, case B supposes that the same output is produced by a plant half as big in which the day shift is followed by a night shift of equal length employing workers of equal productivity. Depreciation, supposed entirely due to wear and tear, is reckoned at 10 and 20 % in the two cases respectively, it being argued that with double the working hours, the machines must wear out twice as fast. In the calculation as set out, no allowance is made for any premium on the hourly wage rate to be paid for night work, i.e. night workers and day workers are both paid the same. It will be seen that even on this unrealistic assumption, the reduction in unit costs between the two cases, at $5\frac{1}{2}$ %, appears quite small. A night-work premium of only 25 % would eliminate the difference altogether. It is not difficult to conclude therefore, that increased utilisation by means of a night shift is hardly worth while.

Costings of this type have so often been shown to the author by business men that it is difficult to know to what extent they embody genuine misunderstanding and to what extent they are rationalisations

† We define the index of utilisation as the planned utilisation, measured in operating hours per annum, expressed as a percentage of 8760, the theoretical maximum.

Table 1.1. *First example of shift-work costing*

	Case A (£)	Case B (£)
Annual gross output	1000	1000
Prime costs and gross profit:		
Raw materials and fuel	200†	200†
Labour	400	400
Gross profit	400	400
Fixed capital costs:		
Capital employed	2000	1000
Index of utilisation	*25*	*50*
Depreciation	200	200
'Interest'	100	50
Total capital charges	300	250
Costs per £ of output:		
Materials	0·2	0·2
Labour	0·4	0·4
Capital	0·3	0·25
Total	0·9	0·85

† In many cases continuous working provides substantial economies in fuel and material costs but here we assume that prime costs vary proportionately with output.

of decisions taken on other less tangible grounds. Of the many fallacies involved, we would emphasise three. First, so long as technical change is occurring, obsolescence cannot, in fact, validly be ignored. To the annual charge for 'wear and tear' must be added the loss of value due to obsolescence. Secondly, it is rarely true that wear and tear varies proportionately with the annual operating time. Many machines deteriorate physically as much or more while they are idle as while they are in use, particularly if the idle periods are short and frequent—the rollers used in the preparatory processes of cotton spinning provide a standard example—and buildings probably decline more rapidly when they are unheated at night rather than used continuously. Finally, the whole method of presentation seems wrong. A small reduction in unit cost may not contribute a startling improvement in competitive market power. But suppose the firm continues to sell at the same prices, and concentrates attention on the rate of profit on capital employed? More precisely, let us examine the behaviour of the rate of net profit, that is of the difference between unit costs, excluding interest charges, and the value of sales, expressed as a percentage of the value of capital employed. In case A (first example) this will be found to be 10 %, in case B 20 %, and it is difficult to believe that to double the rate of profit on capital is not to achieve an economic change of major importance. And when account is taken of the first two points as well, the difference becomes very marked indeed. In Table 1.2 it is assumed that with 25 % utilisation, wear-and-tear depreciation runs at 10 % per annum, but that when utilisation is doubled this charge is increased by only a half. In addition, it is assumed that obsolescence takes a further

5 % per annum off the value of the equipment, the same amount in both cases. The effect of doubling the rate of utilisation is then to increase the rate of net profit *fourfold.*

Table 1.2. *Second example of shift-work costing*

	Case A	Case B
Index of utilisation	*25*	*50*
	£	£
Prime costs per £ of output	0·6	0·6
Gross profit per £ of output	0·4	0·4
Capital employed per £ of output	2·0	1·0
Depreciation per £ of output		
Wear and tear	0·2	0·15
Obsolescence	0·1	0·05
Total	0·3	0·20
Gross profit rate (%)	20	40
Net profit rate (%)	5	20

Except for the omission of a night-shift premium the above figures seem by no means unrealistic. We believe they display the right basis for comparison. That is to say, we believe the rate of profit is what management must aim to maximise when taking investment decisions of this kind. The point will be argued more fully below, but in the meantime consider a simple case where the firm is a typical capitalist corporation, wholly owned by its equity shareholders. If all the profits are distributed, and none of the capital has been raised from non-shareholder sources, the value of a share invested according to the plan represented by case B must be four times the value of a share invested as in case A. So that if the management acts in the interests of the shareholders, it must, at first sight, adopt case B (at second sight, of course, the decision depends on the incidence of the labour shift-premium). In classical economic language, what has happened between the two cases is that the marginal productivity of the capital has increased, therefore its value has increased.

The case for assuming that business men make investment decisions by reference to rates of profit can be supported more generally by noting that the higher the average rate of profit a firm can earn, the faster, on average, it can grow. We suggest that a large proportion of business managements strongly desire to see their organisations grow, and that a good rate of profit is essential to success in this—because the higher the rate of profit, either the easier it is to borrow additional capital, or the faster it is possible to grow by re-investment. Therefore, since the rate of profit on capital is considerably influenced by the rate of utilisation, a firm which chooses correctly according to our criteria will grow faster than a firm that does not.

Something similar can be said of the national economy. However, we cannot analyse the implications of varying utilisation in a whole economy merely by generalisation from conclusions about the individual firm. For a single firm, provided no labour premiums are paid, a higher rate of utilisation must lead to a higher rate of profit and, thus, on one set of assumptions (including the assumption that the firm desires to make use of its opportunities) to faster growth. In an economy as a whole, a general increase in rates of utilisation will be found not unlikely to be associated with faster development, but the set of assumptions required is by no means identical. In order to comprehend the necessary differences of approach, we need to investigate the characteristics of suitably chosen macro-economic 'models' of growing economic systems.

1.3. Utilisation and Economic Growth

Such models should be designed to concentrate attention on our special problem (the effect of variations in planned capital utilisation on economic growth) and to avoid, therefore, complications caused by the intrusion of other problems with which, however important they may be, we are not concerned. Two types of 'complications' in particular need specific elimination; those caused by non-capital factors and those caused by inconsistent behaviour among different decision-taking units of the economy. Economic growth is a complex technical and social process involving *inter alia* the accumulation of productive capital in tangible economic form. But as the literature of the subject increasingly recognises, factors other than capital may be equally significant, especially social and political development, labour skill, technology and foreign trade. Capital accumulation is a necessary but not a sufficient condition of the growth process. Some of the other factors may have direct effects on the rate of utilisation of the capital which is accumulated, others may be themselves significantly affected by it. This study, however, is deliberately concentrated on the more conventional economic aspects of the subject and indirect social factors are ignored. We therefore assume that accumulation is a sufficient condition for growth or, to put the point more favourably, we say that our conclusions may be interpreted as statements that, provided other factors permit, such and such variations in capital utilisation will have such and such associations with accumulation and hence with growth.

The problems arising from decision-making discrepancies arise mainly in unregulated capitalist economies. Here accumulation is undertaken largely through the agency of autonomous privately owned businesses. In order to build new factories, accumulate inventories or otherwise extend capital equipment, the businesses (which are also the owners of the results) require on the one hand a positive desire, in themselves, to make the investments and on the other adequate supplies of purchasing power over capital goods. The latter represent claims on the economy's current supply of real savings—abstentions from consumption out of current income. Thus a general desire to invest and a corresponding desire to save are both necessary conditions for accumulation and hence (in accordance with the preceding assumption) of growth. Many of the problems of particular concern to general growth economics arise from the possibility of inconsistencies between these two desires, and from the consequences of their enforced resolution by indirect means. For instance, if the desire to invest, at a given level of national income, requires less saving than is forthcoming from this income, the inconsistency may be resolved by the occurrence of unplanned under-utilisation of the existing national capital stock, leading eventually to a reduction in the rate of new accumulation. Since, as explained earlier, we are not greatly concerned with discrepancies between planned and actual utilisation (because we are essentially concerned with the role of planned utilisation) such possibilities, also, should be eliminated by our assumptions. We therefore assume there is some mechanism in the economy for ensuring 'Keynesian' full employment so that the available capital stock is always utilised at the average planned rate. More specifically, we shall assume that whatever the level of total output associated with the planned rate of utilisation, the government or some other body ensures that investment, defined as the volume of orders for new capital goods, is precisely equal to the savings forthcoming at this level of output, and total demand is therefore always in balance with total supply. As a corollary we can say that if, under conditions of planned utilisation, there for some reason occurs an increase in the proportion of national income saved, there will instantly occur a corresponding increase in investment. We thus imply that if conditions are such that an increase in investment will have some particular effect on economic growth, the same will apply to an increase in the propensity to save.

1.4. An Under-Developed Economy

An economy is characterised as under-developed when capital is in some sense scarce relative to labour. More specifically, most of the population is engaged in agriculture where their productivity is low because land is overcrowded, their methods are backward, or both. Not infrequently the agricultural sector is so inefficient that marginal transfers of workers to the small industrial sector have little effect on total food production, and food supplies are not a true restraint on development. In such cases the object of progress is to transfer workers as quickly as possible, and thereby generate a sustainable process of capital accumulation, rising output and rising employment. The speed of the process is limited by supplies of social and industrial capital necessary to house and equip the transferred workers, and by supplies of skilled workers, of entrepreneurs and of managers. In other cases there is also a considerable problem of food supply. However, since we are concerned only with the question of capital utilisation, we will for simplicity concentrate attention on the case where the effective bottleneck is solely the rate of domestic industrial capital formation. We exclude the possibility of capital imports and thus imply that the rate of growth at any stage in the process depends exclusively on the ratio, within the industrial sector, between employment in consumer-goods production on the one hand and employment in capital-goods production on the other.

The workers employed on capital-goods production must be maintained, for their output can neither be consumed directly nor exchanged with the peasants for food. This support comes from the community's savings. Where the community is a poor one, such savings as occur will arise mainly from non-wage incomes generated in the industrial sector, either from profits, taxes, managerial incomes or from some combination of the three. In practice it is not unreasonable to assume that, by contrast, savings from wages are negligible. For analytical convenience we will assume that *all* non-wage income is saved, not because the assumption is realistic but because consumption out of non-wage income, although important in many other problems, has no special interaction with the problem of capital utilisation, and because by assuming 100 % saving of profits we avoid some unimportant problems of definition.

We may also assume that the techniques of production embodied in capital goods are fixed, i.e. that not only has there never been a change in the technical knowledge available to industry but also that only one type of equipment is available for producing any given commodity. In effect, then, the average hourly output per man and the average hourly output of a typical unit of equipment (however defined) is 'given' for every industrial activity and so also the *instantaneous employment* provided by every type of equipment, where by this we mean the number of workers required to operate a typical unit of equipment when running normally. It follows, *inter alia*, that the average amount of new capacity for providing instantaneous employment resulting from one hour's work by a capital-goods worker (to be called the 'hourly productivity' of the capital-goods sector, further discussed below) is also given. These assumptions are not intended as realistic but rather as serving to emphasise that the primary problem of economic policy in under-developed countries is usually thought of as the 'widening' of capital to bring more workers into industrial employment with existing types of equipment, rather than of providing those already employed with better equipment.

The usual formula for economic growth on these assumptions, supposing the labour supply to be literally unlimited, is

$$r = s/v, \tag{1.1}$$

where r is the rate of growth of capital stock, employment and output, s is the proportion of national income saved (on our assumptions, this is the same as the proportion of non-wage income to total income in the industrial sector) and v is some measure of the quantity of capital required to support a unit increase in output. Since this 'capital–output ratio' is obviously directly related to the planned rate of capital utilisation, raising the rate of utilisation—a 'capital-saving' re-organisation of production—cannot but be beneficial to growth. We can in fact state the relationship precisely:

$$r = hsk, \tag{1.2}$$

where h stands for the average rate of utilisation† (measured in operating hours per annum, as defined previously), s remains the proportion of income saved and k is the average hourly productivity of the capital-goods industry.‡ This formula has therefore the advantage over the more usual one of making the basic relationships more explicit and, in particular, of distinguishing between the effects of utilisation on the one hand and of technical conditions on the other.

The model confirms that the growth rate varies directly with the utilisation rate. This may be very significant for the welfare aspects of the situation. If the utilisation rate is regarded as a conventional, and unchangeable datum, and k is a technological constant, growth can be accelerated only by increasing the proportion of national income saved (which on our assumptions means reducing real wages). Consumption today must be reduced in favour of an increased growth rate of employment. However, in many under-developed countries the current standard of consumption is already so low that it cannot be reduced further. Productivity being also low, the proportion of wages in output is relatively high and the implied growth rate, therefore, may be more than disappointing. In such a situation the country usually appeals for outside help or attempts Draconian measures against consumption. An alternative policy, we can now see, would be to raise the rate of capital utilisation to an unconventionally high level. If this involves inconvenience for some sections of the population, they should ask whether it is worse to have to work at night or to have no job at all.§ We must re-emphasise, however, that this conclusion depends strictly on the assumption that the supply of industrial capital is the only factor effectively restraining growth.

† Average utilisation is assumed the same in consumer-goods and capital-goods industry.

‡ We can obtain a precise definition of k by first defining the concept of a 'unit of capital'; the average quantum of equipment (e.g. measured by weight of steel) required to provide instantaneous employment for one man, in consumer-goods or capital-goods industry, both quanta being assumed the same. We can then say that k is the average number of consumer-goods units of equipment resulting from one hour's normal operation of a unit of capital in capital-goods industry.

§ There is evidence that in some Asian countries the planned rate of utilisation in cotton spinning is considerably higher than in Western Europe, for example. In Hong Kong, in particular, the rate of utilisation almost approaches the physical maximum and it has been said that 'Hong Kong manufacturers boast they are obtaining from abroad the most modern machinery in the cheapest market, and operating it three times as intensively as in most western countries. As a result, neither capital or labour is allowed to be left idle.' E. Szczepanik, *The Economic Growth of Hong Kong* (Oxford, 1958), p. 72. In India, the mills began to work two shifts in the middle thirties, following an intensification of Japanese competition. Shift-work increased throughout the inter-war period, reaching a peak during the war itself: this coincided with a spurt in the demand for Indian cloth. After the war, double- and treble-

1.5. A Developed Economy

An economy is considered 'developed' when capital has ceased to be scarce relative to labour in the sense that, at the average planned rate of capital utilisation, the capital stock already accumulated is sufficient to employ the available labour. This, of course, by no means implies capital is 'abundant'. Usually there is considerable scope for 'deepening' capital, that is, for providing the labour-force with more capital and thus raising output per man-hour. For example, suppose all the available labour has been equipped with the most labour-saving machinery known, from which they obtain certain rates of output per man-hour and output per machine-hour, and suppose that the rate of utilisation, which determines output per machine-*year*, is a conventional datum. Output per man-year is determined by the average length of the conventional working week of the individual worker and, in the absence of technical change, the activity of the capital-goods industries is entirely confined to making good depreciation caused by wear and tear. Suppose, then, new inventions occur which would permit an increase in output-per-man-hour if associated with a corresponding increase in capital relative to instantaneous employment (capital being measured in terms of embodied capital-goods-industry labour). If the inventions are to be exploited, the necessary re-equipment and capital-deepening in the consumption-goods industry will require both a temporary and a (smaller) permanent increase in the scale of activity in the capital-goods industries. So long as there are technical possibilities to be exploited, therefore, new capital is never useless, and utilisation must remain a matter of importance.

Even in the absence of progress, utilisation may be important. Suppose an economy has reached a high state of development with a rather high conventional rate of utilisation, having used this method, perhaps, for achieving satisfactory growth. Suppose the system finally reaches a position where, given a fair amount of shift-work, all the available labour can be employed with the capital accumulated. Assuming that progress is totally absent and more labour-intensive techniques of production are unknown (most unlikely, of course, in practice) it would normally be supposed that capital accumulation was pointless since, output per man and output per unit of capital being fixed, new capital could not be supplied with labour and could not increase output. However, if now the rate of *utilisation* were reduced (by gradual elimination of shift-work), the workers taken off night shift, if they were not to become unemployed, would have to be provided with

shift working became general. However, in the late fifties the industry experienced a serious recession, and shift-working declined substantially; significantly, the reduction in activity on the third shift was proportionately greater than the corresponding reduction on the second shift, a result which would be consistent with the existence of a higher premium for labour on the third than on the second shift. For information concerning the earlier period, see Report of the *Textile Labour Enquiry Committee, Vol. II—Final Report*, ch. VII; for the later period, see *Report of the Working Party for the Cotton Textile Industry* (Delhi, 1958) and *Indian Textile Bulletin*, August, 1962.

new capital until all were re-employed on day shift. Capital accumulation might be used, therefore, to permit the same national output (and ultimate consumption standard) to be achieved with less shift work. A gain in convenience, perhaps, would have been achieved at the expense of a temporary reduction in consumption; the 'return' on investment, elimination of night work. When the working year of machinery had been brought into equality with the working year of humans, the process could be carried no further. One might thus argue that an economy could not be said to have reached the position sometimes known as 'bliss' until all shift-work, other than that required for purely technical reasons, had been eliminated.

Another aspect of a developed economy without progress arises from the role of population growth. If the working population is growing by natural reproduction, as is still the case even in the United Kingdom and still very much the case in the United States, capital widening will be required to provide productive employment for the additional members. Part of the national income must be saved for this purpose and the usual formula for defining the required proportion is

$$s^* = gv, \tag{1.3}$$

where s^* is the proportion required to be saved, g the natural rate of population growth and v the capital–output ratio. We can make a similar modification as in the previous section and write

$$s^* = g/kh. \tag{1.4}$$

In other words, the higher the rate of capital utilisation, the smaller the saving proportion required to support a given rate of population growth. By agreeing to shift-work, therefore, the present population can reduce the sacrifice of consumption required to provide adequate employment opportunities for their children. If it is assumed that these must and will be provided, an increase in utilisation permits higher *per capita* consumption at all stages in the growth process. Is it the case, then, that the most important role of capital utilisation in developed economies lies in determining the weight of the investment-burden required to support a given rate of population growth? To consider an answer, we must drop the obviously unrealistic assumption of absence of technical progress. What happens in a model which assumes that although the population is constant, technical knowledge is not?

'Technical progress' may be thought of as a state of affairs where the design of equipment and knowledge of its use is steadily improving in such a way as to permit a secular upward trend in output per man-hour. Design improvement, however, is not a sufficient condition for an actual increase in production, because if, for example, machines of the improved designs were rarely ordered, actual productivity in the consumer-goods industries would remain virtually stationary. Therefore, even in the absence of physical depreciation or population growth, economic development requires investment.

In practice, in an economic system where the capital-goods industries continually improve the performance of their products, few machines are replaced with ones whose design and performance (or price-for performance) is identical with their own, because their own design reflects the state of technical knowledge at the date of their original installation, some years back. There is considerable evidence that in these circumstances user-cost and non-user physical deterioration represent relatively unimportant elements in total depreciation. The major factor causing capital goods to depreciate in their owners' balance sheets is obsolescence, i.e. depreciation caused by the marketing of new and better machines doing the same job, or by a decline in the cost of reproducing the original machine. As a corollary, the commonest reason for replacing capital equipment is not wear, tear, rot or rust, so much as the desire to take advantage of new designs. Replacement, therefore, is a necessary condition of rising productivity.

It is therefore convenient to imagine a system in which user-cost and other forms of physical depreciation are absent altogether. Equipment never wears out but is nevertheless from time to time replaced in order to take advantage of improved technique; the average life of a machine is therefore the reciprocal of the proportion replaced annually. Replaced machines are scrapped and their labour transferred to operating the replacement. Since the new machines are always superior, labour productivity rises. But it is by no means certain that this rise in actual productivity will occur at the same rate as the full potential rate, that is to say at the rate of change in output per man-hour available with machines of this year's design as compared with machines of last year's design. The actual rate of change of productivity is what is usually defined as the rate of progress, the potential rate we can call the rate of invention.

At one extreme, it can be seen that if the rate of *replacement* is zero, whatever the rate of invention, the rate of progress must be zero. At the other extreme, if the rate of replacement were infinite, machines would always be replaced before any inventive improvement in design had occurred and the rate of progress would again be zero. Between these two extremes, the position is more complex. If the rate of invention is *independent* of the rate of replacement, in the long run, whatever the rate of replacement, provided it is reasonably greater than zero, the rate of progress will tend to equal the invention rate, because, if machines are replaced more slowly the loss will be offset by the fact that in the meantime more inventive improvement will have accumulated (this can be proved rigorously, provided we ignore short-run effects and define the growth rates by averages taken over very long periods). We may put the point another way by saying that *unless* the invention rate is in some way dependent on the replacement rate, accelerated replacement cannot affect long-run growth, investment becomes valueless and we are back to the state of 'bliss' where, beyond a certain point, the rate of capital utilisation ceases to be of interest. The conclusion is significant, because many argue that the main practical case for high rates of capital utilisation lies in their stimulating effect on replacement (by speeding up the annual rate of wear and tear depreciation) and hence on progress.

In practice, most people believe that demand for capital goods stimulates design improvement. But the question at issue is whether the rate of invention is affected by the *relative size* of the capital-goods industry measured in terms of labour input. Why might this be? We may first note that given the absolute size of the economy as a whole, measured by the size of the labour supply, the relative size of the capital-goods industry also determines its absolute size. We can then see many good reasons for expecting absolute size to encourage invention. The larger the absolute size, the larger either the number of producing organisations into which the industry is divided or the larger the average employment in each organisation. As regards the effect of a large number of organisations, a formal probabilistic hypothesis might run as follows: inventions occur at random among the organisations so that the larger their number the larger the number of inventions occurring annually; inventions in one organisation are quickly imitated by others, therefore the rate of invention, which relates to new designs actually marketed, will also vary directly with the number of inventions and hence the number of organisations. This does not mean that an industry divided into a large number of small organisations will necessarily do better than if divided into a small number of large organisations. For, and this is really a second point, it is known that very small organisations possess a less inherent inventive potentiality; the distribution of inventions is not random in respect of size. Thus, if a large-sized industry leads to large-scale organisation, this, too, may be a cause of fast inventiveness.

Secondly, we may consider stimulus arising in the consumer-goods industry itself. The fact that we have described technical change by reference to changing design of capital goods only does not mean that the causes of change are to be found solely in the capital-goods producing industries; the customers, clearly, play an important role. A production engineer is always aware that he cannot, in general, make big changes in production techniques without also changing his equipment. Often, because he desires to change technique he puts pressure on his equipment supplier to create a new design. But, if the engineer knows that it is the policy of his firm to replace equipment slowly (reflecting, perhaps, the local financial consequences of a national scarcity of abstinence) he will be unable to do this often. Furthermore, if replacement is slow, his own inventiveness will probably stagnate. It is probably more nearly correct to picture the stimulus from consumers of capital goods as represented by 'jolts' of constant strength, occurring successively at discrete intervals of time, with the consequence that the more frequent they are, the greater the average number of jolts delivered and received annually.

If either or both of the foregoing hypotheses is correct—and they no more than rationalise widely held intuitive beliefs—the rate of invention is indeed a dependent function of the rate of replacement, which means in turn that the rate of replacement influences the rate of progress. Since, in the present model, replaced machines are always scrapped, it is easy to see that the rate of replacement is governed by the same formula as the rate of *accumulation* in the previous models, and the rate of capital utilisation plays the same role. Consider, for example, two economies, alike in all respects, except that in one the rate of capital utilisation is generally higher than the other. Both economies employ the same proportion of their total labour force in capital-goods production, therefore the proportion of national income saved is the same and so also total consumer- and investment-goods output; but in the high-utilisation economy as compared with the low, these results are achieved with half the amount of capital in each sector. We have therefore a situation in which the annual output of new capital goods in both economies is the same, but the standing stock in each is not. It follows that the ratio of new flow to old stock—in effect, the rate of replacement—is twice as high in the high-utilisation economy as in the low-utilisation economy. Given the proportion of national income saved, therefore, capital utilisation has a direct relation to replacement.

The relation between replacement and progress, however, will not be so simple. We may imagine that at low rates of replacement, any improvement will have a considerable effect, but when the rate of replacement becomes very rapid, further increases will have less effect: it is not true that given sufficient stimulus, human inventiveness is totally unlimited. We must therefore say that the rate of progress is a rising but flattening function of the rate of replacement, and hence, in turn, of the proportion of national income saved and of the utilisation rate. Thus if we define the functional relationship between replacement and progress as

$$o^{\cdot} = F(r), \qquad (1.5)$$

where $o^{\cdot}$ is the rate of progress measured by the annual rate of growth of labour productivity and r is the rate of replacement, we can then write

$$o^{\cdot} = F(shk), \qquad (1.6)$$

where s, h and k continue to hold their previous meanings. Since F, the functional operator, defines a rising but flattening curve, it follows that in an economy where either the proportion of national income saved or the rate of utilisation or both are very high, further increases in either variable will not have a great effect. There are 'diminishing returns' in a dynamic sense to either increases in saving or increases in utilisation, but it remains true that increased utilisation can provide an increased growth rate of consumption without the need for increased saving, and vice versa. In other words, utilisation and saving are substitutes in the sense that for a given rate of growth, reduced utilisation means reduced immediate consumption, but the rate of exchange is not constant. For a given rate of progress, as utilisation is increased, required savings reduced and current consumption increased, the marginal gain in permissible current consumption for a given increase in utilisation diminishes. As a matter of practical policy, a rational view of the situation will depend on whether the economy is one which could, in fact, benefit from a faster rate of replacement, and whether it seems likely that increased utilisation, rather than increased saving (and reduced consumption) is the most practical way to achieve this. On our assumptions, of course, increased saving means an increased share of non-wage income in total income, but the general conclusion remains valid even when this is not necessarily the case. Despite the simplifying assumptions, our conclusions probably represent real truths. That is to say, if an economy could gradually be reorganised to permit more intensive capital utilisation, it should be able to achieve a faster rate of progress with a given propensity to save: this means that at all future points in history consumption would be higher than would otherwise have been the case. Once a fast rate of progress has already been achieved, however, the marginal effect of further reorganisation is probably rather small.

1.6. The Rate of Utilisation and Economic Welfare

We saw earlier that in the absence of a labour premium for shift-work there is a tendency for the rate of profit in an industrial firm to rise with the rate of capital utilisation. We have now seen that a similar tendency operates with respect to an economic system as a whole and to its rate of growth. A society can balance the social cost, if any, of intensive capital utilisation against the losses or gains of potential growth. Unfortunately there is no way in which this latter decision can be made automatically. A business man may examine the shift-work and overtime premiums that he finds he will have to pay, and by a relatively simple calculation may find the rate of utilisation which maximises his rate of profit. But premiums paid by an individual firm will bear no direct relation to the general 'social disutility' of high rates of utilisation considered from the national point of view. The premium paid by an individual firm will depend on the immediate subjective evaluations of its actual or potential individual employees. These evaluations will depend in turn on factors such as the following:

(i) Instinctive dislike of nightwork.
(ii) Difficulty of obtaining transport at unusual hours.
(iii) Other domestic problems, separation from the family and friends, etc.
(iv) Difficulty of sleeping in the daytime.

Only the first is genuinely independent. All the others themselves depend in some degree on the *existing* extent of shift-working practices in the society in question. If shift-work is extensive, transport will be relatively easy to find, shops may keep special hours, social customs may ameliorate family problems, and so on. To take an extreme (and wholly imaginary) example, suppose a planned economy in which the entire population was divided into two groups, 'day-shift' families on the one hand, 'night-shift' families on the other. The gainfully occupied members of each group would work between fixed hours, and the shifts would not rotate. The non-earning members of the family would appropriately adjust their way of life to match that of the earning members, so that a 'night-shift' family, for example, would sleep in the day and the children would go to school at night. Functioning of schools, shops, places of entertainment, public offices and public transport would be suitably arranged to match the divided industrial schedule (and so provide, in addition, a considerable economy of social capital).

Families could join whichever group they chose but the central planning organisation would have somehow to arrange that the numbers in each group were approximately the same. This could be done by decreeing differential wage rates for the two shifts and by raising the premium for the night shift until the number voluntarily joining this group was equal to the number still asking to be left in the day group. The equilibrium result expressed as a percentage differential could be taken as a measure of the total social preference for day work.

Only by coincidence would the differential reached in this manner approach the figure obtaining in a free market for labour in an otherwise similar society where shift-work was a minority experience. For example, in a real society, such as the contemporary United Kingdom, it may be found that although public transport organisations are willing to provide special services for shift-workers, the demand is often insufficient to permit such services to be operated economically. A situation then arises in which, on the one hand, industrial managements complain that they cannot operate night shifts because of inadequate transport, while, on the other, the transport undertakings complain that industry fails to create an adequate demand for their vehicles at off-peak hours.† Similar situations develop in relation to the other factors mentioned; in towns where one major employment requires shift-work it is easier to operate shifts in other occupations, and vice versa; in areas where shift-work is traditional, shift-work premiums will be low, and in industries where shift-work is very common, they may become absorbed into the general wage structure (i.e. the day workers will be paid much the same as the night workers). Finally, there are factors tending in the opposite direction; for example some workers in real societies prefer shift-work precisely because it is a minority experience offering special opportunities.

We thus face the paradox that only in a society where shift-work was general could the social cost of shift-working be measured. But, as a matter of fact, even the 'social preference' defined by argument from an imaginary planned society where shift-working is general does not

† See Chapter 8.

represent a valid theoretical solution. There are good reasons why the 'equilibrium differential' would by no means adequately estimate the society's collective dislike of the system into which it had been forced. In the first place, this method of measurement takes no account of the *general* social disutility of the compulsion to choose between shifts: given that the system exists, the method indicates only the strength of the preference between shifts and tells nothing of the extent to which the system is disliked as such. The point can be seen more clearly if we drop the arbitrary assumption that shifts do not rotate. Rotating shifts are known to be disturbing and unhealthy, but might nevertheless be generally preferred to fixed shifts. If every member of the working population was employed on a rotating shift system, there would be no reason to expect (provided seasonal complications could be avoided) that one phase would be preferred to another: the 'equilibrium wage differential' might well be zero. This could certainly not be taken as an indication that the society was content. Suppose, for example, the government of this society were democratically elected by universal suffrage. Suppose there were two political parties, one which favoured a system of general rotating shifts and the other which favoured day work only; and suppose the electorate were sufficiently sophisticated to accept an independent estimate of the effect of the alternative systems on the future time-path of consumption. Then, the 'day-shift only' party might well win the election, even though, had the other party won and put its proposal into operation (or for that matter had put a non-rotating shift system into operation) the equilibrium differential would have been zero. This paradox arises because the decision, to be rational, must be collective, but if it is to be collective, because of the interdependence between the actions and desires of the individual members of the society, a free market cannot lead to a valid solution. The determination of the rate of capital utilisation thus provides a classic example of the inability of market mechanisms to make rational choices on society's behalf. And since variations in capital utilisation have powerful effects on over-all economic growth, it is an example of no mean significance.†

In practice, most societies do collectively decide, by default, to live with a fairly low rate of capital utilisation, and thus ensure that shift-work is a minority experience. The determination of the precise extent

† If the 'Compensation Principle' were applied, the procedure would be as follows. Those who had voted for fast growth and compulsory shift-work would offer to 'compensate' the rest by agreeing to pay from their own pockets annually a certain supplement to the others' wages. Unless, after taking account of the supplement necessary to induce the others to collaborate, the expected time-path of the net wages of the shift-working party lay above the path they would have experienced if the shift-working programme had not been adopted, it should not be adopted. It is rather difficult to see how this could be practically applied, because, since the population would subsequently be made up of different people, the necessary premium would always be changing. Also, the groups would have to bargain collectively, thus raising the possibility of bluff. The point is essentially theoretical: one could just as well argue that the leaders of society should impose a decision on the basis of a value judgement.

of this experience is then left in capitalist economies to the market and in planned economies, presumably, to planners. For most of the rest of this inquiry we shall confine ourselves to a more mundane but more practical task, that is to an investigation of the factors which, in a capitalist economy, and in particular in the United Kingdom, in fact determine the actual extent of multiple shift working in manufacturing industry.

1.7. Economic Growth and the Shift-Work Premium

We conclude this chapter with a pause to look ahead into our subsequent findings. We suggested in the preceding section that, given the magnitude of the shift-work premiums he must pay, a business man should be able to calculate whether shift-work is profitable or not. Obviously, if the premiums are high, it is less likely to be profitable than otherwise. But we shall find this is by no means the end of the matter. *Given* the magnitude of the premium, expressed as a ratio of the 'normal' or 'basic' wage for work done on the single-shift system, he will find that shift-work is more likely to be profitable if the basic wage is low, productivity high or his scale of production large. If the basic wage is low relative to productivity, the ratio of wages to profits without shift-work will be low. Therefore a given proportionate increase in wages due to the shift premium will cause a relatively small increase in total costs; hence the premium is likely to be a lesser deterrent to shift-work than would have been the case had the initial ratio between labour costs and profits been high. And if the scale of output is large, shift-work is less likely to be hindered by 'indivisibilities' in capital equipment.

Considering the economy as a whole, it follows from the foregoing that the higher the average level of productivity, the lower the average level of basic wages, and the larger the scale of output from the typical production process, the greater the proportion of plants in the economy likely to work shifts. In other words, the basic wage (expressed in terms of consumer-goods purchasing power), average productivity and average scale of output, together with the average magnitude of shift premiums, are the main factors which determine the average level of utilisation in a price-regulated, profit-rate-maximising economic system.

However, the relations between basic wages and output per man have another significance. They determine, in general, the distribution of income, or more specifically, the ratio, in the economy at large, between total wages and total profits. If wages and profits are thought of as exhausting the sources of income, average output per man-hour and average real wages per man-hour determine the over-all ratio of profits to total income and output.

But the share of profits in the national income must inevitably influence the average proportion of national income saved. Indeed, on the assumptions we were making earlier, the average proportion of profits and the average proportion of savings were identical, and defined by the common coefficient s. This coefficient, in turn, 'determined' the rate of growth associated with any given level of capital utilisation. In other words, we have precisely the type of two-way system of relationships suggested on p. 7. 'Other factors', in the form of income-distribution and average shift-work premium, are associated with capital utilisation in two distinct ways: by their role in business decisions they influence the rate of utilisation actually likely to be chosen and hence the rate of economic growth obtainable from given savings; by their role in the determination of savings they influence the rate of growth obtainable with given utilisation. The situation can be expressed algebraically in the form of a simple growth-model based, for convenience, on the case of a developed capitalist economy without technical progress which must nevertheless accumulate capital in order to support population growth.

$$s^* = g/hk, \qquad (1.7)$$

$$h = h(s, \bar{w}^{\cdot}, O), \qquad (1.8)$$

$$s = s^*, \qquad (1.9)$$

where

g = natural rate of population growth;

k = as defined earlier;

h = average of actual rates of utilisation chosen by individual firms;

$\bar{w}^{\cdot}$ = average level of shift-work premiums, or 'utilisation differential', defined as the proportionate increase in average hourly wages involved in adopting a typical multiple-shift system as compared with a typical single-shift system;

s = proportion of savings in national income (= proportion of profits);

s^* = value of s required to support growth at the rate g;

O = a measure of the average scale of output of individual plants.

The first equation merely repeats equation (1.4), explained earlier. The second states that, because h depends on the proportion of plants being utilised intensively, the average utilisation rate depends on the distribution of income, on the average premium and on the average scale of output. The final equation represents the condition of dynamic equilibrium, namely that, if growth at the required rate is to be achieved, actual savings must equal required savings. Since there are three equations and only three unknowns (s, s^* and h), the model determines both the proportion of savings (distribution of income) and the rate of utilisation. Capital utilisation becomes itself endogenous, and is determined by, rather than determines, the rate of growth. But these relations are not, of course, causal, rather they are relations of consistency. The equations state merely that if the government had the means to ensure a distribution of income such that savings and investment required for growth at the natural rate would in fact be forthcoming, but had no means of determining the rate of capital utilisation (or any of the exogenous 'constants'—average utilisation differential and scale of output, population growth rate and k), then it would be found that the distribution of income necessary to generate the required savings would be such as to stimulate a particular utilisation rate, as indicated by the model.

The real significance of the model lies in the effects of the coefficients. These are k, in effect a measure of the level of productivity, O, in effect a measure of the average extent to which the system exploits economies of scale, and $\bar{w}^{\cdot}$, in effect a measure of the strength of economic 'resistance' or dislike of shift-work. Given the natural rate of growth which is to be supported, and given O and k, the less the resistance to shift-work, the higher the rate of capital utilisation, the lower the required proportion of savings and the higher the level of consumption at all stages of history. Economies of scale, even if they do not interact with k, have a similar effect. But k itself, measuring the general level of productivity, raises the level of consumption without requiring high utilisation. In other words, although capital utilisation has similar effects on the history of consumption to other improvements in efficiency, it is not on all fours with other improvements, because in possibly increasing the 'disutility' of work, it does not unambiguously increase welfare. Unfortunately, for reasons already explained, there is no reason to suppose that the actual average shift-work premium, as measured by $\bar{w}^{\cdot}$, will necessarily develop in such a way as to ensure an 'optimum' choice between shift-work and consumption, even if such choice could be meaningfully defined.

CHAPTER 2

OPTIMUM UTILISATION IN A SINGLE PROCESS

2.1. The Criterion for Decision

We now begin to investigate the factors likely to influence the managers of individual enterprises in planning rates of capital utilisation in the individual plant or process. Essentially the problem is an investment decision, or, as already suggested, it is an aspect of investment planning as a whole: once a decision to undertake a specific expansion of productive capacity (defined as an annual rate of output) has been made, the amount of plant, and hence the capital outlay, depends intimately on the intended rate of utilisation. How should the latter be decided?

There are no generally accepted theories of business investment behaviour. Economists generally assume that decisions concerning particular investments will be closely governed by estimates of profitability, but there is no agreed criterion for determining the minimum rate of return sufficient for justifying an investment, nor method of deciding between alternative projects when both are adequately profitable. Profits, in any case, are by no means the only basic motive of operation in the modern company—growth, employee welfare and prestige of product are some of the others known to be important. Fortunately, these ambiguities are less serious in relation to our problem than to some. For it is difficult to envisage circumstances in which, once it has been decided that an investment should be made for a given purpose, the method of operation should not be chosen in such a way as to yield the best possible return on the capital employed, or, more precisely, it is difficult to see why one should ever choose a particular rate of capital utilisation if another would yield a higher profit rate. A firm which always determined capital utilisation in such a way as to maximise the rate of profit would find almost all other ambitions easier to satisfy—easier to grow, easier to pay good wages, easier to give value for money.

As a matter of fact, this conclusion does require some qualification. Some managers believe all-night work is bad for welfare. Men engaged on permanent night shifts are regarded as committed to a troglodytic existence which is not in their own best interest. Women, it is thought, become promiscuous—an absolute objection for morally minded managers, many of whose fears in this respect are exaggerated. Moreover, since few executive functions are easily divisible, multiple-shift operation often increases, without corresponding remuneration, the effort and anxiety of managers themselves, particularly, for example, the anxiety of works' managers: although such men are not usually required to work shifts themselves, they may live in permanent fear of telephone calls summoning them to deal with breakdowns. All these factors are real. Some have been the subject of other inquiries. Our task is to treat them, as far as possible, analytically. While we shall not investigate the theoretical consequences of society's fear of promiscuity, since these are more or less obvious, we shall indeed investigate the consequences of the fact that such fears are reflected in legislation prohibiting the employment of women and children at night (the extra cost of shift-work then including the cost of substituting male workers for underpaid females). We shall not conduct a medical investigation of managerial ulcers, but we shall consider the general theoretical implications of the indivisibility of executive functions.† In other words, we shall seek for the optimum rate of capital utilisation—where this is defined as the rate which maximises the rate of profit on the investment—subject to various practical conditions and restraints.

2.2. The Unit of Equipment

The fixed capital employed in a typical manufacturing establishment consists of a wide variety of inter-connected equipment, all collaborating in final output. But although the various items are usually essential to one another, i.e. are inter-dependent in the general production-process, it is by no means essential that all be operated at identical rates of utilisation. The buildings exist and depreciate whether the machinery is operating or not; some processes can conveniently be run in daytime only, others must be kept going round the clock. In principle processes can be regarded as independent in respect of the rate of utilisation wherever components can be stored between processes without incurring undue extra cost (such as the cost of re-heating molten metal). In practice, some processes will be independent in this sense, others not.

Having defined a 'unit of capital'‡ as the quantum of equipment corresponding to one worker, we can define a 'unit of equipment' as a group of units whose members *cannot* be operated independently, but which, as a group, may operate independently of all other such groups. In some cases the group will contain only one member; if so, the unit of capital and the unit of equipment are co-extensive. More typically, the unit of equipment would consist of several units of capital, for example a lathe (operated by one man) together with a truck (operated by one man) to bring materials and to take away products. If one truck is capable of serving a number of otherwise independent lathes, all the units of capital served by the truck, together with the truck itself, constitute one unit of equipment.

A typical manufacturing establishment will also contain a number of different *types* of units of equipment, each type carrying out a charac-

† Chapter 4, §4.7. ‡ Chapter 1, p. 14 (n.).

teristic process or 'activity'. Thus the complete description of a factory requires a description of the different types of equipment (including an indication of the units of capital which constitute one unit of each type of equipment), a statement of the number of units installed in each category and an account of the scale and cost of the buildings and common services. The problem of decision with which this study is concerned is the problem of how to specify the factory, in the foregoing sense, in such a way that in order to produce a given output at a given price the average rate of profit on capital employed is maximised. In short, how to design the factory in what is expected to be the most profitable way for the task required?

The first task of the designer is to discover how many intermediate 'products'—how many separate 'activities' and the output of each—are required in order to obtain a given quantity of final output. Each intermediate activity is presumed to be undertaken by one particular type of equipment;† therefore, if we know the output required from each activity to produce one unit of final output, and if we know the magnitude of the final output itself, we know the number of types of equipment and the total intermediate output required from each type. We do not know, however, how *many* units of equipment should be installed in order to meet these requirements—because the number of units required depends not only on the output required but also on the rate of utilisation, and, at this stage of the argument, we do not know how rates of utilisation shall be chosen. It is this last aspect of the problem which is usually overlooked in theoretical studies of the economics of factory design. The problem is to find the rate of utilisation on each type of equipment which, taken together, maximises the rate of profit on the factory as a whole.

It would appear that for each type of equipment there should exist an 'optimum rate of utilisation' which maximises the type's contribution to the general rate of profit. If this optimum rate of utilisation for each type of equipment could be determined independently of the factors influencing the optimum rates of the other types, the problem would be simple. We would find each type's independently determined optimum rate and then compute the number of units required, by dividing in each case the required output by the product of the hourly rate of output of that type of equipment and the optimum rate of utilisation expressed in machine-hours per annum. Unfortunately, this solution is rarely available. Because intermediate outputs are usually required in virtually fixed proportions, the optimum rate of utilisation on any one type of equipment is inevitably affected by the operating conditions of the other types, and these in turn depend on what has been decided about the first type. The solution is therefore inevitably simultaneous and inevitably complex; but it is convenient to begin with a simplified example in which the whole final product is made with only one type of equipment. For the sake of argument the factory will

† We introduce alternative techniques of production later—§2.10 *et seq.*

be presumed to consist of a battery of identical units of equipment, each of which is capable of fabricating the complete finished product from the same raw material—in this factory, therefore, there is only one activity. The analytic task is no more than to decide how many units of this one type of equipment should be installed to produce a given total output, which means of course no more than deciding optimum rate of utilisation of one unit. As a further simplification we will assume that the cost of the buildings varies exactly in proportion to the total number of units housed, a particularly unrealistic postulate. However, there is no need to be alarmed because unrealistic assumptions are necessary to obtain easily intelligible solutions. We shall find that the simple example demonstrates important tendencies which cannot be reversed by investigating more complex realistic cases.

2.3. Definition of the Rate of Profit

When each unit of equipment is capable of producing the finished product, each unit can be assigned its own rate of profit. The rate of profit with which we are concerned (for a single unit) is defined as follows:

O = annual output of the unit;

P = selling price of the product;

W = total wages paid to the unit's operatives, per annum;

N = other prime costs incurred when operating the unit (materials, fuel, etc.), per annum;

C = original capital cost of the unit;

D = annual depreciation of the unit;

r = 'crude net profit rate' of the unit.

Then
$$r = \frac{OP - W - N - D}{C}. \tag{2.1}$$

That is to say, the crude net profit rate is defined as the ratio of current net profit to the *initial* capital cost. Normally, a profit rate is defined as the ratio of net profit to the written-down value of the capital, and the latter in turn depends on the age of the equipment in question. But it is clear that in most cases the rate of utilisation which maximises this crude net profit rate will also maximise the true net profit rate; therefore, for this problem it is sufficient to concentrate on the crude rate alone. Indeed, as we have already implied, given the assumptions of the simple case we are considering, since each unit of equipment has identical characteristics, the optimum operating conditions for each must be identical. In other words, the crude rate on one unit is the same as the crude rate for the factory: on these special assumptions if we know the conditions for maximising the profit rate on one unit of equipment, we know the conditions for maximising the general profit rate in the whole factory (the profit rate on one unit is in fact the same thing as the general profit rate).

The capital cost of one unit of equipment (C) is fixed. Therefore to maximise its *rate* of profit we have only to maximise its annual total profits or earnings. We may begin the analysis for finding this position by considering the various elements in the formula for the rate of profit in turn. If we take the price of the product (P) and the cost of the equipment (C) as given, we are left with only four variables, O (annual output), W (wage bill), N (other prime costs) and D (depreciation). Given the hourly rate of output of the particular type of equipment, the annual output depends exclusively on the rate of utilisation. The wage bill is the product of the rate of utilisation, measured in operating-hours per annum, and the average hourly wage rate; other prime costs are the product of the rate of utilisation and the hourly rate at which these costs are incurred. It is therefore possible to re-write the formula for the 'crude net profit rate' as follows:

$$r = \frac{h(Po - w - n)}{C} - d, \qquad (2.2)$$

where

h = rate of utilisation measured in operating hours per annum;
P = selling price of the product;
o = hourly rate of output of one unit of equipment;
w = hourly wage bill of one unit of equipment;
n = hourly rate of other prime costs;
d = annual rate of depreciation ($= D/C$).

Evidently, if the wage rate and the rate of other costs are independent of the rate of utilisation, any increase in the rate of utilisation must increase the profit rate. But if increases in the rate of utilisation cause increases in the wage rate, the net result is uncertain.

2.4. Definition of a System of Operation

The rate of utilisation can be varied by the use of overtime and shift systems, and there is a considerable variety of possibilities. The 'normal' working week may be 40 hours, 45 hours or even 50 hours, and to this can be added as much as 10 or even 20 hours of overtime. A double-day shift system of $7\frac{1}{2}$ hours per shift, two shifts per day, 5 days per week, yields 75 machine-hours; a 5-day day shift combined with a permanent 5-day night shift, each shift of 8 hours, yields 80 machine-hours per week; a 6-day day-and-night-shift yields 96 hours; a continuous three-shift system, halted on Sundays, 140 hours; a fully continuous system, 168 hours. There are also intermediate possibilities, for instance, a day-and-night-shift system with overtime on one or both shifts.

Both 'overtime' and shift-work are likely to involve increased labour costs per unit of output. In the case of shift-work the result comes about in several ways. The most obvious way is when, on account of the subjective 'disutility' of labouring in unusual hours it is necessary to offer shift-workers an overt premium on the basic normal hourly wage. Less obviously, a shift-working plant may be forced to pay all its employees, shift-workers or not, at a higher-than-normal rate because willingness to undertake shift-work must be a general condition of employment at the plant; in other words, because of the 'risk' of being required to work shifts, the general level of wages for given grades of labour must be higher than in comparable plants where the risk does not exist. Or, where shift-work is a general practice throughout a whole industry, the level of wages in the industry may be higher than would otherwise have needed to be the case, even though non-shift workers, if any, are paid the same rates as the rest. Finally, protective social legislation may prohibit the employment of women and juveniles outside 'normal' hours so that the operation of a night-shift involves the employment of expensive male labour where cheaper female or juvenile labour would otherwise be more economical. For all these reasons it is generally the case that the hourly 'efficiency-wage' rises as the rate of utilisation is increased.

The increases in unit prime costs which come with increases in utilisation rates may or may not be progressive and are unlikely to be smooth. The premium for a double-day shift may be, or may not be, higher than the premium for the first few hours of overtime, and whether it is or not, there is inevitably a discontinuous jump in conditions when changing from overtime to any sort of shift system. Nevertheless, it is not difficult to arrive at general rules for determining the optimum system of operation and hence the optimum utilisation rate.

By a 'system' we mean a specific plan of overtime or shift-working such as described above. Each system implies a rate of utilisation, a wage rate and a depreciation rate. For each system there is a characteristic rate of profit, that is, a determinate value of r as defined in equation (2.2). We can summarise this profit rate by

$$r = \frac{hm}{C} - d, \tag{2.3}$$

where m, which can be called the *hourly profit margin*, stands for the amount of gross profit, measured in money, earned per hour of operating time, with that system. A 'system' is a method for operating a given type of equipment, therefore the equipment's cost, C, is unaffected by change of system. Variations in system can affect h, m and d only. However, if there is no user cost, if depreciation is entirely attributable to obsolescence, d also remains unchanged between systems. Where this occurs, the comparisons can as validly be made on the basis of the gross profit rate as of the net rate—that is to say wherever the gross profit rate is greater on one system than another, so also will be the net rate. In order to simplify the argument for the time being we shall assume this to be the case, making the necessary adjustment for user cost later. We shall also for the time being assume that the hourly rate of other prime costs, n, does not vary between systems: in many industries, particularly metals and chemicals manufacturing, other prime costs fall markedly as utilisation rates rise and although our study is not primarily concerned with such cases, we will in due course demonstrate the necessary adjustment for this also.

In comparing two systems, say 'system 1' and 'system 2', we shall refer to the proportionate increase in average hourly efficiency-wages (i.e. the proportionate increase in labour costs per hourly unit of output) caused by changing from 1 to 2 as the *utilisation differential*.

2.5. The Incentive to Utilise

We ignore depreciation, then, and concentrate on the behaviour of the gross profit margin and the gross rate of profit on capital, i.e. on r, where r is re-defined as

$$r = \frac{mh}{C}. \tag{2.4}$$

Let us compare two alternative systems of operation for a given activity with a given type of equipment. Since the type of equipment is fixed, the systems differ only in respect of the rate of utilisation (h) and the profit margin (m). In system 1, we may suppose, the rate of utilisation is lower and the profit margin is higher than in system 2, because in 2, on account of a utilisation differential, the wage rate is higher. In moving hypothetically from system 1 to system 2, the proportionate change in the profit rate depends on the interaction between the proportionate changes in the rate of utilisation and profit margin in the following manner;†

$$r^{\cdot} = h^{\cdot} - m^{\cdot} - h^{\cdot}m^{\cdot}, \tag{2.5}$$

where $h^{\cdot}$ is defined as the proportionate increase in rate of utilisation and $m^{\cdot}$ as the proportionate *decrease* in profit margin. For example if the rate of utilisation is doubled while the profit margin is halved, $h^{\cdot}$ is equal to 1·0 and $m^{\cdot}$ is equal to 0·5; $r^{\cdot}$ is therefore zero. In this case there is no gain or loss of profitability in moving from system 1 to system 2.

If $r^{\cdot}$ is positive, system 1 is more profitable than system 2, and vice versa. $r^{\cdot}$ will always be positive wherever

$$m^{\cdot} < \frac{h^{\cdot}}{1+h^{\cdot}} \quad \text{or} \quad h^{\cdot} > \frac{m^{\cdot}}{1-m^{\cdot}}, \tag{2.6}$$

i.e. wherever the proportionate decline in the profit margin is less than a certain function of the proportionate increase in the rate of utilisation. For an increase in utilisation to be profitable it must exceed the reduc-

† Throughout this study we use the symbol $x^{\cdot}$ to indicate a *proportionate* change in some variable, x. In Chapter 1, the change related to a period of time; in this and the remaining chapters of Part I, the change is that occurring when moving from one method of production to another, and may for this reason be large.

tion in the profit margin by a definite amount. This amount increases with the magnitude of the reduction in the profit margin itself. Where conditions are such that the decline in the profit margin is large, only a very large increase in the rate of utilisation indeed can provide the necessary offset. In the limiting case, if the profit margin declines by 100 %, profits have become zero and no increase in the rate of utilisation, however large, can be profitable—if each unit of output earns no profit, annual profit remains zero however many units are annually produced.

To sum up: we have defined the coefficient $r^{\cdot}$, which measures the proportionate difference between the rates of profit associated with any two specific systems for operating a given type of equipment in a given economic activity. The comparison is always to be made in terms of a movement from the system of lower to the system of higher utilisation. Hence, a positive value of $r^{\cdot}$ indicates that the system of higher utilisation is the more profitable, a negative value indicates that it is the less profitable. Henceforth we will call $r^{\cdot}$ the *incentive to utilise* or, alternatively, the *utilisation incentive*.

We have seen that the value of the utilisation incentive depends on the opposition of two factors, the increase in the rate of utilisation on the one hand and the fall in the profit margin per unit of output on the other. Given the magnitude of the proportionate reduction in the profit margin (and provided this is not greater than one, i.e. provided profits do not become losses) we can say that the greater the magnitude of the proportionate increase in rate of utilisation, the greater the value of the incentive to utilise and the more likely this coefficient to be positive. Alternatively, given the increase in the rate of utilisation, the greater the proportionate reduction in the profit margin, the smaller the coefficient of incentive to utilise and the more likely it is to be negative. Thus we confirm the intuitively obvious conclusion that the smaller the fall in the profit margin relative to any given proposed increase in rate of utilisation, the more likely is that increase to be profitable.

2.6. The Optimum Rate of Utilisation

All possible systems relating to any given activity can be compared by reference to the utilisation incentive. If the comparisons are strictly confined to the effects of changes from systems of lower to systems of higher utilisation, there is little difficulty in finding the system which is most profitable of all. Thus, suppose there are four available systems, 1, 2, 3 and 4, the numbers representing the ordering of the systems in terms of rate of utilisation: system 1 might be a single-shift system, 2 might be a double-day-shift system, 3 a rotating day-and-night-shift system and the last a three-shift system. Each system should be compared with all others more highly numbered. Thus 1 should be compared with 2, 3 and 4; 2 with 3 and 4; 3 with 4; and 4 with none. From each such comparison there is a value of the utilisation incentive,

$r^{\cdot}$. Wherever $r^{\cdot}$ is positive the lower-numbered system can be rejected and in due course the optimum system (i.e. the most profitable of all) will be found.

For every comparison between pairs of systems, then, there is a value of the incentive to utilise. If there were only two systems, a change in this value would not necessarily change the optimum, but might well do. If the change were large enough and in the right direction (i.e. sufficient to change the sign of the coefficient) a change of optimum would be inevitable. We can therefore say more loosely that in this case an increase in the incentive to utilise must *tend* to raise the optimum rate of utilisation, that is, must increase the likelihood that the system of higher utilisation will become optimum. When there is a number of systems to compare, this conclusion becomes more general. If something occurs to raise the average value of all utilisation incentives through the whole matrix of pairwise comparisons, there will be a tendency to optimise a system of higher utilisation than was the case before the change occurred. If the increase in the general level of the incentives is large enough, some increase in the optimum rate of utilisation is inevitable unless the system of highest utilisation has been optimised already.

The factors determining the optimum system, then, are the factors influencing the general level of incentives to utilise. These are investigated in the next section.

2.7. Factors Determining the Incentive to Utilise

From what has been said up to this point, it will be clear that the kernel of the problem lies in those factors which determine the extent of the fall in the profit margin for a given increase in rate of utilisation. The profit margin falls when the rate of utilisation increases because the wage rate rises. Obviously then, the greater the utilisation differential in wages—i.e. the greater the proportionate increase in average hourly wage costs associated with moving from the system of low to the system of high utilisation—the greater the fall in the profit margin and the smaller the incentive to utilise. But it is unusual for profits and wages to represent equal proportions of the value of output; normally wages are larger than profits. Therefore an increase in wage costs must cause a disproportionate fall in profit margin. In fact there is a predictable ratio between the proportionate rise in unit wage costs and the proportionate fall in profit margin. Precisely, if the economic conditions associated with the system of lower utilisation, which we will continue to refer to as system 1, are called the 'initial' conditions, then the higher the ratio of wages to profits in the initial conditions, the greater the proportionate fall in profit margin for any given utilisation differential. Algebraically, the proportionate fall in the profit margin is given by

$$m^{\cdot} = w^{\cdot}w', \qquad (2.7)$$

where w' is the initial ratio of wages to profits and $w^{\cdot}$ the utilisation differential. Given $w^{\cdot}$, $m^{\cdot}$ varies directly with w', and hence given both the increase in utilisation and the associated wage differential, the incentive to utilise depends on the initial value of w' alone. This value therefore deserves further analysis. By applying the additional notation set out on p. 30,† we can show that

$$w' = \frac{1}{(oP/w)-(n/w)-1}. \tag{2.8}$$

In other words w' is greater:

(i) the greater the initial wage rate;
(ii) the lower the price of the product;
(iii) the lower the hourly rate of output of the equipment (productivity);
(iv) the greater the hourly rate of other prime costs.

The foregoing result can be stated in a more sophisticated manner by taking fuller account of the factors determining n. This variable, evidently, depends both on the quantities of the raw materials and fuel, etc., consumed by the equipment each hour, and on the average price of these inputs. Suppose their average price is expressed as a fraction, a, of the selling price of the final product, and that the quantities can be expressed as another fraction, b, of the hourly rate of final output. Then

$$w' = \frac{1}{(Po/w)(1-ab)-1}. \tag{2.9}$$

The ratio of wages to profits is therefore greater the greater the wage rate *relatively* to selling price or productivity; it also varies directly with the ratio of input prices to output price and with the quantity of input required to produce a unit of final output.

The following therefore emerge as factors capable of influencing the initial ratio of wages to profits and hence the utilisation incentive:

the initial wage rate;
the hourly rate of output;
the selling price;
the ratio of input prices to output prices;
the ratio of input quantities to output quantities.

Except for the initial wage rate, none of the above are factors which vary between systems; their influence, therefore, is straightforward: the higher the hourly rate of output ('hourly productivity') or selling price, or the lower the ratios of input to output quantities or prices for other prime costs, the greater will be the incentive to utilise.

The initial wage rate varies between systems because it is associated with the rate of utilisation; for each system and rate of utilisation, there is a wage rate,‡ and vice versa. Nevertheless, the wage rate is also

† Reminder: o, hourly output; w, initial hourly wage; P, price of the product; n, hourly rate of other prime costs; w', initial ratio of wages to profits ($= w/m = w/o-w-n$).

‡ Where the system involves different wage rates on different shifts, this is an average of, for example, day and night rates.

evidently susceptible to general influences. A rise in the 'basic' or normal wage for day shifts will usually be associated with an equivalent rise in the rate payable on multiple-shift systems. If the *utilisation differentials* between all systems from a given set are constant, a rise in the wage rate on one system implies, by definition, an equal proportional rise in all others: such a development may be called a rise in the general level of wages and this level may itself be defined by reference to the rate payable for 'normal' hours. A rise in the general level of wages, unless offset by a corresponding increase in selling price or productivity, must lower the general level of the incentive to utilise.

We may now combine the results of our dissection of the wage–profit ratio with the earlier equations. The combination of equations (2.5), (2.7) and (2.9) yields the following complete formula for the incentive to utilise:

$$r^{\cdot} = h^{\cdot} - \frac{w^{\cdot}(h^{\cdot}+1)}{(Po/w)(1-ab)-1}. \tag{2.10}$$

There must evidently be some connection between $h^{\cdot}$, the proportionate increase in utilisation, and $w^{\cdot}$, the utilisation differential (difference in wage cost). For example, if the comparison relates to two systems with a moderate increase in utilisation such as is obtained in changing from a single day shift to a double-day shift, both employing women, the utilisation differential may represent no more than the premium implicit in allowing the workers a slightly shorter individual working week for the same weekly wage.† If, on the other hand, the single-shift system is compared with a system involving night work, not only is the increase in utilisation proportionately greater, but so also the cost in terms of utilisation differential, because it will now be necessary to employ men. The precise relationship between $h^{\cdot}$ and $w^{\cdot}$ will depend first on the character of the two systems being compared and secondly on general conditions in the industry. Unfortunately it is not easy to separate the latter from the former. Clearly, however, there will be circumstances—for example, economic conditions otherwise favouring employment of females or strong local resistance to shift-work owing to absence of other shift-working firms—when we can say that the 'general level' of the differential is high.

This concept of general level of utilisation differential is more difficult to define than the concept of a general level of wages,‡ but we may say

† In many double-day arrangements this is the only 'price' the employer has to pay, and the effective utilisation differential is sometimes less than 10%. For empirical data, see Chapter 7, Table 7.3.

‡ The mathematical reader will appreciate that the difficulty arises because the hierarchy of systems of operation is discontinuous. There are no intermediate positions between adjacent systems. A system is defined by two variables, wage rate and utilisation rate. Both are discontinuous. We cannot say what wage rate would be paid for a utilisation rate that is not feasible.

Were the variables continuous, we could write the wage rate as a function of the utilisation rate, in which case the optimum rate of utilisation is found by increasing the rate until $d(\log w)/d(\log h) = 1/w'$, where w' continues to stand for the wage–profit ratio. Since w' rises with h, it is possible that in the absence of boundaries, the 'optimum' would be plus or minus infinity.

that the general level has increased if, for any given set of systems relating to one process (and hence given set of values of $h^{\cdot}$), one or more of the corresponding utilisation differentials between the systems has increased while none has decreased, and vice versa. If the reader will then permit us to slide from defining a change in the general level of differentials to writing as if we could define the level itself, we can summarise the complete list of factors influencing the general level of the incentive to utilise:

(i) the general level of utilisation differentials;
(ii) the general level of wages;
(iii) the level of other factors influencing the ratio of wages to profits (product price, hourly productivity, input–output ratios of the prices and quantities of raw materials and fuel, etc.).

All, with the exception of the product-price and hourly productivity, operate with inverse effect. It follows that with the two exceptions mentioned, an increase in any of the above will tend to reduce, but will not necessarily be sufficient to change, the optimum rate of utilisation. An alternative formulation states that the incentive to utilise depends on the general level of utilisation differentials and the initial wage–profit ratio (w') only. The level of utilisation differentials expresses labour's 'resistance' to shift-work in monetary form, the wage–profit ratio measures the distribution of the proceeds of production within the firm. The connection between this analysis of the situation in a single process and the analysis for the economy as a whole (especially as discussed in the final section of Chapter 1) should now be clear.

2.8. Economies in Other Prime Costs

So far we have assumed that the hourly rate of other prime costs, n, is constant between systems, i.e. we have ignored important economies in fuel and raw materials which may be achieved in many industries by continuous or semi-continuous operation involving high rates of utilisation. In chemicals and metal manufacture, for example, these economies may be so significant that economies in capital cost associated with high utilisation may represent little more than an incidental factor in the managerial decision. Not much needs to be said on the point, however, because it presents few analytical problems. If the hourly rate of other prime costs, n, varies between systems—for example, because the cost of fuel per unit of output is lower in the higher-utilisation systems—the effect falls on the profit margin in a similar manner, although usually in the opposite direction, to that of the wage differential. In the formula $m = Po - w - n$, the proportionate influence of a given proportionate change in n depends on the initial ratio of other prime costs to profits. As we said earlier that given n, the ratio of wages to profits depended on the share of wages in the proceeds of output, so we say now that given the share of wages in the proceeds of output, the higher the share of other prime costs, the higher the ratio of other prime costs to profits. And the factors influencing the share of other prime costs in the proceeds of output have already been analysed above (p. 35). In short, in an industry where other prime costs are a heavy element in total costs, economies in these costs, achieved by shift-working, will be well worth while. It is possible that they will be so important that in changing from a system of low to a system of high utilisation, their effects may oppose the effects of the wage differential to such an extent that the profit margin, instead of falling, rises. In such cases there would be a gain in profitability even if there were no reduction in capital cost: the incentive to utilise, in these cases, must inevitably be positive.

2.9. Depreciation

We say in Chapter 1 (p. 8) that depreciation should be divided into two parts, a part attributable to wear and tear or 'user cost' and a part attributable to other causes, such as rusting, rotting and technical obsolescence. The first part varies with utilisation, the second does not. In order to consider the effects of introducing depreciation we need to restore the notation in which r was defined as the rate of net, rather than gross profit. Suppose we adopt the following notation:

C = value of the capital unit;
u = user-cost depreciation per hour of operating time, as ratio of C;
z = annual rate of other depreciation (total annual cost expressed as a ratio of C);
m = hourly gross profit margin;
u' = initial value of the ratio uC/m.

Then
$$r = h\left(\frac{m}{C} - u\right) - z, \qquad (2.11)$$

$$r^{\cdot} = h^{\cdot}\left(1 - \frac{m^{\cdot}}{1-u'}\right) - \frac{m^{\cdot}}{1-u'}. \qquad (2.12)$$

For example, if a machine depreciates by 5 % per annum through obsolescence and other non-user depreciation, z is 0·05. If, on account of user cost, the machine depreciates by another 2 % per annum for every 1000 hours of annual operation, u is 0·00002. With h at 2000, C at, say, £1000 and m at, say, £0·08, r, the net profit rate, would be 7 %.

For reasons also discussed in Chapter 1 (p. 9) it is likely that u, the hourly rate of user cost, will vary between systems, often falling as utilisation rises. Where, however, u is constant between systems, we can see from equation (2.12) that the higher the initial burden of user cost, expressed in the ratio u',† the lower the general level of the incentive to

† u is the proportion by which the value of the equipment depreciates, due to user cost, per hour of operating time. u', defined as the initial value of uC/m, is the initial value of u to the *hourly* gross profit *rate*, the latter being the amount of profit earned in an hour of operating

utilise. This ratio will tend to be high, given product price, productivity, and wage rate, if the value of u itself is high, in other words if the machine is one which wears badly. Other things being equal, therefore, it is likely that the optimum rate of utilisation for a machine which wears well will be higher than that for a machine which wears badly.

Where the hourly rate of user cost declines with utilisation, the optimum rate of utilisation will, of course, tend to be higher (other things again being equal) than where this is not the case.

User cost, therefore, behaves much as 'other prime costs', measured by n, in the earlier analysis. Our main reason for treating it separately was to distinguish its role from that of the other main element in depreciation, obsolescence. At first sight the annual rate of obsolescence appears to have no influence whatsoever on the coefficient of incentive to utilise, because it is unaffected by the rate of utilisation and does not vary between systems. But this conclusion is valid only if the hourly rate of *user cost* is itself independent of the rate of obsolescence, and it is frequently argued that obsolescence and wear-and-tear depreciation cannot be separated, because the amount of value lost through wear and tear depends on the amount already lost through obsolescence: no 'user cost' occurs with a machine which, having become totally obsolete, is valueless. By contrast, in the argument of the preceding paragraphs, the rate of user cost (u) and the rate of obsolescence (z) are treated as separate, and, in effect, additive.

The problem may be analysed by imagining a state of affairs where there is a well-developed and clearly defined market for second-hand equipment, as, for example, in the case of transport vehicles. In this market vehicles change hands at prices reflecting current relative earning power, which depends in turn on their condition and the extent of competition from later models. Thus the second-hand value of the equipment depends partly on age and partly on use; for example, in the case of an aircraft, partly on age and partly on mileage. On these assumptions the two forms of depreciation may be considered quite independent: the cost of wear and tear depreciation reflects the loss of earning power due to rising maintenance bills, depends exclusively on the aggregate operating hours and is entirely unaffected by the extent to which the machine has or will depreciate through exogenous obsolescence.

Where, as in many cases in real life, there is no clearly defined second-hand market, the character of the problem remains basically the same, although conceptually more delicate. The true depreciation of the machine essentially derives from the decline in earning-power; when earning-power becomes zero, the machine is valueless, and must be replaced. When obsolescence is rapid, a machine may become valueless

per £ of capital. u' is a good measure of whether a machine wears 'well' or 'badly' because it takes account of both the cost, and the output of a machine. Thus if the hourly user depreciation of two machines is identical, but one has higher hourly productivity, this one will display a smaller value of u'.

long before the end of its physical life, but the date of economic death depends not only on obsolescence, but also on interim wear and tear. For example, suppose a machine is bought at date t but never used. Then suppose that seven years later, the machine, if now used for the first time, can earn nothing because, owing to technical progress, the selling price of the product has become less than unit prime costs. But, if the machine had been used, the date of decease would have been earlier, because rising maintenance costs or falling labour productivity (reflecting wear and tear) would have added to the losses caused by obsolescence, and advanced the date at which no profits could be earned. The more intensively the machine had been used, the more powerful this second effect, and the two effects are additive. Provided the economic effect of wear and tear, per hour of running time, is constant over the life of the machine, intensive utilisation must advance the date of economic death, in other words must accelerate total depreciation and continue to function in the manner assumed above.

Nevertheless, it is widely believed in industry that where, due to fast technical change, obsolescence is rapid, the economic significance of wear and tear depreciation is reduced and, other things being equal, the case for shift-work strengthened. There are two reasons for this, both, despite our arguments, perfectly rational.

In the first place, wear and tear depreciation often fails to progress smoothly, as we have assumed, but instead is slight during the early stages of working life, then, after a certain point, increases rapidly. If this point occurs at a date in time *after* the machine has become virtually valueless due to obsolescence, the incidence of any subsequent 'user cost' becomes academic, since the machine has ended its economic life anyway. For example, suppose a machine would become obsolete in five years, but would not begin to show signs of wear and tear until it had been run for ten years on single shifts. Suppose the technical conditions are such that doubling the annual rate of utilisation will have an exactly proportional effect and thus advance by five years the date when rapid wear begins. Then, whether the firm chooses double shifts or single shifts, no user cost can be experienced during the maximum economic life of the machine, or more precisely, wear and tear cannot affect the length of this life. It follows that user cost may be ignored in determining the optimum rate of utilisation, and the formula based on gross profits, developed in the preceding sections, may be applied without modification. Given the necessary 'non-linear' development of the rate of wear and tear, the faster the rate of obsolescence, the more likely is this situation to be found. Provided there is a tendency to the necessary non-linearity, there will be a tendency for user cost to be less significant, and hence for shift-work to be more attractive, wherever obsolescence itself is rapid.

That, however, is not the end of the matter. If an industry experiences rapid obsolescence it will have to develop a structure of prices, relative to prime costs, such that the average firm can earn reasonable profits. This will mean that as compared with otherwise similar industries in which obsolescence is less rapid, the ratio of gross profits to wages will tend to be higher, and intensive capital utilisation, according to the principles explained above, more attractive. It is therefore to be expected that in industries with rapid obsolescence, other things being equal, both profit margins and optimum utilisation rates will tend to be relatively high and it is true, therefore, that obsolescence can be said to encourage shift-work. To the extent that the rate of obsolescence in an industry is partly a reflection of the industry's own inner dynamism (rather than of purely 'outside' forces, such as technical change in the relevant capital-goods industries), the conclusion implies an interconnecting causal chain similar to the one we previously identified for the economy as a whole. An industry or an economy which is developing fast should tend to display high profits, rapid replacement, rapid obsolescence and relatively high capital utilisation.

Rates of obsolescence are difficult to measure and we were unable, therefore, to undertake quantitative tests of either of the above hypotheses. We did, however, find considerable qualitative support in industrial interviews: for example, the manager of a ball-bearing plant argued graphically that since technical progress would render his machines obsolete in five years, he aimed to 'wear them out as quickly as possible', by means of extensive shift work. This discussion emphasises the limited nature of our inquiry so far. We have so far merely developed an objective formula listing the factors affecting the optimum utilisation in a single process. It may be that in order to explain what happens in real life we shall have to go outside the firm and try to discover why particular variables in the formula take on particular values in particular situations. As the argument develops we shall make such excursions more frequently.

2.10. Alternative Techniques of Production: Basic Definitions

So far we have assumed that when a plant was designed, only one type of equipment was available for the intended purpose; therefore, given the desired rate of output, the designer had only to determine the rate of utilisation in order to know how many units of the equipment he would require. If, instead, the market for capital goods offers a number of alternative types of equipment, the specification of the plant design must indicate not only the number of units required but also their type. The specification of type we call a 'technique of production'.

A technique of production is a method of producing a given product with a particular type of capital equipment. A full description of a technique, therefore, includes not only a description of the equipment but also of the mode of operation. In order to avoid the length and difficulty involved in complete descriptions, techniques are usually given names derived from a salient characteristic in equipment or method. Sometimes a technique is named after the equipment used ('Lancashire Loom', 'Automatic Loom') sometimes after a chemical feature of the production process ('Cold Rolled', 'Hot Rolled'); in all cases the name is intended to convey a general specification of a production process, equipment type and labour requirement. In what follows we shall refer to techniques by numbers, each number representing, as it were, the code-name of a distinct technique. The code-name of a technique relates to a dictionary of technology, but each item possesses measurable economic characteristics, such as capital cost, instantaneous employment, other prime costs, hourly user cost, hourly output and annual obsolescence, which directly affect the rate of profit. The rate of profit, however, is determined not only by these characteristics but also by the system of utilisation. We shall call a statement of the name of the technique and the planned system of utilisation in a given process an *activity programme*. The set of activity programmes required to determine the design for all the processes of a multi-activity plant we call a *plant programme*. Where, as in the present chapter, plants are presumed to comprise only one activity (so that plant and activity programmes are identical) we speak simply of 'the programme'.

Table 2.1. *Matrix of activity programmes*

Technique	System 1	2	3
1	1, 1	1, 2	1, 3
2	2, 1	2, 2	2, 3
3	3, 1	3, 2	3, 3

As we numbered systems of operation in order of their utilisation rates so we may number techniques of production in order of output per man-hour. Then, in an example containing three alternative techniques and three alternative systems, there are nine alternative programmes, indicated as in Table 2.1. Thus programme 2, 3 is the programme employing technique 2 on system 3. As we move from left to right along a row we increase utilisation with given technique; as we descend a column we increase hourly productivity with given utilisation. Any increase in hourly productivity, represented by a change to a higher-numbered technique, will be referred to as an increase in *mechanisation*. Therefore a diagonal move, such as from 1, 1 to 2, 2, represents an increase in both mechanisation and utilisation—more mechanised equipment, more intensively utilised. Where there are more or less than three techniques or systems, the dimensions of the matrix will, of course, be modified accordingly.

We may signify the profit rate associated with the employment of a given programme by, say, $r(2, 2)$, where this is the rate for programme 2, 2. In order to compute the profit rate of a particular programme we need not only the economic details of the named technique but also the wage rate and utilisation rate of the system of operation. We also need the selling price of the product. If we postulate a 'basic' wage rate to be paid on system 1 (which may generally be thought of as the single-shift system) the wage rate payable on all other systems is given by the various utilisation differentials. We may refer to the technique details, the utilisation differentials and the utilisation rates of the various techniques and systems respectively as the *data* of the programme matrix. Given the data, the basic wage and the price of the product, each programme matrix implies a unique profit-rate matrix, that is, a list of programme profit rates arranged in rows and columns corresponding to those in Table 2.1. With given data, variations in basic wage rates or product prices affect every profit rate in a predictable manner. In order to analyse the more fundamental aspects of these relationships, we shall make a series of rather unrealistic simplifying assumptions, some of which will later be relaxed. For the time being we assume that all techniques are identical in every characteristic influencing the shift-work decision *except* in the relationship between output per man-hour and capital cost per unit of instantaneous employment. More specifically, the techniques are assumed to be identical in respect of:

(i) Value of other prime costs per £'s worth of final output (i.e. they are identical in respect of the product ab in equation (2.9)).

(ii) The incidence of user cost in the 'incentive to utilise' (see § 2.9; in effect, we assume that u is zero on all techniques, at least within the obsolescence life of the equipment at the highest rate of utilisation).

(iii) The utilisation differential between any pair of systems in the data (e.g. the proportionate increase in average hourly wage bill in changing from one shift to two shifts is assumed the same whatever type of equipment is used).

(iv) Instantaneous employment, per unit of equipment.

These admittedly unrealistic assumptions are designed to help bring out the essential characteristics of the economic problem that is involved when a manufacturer is faced with the alternative methods of increasing capital intensity: on the one hand, increased mechanisation, on the other, reduced utilisation. They have the effect of making the ordering of gross profit rates of all programmes identical to the corresponding ordering of net profit rates, and they simplify the definition of the data. In real life examples, the necessary modifications to take account of varying burdens of other prime cost and of user cost can be fairly easily made, and in § 2.12 below we specifically consider the effects of dropping the assumption of equal utilisation differentials. The final assumption (equal instantaneous employment), which has little economic significance as such, is relaxed in Chapter 4. We consider, then, a matrix of gross profit rates and define the *optimum programme* as the one whose gross profit rate is highest.

We have seen that when utilisation is varied with given technique, changes in labour cost, expressed in the utilisation differential, are exchanged for offsetting changes in capital cost, caused by the variation of utilisation. If the initial ratio of wages to profits in the proceeds of output is sufficiently high, a reduction in utilisation may thus yield an increase in the rate of profit, even though the reduction in utilisation is proportionately considerably greater than the associated reduction in wages. *Given* the initial wage–profit ratio, however, the profitability of a change in utilisation depends on its quantitative relation to the associated change in wage cost.

The effect of variations in technique is analogous. With given utilisation, a change of technique will not be considered unless it offers some exchange between labour cost and capital cost; if capital cost, for example, were to increase with no reduction in labour cost, the variation would be unprofitable. In general, 'mechanisation' involves a reduction of labour cost (through increased productivity) in exchange for increased capital cost through the use of more expensively designed equipment. Where an increase in productivity can be achieved without increase in the cost of the equipment, the 'inferior' equipment will not be employed in any circumstances. Therefore we may say that the invention of techniques which are superior, in this sense, to techniques currently in use represents an 'improvement in technical knowledge'—an aspect of technical progress. For the moment we shall rule out technical progress and consider the implications of a fixed hierarchy of techniques, none of which is inferior to any other in the sense of offering, with given utilisation, lower labour cost or higher capital cost without *some* opposing variation in the other. This means that the 'data' of the programme matrix relates only to techniques whose ordering in terms of hourly productivity is identical to their ordering in terms of capital value per unit of equipment; that is to say, the ordering of o is the same as the ordering of C.

Since the character of the variation is essentially the same—an exchange between labour cost and capital cost—we can expect that the 'optimum' among a set of non-inferior techniques, assuming given utilisation, will be determined in a similar manner to the optimum utilisation of a given technique. That is to say, whether an increase in mechanisation will be profitable will depend on the initial wage–profit ratio. The higher the initial burden of labour costs, the more likely is any specified increase in mechanisation to be profitable. *Given* the initial wage–profit ratio, the result should depend on the relation between the proportionate change in productivity and the proportionate change in capital cost. It is therefore convenient to define two coefficients designed to summarise the relations between the forces making for increased mechanisation and the forces making for increased utilisation respectively. We define,†

† The corresponding section of the mathematical appendix is A. 2. The greater generality of the Appendix required a more complex notation (first explained on pp. 64–9 below), but

(i) *The Elasticity of Utilisation*

The elasticity of utilisation between two systems of operation is defined as the proportionate increase in utilisation rate, when moving from the lower-numbered to the higher-numbered system, divided by the corresponding utilisation differential. Therefore, in the notation developed in the preceding sections, the elasticity of utilisation, which we shall call E_u, is given by

$$E_u = h^{\cdot}/w^{\cdot}. \tag{2.13}$$

(ii) *The Elasticity of Mechanisation*

The elasticity of mechanisation between two techniques is defined as the proportionate increase in hourly productivity (in effect, output per man-hour) when moving from the lower-numbered to the higher-numbered technique, divided by the corresponding increase in capital cost of one unit of equipment (in effect, given the simplifying assumptions, increase in capital per unit of instantaneous employment). Therefore,

$$E_t = o^{\cdot}/C^{\cdot}. \tag{2.14}$$

The elasticity of utilisation has a direct, though slightly complex, relationship to 'the incentive to utilise' in the case where there is only one technique: clearly, other things being equal, the higher this elasticity, the higher the 'incentive'. Similarly, the elasticity of mechanisation can be thought of as indicating the 'incentive' to mechanise; given the rate of utilisation, the higher this elasticity, the

the reader wishing to verify the results of the present chapter may translate as follows:

v (output per man-hour in the Appendix) may be treated as identical with o, hourly productivity.

q (capital per man in the Appendix) as identical with C, capital per unit.

$\overline{\overline{w}}$ in the Appendix stands for the real basic wage (wage rate on system 1, divided by selling price of product).

f stands for the ratio of the wage paid on a particular system to the basic wage.

In the Appendix, when considering a particular change, the data in the programme *to* which the movement is to be made are primed, those in the programme being 'left behind' are unprimed. Thus in considering a change from system 1 to system 2, the utilisation rate from system 1 is indicated by h, for system 2, by h'. It follows that in considering a change from 1 to 2, the translation of $h^{\cdot}$, as used above, is

$$h^{\cdot} = \frac{h'-h}{h}. \tag{2.15}$$

If, however, the contemplated change is from system 2 to 1, the definition of $h^{\cdot}$ is reversed, i.e.

$$h^{\cdot} = \frac{h-h'}{h'}. \tag{2.16}$$

(This is because $h^{\cdot}$ always related the system of lower utilisation to the higher.) Other items translate similarly. For convenience we note that when the contemplated change represents an increase in utilisation, the elasticity of utilisation, as defined above, translates

$$E_u = \frac{f'-f}{f}\,\frac{h}{h'-h}. \tag{2.17}$$

Where an increase in mechanisation is contemplated, the elasticity of mechanisation translates

$$E_t = \frac{v'-v}{v}\,\frac{q}{q'-q}. \tag{2.18}$$

more likely, at any given wage rate, the more mechanised of two techniques to be the most profitable. If the elasticity of mechanisation between any two techniques exceeds unity, the less mechanised technique will never be the more profitable at any wage rate on any system; in other words, in these circumstances the less mechanised technique is 'inferior' and will not be included in the matrix. Alternatively, if the elasticity of mechanisation between two techniques is negative, the more mechanised technique must be inferior. Therefore, given the assumption that inferior techniques are excluded, the elasticity of mechanisation is a number lying between zero and plus one. This simplifies the data.

2.11. The Optimum Programme

The relationship between utilisation and mechanisation may be thought of in the following manner. Select for consideration a non-optimum programme so placed in the matrix that there are more profitable programmes both immediately to the right and immediately below; in other words, imagine a state of affairs where either an increase in mechanisation or an increase in utilisation would prove profitable. Of these two possible 'moves', one, except in a special case, will prove more profitable than the other, i.e. will increase the rate of profit most. It will be found that the factors determining which type of move is likely to be the better are also the factors explaining the basic relationship between capital utilisation and the technical characteristics of the production function. This relationship is of considerable practical importance, because, in industry, the two types of decisions often go hand in hand.

For purposes of clarification we shall use the analytical device of imaginary variations in basic wage rate. We shall first consider a situation in which the basic wage rate is low, then envisage the changes in the programme matrix which would occur if, with the same data, the wage rate were gradually raised. These variations are not to be thought of as simulating historical changes in a real economic system; they represent a method of static comparison only.

For example, consider the matrix of nine profit rates in Table 2.1. Of the nine, one may be optimum, i.e. higher than all the rest. Alternatively, one or more profit rates may be equal and no programme optimum. However, we know that any change in the basic wage rate will change all the elements in the matrix, therefore if several profit rates are equal at some wage rate, they are unlikely to remain equal if the wage rate is different. Conversely, we may describe a wage rate which equalises the profit rates of a pair of adjacent programmes, the '*critical wage*' between the programmes, because this wage represents a watershed between profitability and non-profitability of a change from the one programme to the other. If the assumed wage rate is progressively raised, the average rate of profit falls throughout the matrix, but because the wage rate also affects the initial wage–profit ratio, some profit rates decline more than others and so, in due course, the ordering relationship between the programmes is changed. The relative profitability of programmes of lower utilisation or of more mechanised technique will increase, that of the others decrease. A decline in assumed wage rate will have the opposite effect. Thus, if we know the critical wage between two programmes, we know the direction in which their relative profitability will 'tip' in face of any small assumed variation in wage rate. We also know that at some wage rate sufficiently low, the programme of maximum utilisation and minimum mechanisation (top right of the matrix) must become optimum and that at some wage rate sufficiently high, the programme of minimum utilisation and maximum mechanisation (bottom left) must become optimum. These conclusions are of considerable analytical value.

For, consider the state of affairs where the top right programme has become optimum. If the assumed wage rate is progressively raised, we shall eventually reach critical levels between this programme and the various adjacent programmes below, to the left and to 'south-west'. But except in a special case, *one* critical wage will be reached before all the others, i.e. the critical wages can be ordered, and one will be lower than the others. What then determines which move will be first, i.e. which type of programme will next become optimum? The forces pulling to the left are the forces favouring *reduced* utilisation; the forces pulling downwards are the forces favouring *increased* mechanisation, both, in effect, representing 'substitution' of capital cost for labour cost. The strength of the force for reduced utilisation is indicated by the elasticity of utilisation; the *lower* this elasticity, the greater the incentive to eliminate shift-work or, more precisely, the more likely it is that a given increase in basic wage will make shift-work unprofitable. The strength of the force for increased mechanisation is indicated by the elasticity of mechanisation. The greater the elasticity of mechanisation, the more likely is the 'first move' to be downwards, i.e. the rising wage rate is more likely to stimulate increased mechanisation, rather than reduced utilisation.

More generally, we can show that if *any* programme has become optimum at some wage, the next first move will be downwards if, and only if,

$$E_t(E_u + h^{\cdot} + 1) > 1, \tag{2.19}$$

where E_t is the elasticity of mechanisation between the initial technique and the next highest technique, and E_u is the elasticity of utilisation between the system immediately to the left of the initial system and the initial system itself; $h^{\cdot}$ is the corresponding increase in utilisation. This result is obtained by finding the conditions in which the critical wage for the downward move will be smaller than for the leftward move.† The essential conditions, it will be seen, depend exclusively on the data, and are independent of the level already reached by the wage rate.

It is not impossible, of course, that the first move from some initial

† See Mathematical Appendix.

optimum be diagonal; for example, as the wage rate rises the next optimum programme may represent increased mechanisation combined with reduced utilisation. In general, however, these cases require either unrealistically extreme or otherwise freakish values in the data, and can for practical purposes be ignored. If diagonal moves are ignored, the first move from top right must either be to the left or downwards, depending on the values of the elasticities in equation (2.19). The higher the elasticities of mechanisation *and* of utilisation, the more likely is the first move to be downwards, i.e. the more likely is the rising wage to lead to increased mechanisation without change of utilisation. Suppose the conditions are such that the first move is, in fact, downwards. If the next relevant pair of elasticities (elasticity of mechanisation between techniques 2 and 3, elasticity of utilisation as before) are still sufficiently high, the next first move will again be downwards. At this point, however, further mechanisation is impossible, no more-mechanised techniques being known to the industry. Therefore it is inevitable that if the wage rate is again raised, the optimum utilisation rate will decline, and the optimum programme eventually reach the position at bottom left. It follows that if high values of the elasticities prevail throughout the data, the path of the optimum programme, as the wage rate is raised, will be to travel downwards along the right-hand edge of the matrix and leftwards along the bottom edge. If the wage rate is then lowered, the optimum position will return by the same route. In these circumstances, only the programmes along these edges will ever be optimum. The others will never be optimum at any wage rate; in other words, given the data, they will not be optimum under any circumstances at all. Conversely, if the elasticities are *low* throughout the data, the path will be along the top edge of the matrix and down the left edge. Unless, therefore, the data contain irregularities, involving sharp *changes* in the elasticities as one moves through the matrix, the set of possible optimum programmes is much simplified; it has either the shape of a reversed L or that of an inverted L. Where, with low elasticities, the L is inverted, we have conditions in which high utilisation is optimum only when the wage rate is so low as to encourage minimum mechanisation. Where, on account of high elasticities, the L is reversed, we have conditions in which high utilisation continues until the wage rate is so high as to encourage maximum mechanisation.

The significance of this finding is that the *elasticity of mechanisation* now appears as a separate factor encouraging capital utilisation. Imagine a case in which all elasticities of mechanisation and of utilisation, respectively, were equal to one another, i.e. there was one common value of E_t and one common value of E_u. Then consider alternative matrices with the same property but different common values of the elasticities. The precise outcome of any wage rate in any matrix depends, among other things, on the positions of the matrix boundaries; if the optimum programme has reached the lower horizontal boundary, nothing can prevent reduced utilisation as the wage rate is raised: at the lower boundary of a matrix the elasticity of mechanisation is always in effect zero. It is nevertheless true that, in the case suggested, other things being equal (wage rate, elasticity of utilisation, other data), the higher the common value of the elasticity of mechanisation, the higher would be the *tendency* of the optimum rate of utilisation. More generally, if an industry is faced with a production function in which capital is generally a 'good' substitute for labour, in the sense that relatively moderate increases in capital can yield substantial increases in labour productivity, the average optimum rate of utilisation in the industry, other things being equal, is likely to be relatively high. This conclusion is of considerable economic significance. It is generally recognised that high rates of utilisation are more likely to be profitable in an industry using highly mechanised techniques than in an industry which is not, but since the profitability of any technique partly *depends* on the rate of utilisation, little is thus explained. We now see that the choice of optimum technique and the choice of optimum system are intimately connected. The higher the elasticities of utilisation and of mechanisation, the more likely is the optimum choice to involve both high utilisation and high mechanisation. Furthermore, since the elasticities interact (see equation (2.19)), an industry in which the elasticity of mechanisation is modest may nevertheless be encouraged to adopt relatively mechanised techniques, because favoured with a high elasticity of utilisation; and an industry with an attractive elasticity of mechanisation may have to adopt less mechanised techniques because faced with a low elasticity of utilisation. Conversely, an industry faced with a low elasticity of utilisation may nevertheless adopt relatively high rates of utilisation, because it has a high elasticity of mechanisation, and vice versa.

If we observe an industry using a particular technique of production at a low or moderate rate of utilisation, we may be told that increased utilisation would be unprofitable because, in effect, the elasticity of utilisation is inadequate (probably on account of a high shift-work premium, or of other factors affecting the utilisation differential). This explanation may be inadequate. A complete explanation would include the elasticity of mechanisation. For example, consider a matrix of two systems and two techniques. The wage rate is such that the optimum programme uses the least mechanised technique with the lowest rate of utilisation (top left). Although the industry may never historically have used the programme at top right, we can nevertheless think of the current position as having been reached by a 'move', as the wage was raised, from right to left. And we know that this 'move' would not have occurred had the elasticities of utilisation and of mechanisation, in combination, been such that the first move from top right would have been downwards. In other words, we know that at the wage rate which now exists, had the elasticities been higher, the optimum programme, instead of being at top left (low utilisation, low technique) would have been at bottom right (high utilisation and high technique). *Thus the elasticity of mechanisation, as well as the elasticity of utilisation, is required to explain the low optimum rate of utilisation*, as well, of course, as explaining the low degree of mechanisation.

These theoretical results have important implications in application. Given realistic data, most programme matrices would be of the type in which the path of the optimum programme formed the reversed L, i.e. favoured high rates of utilisation except at wage rates so high that the bottom edge had been reached (i.e. when the most mechanised of all known techniques of production was the most profitable at any rate of utilisation). Therefore, if it is observed in real life that intensive capital utilisation is not, in fact, general, either our theory must be wrong or incomplete, or the majority of industries must be faced with technical and economic conditions forcing them to the bottom-edge situation. In practice, as we shall see, the 'prediction' that in a typical industrial economy shift-work should be general (i.e. that the size and character of the national capital stock should be such as to provide full employment for the working population only at a high average rate of utilisation) turns out to be false,† and, furthermore, it is difficult to believe that cases of constraint by the edge of the production function could be sufficiently common to provide a satisfactory alternative explanation of the results to be reported in Part II. The true explanation, we believe, is that our theory is at present incomplete, because by implication it assumes that all equipment is infinitely divisible. In Chapter 4 we investigate the consequences of dropping this assumption, and develop a more complete theory which, as we shall see in Part II, is more successful in its predictions.

2.12. Effects of Interdependence in the Elasticities

One of the implications of the simplifying assumptions made on p. 43 was that the elasticity of utilisation was independent of the techniques of production, i.e. was the same for all pairwise comparisons between adjacent *columns* of the programme matrix. This is an assumption which is not only unrealistic but has significant implications when relaxed. For example, suppose the ratio between the efficiency wages of women and men differs between a pair of adjacent techniques—one type of machinery is easily worked by women, so that any difference in their hourly productivity as compared with men is more than offset by the difference in wages, while the other type of machinery, perhaps, requires a strength or skill which women are unable to acquire. Consider then three systems; single shift (1), double-day shift (2) and rotating double day-and-night shift (3). As between 1 and 2, the elasticity of utilisation might well be the same on both techniques. As between 2 and 3, we have

† A typical value of E_u is about 3·0, and of $h^{\cdot}$ about 0·83. Therefore the critical inequality for first move downwards (equation (2.19)) is typically satisfied if E_t exceeds 0·225. There is good reason to suppose that the typical empirical value of E_t is considerably higher.

$h^{\cdot}$ at about 0·07 (ten $7\frac{1}{2}$-hour shifts per week compared with ten 8-hour shifts) and, for male workers, $w^{\cdot}$ small or zero. Hence, for the technique favouring the employment of male workers, the elasticity of utilisation between systems 2 and 3 may be so high as to render the former unprofitable at any wage rate. For the other technique, however, the utilisation differential, which, in combination with $h^{\cdot}$, determines the elasticity of utilisation, must take account of the legal requirement to substitute men for women when adopting the rotating night shift. Clearly, we have a situation which cannot be analysed by the rules outlined so far.

The problem arises from the ambiguous status of women in modern industrial society: women are paid less than men not only because they are sometimes less efficient but also because convention and the domestic situation depress the 'supply price'. In the absence of a one-for-one relation between their relative efficiency and their relative wages in different occupations, the ratio between their efficiency wages and those of men varies between techniques of production. This, coupled with the fact that the dual role as mates and producers leads to legal exclusion from industrial night-work, creates the situation described. We cannot generalise about the economic effects because there is no obvious correlation between the degree of mechanisation of a technique and its wage–sex–efficiency ratio. In the phase of mechanisation reached in manufacturing industry immediately after World War I —the phase of the first assembly lines—it did seem that some methods of production had become considerably more suitable to women than hitherto. Or, to give a more specific example, the ring spindle, which is little more a mass-production technique than the mule spindle, owes much of its economic attraction to the fact that it can be minded by women alone. If one could find a general tendency for mechanisation to be associated with 'feminisation', it would not be difficult to conclude that the invention of such techniques must reduce the optimum rate of capital utilisation in the economy at large. However, more recent trends might seem to point in the opposite direction. For good reason or bad, women are not often employed to control or maintain complex automated machines. If it is true that women are inherently less able in the mechanical and electrical arts, and if it is true that automation must increase the relative importance of what is now termed 'maintenance' labour, then we may expect a trend to higher utilisation. However, since maintenance may often be undertaken at hours chosen to suit the workers' convenience, it is possible that this trend will be accompanied by a reduction rather than an increase in the proportion of the working population required to work shifts. In other words, it may prove to be a major advantage of current technical trends that they can exploit high rates of capital utilisation against a small cost in social inconvenience. This point is discussed further in the industry study of Chemicals and referred to again in the final chapter on policy. That chapter also discusses the wider implications of the feminine employment situation and the possible consequences of changes.

2.13. Example from the Cotton Industry

The conclusions of the previous section are of considerable practical significance. In a condition of stationary technical knowledge an industry may be faced with a number of alternative, non-inferior, techniques which have all been known for some time. The more mechanised, however, may not be used because the basic wage rate is too low to render them profitable. Nevertheless, the wage is high enough to rule out intensive utilisation of the less mechanised techniques. In the course of time, outside forces raise the market rate of wages relative to prices, thus, in the absence of technical progress, reducing the rate of profit. But we have seen that if the wage increases sufficiently, the decline in the profit rate can be retarded by now adopting the more mechanised techniques. These are techniques which, had they been profitable at the old wage, would have favoured intensive utilisation, but the wage which is now sufficiently high to encourage their use is also sufficiently high to discourage shift-work. Shift-work, therefore, does not occur.

The history of the British Cotton industry since World War II provides a good example. During the past thirty years technical progress in the world's textile industries has consisted more in the discovery of new fibres than of new ways of processing traditional fibres. Many of the most mechanised techniques for both spinning and weaving cotton have been known for some time. In Britain, their adoption has been delayed by the low elasticity of mechanisation between semi-automatic and fully-automatic techniques (for example between modified Lancashire looms and fully-automatic looms) and by the high relative efficiency of low-paid female labour, implying in effect a low basic efficiency wage rate.

By the middle 1950's the British industry was unmistakably declining and many firms were going out of business. The survivors, however, appreciated that in due course they would need to 're-equip' with more mechanised machinery, but they found that this would not be profitable unless multiple shift-work, which had previously been opposed by the local trade unions, were now adopted. The unions, after negotiation, agreed to permit shift-working where re-equipment was actually undertaken, and there then occurred a considerable debate as to a reasonable level of premium. The employers contended that the figure asked by the unions was excessive, and they had collected information suggesting that premiums agreed in most other industries were lower. However, the data presented in Chapter 7 below imply that when account is taken of hidden bonuses and other financial benefits of night workers, the cost of the premiums demanded by the Cotton unions would probably not have exceeded the average differential actually prevailing in manufacturing industry as a whole. Yet the employers were almost certainly correct in arguing that the unions' demands would render the proposed change of 'programme' unprofitable. Neither side fully appreciated that the fundamental cause of the difficulty lay not so much in the workers' resistance to shift-work as in the technical conditions which caused the low elasticity of mechanisation.†

In terms of the analysis of § 2.10, the 'move' under discussion was a south-east one, that is a move from system 1 (single shifts) with technique 2 (moderate mechanisation) to system 2 (double shifts) with technique 3 (substantial mechanisation). We have seen that in the conditions described, such a move will nearly always prove unprofitable, and the initial programme will not be abandoned until the wage rate has risen sufficiently to optimise programme 2, 1. Why then was the matter being discussed in the cotton industry at all? The answer lies in a peculiar aspect of the industry's situation, namely that the unions, irrespective of the question of sex, were asking for the establishment of a considerably lower utilisation differential on the less mechanised technique than on the higher. In effect, they were hardly prepared to countenance shift-work at all except in firms which agreed to re-equip. They realised that, owing to international competition, unless the more mechanised technique were generally adopted, real wages in the industry could not rise. Therefore, it seemed not unreasonable that they use the shift-work agreement as a weapon to stimulate mechanisation. Obviously in such a case the south-east move may well become profitable and even save the industry. But whether the move becomes profitable, and how profitable it becomes will depend both on the elasticity of mechanisation and on the elasticity of utilisation, hence the employers' necessary toughness. Had the elasticity of mechanisation been higher, the move could have occurred on the basis of an elasticity of utilisation more easily acceptable to both sides and more comparable with conditions elsewhere. It will be noted, however, that the low elasticity of mechanisation was not the only difficulty here. This industry, especially in the spinning section, was particularly affected by the 'feminisation' problem discussed in the preceding section. Had this not been the case, a more attractive utilisation *differential* (paid to men) would have yielded a similar elasticity of utilisation, and vice versa.

† For an account of the Cotton unions' previous attitude to shift-work, see Chapter 8, §8.5. For an account of the 1955 negotiations, see 'New Phase in the Cotton Industry', *The Financial Times*, London, 5 November 1955. For utilisation differentials in manufacturing, see Chapter 7, §7.2. For an indication of how the basic paradox remained misunderstood and substantially unresolved during the following years, see 'The Halfpenny and the Cake', *The Observer*, London, 26 March 1961. This last article stated 'A big break through could be made if Lancashire would accept shift-working. The chairman of another spinning combine went so far as to say that shift-working was a condition of re-equipment. Some progress has been made in the last eighteen months—enough to astonish people who know the conservatism of workers and employers alike in the trade. But the typical mill hand is female and elderly, and doesn't like night work.' The economic logic of this argument is analysed below, but we may note here that if by 'night work' is meant work after 10 p.m. or before 6 a.m. it is *illegal* for all females, however elderly, in the U.K. If the reference is to evening work under the double-day system, research has shown that workers of both sexes vary considerably in their attitudes to the system, some actually preferring it to single-shift day work (see the study by Hilda G. Brown, referred to in the Foreword, p. xiv).

As a matter of fact, by the middle 'fifties a small minority of spinning firms had already adopted the double-day system. But these were firms who by superior methods of organisation had considerably raised the productivity of workers engaged on the more mechanised techniques.† They had not so much raised the hourly productivity of the spindles, as reduced the number of girls required to mind a given number, i.e. they had altered the ratio of units of capital to units of equipment. They had therefore *raised* the elasticity of mechanisation; in effect they had provided themselves with a 'superior' production function. The theory correctly predicts that these firms would find a higher utilisation rate to be optimum.‡

2.14. A Dynamic Model

Table 2.2 represents the results of applying varying 'basic' wage rates to a constant set of data. The data relate to a model containing three techniques and three systems. *System 1* is a single-shift 40-hour week, yielding 2000 operating hours per year ($h_1 = 2000$).§ Workers employed on this system are paid at the basic rate. *System 2* is some kind of double-shift system, each shift being of 8 hours, 5 days a week, 4000 operating hours a year ($h_2 = 4000$; $h^{\cdot} = 1$). The utilisation differential between systems 1 and 2 is 0·15, that is to say, the average hourly efficiency wage is 15 % higher on 2 than on 1. *System 3* is a three-shift system, operated 5 days a week, yielding 6000 operating hours per annum ($h_3 = 6000$; $h^{\cdot} = 0{\cdot}5$). The utilisation differential between systems 2 and 3 is 0·10. A unit of equipment of the *first technique* costs £20,000 and yields 4 units of final output per hour. A unit of the *second technique* costs £50,000 and yields 7 units per hour. A unit of the *third technique* costs £100,000 and yields 9 units per hour. All three types of unit of equipment require an instantaneous employment of 20 workers: therefore, the hourly wage bill is 20 times the hourly wage rate. We may summarise these data as follows:

System 1 to 2	$h^{\cdot} = 1$,	$w^{\cdot} = 0{\cdot}15$,	$E_u = 6{\cdot}66$
System 2 to 3	$h^{\cdot} = 0{\cdot}5$,	$w^{\cdot} = 0{\cdot}10$,	$E_u = 5$
Technique 1 to 2	$o^{\cdot} = 0{\cdot}75$,	$C^{\cdot} = 1{\cdot}5$,	$E_t = 0{\cdot}5$
Technique 2 to 3	$o^{\cdot} = 0{\cdot}286$,	$C^{\cdot} = 1$,	$E_t = 0{\cdot}286$

We next define a real *basic wage rate*, ($\overline{w}$), the money basic wage paid on system 1 (i.e. the money wage per man-hour) divided by the price of

† For example, Hayeshaw Ltd., of Manchester.

‡ It is of considerable significance that in the weaving of *Rayon*, shift-work has always been very much more prevalent than in Cotton (see Appendix Tables I and II). As a result of exceptional assistance from Messrs Courtaulds Ltd. we were able to establish that this was substantially due to a difference in technical conditions yielding a more favourable elasticity of mechanisation. However, the commercial structure of the industry (a virtual monopoly) was also important: Courtaulds, compared with the typical Cotton weaver, were rapid innovators and able to produce on a large scale. The significance of these factors will become apparent to the reader in the section immediately following, in Chapters 4 and 7.

§ We assume that the equivalent of 10 working days are lost each year through holidays and other stoppages.

the product, which latter for convenience is assumed to be £1. The nine profit-rate matrices shown in Table 2.2 represent the result of applying varying values of the real basic rate to the specified data. In profit-rate matrix number 1, the real basic wage is 0·363 per hour, which means that, for twenty men, the hourly wage bill for operating system 1 is £7·26. In matrix 2 the basic wage is 18½ % less than in matrix 1; in matrix 3, 18½ % less than in 2, and so on.

Table 2.2. *Sample profit-rate matrices for varying real basic wage rates*

(Annual gross profit rates, in percentages.)

Matrix no. ...	1			2			3		
System no. ...	1	2	3	1	2	3	1	2	3
Technique no. 1	−33|	−87	−156	−20|	−58	−108	−10|	−34	−68
2	−1|	−11	−26	4|	1	−7	*8*	10|	9
3	***3***|	*3*	*1*	*6*	***8***|	*8*	8	*13*	***16***|
Matrix no. ...	4			5			6		
System no. ...	1	2	3	1	2	3	1	2	3
Technique no. 1	−1|	−14	−36	6|	2	−9	12	16|	14
2	*12*	*18*	22|	*14*	*25*	***33***|	*17*	*30*	***42***|
3	10	17	***23***|	11	20	28|	12	23	33|
Matrix no. ...	7			8			9		
System no. ...	1	2	3	1	2	3	1	2	3
Technique no. 1	17	27	32|	*21*	36	47|	*26*	*44*	***60***|
2	*19*	*35*	***49***|	20	*38*	***55***|	22	41	60|
3	13	25	36|	14	27	39|	15	29	42|

N.B. For explanation, see text, pp. 54–5. The data have been rounded to the nearest whole number; indicated maxima are based on the unrounded figures.

The highest profit rate in any row is marked with a bar to the right, the highest in any column is in italic and the highest in the matrix, indicating the optimum programme, is in bold. Evidently, where the optimum programme is located, we must have both a row maximum and a column maximum. The bold profit rates, therefore, are also row and column maxima. The movements of the row, column and matrix maxima, as the wage rate is changed, illustrate the theorems derived above. Thus in matrix 1, all row maxima lie on system 1—the wage rate is so high that whatever the technique of production, shift-work is unprofitable. As the wage is reduced (through matrices 2, 3, ..., 9) the line of row maxima begins to move to the right. Since hourly productivity is higher in the higher techniques, the initial wage–profit ratio is lower and the incentive to utilise, in turn, higher. Therefore, as the wage is reduced, it is impossible for the first move of the row maximum on any technique to precede that on some higher technique; in general, the line of row maxima advances in zig-zag formation, with the higher techniques in the lead. This theorem will be of considerable importance in Chapter 4.

When the wage rate is very high, as in matrix 1, the line of column maxima is the bottom edge: whatever the system of operation, the most mechanised technique is most profitable. As the wage is reduced, the line of column maxima rises and we may deduce a 'zig-zag' theorem similar to the one governing row maxima. The 'incentive to mechanise', we have seen, depends directly on the initial ratio of wages (including utilisation differential) to profits. The utilisation differential is higher on the higher systems, so also therefore is the incentive to mechanise. When mechanisation is being reduced, as the basic wage falls, the systems of lower utilisation will inevitably be the first to move. (Sometimes of course, when the basic wage is varied discretely, several techniques or systems may move together; for precision we should confine ourselves to the statement that the most mechanised techniques and the least intensive systems will never change before the others, and vice versa when the wage is raised.)

The optimum programme in matrix 1 is at the bottom left-hand corner; in matrix 9 it is at the top right. The chosen range of wage-rate variations therefore exhausts the range of possible moves with this set of data. The path followed from the one corner to the other is as predicted by equation (2.19); for the first move from the top right corner $E_t(E_u+h^{\cdot}+1)$ is greater than unity (it is 3·25) and is again greater than unity (1·86) for the move from programme 2, 3; therefore it is inevitable that the optimum programme first travel south down the right-hand edge, then west down the south edge. This is a case where the general level of the elasticities of mechanisation and of utilisation is so high that the most intensive capital utilisation possible will always be profitable until the wage has risen so far that the possibilities of mechanisation are exhausted. With these data, shift-work is likely over a wide range of wage rates. The data were chosen because, despite the fact that, for reasons which will become apparent later, shift-work is not frequent in real life, the values chosen are realistic and typical.

So far, in speaking of variations or 'changes' in the real basic wage and other variables in the shift-work equation, we have been asking the question: 'If, with given data, and given basic wage, a designer would plan such and such a utilisation rate, what utilisation rate would he have chosen had his variables been different?' The variations discussed were not changes in time, but alternatives relating to a given point in time. In real life, as time passes, the data change; in particular, technical progress leads to the introduction of new techniques into the data-matrix and to the elimination of old techniques through inferiority. If we consider our problem in a dynamic context, we may find a better explanation of observed facts.

Suppose in '1950', the prevailing level of wages and prices, as represented by the state of competition in the industry and general conditions in the economy at large, were such as to face employers with a real basic wage equivalent to matrix 5 in Table 2.2. But suppose that, in contrast to the data presented in the table, at that time only technique 1, or inferior techniques, were known, the equipment for techniques 2 and 3 not having yet been invented. In effect, only the first row of the matrix is operative. The optimum rate of utilisation is system 1, and this, with technique 1, yields a 6 % profit rate. Suppose every firm in the industry is equipped with just enough units of technique 1 to meet a given, constant, annual demand for the output of the industry as a whole, using system 1. Suppose, somewhat unrealistically, that the 6 % gross profit rate proves just sufficient to meet wear and tear depreciation and to provide the modest return on capital which is appropriate in a static industry. Prices and wages are constant and the industry maintains its total output capacity by replacing worn out equipment with new equipment of the same type, at a constant annual rate.

Then technique 2 is invented. Technique 2 does not render technique 1 inferior, but it does fundamentally alter the data. In place of three programmes only we now have six, each representing the three alternative systems of operation for the new technique and the old. One of the added programmes, 2, 3, shows a very much higher profit rate than the rate associated with the original optimum programme: by employing technique 2 on treble shifts it is possible to raise the profit rate from 6 to 33 %. Programme 2, 3 is now the optimum programme.

It is not to be supposed, however, that the new optimum programme will immediately be adopted throughout the industry. In the first place the industry's existing capital is already embodied in a form appropriate to programme 1, 2. The number of units of capital will be greater, and the type of equipment less mechanised than is required for the new programme. The 'optimum programme', as we have defined it, relates to a *planned* rate of utilisation combined with a planned technique of production and can be changed, therefore, only when new plant is installed. In the second place, to employ the new technique may involve more than the mere purchase of new equipment; it may involve new 'know-how' and new types of labour skill. It is likely that only a minority of firms will have the ability to pioneer the new methods. To other firms, possessing less internal skill, the new method might fail to provide the reduction in labour costs necessary to justify the increased capital cost. Some firms, also, may recently have installed new equipment of the old type and be unprepared to face the rapid rate of obsolescence implied in now replacing it.† For all these reasons we may assume that only a relatively small minority of firms will immediately change over to the new optimum programme. These firms

† It may be argued that the obsolescence occurs anyway, since the value of the old machinery suffers a once-and-for-all decline as a result of the invention of the more profitable equipment. This is not necessarily so. If the firms could rely on no competitor undertaking the innovation, there would be no abnormal depreciation of the old equipment, since it would still be capable of earning the old profit rate. The 'external' rate of obsolescence of the old equipment depends on the extent to which competitors buy the new equipment and make use of its advantages to force down prices and reduce the profitability of the old.

will borrow new capital or liquidate reserves in order to buy and install the new equipment. Assuming for the moment they expect to continue to sell the same output, they will order only the number of new equipment units necessary for system 3. They will order approximately one-third as many units as were required for the old programme but, since the new units cost five times as much as the old, the replacement cost of their investment will rise by two-thirds. Output per man-hour, however, has more than doubled and this fact, despite the slightly higher wages implied in the change of system, is sufficient to provide the considerable increase in profit rate indicated in the table. (Capital per unit of output increases by two-thirds, labour costs per unit of output fall by 40 %, and, wages representing a considerably larger proportion than profits in the initial condition, the rate of *profit* on capital rises.) We then have a situation in which a minority of pioneers employs advanced techniques and shift-work, and earns a considerably higher rate of profit than the majority. It is this situation which is so often empirically observed.†

What is to happen next? We can hardly expect nothing further to change. It is rare that innovating enterprises intend no more than to earn higher profits on a static output. Assuming that they continue to be endowed with a pioneering psychology we may expect they intend to exploit their more profitable programme in order to strengthen their general competitive position. With a higher potential profit rate they may at one and the same time increase their share of the market by price cutting and increased selling expenditures (while still maintaining a reasonable profit) and they may obtain by re-investment or by borrowing the necessary capital funds for this expansion. If we assume there is a definite relationship between the rate of profit and the supply of capital, and another between the rate of profit and the rate of increase in the share of the market,‡ one particular commercial policy (i.e. combination of prices and selling expenditures) combined with an associated rate of profit will ensure that the firms' expansion will be 'balanced', i.e. that the rate of growth of their sales will be equal to their rate of growth of capital capacity (assuming the optimum programme). This profit rate will lie between the maximum obtainable with the new programme and the old commercial policy—i.e. in the example, 33 %—and the 'old' 6 % rate. Armed with this profit rate, policy and programme, the firms will steadily expand their sales, which means that, unless the demand for the industry's products as a whole is expanding very rapidly for 'outside' reasons, the sales of the 'rump' firms will decline. If the latter continue to employ their original stock of equipment, they will be forced to reduce its utilisation, because there is no other way, in the short run, by which output may be reduced.

† See Chapter 7.

‡ See J. Downie, *The Competitive Process* (Duckworth, London, 1958), chapters 7–10: this was another conditional aid project. See also an article by the present main author in the *Quarterly Journal of Economics*, May, 1963.

This, of course, represents an 'unplanned' change in utilisation. Eventually, however, these firms will be required either to go out of business or to copy the pioneers. Here we reach the nub of the argument. The outcome of the competitive process resulting from retaliation by the 'sheep' is uncertain. Selling prices may be driven down and sales increased, or wages may rise in accordance with an exogenous secular trend. In all circumstances it is unlikely that the industry will find stability on the new programme with a general level of profits yielding typical rates of return as high as the figure of 33 % obtained (in this example) by the pioneers during their period of leadership. More likely prices and wages will end up in some relationship such that, using the new technique, the maximum obtainable rate of profit is not greatly in excess of the rate ruling before the original change occurred, i.e. in the example, 6 %. In other words, the 'sheep' will find that in order to continue to earn a 'normal' rate of return they will now have to use the new technique, a condition which implies, of course, that the real basic wage rate has increased. *But this means it will not be profitable to operate the new technique so intensively as was the case in the conditions originally facing the pioneers.* The new optimum programme—i.e. programme just able to earn about 6 %—will probably be technique 2 on system 1. The sheep, then, when they follow the pioneers in respect of technique, should not plan to follow them in respect of utilisation, and the original pioneers will find themselves equipped with a stock of capital appropriate to a programme which is no longer optimal.† Thus stability may be restored to the industry with a more normal profit rate, obtained with the original, relatively low utilisation rate. But, with the aid of the new technique, output per man-hour is higher, and so also the real basic wage rate. Because the real basic wage is higher, intensive utilisation of the new technique is no longer profitable.

There, in principle, the story could end. The appearance of shift-work among the pioneering firms could be classed as an interlude in a once-and-for-all historical process of change. In practice, however, in an economy where technical progress is continuous, we would next expect technique 3 to be invented and the process to be repeated. Indeed, since there is no reason why technique 3 should not have been invented before the final 'programme 2, 1' equilibrium was reached, the process cycles may well overlap. Although technical change in an individual industry is rarely continuous, the jumps are fairly frequent. Therefore we can generalise to the extent of saying that where shift-work is observed among a minority of the firms in an industry, the firms will tend to be the ones who have most recently innovated, in the sense of having adopted a technique more mechanised than prevailed

† How the pioneers will react depends on the details of the intervening events. One possibility is that they are forced back to their original share of the market, and the latter, in turn, has not expanded. They will therefore be compelled to reduce their output, an adjustment which may be achieved by reducing utilisation of a capital stock originally designed to produce a larger output by higher utilisation. I am very grateful to Mr K. P. Norris of the Shirley Institute, Manchester, in connection with this analysis.

in the industry previously. Conversely, we can say that even where, in a static system, the elasticities of utilisation and mechanisation would not favour shift-work, the occurrence of technical progress will tend to induce shift-working among the more rapidly innovating minority. These theorems hold under all circumstances where there are significant differences between individual firms' reactions to progress. As experimental predictions they turn out to represent an important part of the empirical truth.†

† See Chapter 7. The predictions apply, of course, to genuinely comparable firms only. Where the firms who happen to be classified statistically in one industry are engaged in widely differing economic activities it is possible that one group may adopt shift-work simply because they are producing a different product, with a different production function, for a different market.

CHAPTER 3
MANY PROCESSES

3.1. The Character of the Problem

We are now ready for the problem of the real-life factory where more than one process or 'activity' is required to manufacture the final product. Typically, at least half a dozen distinct activities are required, although the number identified will, of course, depend partly on how finely they are distinguished. There are many criteria for distinguishing activities, but we need one only—the capacity for independent utilisation. If, of two processes, one cannot be operated unless the other is being operated at the same time, both must be treated as the same activity. An activity, then, is a process with distinguishable inputs and outputs both capable of being stored between adjacent activities in the production line. Thus, for example, in brick manufacturing the process of transporting clay from the pit or 'knothole' to the kiln could be considered a distinct activity, provided it were feasible to store clay both before transportation and after.†

The introduction of the concept of an activity modifies the concept of a technique of production. Techniques must now be defined in relation to activities. A particular technique is represented by a particular type of equipment for undertaking a particular activity. There may or may not be more than one technique available for a particular activity at any moment of time, but in any multi-activity plant there must be at least as many different types of equipment as there are activities: an excavator cannot do the work of a kiln and techniques for different activities cannot directly be compared. In this situation the rate of profit in the plant as a whole can no longer be identified with the rate earned by a single unit of equipment; and indeed, wherever the outputs of the various activities are required in fixed proportions (as we shall generally assume to be the case), no simple meaning can be given to the concept of a single-activity profit rate.

Many factories house equipment for more than one final product. This is not the problem we are discussing. Here we are concerned with the theoretical difficulties which arise even when the final product is unique. We shall use the expression 'a plant' to indicate the collection of equipments required for the production of complete units of a single final product, leaving 'factory' to refer more loosely to a single manu-

† As it happens, clay is normally stored after transportation, in order to dry, but must be taken from pit to storage bins while wet, since hardened clay could not be transported. Therefore transportation to bins must be regarded as part of the activity of excavation, since the two tasks must be carried on simultaneously.

facturing establishment. In this terminology, then, a 'factory' may contain several 'plants'. In such cases, some equipment is often shared by more than one plant—the case of so-called 'joint-production' which has been considerably investigated in theoretical economic literature. We have been unable to investigate the theoretical implications of joint-production for our problem. All our final products are dis-joint.

We are, of course, concerned only with those theoretical aspects of the matter which are special to the case. The major generalisations, developed in the analysis of the simplified, single-activity case, will be found to remain valid, but at the same time to require extension. Thus an intuitive development would suggest that as the ratio of basic wage rate to selling price influences the optimum rate of utilisation of a single activity, so the ratio of wage rate to final selling price would influence the *average* optimum rate of utilisation over a group of activities—average rate being defined as the sum of the individual rates divided by the number of activities. This turns out to be true, but of attenuated significance. In a single-activity model, when we know the wage rate and other relevant 'initial' data, we know precisely the optimum rate of utilisation. But in a multi-activity plant, in order to determine the optimum utilisation of a particular activity, not only must we know the data relating to that activity, but also to all the others (and the same, of course, applies in turn to each of them). Therefore, the actual level (as against the tendency) of the average rate of utilisation in the optimum plant-programme is determined only as a result of the determination of its individual components.

The general character of the interdependence can be seen by imagining an example with two activities: say 'Grinding' and 'Polishing'; final product, 'bearings'. The gross rate of profit in the plant as a whole —which we call the plant rate of profit—is the annual value of output,† less the wages bill in Grinding, less the wages bill in Polishing, all divided by the sum of the values of the equipment employed in each. Suppose we have designed a plant intended to produce a certain output of bearings on the assumption that both activities operate single shifts only. A critic then asks us to consider double-shifts. We decide, however, that as Polishing mainly employs women, we will consider the shift-working possibilities in Grinding only. We calculate a new plant profit rate on the assumption that the rate of utilisation in Grinding is doubled and that, to this end, we shall have to pay the grinders' a shift premium of 20 % on their basic rate. What factors determine whether the second estimated profit rate is higher than the first?

The prospective capital cost in Grinding is halved, but this does not mean, of course, that the capital cost of the whole plant is halved, because Grinding is only one of two activities. In order to compute the proportionate reduction in total capital cost, we need to know the *initial* proportion of Grinding capital to Polishing capital; the higher

† Throughout the present analysis, final output is assumed to be valued net of all prime costs other than wages.

this is, the greater the reduction in total capital for a given reduction in Grinding capital. Other things being equal, the proportion will be higher and the attractiveness of shift-work for Grinding greater, the more 'capital heavy' the technique of production used in Grinding relative to that of Polishing and vice versa. But other things are not equal. We know that in the numerator of the formula for the profit rate the effect of the rise in the Grinding wage rate will depend on the initial ratio of the *Grinding* wage bill to *total* profits. Total profits depend, *inter alia*, on the productivity of labour both in Grinding and in Polishing. The higher the productivity of labour in Polishing, the lower the ratio of Grinding wages to total profits in the initial condition; *therefore, the higher the productivity of labour in Polishing, the greater the attractions of shift-work in Grinding*. And if the basic design be changed to employ a more mechanised technique in Polishing, involving more capital and higher labour productivity, the effect on the numerator is to favour shift-work in Grinding, but the effect on the denominator is contrary: and so on.

Suppose, after taking account of all these factors, we discover that double shifts in Grinding would indeed be more profitable than single shifts. We may then begin to wonder whether we had not perhaps been over-hasty in dismissing the possibilities in Polishing. What would happen if men on double shifts were substituted for women on single shifts? Suppose after inquiry it is learnt that although men are paid 50 % more than women, their output per man-hour, using the same equipment, is 25 % higher; so that even after allowing the men a modest shift-work premium the effective utilisation differential turns out to be only a little higher than in Grinding. The original arguments concerning the effect of conditions in Polishing on the profitability of shift-work in Grinding are now precisely applicable in reverse. However, we face an additional and fundamental complication. The proportions of capital initially involved in Grinding and Polishing must depend not only on techniques of production, but also on rates of utilisation. Similarly, the ratio of polishing wages to total profits is influenced by the fact that we are now assuming wages in Grinding to have been raised (and hence profits reduced) by a shift-work premium. In other words, the profitability of shift-work in Polishing may be affected by whether or not we had, in fact, already decided on shift-work in Grinding. It would seem, therefore, that in order to obtain the 'general optimum'—the plant programme which maximises the plant rate of profit—we must consider all the four possible combinations; both activities on single-shifts, both on double-shifts, Grinding on double with Polishing on single, and Polishing on single with Grinding on double. In other words, the solution has to be simultaneous.

This is not a problem of true mathematical depth or complexity. Rather than complex, it is intricate. For each activity, there are a number of alternative systems (combinations of utilisation rates and differentials), together, more than likely, with a number of alternative techniques of production. The spectrum of systems may in certain circumstances be identical for all activities, but never the spectrum of techniques. Nor will each activity contribute equally to final output; for each, we must find a 'combination coefficient' indicating the output required from the activity in order to produce a given quantity of final output, and one might expect these coefficients to play a significant role in the solution. Thus, if the number of activities is n, the number of techniques available to each m and the number of alternative systems l, the number of possible plant programmes is lmn (e.g. three activities, three techniques each and four systems: 36 programmes)—our problem is to select the most profitable. Inevitably, however, we shall be forced to employ more overtly mathematical modes of argument, and at times to make use of vector notation. We shall attempt to state conclusions in non-mathematical terms also, but some important results do not easily lend themselves to verbal or 'common-sense' interpretation.

3.2. Notation

We have to develop a comprehensive algebraical notation adapted to the problem and set up the basic equations defining the plant profit rate over many activities. There are a number of activities, a certain amount of output being required from each to produce a given amount of final output. To each activity there is available at least one technique of production characterised by particular values of three technical coefficients; and there may be alternative techniques, characterised by other values of the coefficients. In addition, for any activity-technique pair, there are available a number of alternative discrete systems of operation, each characterised by a rate of utilisation and a wage rate. We shall find it convenient to modify our previous method of describing the relations between the wage rates and utilisation rates by defining a 'relative utilisation rate' and a 'basic differential'. The relative utilisation rate of a given system is the ratio of its absolute utilisation rate, expressed in hours per annum, to the absolute utilisation rate of system 1. The 'basic differential' is the ratio of the wage rate paid on a system to the basic rate paid on system 1. Thus, in the previous notation, the relative utilisation rate of system 2 is $1+h_1'$, of system 3, $(1+h_1')(1+h_2')$ and so on, where h_1' relates to the comparison between systems 1 and 2, and h_2' to the comparison between systems 2 and 3. A similar translation applies to the 'basic differential'.

The basic differential is an increasing step function of the relative utilisation rate. This function is described in Fig. 3.1. We shall usually assume this function to be the same for all activities (in real life, especially when complications involved in the substitution of male for female labour are considered, this is often not the case) and we shall continue to assume that utilisation at rates between the steps is impossible.

For the present problem we will further simplify by assuming that there are no 'other prime costs' and that depreciation occurs only from obsolescence. Programmes can therefore continue to be compared on the basis of gross profit rate alone. We shall also modify our previous method of specifying techniques: given hourly output per unit of equipment, workers per unit and capital per unit, we know output per man-hour and capital per man (the ratio of capital per unit to instantaneous employment per unit), and it is these last two, together with the first, we shall find most convenient to employ in the equations.

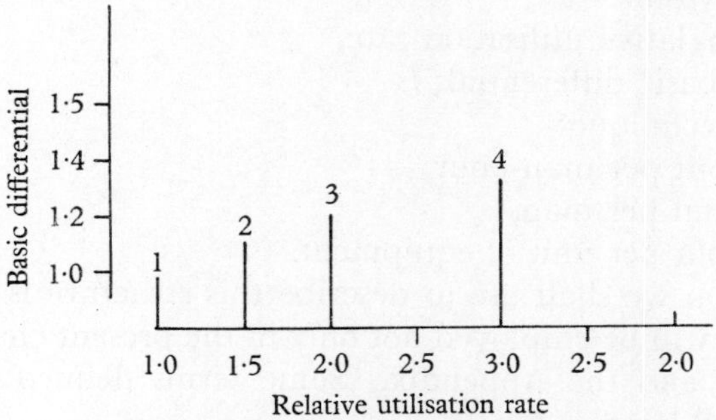

Figure 3.1. The system step-function.

We first describe the final product and the activities required to produce it. For our purposes the final product may be said, indeed, effectively to be characterised by its activities, since no other aspect is of direct concern for our problem. A list of activity descriptions might read as shown in Table 3.1 (the example is again taken from brick manufacture).

Table 3.1. *Example of specification of activities. Manufacture of building bricks*

Activity no. ...	1	2	3
Trade name	Winning	Grinding	Pressing
Task	Extracting and transporting clay	Pulverising dried clay	Forming powdered clay into brick moulds
Output	Wet clay	Powdered clay	Shaped unfired bricks
Units	Cu. yards	Tons	Numbers of shapes
Activity no. ...	**4**	**5**	**6**
Trade name	Setting	Firing	Drawing
Task	Stacking shapes in kiln	Operation of kiln	Removing, sorting and despatching bricks
Output	Stacks of shapes	Finished bricks	Bricks on lorries
Units	Numbers of stacks	Numbers of stacks	Lorry-loads

Given the description of the activities, and the definitions of their units of output, there is for each activity a combination coefficient. In the above example, all the output measures could reasonably be converted into tons, in which case the combination coefficient of the first activity would be some number greater than unity (tonnage of clay required for a ton of bricks) and the subsequent coefficients would progressively decline towards unity as the material lost weight in the process of manufacture.

Then, to specify a plant programme we indicate for *each activity*:

(*a*) the system,

(*b*) the technique;

implying—

(*a*) of the system:

(i) the relative utilisation rate,

(ii) the basic differential;

(*b*) of the technique:

(i) output per man-hour,

(ii) capital per man,

(iii) output per unit of equipment.

The notation we shall use to describe this structure is given below. This notation will be employed not only in the present chapter but also in Chapter 4 and the Appendix. Some terms defined here are not employed until later.

(1) *Activity variables*

There are 1 ... i ... n activities.

Let k_i be the combination coefficient of activity i.

Then $\mathbf{k}$ denotes the vector, $k_1 \ldots k_i \ldots k_n$.

$\mathbf{k}$ therefore represents the sufficient specification of the final product.

Define h_i as the relative rate of utilisation in activity i.

h_i is a discrete variable.

Then if $\bar{h}$ is the rate of utilisation on system 1, the absolute rate of utilisation in activity i is $\bar{h}h_i$.

In each activity various alternative techniques of production are available. We use t_i to denote the technique being used in activity i.

t_i will be characterised by:

$o_i(t_i)$ = hourly output per unit of equipment in activity i, when using t_i;

$v_i(t_i)$ = output per man-hour, in activity i, when using t_i;

$q_i(t_i)$ = value of capital per man in t_i, when the equipment is in operation.

Let w_i be the average hourly wage rate in activity i.

Then if $\bar{w}$ is the wage rate on system 1, i.e. the basic wage rate

$$w_i = \bar{w}f_{h_i},$$

f_{h_i} is an increasing step function of h_i and is generally independent of i; when $h_i = 1, f_{h_i} = 1$.

We employ $\dot{h_i}$ to indicate the proportionate change in h_i when h_i is increased by one step, and we employ $\dot{f}_{h_i}$ to indicate the associated proportionate change in f_{h_i}.

(2) *Aggregates*

O = annual output of final product.

P = net selling price of final product.

OP = net value of final output.

$$W_i = \frac{Ok_i w_i}{v_i} = \frac{Ok_i \overline{w} f_{h_i}}{v_i} = \text{annual wage bill in activity } i.$$

$$N_i = \frac{O}{\bar{h}}\frac{k_i}{o_i h_i} = \text{number of units of equipment installed in } i.$$

$$C_i = \frac{O}{\bar{h}}\frac{k_i q_i}{v_i h_i} = \text{aggregate capital cost of equipment installed in } i\text{: that}$$

is to say, the product of N_i and the cost of a unit of equipment of technique t_i: $(N_i q_i o_i)/v_i$.

(2) *Specification of programmes and associated profit rates*

We can specify any plant programme by the matrix

Activity	1	...	i	...	n
Combination coefficient	k_1	...	k_i	...	k_n
Relative utilisation	h_1	...	h_i	...	h_n
Basic differential	f_{h_1}	...	f_{h_i}	...	f_{h_n}
OPUH	$o_1(t_1)$	...	$o_i(t_i)$	...	$o_n(t_n)$
OPMH	$v_1(t_1)$	...	$v_i(t_i)$	...	$v_n(t_n)$
CPM	$q_1(t_1)$	...	$q_i(t_i)$	...	$q_n(t_n)$

For convenience, where the meaning is obvious, we will write $o_i = o_i(t_i)$ and correspondingly, v_i and q_i.

Since f_{h_i} is a function of h_i, and t_i determines o_i, v_i and q_i, we can compress the specification of a programme into a $3 \times n$ matrix such as

$$\begin{matrix} k_1 & \dots & k_i & \dots & k_n \\ h_1 & \dots & h_i & \dots & h_n \\ t_1 & \dots & t_i & \dots & t_n \end{matrix}$$

Then if **h** indicates the vector of h_i and **t** the vector of t_i, the programme specification can be further compressed to read **k**, **h**, **t**.

(4) *Composition of the rate of profit*

The plant profit rate, R, is given by

$$R = \frac{PO - W_1 - W_2 - \dots - W_n}{C_1 + C_2 + \dots + C_n}$$

$$= \frac{PO - \sum_{i=1}^{n} W_i}{\sum_{i=1}^{n} C_i}$$

$$= \frac{PO - \sum_{i=1}^{n} \frac{Ok_i \overline{w} f_{h_i}}{v_i}}{\sum_{i=1}^{n} \frac{Ok_i q_i}{v_i h_i \bar{h}}}. \qquad (3.1)$$

Define the 'real basic wage' $\bar{\bar{w}}$, so that $\bar{\bar{w}} = \bar{w}/P$. Also measure all q_i in units of P. That is to say, if the cost of a unit of machinery in some activity, j, is £1000 (for example, the cost of a unit of equipment £2000, instantaneous employment, two workers) and P is £4, q_j is 250. Assume that $\bar{h}$, the rate of utilisation in system 1, may be treated as unity.†

Then, since O and P are independent of i,

$$R = \frac{1 - \bar{\bar{w}} \sum_{i=1}^{n} \frac{k_i f_{hi}}{v_i}}{\sum_{i=1}^{n} \frac{k_i q_i}{v_i h_i}}. \tag{3.2}$$

Then R is a continuous decreasing function of $\bar{\bar{w}}$ and a step function of **h** and **t**.

Let $R(\mathbf{k}, \mathbf{h}, \mathbf{t}, \bar{\bar{w}})$ be the plant profit rate earned by plant programme **k**, **h**, **t**, at real basic wage $\bar{\bar{w}}$.

(5) *Optimum programmes*

$\mathbf{h}^*(\mathbf{k}, \mathbf{t}, \bar{\bar{w}})$ denotes that **h** which sets $R(\mathbf{k}, \mathbf{h}, \mathbf{t}, \bar{\bar{w}})$ at maximum for given **k**, **t**, $\bar{\bar{w}}$.

$\mathbf{t}^*(\mathbf{k}, \mathbf{h}, \bar{\bar{w}})$ is that **t** which sets $R(\mathbf{k}, \mathbf{h}, \mathbf{t}, \bar{\bar{w}})$ at maximum for given **k**, **h**, $\bar{\bar{w}}$.

$\mathbf{h}^*, \mathbf{t}^*(\mathbf{k}, \bar{\bar{w}})$ is that plant programme which sets $R(\mathbf{k}, \mathbf{h}, \mathbf{t}, \bar{\bar{w}})$ at a general maximum. It is a function of $\bar{\bar{w}}$ controlled by the lists of techniques available to each activity.‡

$R^*(\mathbf{k}, \mathbf{t}, \bar{\bar{w}})$, $R^*(\mathbf{k}, \mathbf{h}, \bar{\bar{w}})$, and $R^*(\mathbf{k}, \bar{\bar{w}})$ are the corresponding profit rates.

(6) *Expanded notation*

We could represent the state of technical knowledge by an $m \times n$ matrix,

	Activity	1	...	i	...	n
Technique	1	t_{11}	...	t_{1i}	...	t_{1n}
	⋮					
	j	t_{j1}	...	t_{ji}	...	t_{jn}
	⋮					
	m	t_{m1}	...	t_{mi}	...	t_{mn}

the column $t_{1i} \ldots t_{ji} \ldots t_{mi}$ representing the set of techniques available to activity i.

Let **T** represent such a matrix. Then **T** has the following properties:

† In reality, of course, this variable is usually a number around 2000, but since it cannot affect the ordering of programme profit rates, its value is of no significance in the problem of selecting optima. For analytical purposes, $\bar{h}$ may here be ignored.

‡ These lists limit the variation of t. If, due to a change in technical knowledge, a new technique is added to the list of those available to any activity or activities, the functional form for t^*, $h^*(k, \bar{\bar{w}})$ may be changed: for an alternative statement, see expanded notation, below.

(i) each column has at least one non-void element, and m is the maximum number of non-void elements in all the columns;

(ii) each non-void element, t_{ji}, implies a triad of values of o_{ji}, v_{ji} and q_{ji}, where o_{ji} is the hourly rate of output of the jth technique for the ith activity, and v_{ji} and q_{ji} are the corresponding values of output per man-hour and capital per man respectively;

(iii) the column ordering of techniques is that of v_{ji};

(iv) the column ordering of q_{ji} must be the same as that of v_{ji}; if at any time this condition is violated, techniques shall be eliminated until the correct ordering is restored;

(v) if it is necessary to eliminate techniques for the reason given in (iv), the following rule shall govern the selection of those to be eliminated—

if some $v_{ji} \geqslant v_{ki}$ while $q_{ji} < q_{ki}$, then eliminate t_{ki}.

Note. The above rules ensure that **T** will contain no inferior techniques. **T** may be changed by the addition of new techniques and the consequential elimination of old techniques now rendered inferior. Such a change constitutes a definition of an economically relevant change in technical knowledge. (It is to be noted that **T** is defined in respect of a particular set of activities only. A change in technical knowledge in the economy at large is relevant, therefore, only if it affects these activities.)

We could also define the step function f_{h_i} by an $l \times n$ matrix:

Activity		1	...	i	...	n
Relative utilisation	1	$f_{h_1 1}$	...	$f_{h_1 i}$	...	$f_{h_1 n}$
	2	$f_{h_2 1}$	...	$f_{h_2 i}$	...	$f_{h_2 n}$
	$\vdots$					
	j	$f_{h_j 1}$	...	$f_{h_j i}$	...	$f_{h_j n}$
	$\vdots$					
	l	$f_{h_l 1}$	...	$f_{h_l i}$	...	$f_{h_l n}$

But since $f_{h_j i}$ is generally independent of i, we can normally represent the function adequately by the single column-vector **f**, where **f** denotes

$$f_{h_1} \cdots f_{h_j} \cdots f_{h_l}.$$

It follows that we can represent the general optimum for a given product, wage rate and state of technical knowledge by

$$\mathbf{h}^*, \mathbf{t}^*(\mathbf{k}, \mathbf{T}, \mathbf{f}, \overline{\overline{w}}),$$

and the corresponding profit rate, as

$$R^*(\mathbf{k}, \mathbf{T}, \mathbf{f}, \overline{\overline{w}}).$$

These functions are unique.

This completes the description of the notation.

3.3. Fixed Techniques

We have to investigate the factors which determine the character of the general optimum, **h***, **t***. To this end, following the previous practice, we first investigate the case where techniques are fixed, and then proceed to the more general problem. That is, we first investigate **h***(**t**) and later return to the problem of determining **h***, **t***.

Consider the formula for the plant profit rate (3.2). All the variables in this formula are specified by any programme, combined with some real basic wage. Both a change in programme with given wage rate and a change in wage rate with given programme affect the profit rate in a predictable manner. The effect of a change in programme, however, depends on the initial wage rate, and vice versa. Consider, therefore, changes of programme made in one activity at a time, beginning (for convenience) with the programme in which each activity is operated on system 1, at a wage rate at which this programme happens to be optimum. Without varying the wage rate, raise the rate of utilisation by one step in one activity, say activity j. What determines the effect on the plant profit rate, R? The change affects both numerator and denominator. In the summation in the second term of the numerator, f_{h_j} is increased from unity to some higher value. In the summation in the denominator h_j is likewise increased. Evidently the effect on R will depend on the magnitudes not only of these changes themselves but also of the initial 'weight' of the activity in question in the respective summations. The greater the initial value of k_j/v_j relative to the corresponding value in other activities, the greater the effect of the change in f_{hj}; and the greater the relative initial value of $k_j q_j/v_j$, the greater the effect of the change in h_j.

Now suppose the basic wage is lowered and new profit rates computed for both original and modified programmes. In the modified programme the wage-bill summation in the numerator of the profit rate is higher and the capital-cost summation is lower, than in the unmodified programme, but the change in the basic wage rate alters the relative significance of these differences in a manner with which we are already familiar. Consequently, although the profit rate on both programmes rises, the profit rate on the modified programme rises faster, until eventually we find a critical wage at which both rates are equal. The farther it is necessary to lower the wage rate to obtain parity, the lower, evidently, the critical wage. It seems intuitively obvious that the necessary reduction varies directly with the initial distance between the profit rates (the 'incentive to utilise' of Chapter 2) and therefore the critical wage depends on the factors determining this distance. These factors, we saw, were those which determined not only the magnitude, but also the relative weight of the changes in basic differential and relative utilisation associated with the change from original to modified programme.

We may thus visualise the optimum programme developing by a

succession of changes, as the basic real wage is raised or lowered, much in the manner of the single-activity, many-technique example in Chapter 2. In order to determine the character of the path of the optimum programme we again have to discover, from any initial optimum position, which next change will be the first. Now, however, instead of a choice between change of technique or change of system, in one activity, we have to decide which of several activities, using fixed techniques, will be first to change their systems.

The 'next change' for any activity is a change of programme in which that activity changes utilisation by one step, all other activities remaining unchanged. Thus, moving in one direction from any initial optimum, there are as many 'next changes' as there are activities, each change representing a particular modification of the programme. For each there is a critical value of the real basic wage, that is, value at which this particular modified programme will exhibit the same profit rate as the initial programme. Clearly, the next change in the optimum programme itself will be the first of these activity 'next changes', that is, the change for which the critical wage, in the case of falling wage rate, is highest or, in the case of rising wage rate, lowest. If therefore we can determine the critical wages for all next changes after each initial optimum, we can solve our problem.

At first sight it might seem we need be concerned only with those factors which affect the *ordering* of the critical wages for the various changes. This, however, would resolve only one aspect of the problem. Suppose we found that some variable influences the level of all critical wages equally and positively. Then, without any change in the basic wage, a rise in this variable must influence the optimum programme in the direction of higher utilisation on *all* activities. For example, suppose there were a uniform change in all the v_i (output per man-hour). This would raise the profit-rate numerator and lower the denominator, thus raising all profit rates. It would also, however, reduce the initial wage–profit ratio in the numerator as a whole, and therefore generally encourage programmes containing higher utilisation rates. However, since all the v_i changed together, no one critical wage would change more than any other, and the effect must therefore be general.

We define $\bar{\bar{w}}_j$ as the critical wage for the next change in activity j, that is, the value of the real basic wage at which a programme in which activity j was changed by one step, all others remaining unchanged, would exhibit the same profit rate as the initial programme. Then it can be shown that

$$\bar{\bar{w}}_j = \frac{1}{\sum_i \frac{k_i f_{h_i}}{v_i} + \frac{1+h_j^{\cdot}}{Eu_j}\left(\frac{f_{h_j} h_j}{q_j}\right) \sum_i \frac{k_i q_i}{h_i v_i}}, \tag{3.3}$$

where Eu_j is the elasticity of utilisation for the change and $h_j^{\cdot}$ the corresponding utilisation increase.† This formula is less formidable than it

† See Appendix.

seems and can easily be intuitively related to the basic theory first set out in Chapter 2. The first term in the denominator amounts to a weighted average, taken over the plant as a whole, of relative labour costs per unit of output in the various activities, the weights being the k's. In the second term, the first part takes appropriate account of the elasticity of utilisation (a rise in utilisation differential, relative to $\dot{h}_j$, reducing, as it were, the appropriate 'incentive to utilise'—therefore *lowering* the critical wage); the second part is a weighting factor depending on the initial state in activity j and the third part represents the overall capital-output ratio.

Notice that the critical wage for any change depends intimately on the initial conditions. Not only the changes in f_h and h_j as expressed in the elasticity of utilisation (ratio of $\dot{h}_j$ to $\dot{f}_{h_j}$) but also the initial values of these variables affect the result, as they did, of course, in the single-activity case. The procedure for computing the path of the optimum programme is therefore as follows: from the initial position, find the critical wage for next change in all activities. Then take the highest or lowest critical wage as the case may be and assume that this change is made. The result indicates the new optimum programme and the new set of initial values. With these new initial values again compute all critical wages, and repeat until no further changes are possible. The Mathematical Appendix describes a general method for simulating this procedure which enables us to find the optimum programme for any wage without actually computing the programme for other wages, and which also deals with certain complications here omitted.†

It is of considerable interest to investigate how the parameters of equation (3.3) affect the relation between critical wage rates. Since only one technique, at this stage of the argument, is available to each activity, all k_i, v_i and q_i may be regarded as parameters. For example, it is clear that the higher q_j (the cost of capital per man in activity j) the higher the critical wage for the next change in this activity, because q_j is more significant in the second part of the second term than in the third part. A common-sense explanation of this result is that if capital per man in a particular activity is high, the proportion of plant capital in that activity is likely to be high. Therefore a reduction in utilisation in the activity will imply a relatively large reduction in average utilisation in the plant as a whole. Given the saving in labour costs expressed in the utilisation differential, this discourages the change and raises the critical wage. In other words, the higher the capital per man in an activity, other things being equal, the greater the reduction (or the smaller the increase) in plant profit rate to be expected from reducing utilisation in that activity. It will be noted that a rise in capital per man in a particular activity with no rise in output per man implies that the

† The most important is the case of a 'double-jump' change. It is found that some systems of utilisation are inferior in one activity but not in others, and that the likelihood of inferiority depends on all the values in the equation. It is therefore impossible to eliminate this type of inferiority, and double jumps of system may occur.

technique of production in the activity has economically deteriorated. Since this is historically unlikely it is more fruitful to interpret the effect in reverse: if technical progress cheapens the capital cost of obtaining a given output in some activity, labour cost remaining constant, that activity will tend to show a higher utilisation rate in the optimum programme than would otherwise have been the case. Notice, however, that the effect on other activities is reverse. In their cases (as may be seen also in the critical-wage formula) their relative weight in the plant's total capital is reduced by virtue of the first activity's increase, therefore they will tend to be utilised less intensively. The effect on average rate of utilisation in the plant as a whole is therefore ambiguous: certainly, if all q_i change together, there is no effect whatsoever. This is confirmed in the absence of initial capital cost in any of the formulae relating to the single-activity case.

As regards k_j and v_j it will be noticed that since both these enter the formula only as part of summations they can have no specific effects. If v_j increases, the critical wage for next change in activity j is raised but so are the critical wages for all other activities, and to the same extent. *Therefore the levels of productivity in the different activities, given the levels of capital per man, cannot in fact affect the ordering of the critical wages.* A rise in productivity in an activity, due to technical progress, reduces the initial wage–profit ratio in the plant as a whole and affects the average rate of utilisation, but the effect is general and is not confined to the activity where the improvement occurred.† Changes in the combination coefficients k_i are similar to reverse changes in productivity. If some k_i increases, other things being equal, more resources are required in that activity to produce a given quantity of final output; this is equivalent to a decline in the productivity of the activity. Therefore all that has been said about v_i applies, inversely, to k_i.

Finally we may note a more sophisticated effect. The critical wage for a specific activity is affected, relatively to the others, by the level of utilisation already obtaining in that activity, because the higher the utilisation, the lower the proportion of plant capital found in the activity and the higher the proportion of plant wages (on account of utilisation differential). This effect is expressed in the denominator of the second part of the second term of the denominator of (3.3). It is stronger, of course, the greater the basic differential for given utilisation.

† An intuitive explanation of this perhaps surprising result may be found by again considering the rate-of-profit formula (3.2). A change in output per man, in a given activity, other things being equal, reduces the weight of the activity in the initial wage bill, thus influencing its critical wage in one direction. But the number of workers required in the activity, and hence, given capital per man, the amount of capital, is also changed and in the same direction, thus changing the weight of the activity in the initial capital stock. Since the one change operates in the numerator of the profit rate, the other in the denominator, they are offsetting. The critical wage of the activity, *relative* to that of other activities is, on balance, unaffected. There is, however, a general change in the initial wage–profit ratio whose effect cannot be offset by a change in the denominator, any more than would have been the case in a single-activity model. Therefore all critical wages, including that of the affected activity, are to some extent changed.

3.4. Arithmetical Example with Fixed Techniques

An arithmetical example of the foregoing is useful. The data and chart below relate to a matrix with three activities, but only two alternative utilisation systems. Each activity may either be worked on double shifts or single shifts only, and the elasticity of utilisation for this change is the same for each. We investigate the critical wages for first change after an initial optimum in which all activities are on single shifts, that is, the initial programme is 1, 1, 1. The data are as shown in Table 3.2. These data are concerned with the effect of changes in the coefficients of the technique of production in one activity, all other activities remaining unaffected. Taking case 1 as the basis of comparison, case 2 investigates the effect of a change in the cost of capital per man in activity 2 (due perhaps to a rise in the relative price of this type of machinery), output per man remaining unchanged. In case 3 the same effect is carried further. In case 4, output per man is raised, capital per man remaining constant. In all these cases either the old or the new technique is inferior to the other, but in case 5 both output per man and capital per man are raised, that is to say, the degree of mechanisation in activity 2 is intensified.

Table 3.2. *Data of example*

Activity no. ...	1		2		3	
Variable ...	v_1	q_1	v_2	q_2	v_3	q_3
Case no. 1	10	9	2	3	4	2
2	10	9	2	8	4	2
3	10	9	2	12	4	2
4	10	9	6	3	4	2
5	10	9	3	6	4	2

$h^{\cdot}$ (between systems 1 and 2) $= 1$; $E_u = 5$. All $k_i = k_j = 1$. $P = 1$.

Fig. 3.2 shows the resulting critical wages for the next change in each activity in the different cases. Each transverse line intercepts the vertical lines at the level of the critical wage, measured on the vertical scale. One transverse represents case 1, with which the other cases may be compared. Thus in case 2 a rise in the relative cost of capital per man in activity 2 raises the critical wage in 2, lowers it in 1 and 3. In case 3 the same effect has been carried so far that the ordering of critical wages is now changed; because capital per man in activity 2 is now higher than in any other activity its next change is first change. In case 4, the rise in output per man-hour does not affect the relative position of activity 2; in conformity with the theory, all critical wages are raised, and the line is moved bodily upwards. In case 5 mechanisation of activity 2 raises all critical wages, more in activity 2 than in the rest. This case, also predicted by the theory, has not previously been mentioned, but will be important later.

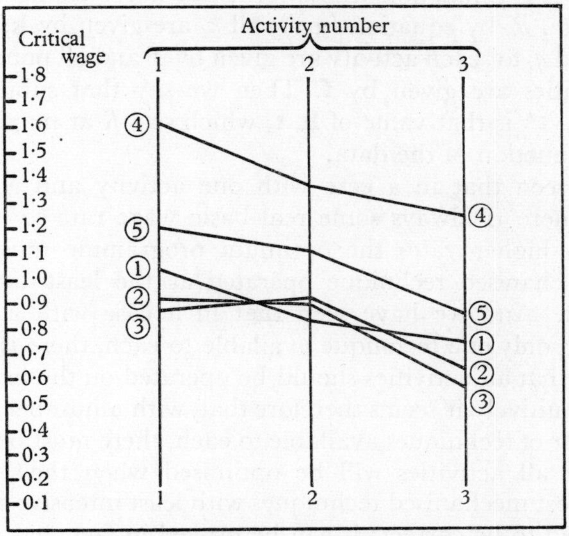

Figure 3.2. Values of critical wages.

3.5. Variable Techniques

Finally we reach the problem where, having discovered how to find the optimum programme in n activities with a fixed set of techniques, we consider a whole spectrum of techniques available to each activity; so that, in effect, there are a number of fixed-technique optima and we must choose the most profitable. In the basic notation we have learnt how to find $\mathbf{h}^*(\mathbf{k}, \mathbf{t}, \bar{\bar{w}})$ and we have investigated the effects of various types of changes in $\mathbf{t}$. Now we consider the position where, alternative techniques being available to each activity, there is rather a large but limited number of possible values of the vector $\mathbf{t}$ for each of which there is a value of the optimum-programme vector, $\mathbf{h}^*$. We wish to choose those values of $\mathbf{h}^*$ and $\mathbf{t}^*$ for which R is highest. In other words, in basic notation, we wish to find $\mathbf{h}^*, \mathbf{t}^*(\mathbf{k}, \bar{\bar{w}})$.

In order to visualise the problem more comprehensively it is convenient to employ the expanded notation. This enables us to specify $\mathbf{h}^*, \mathbf{t}^*$ in such a manner that its functional dependence is unique. We write $\mathbf{h}^*, \mathbf{t}^*(\mathbf{k}, \mathbf{T}, \mathbf{f}, \bar{\bar{w}})$ where $\mathbf{T}$ is a matrix stating all the techniques available to all activities, implying, that is, complete sets of interlocking alternative values of v_i, q_i, and o_i. $\mathbf{f}$ specifies the step function of wage rates on utilisation rates, so that for any relative utilisation rate, whatever the activity, when we know $\mathbf{f}$, we know the basic differential which must be paid. $\mathbf{k}$ relevantly specifies the final product, $\mathbf{T}$ relevantly defines the state of technical knowledge, and $\mathbf{f}$ measures the prevailing economic resistance to shift-work.

What is precisely meant in saying that the function **h***, **t*** is unique? We mean that, given the definition of the concepts of an optimum programme, it is a function whose form can never change. We define the profit rate, R, by equation (3.2): all k_i are given by **k**, all possible pairs of v_i and q_i for each activity are given by **T** and all pairs of h_i and f_i for all activities are given by **f**. Then we say that subject to these restraints **h***, **t*** is that value of **h**, **t**, which sets R at maximum. This is a unique function of the data.

We have seen that in a case with one activity and a number of techniques there is always some real basic wage rate so high that at this and all higher rates the optimum programme must consist of the most mechanised technique operated at the least intensive rate of utilisation. And we have seen that in a case with a number of activities, but only one technique available to each, there is some wage rate so high that all activities should be operated on the least intensive system.† Intuitively it seems therefore that, with a number of activities and a number of techniques available to each, there must be some wage so high that all activities will be optimised when they adopt their respective most mechanised techniques with least intensive system. This can be proved to be correct: it can be proved in fact that as the wage rate is raised and the general programme changes, no single activity-programme will ever become less mechanised or more intensively utilised.‡

As in the fixed-technique case, when the wage rate is lowered from the high-extreme value, the optimum programme will change. But now, however, the range of possible changes is much wider. With fixed techniques, the minimum number of possibilities for the first change is no greater than the number of activities: with variable techniques, in a three-activity, three-technique-per-activity example, the minimum possibilities for the first change would appear to be nine: three activities × three possible changes per activity (reduced mechanisation, increased utilisation or both).

Fortunately, it is possible to reduce the problem considerably by taking advantage of theorems which are proved in the mathematical appendix. Not only is it possible to show that as the wage is reduced no activity will ever change to lower utilisation or higher mechanisation, but also that no activity will ever change to a programme which involves an increase in the ratio q/vh.§ The actual change which will be made, and the corresponding critical wage, can be determined by an extension of the formulae given for the fixed-technique case at the end of the preceding section. More loosely we can say that if an activity is the leading activity, it will make that change which would be its next change if it were the only activity in the plant. And an activity will in fact become the leading activity if its critical wage for this change is

† Of course, these wage rates may be so high that the optimum-programme profit rate is negative.

‡ See Mathematical Appendix, p. 104.

§ Appendix, p. 104.

higher than the critical wage for the next possible change in any other activity.

The mathematical analysis therefore leads to a computation procedure which considerably reduces the labour of finding the optimum programme for any given wage rate; we find the critical wage for every change of programme—including both changes of technique and changes of system—in a similar fashion to the procedure for the fixed-technique example. Bearing in mind that the critical wage is more accurately described as the basic real critical wage—i.e. it incorporates both the money wage and the product selling price—we can see that the procedure implies that once the basic data concerning techniques and utilisation steps and differentials have been 'fed into' the computation, the resulting tables must show at a glance the general optimum for any combination of price and wage. The adjustments necessary to take account of the incidence of other prime costs and of wear-and-tear depreciation (which are not considered in the example) are obvious and straightforward: other prime costs per unit of output, provided they do not vary between systems, can be deducted from the selling price. If the incidence of these costs does vary between systems, their effect can be included in the wage-utilisation differential, and so on.

The computation procedure is described in the Appendix, p. 111 *et seq.* and is followed by an example of its working. This example is based on the data shown in Table 3.3.

Table 3.3. *Example of optimum programmes with three activities, and three systems and three techniques for each activity*

(1) Techniques

Activity ...	1		2		3	
Alternative techniques	v	q	v	q	v	q
1	2	300	4	200	4	300
2	4	800	7	500	10	900
3	5	1300	9	1000	13	1600

N.B. v and q were defined on p. 66 (v represents output per man-hour and q capital per man measured in terms of the price of the final product, which is £1)

(2) Combination coefficients

All $k_i = 1$

(3) Step function

$h_i = 1$ $\quad h_i = 2$ $\quad h_i = 3$

$f_{hi} = 1$ $\quad f_{hi} = 1{\cdot}15$ $\quad f_{hi} = 1{\cdot}15 \times 1{\cdot}10 = 1{\cdot}26$

(4) Wage steps—in critical wages. The real critical wage for the change from one programme to the next is printed between each, in fig. 3.3, below.

The optimum programmes and critical wages work out as in Fig. 3.3. It will be seen that this example behaves in three dimensions rather as the single-activity example behaved in two. This, of course, is by no means inevitable since the elasticities of mechanisation in the various activities may differ by considerably more than is assumed here. Notice that as the programmes unfold the positions of different activities in the 'race' for the finishing post at 1, 3 may change. In programme 8 activity 3 is in the lead, but the final winner is activity 1 (programme 11).

Can anything general be said about the effects of the elasticities of mechanisation and of utilisation in this intricate structure? Where the relative efficiency wages of men and women are the same on all techniques for all activities we can say that the elasticity of utilisation is likely to be much the same for all activities. If so, the elasticity of utilisation becomes a general variable influencing all critical wages equally and thus behaving in exactly the same way as in the one-activity model. Where this assumption does not apply, each case must be analysed separately. What of the elasticity of mechanisation? Intuitively (confirmed by the mathematical results) one would expect that the higher the elasticity of mechanisation between the technique now used in some activity and the next more mechanised technique, the greater the likelihood that the next change in the whole programme will be an increase in mechanisation in that activity, rather than any other change (either of mechanisation or of utilisation) in any other activity. However, until the change occurs, the characteristics of the next technique in this activity cannot affect the rest of the plant, since the technique is not in use. Once, however, the change is made, all future possible changes are affected. Both capital per man and output per man in one activity have increased. This has the consequences which were described in case 5 in Fig. 3.2: all critical wages for change of *system* are raised. It follows that the higher the general level of the elasticity of mechanisation between all pairs of adjacent techniques in any activity, the more likely, at any given wage rate, that not only this activity, but all others, will be relatively intensively utilised in an optimum programme. The elasticity of mechanisation thus plays the same general role as in the single-activity model, as well, of course, as a new more specific role in encouraging both mechanisation and intensive utilisation in activities where it is above average. As a very loose generalisation we can say that if the elasticity of utilisation is much the same for all techniques and activities, but utilisation rates are nevertheless observed to differ between activities, it is probably because the elasticity of mechanisation in the intensively utilised activities is higher than in the rest. The position, however, is complicated by the fact that an attractive elasticity of mechanisation in one activity encourages shift-work in others.† We would expect, and we observed, an ex-post inter-activity correlation between capital per man and intensity of utilisation, but we could not expect, and did not find, that capital per man was widely used as the main criterion for deciding which activities in a given plant should be considered for shift-work.

Our investigation of the multi-activity case, then, has not thrown up

† A good example was found in the manufacture of electric light bulbs. A very high elasticity of mechanisation in the basic process led the relatively labour-intensive packing process to be worked on a shift-basis, although the labour was exclusively female.

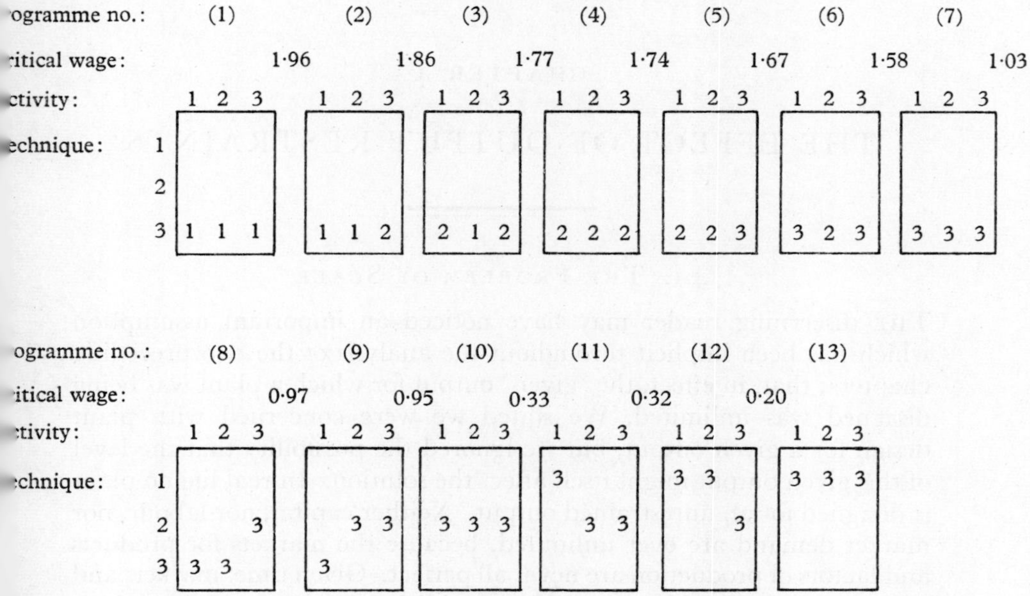

Fig. 3.3. Example of optimum programmes and critical wages for the general case.

N.B. Each box specifies an optimum programme, and each adjacent pair of boxes indicates the programmes separated by the critical wage printed above and between them: thus at any wage below 1·96, programme (1) will always be optimum, and at any rate between 1·96 and 1·86, programme (2) will always be optimum. The numerical elements represent systems, the column numbers, activities, and the row numbers, techniques. Thus in optimum programme (6), activity 1 uses technique 3 on system 3, activity 2 uses technique 3 on system 2 and activity 3 uses technique 3 on system 3; in optimum programme (8), activities 1 and 2 use technique 3, but activity 3 uses technique 2 while all use the same system, namely 3. The data are given in Table 3.3 above.

new fundamental theorems of wide significance. It has however given us greater insight into the finer structure of our problem and it has confirmed that generalisations from the single-activity model are unlikely to be invalidated by the reality of the multi-activity plant. And we shall depend heavily on the apparatus we have developed here in the next chapter, where we consider the effects of restraints on output.

CHAPTER 4

THE EFFECT OF OUTPUT RESTRAINTS

4.1. The Problem of Scale

The discerning reader may have noticed an important assumption which has been implicit throughout the analysis of the two preceding chapters; that, in effect, the 'given' output for which a plant was being designed was unlimited. We stated we were concerned with plant design for a given output, but we ignored the possibility that the level of this given output might itself affect the solution. In real life no plant is designed for an unrestrained output. Neither capital, nor labour, nor market demand are ever unlimited, because the markets for products and factors of production are never all perfect. Given time, markets and labour supplies may be expanded or additional capital obtained from re-invested profits or from the outside monetary system. But a plant design must relate to a definite period of time, and must take account of prospective average demands and supplies over the plant life; therefore, inevitably, the size of the plant is restrained; a designer who ignored this would soon bankrupt his employers. In the present chapter we investigate the possible effects of such restraints on the optimum planned level of utilisation. We also consider, in § 4.8, the effects of expected *fluctuations* in maximum output, caused by fluctuations in demand, for these present analogous problems.

In the preceding chapters we appear to have found methods of determining the optimum programme in various types of economic conditions. The programme stated the technique of production and system of utilisation to be adopted in every process or 'activity'. That is to say, for every activity the programme implied specific values of output per man-hour, output per unit of equipment, capital per man and the relative rate of utilisation. If this were really the end of the matter, the face of modern industry would be very different from the face we see.

An optimum plant-programme specifies values of q_i, v_i o_i and h_i for every activity. These values, when combined with the figures of the required volume of final output and the basic rate of utilisation imply unique values of N_i—the number of units of equipment to be installed in each i. The vector of N_i we will call the vector of *unit requirements*. Now it will be remembered that†

$$N_i = \frac{O}{\bar{h}} \frac{k_i}{o_i h_i}. \qquad (4.1)$$

† See p. 67.

The first part of this expression is common to all techniques, systems and activities; the second is particular to each *activity-programme*. It will be convenient to refer to the second part as a *scale-coefficient*, defined as

$$z_i \equiv \frac{k_i}{o_i h_i}. \tag{4.2}$$

There is one scale-coefficient for each activity-programme, and the specification of the programme is sufficient to determine the value of the coefficient. Therefore, a plant programme, optimum or otherwise, can be expressed as a vector of scale-coefficients, $\mathbf{z} = z_1, \ldots z_i \ldots z_n$.

We can call the fraction $O/\bar{h}$ the *output scalar*. Then the unit requirement in any activity can be determined by multiplying the appropriate scale coefficient by the output scalar. *Our arguments so far have assumed that the optimum programme is unaffected by the size of the output scalar*: we could, apparently, fully characterise an optimum programme in terms of the vector of scale-coefficients alone, leaving the unit requirements to be determined by whatever volume of output we subsequently chose to require. The problem which must now be faced is that we have in effect been assuming that the unit requirement is an unrestrained variable. But if a programme is to be practicable it is essential that equipment can be ordered in precisely the quantities specified: if not, the programme is of academic interest only. In reality, the practicable values of N_i are free by no means.

If a unit requirement works out at a whole number such as 1 or 2 or 10, no difficulty arises; one, two, or ten units of the appropriate type of equipment can be purchased in the usual manner. But if, as is far more likely, a unit requirement works out at a fraction such as 0·5, or 1·25, we are obviously in trouble. Such programmes require us to order units of equipment in divided parts, and it is inherent in the whole concept of a unit of equipment that this is impossible: one cannot cut a lathe in half nor, for that matter, a machinist.

To put the point another way, we have previously been assuming that each unit of equipment is operated by a fixed (integral) number of workers and produces a fixed amount of output per hour. Because no unit can be further subdivided so as to produce a fraction of the output a unit produces, if actual output produced during the whole shift by a unit is less than the potential maximum, the rate of profit is necessarily depressed. When the plant consists of a number of different types of equipment, each with a different maximum hourly output per unit, if the rate of profit is not to be depressed, the hourly final output must equal the least common multiple of the individual maximum hourly outputs, or some integral multiple of this least common multiple. When total final output is restrained, therefore, some units of equipment may perforce be under-utilised, and in varying degree; hence the profit rates on the individual programmes may be differently affected, and hence their profitability ordering. Thus output restraints inevitably influence the determination of the optimum programme.

4.2. Degradation of Techniques

This does not mean, of course, that only programmes in which all unit requirements are precise integers can be adopted. Such a conclusion would be absurd. For example, supposing the unit of equipment for a particular technique were defined as *ten* lathes, served by *one* truck, involving ten machinists and one driver. Suppose we wished to adopt a programme which implied a unit requirement no greater than 0·5. To meet the difficulty we could in various ways 'degrade' the technique: we could dispense with truck and driver and require each machinist to undertake his own fetching and carrying, thus making the original unit divisible into ten; or we could use five lathes and one truck. In the first case, provided the truck were more expensive than a lathe, capital per man would be slightly reduced, so also, by an unknown amount, output per man-hour—for the familiar reasons first described by Adam Smith. In the second case capital per man would be increased and output per man-hour reduced, truck and driver now being under-employed. (In both cases we must experience the consequences of despecialisation of men and machines.) Finally, we might simply allow both men and machines to operate more slowly, reducing output per man-hour *pro rata*, leaving all other variables unchanged. In the second and final cases the degraded technique would be formally inferior to its original; in the first case, owing to the slight reduction of capital per man, this would not be so. Therefore 'techniques' such as the one in which no truck was used at all should in principle be included in the basic hierarchy of techniques from which any optimum programme is derived, allowed, as it were, to take their chances in the optimising process. At some sufficiently low wage rate, this might be an optimum technique. Hence it is best if the expression 'degraded technique' is confined to cases where, if output were unrestrained, the alteration would render the adjusted technique strictly inferior to its original, in the sense defined in Chapter 2.

If a technique is degraded, then, either $v_i(t_i)$ falls or $q_i(t_i)$ rises, or both. Therefore the substitution of a degraded technique for its original must reduce the rate of profit.

It follows that a practicable programme cannot be determined without reference to the output scalar. From any initial or 'theoretical' programme, optimum or otherwise, we deduce a vector of initial scale coefficients. We apply the chosen output scalar and obtain the vector of unit requirements. To obtain the corresponding *practicable* programme we must then adjust each scale coefficient, by degradation of technique, until each unit requirement has been raised to the next highest whole number.

The method of degradation chosen to achieve each adjustment will vary from activity to activity and from technique to technique. In any particular example, the collection of methods chosen should be those which minimised the overall reduction of the rate of profit. In a multi-activity example, the implications of this proposition are obviously going to be complicated, and for the time being we shall revert to discussing a one-activity problem only. We can therefore drop the *i*-suffixes to the various coefficients and analyse a situation where there is only one scale coefficient of each plant programme.

With one activity and one technique of production, if degradation of techniques were impossible the result would be so simple that we would hardly need an extensive theoretical apparatus for our argument. If a business cannot sell enough output to justify multiple shifts, multiple shifts cannot be operated. More precisely, the value of o is fixed, therefore only by reducing h can we raise z. If degradation is permissible, small adjustments may profitably be achieved by this means, but since degradation by definition 'inferiorises' the technique, whereas reduction of utilisation, although raising capital costs, does lower labour costs, it is almost certain that when large adjustments are required utilisation adjustments will prove the best method. The general tendency of effect of restraints on output must inevitably be in the direction of reducing optimum practicable rates of utilisation.

4.3. Scale Inversion

We shall find that this broad conclusion is not reversed when the assumption of alternative techniques is restored, but it does become less obvious. In order to see the difficulty we must consider more carefully than hitherto the relation between the coefficient o (output per unit of equipment) which determines the magnitude of the unadjusted scale coefficient, and the coefficient v (output per man-hour) which determines the rate of profit.

The connection between o and v is

$$o = lv, \tag{4.3}$$

where l, it will be remembered, stands for the number of workers required to 'man-up' the unit of equipment (i.e. instantaneous employment). If l is the same for all techniques in the hierarchy, the ordering of techniques in terms of o is identical with the ordering in terms of v. In this case, therefore, a change of technique in the direction of lowering v implies the same proportionate reduction of o and vice versa. A set of scale coefficients for activity programmes with varying techniques but the *same* utilisation rate will then be ordered precisely as the ordering of the v of the techniques. It follows, then, that we have now three ways of reaching a practicable optimum programme when the initial or 'theoretical' optimum is ruled out by output restraint. We may degrade the technique and employ the same programme. We may adopt an alternative programme containing a lower rate of utilisation or we may adopt an alternative programme containing a less mechanised technique (if l is constant, a fall in v must mean a fall in o). It is not by any means obvious which method would be the best, i.e. it is not obvious which adjustment will depress the rate of profit least. Therefore, since only one of these methods involves reducing utilisation, it is not obvious how output constraint will affect optimum utilisation rates.†

In real life there is no reason to suppose that l will be constant for all techniques. If l varies, the ordering of techniques in terms of o may differ from the ordering in terms of v and it will be extremely difficult to say anything general at all: the direction of effect of output restraints both on optimum technique and on optimum utilisation will seem to be indeterminate. It is therefore of the utmost importance to consider the relation, in a hierarchy of non-inferior techniques, between o and v, that is, in effect, the relation between v and l. Do the more mechanised techniques tend to exhibit the larger values of output per unit of equipment or do they not?

Imagine a unit of equipment consisting of one machine, operated by one machinist. Suppose mechanisation in this case would involve replacing the one machine by another more expensive, still operated by one man who, on account of the superiority of the more expensive machine, is able to produce more rapidly. o and v rise in the same proportions, l remaining constant. Even if the more expensive machine requires two operators (but is not inferior because its hourly rate of output is more than twice that of the cheaper machine) the ordering relation is sustained, that is, l having risen, o has risen also. But suppose the *cheaper* machine had required two operators while the dearer machine required only one, then provided the hourly rate of output of the dearer machine were at least 50 % of that of the cheaper machine, its output per man-hour would be greater and so also, evidently, its capital per man; therefore neither technique would be inferior to the other. Obviously such cases must be possible. We will refer to them as cases of *scale inversion.* Scale inversion may occur between any pair of adjacent techniques in a hierarchy or even between all techniques. However, we need to define the concept a little more precisely. What is required is that as we move from one technique in a hierarchy to the next above it, output per unit of equipment falls while output per man rises. The proportionate change in output per unit, $o^{\cdot}$, is given by

$$o^{\cdot} = v^{\cdot} - l^{\cdot} - l^{\cdot}v^{\cdot},$$

where $l^{\cdot}$, the proportionate change in instantaneous employment, is defined negatively. We require that $o^{\cdot}$ be negative. The formal condition for inversion is, therefore,

$$v^{\cdot} < \frac{l^{\cdot}}{1 - l^{\cdot}}.$$

Scale inversion therefore requires not only that the number of men per machine be reduced with mechanisation but that the proportionate decline in the number of men must exceed the proportionate increase in

† Strictly we should also consider the possibility of raising technique while lowering utilisation to an offsetting extent, or vice versa. These cases will be discussed later.

output per man-hour by a definite amount, which increases with the magnitude of $l^{\cdot}$ itself.

There is a considerable quantity of empirical evidence that production functions in which scale inversion predominates are unusual† and we shall for the moment assume it to be non-existent. Later, in §4.6, we consider the theoretical consequences of dropping this assumption.

4.4. Determination of the Optimum Practicable Programme

We are now in a position to describe the procedure for finding the optimum practicable programme when there is more than one technique. In effect, the adjustments described in §4.1 must be considered for each technique in turn and the total number of alternative practicable programmes is correspondingly increased. For any given utilisation rate there is a different scale coefficient for each technique and similarly a different unit requirement; in other words there are coefficients for all programmes. We can also define for each programme a *scale adjustment coefficient*—the factor by which the unit requirement must be divided in order to bring it to a whole number.

Then if z_{ii} stands for the scale coefficient of programme i, i (that is of the programme in which the ith technique is employed at the ith rate of utilisation) while u_{ii} and a_{ii} stand for the programme unit requirement and scale adjustment coefficient respectively, we can visualise a succession of 'operating' matrices defining the adjustments necessary to obtain the matrix of practicable, i.e. adjusted, programmes from the initial data, as follows:‡

Matrix of initial scale coefficients, $\mathbf{Z}$, where $z_{ii} = k_i/o_i h_i$.

Matrix of unit requirements, $\mathbf{U}$, where $u_{ii} = z_{ii}(O/\bar{h})$.

Matrix of scale adjustments, $\mathbf{A}$, where $a_{ii} = u_{ii}/y_{ii}$
(y_{ii} being the next whole number greater than u_{ii}).

Matrix of initial profit rates, $\mathbf{R}$, where $r_{ii} = r(i, i)$.

Matrix of adjusted profit rates, $\mathbf{R}'$, where r'_{ii} is defined below.

r_{ii} is determined by the technique of production, t_i, the system of utilisation, h_i, and the basic real wage, $\bar{\bar{w}}$. Since z_{ii} is also uniquely determined by t_i and h_i we can write

$$r_{ii} = r_{ii}(z_{ii}, \bar{\bar{w}}). \qquad (4.4)$$

† It seems that the comparison between 'mule' spindles and 'ring' spindles in the textile industries might provide an example of inversion, although when ring spindles are operated with the most advanced methods of labour deployment, the number of 'Sides' of spindles tended by each operative may represent a unit of equipment whose output is considerably greater than the unit managed by the three-person team of mule operators: in defining a unit of equipment, we should remember to take account of the indivisibility of the operatives as well as of the machine.

‡ In this paragraph and in what follows, the two i's used as subscripts are not necessarily equal. Thus z_{ii} might stand for z_{12}.

Unfortunately the determination of r'_{ii}, the adjusted profit rate, is less unique. The adjustment results from degradation. Without knowing the degradation possibilities of each technique precisely, we cannot specify the degree of profit reduction associated with a given amount of adjustment expressed in a_{ii}. Clearly there is a functional relation between r_{ii}/r'_{ii} and a_{ii}, but this will vary between techniques and will be by no means necessarily homogeneous. The information required is inherent in the specification of a technique, but we cannot generalise about it. For the time being we shall proceed on the sweeping assumption that the function takes the simplest form imaginable, to wit, for all i,

$$r'_{ii} = r_{ii} a_{ii}. \tag{4.5}$$

We discuss the implications of this assumption later.

The matrix of initial scale coefficients is given by the programme data. The unit requirements and scale adjustments are derived from this and from the output scalar. The same information, with the addition of the basic wage, provides the initial profit rates. The *adjusted* profit rates r'_{ii} can then be derived by assumption (4.5). The *optimum practicable programme* is that programme displaying the highest adjusted profit rate. It follows that the optimum practicable programme, given our assumptions, is fully determined by the programme data (that is to say the vectors of available techniques and systems), the basic wage and the output scalar, the latter in turn depending on the desired output and the basic rate of utilisation (operating hours per annum on 'normal' one-shift basis). In a real-life case the same result can in principle be obtained without the strong assumption (4.5) if the data indicate all the possibilities and consequences of degradation in each technique. However, if we are to continue to analyse the relation between optimum practicable and optimum initial programme we must continue to make use of this or some other specific simplifying assumption. We now investigate the relationship in question by means of examples.

4.5. Examples of Adjusted Programmes

Consider the initial profitability matrix for the example given in Chapter 2, p. 55 for wage rate 3.

	System... 1	2	3
Technique 1	−10	−34	−68
Technique 2	8	10	9
Technique 3	8	13	**16**

(= **R**) (4.6)

From the basic data of the example we can also compute a matrix of *scale coefficients*,

$$\begin{matrix} 0{\cdot}250 & 0{\cdot}125 & 0{\cdot}083 \\ 0{\cdot}143 & 0{\cdot}072 & 0{\cdot}048 \\ 0{\cdot}111 & 0{\cdot}055 & 0{\cdot}037 \end{matrix} \quad (= \mathbf{Z}) \tag{4.7}$$

If the output scalar were 16, implying an annual turnover of £32 000, the matrix of *unit requirements* would be

$$\left.\begin{matrix} 4\cdot00 & 2\cdot00 & 1\cdot33 \\ 2\cdot28 & 1\cdot15 & 0\cdot77 \\ 1\cdot78 & 0\cdot88 & 0\cdot59 \end{matrix} \quad (= \mathbf{U})\right\} \qquad (4.8)$$

$$[O/\bar{h} = 16].$$

The corresponding *scale adjustments* are

$$\left.\begin{matrix} 1\cdot00 & 1\cdot00 & 0\cdot67 \\ 0\cdot76 & 0\cdot57 & 0\cdot77 \\ 0\cdot89 & 0\cdot88 & 0\cdot59 \end{matrix} \quad (= \mathbf{A})\right\} \qquad (4.9)$$

$$[O/\bar{h} = 16].$$

Ignore programmes showing a negative initial profit rate, then we have a matrix of *adjusted profit rates*

$$\left.\begin{matrix} \ldots & \ldots & \ldots \\ 6 & 6 & 7 \\ 7 & \mathbf{11} & 9 \end{matrix} \quad (= \mathbf{R}')\right\} \qquad (4.10)$$

$$[O/\bar{h} = 16].$$

The optimum programme has been displaced from 3, 3 to 2, 3. The optimum practicable rate of utilisation is less than the optimum theoretical rate, but the technique is unchanged. The maximum profit rate, of course, is considerably reduced.

If the output scalar were halved, implying a turnover of £16 000 per annum only, we should have *unit requirements*

$$\begin{matrix} \ldots & \ldots & \ldots \\ 1\cdot14 & 0\cdot57 & 0\cdot38 \\ 0\cdot86 & 0\cdot44 & 0\cdot28 \end{matrix} \quad (= \mathbf{U})$$

$$[O/\bar{h} = 8].$$

Scale adjustments

$$\begin{matrix} \ldots & \ldots & \ldots \\ 0\cdot57 & 0\cdot57 & 0\cdot38 \\ 0\cdot86 & 0\cdot44 & 0\cdot28 \end{matrix} \quad (= \mathbf{A})$$

$$[O/\bar{h} = 8].$$

Adjusted profit rates

$$\begin{matrix} \ldots & \ldots & \ldots \\ 5 & 6 & 3 \\ \mathbf{7} & 6 & 4 \end{matrix} \quad (= \mathbf{R}')$$

$$[O/\bar{h} = 8].$$

The optimum rate of utilisation is further reduced, together with the profit rate.

However, had the output scalar been *doubled*, so that turnover was £64000, the *adjusted profit rates* would have been:

$$\begin{matrix} 7 & 8 & 7 \\ 7 & \mathbf{11} & 9 \end{matrix} \quad (= \mathbf{R}')$$
$$[O/\bar{h} = 32].$$

The optimum programme moves back to 3, 2. Had the output scalar again been doubled,

$$\begin{matrix} 7 & 9 & 7 \\ 7 & 11 & \mathbf{13} \end{matrix} \quad (= \mathbf{R}')$$
$$[O/\bar{h} = 64].$$

The optimum practicable programme, but not the optimum practicable profit rate, has become the same as in the optimum initial position. We have thus observed the following development. As the value of the output scalar is progressively increased, the value of all the scale coefficients is increased. When any set of numbers increases, the ratio between any one member and the nearest whole number tends to rise: as the output scalar becomes large the adjustment coefficients tend to unity. Therefore as the output scalar becomes large, the unadjusted profitability matrix becomes increasingly valid and the problems of indivisibility disappear. In the example the figures for this development were as shown in Table 4.1.

Table 4.1. *Results of example*

Annual turnover (£)	Optimum practicable programme	Profit rate (%)
16000	3, 1	7
32000	3, 2	11
64000	3, 2	11
128000	3, 3	13
Large	3, 3	16

4.6. Effects of the Constraint

Reading up the table, the constraint on output progressively reduces both rate of utilisation and rate of profit. At a turnover of £16000 no further reduction of utilisation is possible, and the only method of reducing the scale coefficient would have been to reduce technique. Therefore in due course technique also must be reduced. Evidently, however, with slightly different basic data, technique might have been reduced first and subsequently utilisation. But it can be shown that at no stage is it likely that the restraint would suggest *raising* utilisation while lowering technique, even though, at first sight, this appears a possibility. The point can best be seen by postulating a rather large, say 4×4, unadjusted profitability matrix—representing a case with four techniques and four systems, as shown in Table 4.2. Suppose the adjusted optimum happened to occur at r_{33}. Then (on our present assumptions) the scale coefficients for programmes 3, 4, 4, 3 and 4, 4 must all be lower than that of 3, 3. Whatever the output scalar, therefore, the scale adjustments for these programmes will tend to be higher and the adjusted optimum is unlikely to lie in the quadrant to the south-east of the theoretical optimum. But we have to ask whether it is likely that the adjusted optimum could be for example 2, 4 rather than 2, 3 or 3, 2.

Table 4.2. *Large matrix*

r_{11}	r_{12}	r_{13}	r_{14}
r_{21}	r_{22}	r_{23}	r_{24}
r_{31}	r_{32}	$\mathbf{r_{33}}$	r_{34}
r_{41}	r_{42}	r_{43}	r_{44}

If 3, 3 is the optimum theoretical programme, r_{33} is a row maximum. Then the maximum of row 2 cannot lie to the right of this position.† Therefore the unadjusted value of r_{23} cannot be higher than that of r_{24}. But the scale coefficients of programme 2, 4 must be lower than that of 2, 3 (higher rate of utilisation, same technique): therefore not only is the initial value of r_{24} lower than the initial value of r_{23} but is also likely to require greater adjustment. Therefore it is most unlikely, on our present assumptions, that the adjusted value of r_{24} will exceed that of r_{23}. Therefore wherever the adjusted optimum lies it does not lie at 2, 4. The argument can easily be extended to eliminate programme 1, 4 also. For movements in the south-westerly direction, however, the argument is reversed: an adjusted optimum at 4, 2 is not only possible but likely.

Despite the strong assumptions on which it is dependent, this conclusion is of very considerable economic importance indeed. The theorems proved in the mathematical appendix‡ imply that in the absence of degradation, constraints on the scale of output can never encourage utilisation. Where degradation takes a simple form, such as we have been assuming above, constraints must in general discourage utilisation, although occasionally they may lead to increased mechanisation at the expense of reduced utilisation. As constraints increase in severity they must eventually reduce both mechanisation and utilisation. In all cases constraints depress the rate of profit. Conversely if the permitted rate of output is increased from a low level, both mechanisation and utilisation are encouraged and the rate of profit obtainable with given wages and prices is increased. This is a fundamental cause of the economic phenomenon known as 'economies of large scale production'.

Our arguments have necessarily been loose because we have been unable to specify with any generality the way in which particular techniques are degraded. We have relied on the strong assumption that the relation between scale adjustment and profit-rate adjustment is

† See p. 55 above. ‡ See Mathematical Appendix, p. 108.

homogeneous. If as seems not unlikely the effects of degradation were more severe in the more mechanised techniques (i.e. if the proportionate depression of profit rate for a given scale adjustment tended to be larger for those techniques with higher output per man-hour) the adjusted profitability matrix will be modified in a direction favouring lower levels of mechanisation. This would weaken the basis of the argument from which we concluded that output constraints would never be likely to encourage an increase of utilisation: if the extra encouragement to de-mechanisation were strong enough, a north-easterly movement of the optimum position could well be possible. But clearly the paradox is limited to certain ranges of the output scalar: if the scalar is small enough, the reduction of utilisation is inevitable.†

The various methods of degrading techniques do not in fact exhaust the possibilities for making the required scale adjustments. An alternative method would be to reduce the length of each shift when using the programme in question. It is unlikely that this change would be accompanied by a reduction in unit labour costs (and indeed, costs might well be raised) so that the programme profit rate could be assumed to be reduced at least *pro rata*. If this were the method adopted for all adjustments, our assumption that the profit rate adjustment is homogeneous in the scale-coefficient adjustment is validated, together, of course, with all the conclusions based on it.

Another alternative method of adjustment raises more difficult questions. Suppose the unit requirement of a certain programme were 1·10. If we are to raise this to the next whole number we face a reciprocal scale adjustment of 0·55, which is severe. Paradoxically, had the value of the required output scalar been 10% *lower*, the required scale adjustment would have been no greater than unity. Indeed, any reduction of the output scalar greater than 10% and less than 50% would have improved the position. One useful 'adjustment', then, would be to decide to produce a smaller output. This is a possibility of particular importance where unit requirements lie between 1·0 and about 5·0—a range which is likely to be common. We have therefore to ask whether the constraint on the output scalar is to be regarded as both a maximum and a minimum (as we have assumed so far) or as a maximum only.

It is a question which is impossible to answer. To say that, *given* the desired output, firms should maximise the rate of profit is one thing: to say how they might choose between a larger output versus a lower

† There is a special, and possibly important, form of 'degradation', concealed by our earlier assumptions, which may also have paradoxical effects. Our basic assumptions eliminate from the data all 'inferior' techniques, i.e. techniques which, with *unrestricted* output, could not be profitable with any wage rate on any system. When output is restricted, however, it is possible that some such techniques (depending on the extent and character of the constraint) may no longer be inferior, and they should, therefore, be restored to the data. The implications are similar to those of non-linear degradation: it becomes possible that, over certain ranges of output, an increase in the severity of the constraint may lead to increased utilisation accompanied by decreased mechanisation. Eventually, however, as the constraint becomes verv severe, utilisation must again be depressed.

rate of profit, and vice versa, is another. Professor William Baumol† has suggested that many firms in practice aim for the largest possible value of turnover subject to the earning of a certain minimum rate of profit, the hypothesis known as 'revenue maximisation subject to minimum profit restraint'. The present main author, however, believes that when considered dynamically this hypothesis has certain weaknesses: for if the rate of profit, as the author believes, is closely associated with the *financial* limits on the growth of firms, then in certain circumstances the firm may in the long run grow faster if content with a lower absolute level of output in the first stage of expansion in order to earn a larger rate of profit and hence grow faster later.

However, it is illuminating to investigate the consequences of going to the extreme of assuming that the output restraint is a maximum only. We may imagine, for example, that the firm is concerned only with the rate of profit, and finds that the size of its market is limited by the usual economic factors (known generally in economic theory as 'imperfections' of competition). There is some 'right price' for the product; at this price the output O can be sold; if price is lowered, no more can be sold; if price is raised little or nothing can be sold. Therefore price is 'given' and the firm is seeking that programme which will maximise the rate of profit subject to the output restraint. It is completely indifferent about actual output, provided it is less than the indicated maximum. (These assumptions are clearly absurd if carried to extremes.) Then the only programmes to require scale adjustment will be those whose unit requirements, computed with the output scalar corresponding to O, are less than unity; i.e. those programmes which require the designer to order less than one whole unit of equipment. Any unit requirement greater than unity can be adjusted *downwards* by reducing the planned volume of output, that is to say, by consciously planning to leave part of the market unsatisfied. If at the same time we ignore entirely the possibility of degrading techniques, the analysis of the whole problem is considerably simplified. The programme with the highest unit requirement (calculated at the maximum permissible value of the output scalar) below unity must be eliminated from consideration altogether, along with all those programmes due east, due south or south-west of it. Therefore the practicable programmes are unambiguously located to the north-east, north, north-west, west and south-west. In this situation, our argument that the adjustment will never move in the direction of raising utilisation becomes rigorous and thus lends support to the broader general conclusions.

Finally, we must reconsider the question of scale-inversion. We are now in a much better position to understand the implications of the assumption that scale-inversion is rare. If scale inversion occurs between any pairs of techniques in **T**, the relation between the patterns of the matrix **R** and of the matrices **Z** and **A** break down. We can no longer say anything definite about the effect of output restraints on either

† William Baumol, *Business Behavior, Value and Growth* (Princeton, 1959).

utilisation or technique: *in certain conditions the imposition of a restraint might lead to an increase in utilisation or of mechanisation or both.* If inversion occurs between *all* adjacent pairs in **T**, however, we obtain a bizarre result: all our arguments are reversed; output restraint may encourage the adoption of a *more* mechanised technique at the same rate of utilisation or a lower rate of utilisation at the same technique or even to a combination of less mechanised technique and higher (!) rate of utilisation. Even here, however, if the restraint becomes sufficiently severe reduced utilisation is inevitable. The conclusion that output restraints tend *in general* to reduce utilisation seems to remain valid, but a state of affairs where inversion predominated would imply another general tendency that no business man would believe—to wit that output restraints *encouraged* mechanisation.

4.7. 'Indivisibility' in Management

It is often argued that rather than indivisibilities of fixed capital, problems of management are the largest single factor preventing shift-work among small firms. In large and medium firms, only a relatively small proportion of the managerial staff is directly involved in routine supervision of production: the rest are concerned with the sales, purchases, finance and policy. If there were a perfect separation of function between routine supervision and other work, multiple-shift operation would present no special difficulties. The salaries of supervisors, if any, required to work shifts would be included in the wage bill of operatives and treated on precisely the same analytical footing: in practice, with permanent night-shifts, supervision is often reduced to a minimum, with the result that, contrary to what might be expected, output per man-hour is often increased.†

But this kind of arrangement is usually possible only in certain processes. A single activity can run without close supervision, but when many activities are operating simultaneously, troubles arise immediately. One of the most important tasks of medium-level management is co-ordination. When a hitch occurs in department *A*, disrupting the work of departments *B* and *C*, it is the task of management to decide what is to be done. Furthermore, the division of functions is rarely as perfect as we have postulated. A works manager, for example, does much that is similar to general administration and which need not be undertaken directly in phase with production. Many of the functions of the personnel manager, such as the hiring of new employees, can easily be

† A shift-worker told the author, 'We are paid on piece rates and I always choose the night-shift because you can earn more then. You don't get so much messed-about at night. You are rarely kept waiting for material, because the day-workers leave behind a sufficient supply, and the machines are left ready set up for us. There are no women and no supervisors in the factory at night; that speeds up production a lot!' This man was earning about £20 a week, and was saving up to buy a house. His wife had recently been ill, forcing him to go on to the day-shift—a financial disaster, for his earnings, he said, were almost halved.

concentrated into a day-shift, but his other functions, such as welfare work, and the firing of employees, require his presence at the time when the workers themselves are present. More generally, the personnel manager is not likely to be very efficient if half of his charges are never in the factory at the same time as he. On the other hand, if the whole of the middle management staff is duplicated (two works managers, two personnel managers, and so on) while the scale of output is constrained to a fixed level, at least one-half of the managerial staff concerned are likely to be considerably under-employed. There are also likely to be problems of co-ordination and integration of leadership.

One solution might be to hire a 'junior team' of supervisory managers for the second shift, that is, to hire a deputy works manager, a deputy personnel manager, deputy production engineers, and so on. But again a number of serious difficulties arise. One is that although manual workers by no means dislike the shift system, and some prefer it, to the middle-class person shift-work seems not only inconvenient but undignified. One of the most valued middle-class privileges is that of getting out of bed an hour later than the rest of the population, and since few professional workers are under economic pressure to work shifts, an industrial manager working unusual hours will find himself in a much smaller minority among his friends than would a manual worker.† A second difficulty lies in the implications for management training. The 'junior team' is being trained not only to supervise routine production but also, ultimately, to take on wider and more transcendent roles. The first will be learnt considerably more quickly than the second, and it would then seem reasonable to set these partly trained employees to the task of supervising production at night. Unfortunately, if the young men are isolated on one shift, while their principals remain on the other, little broader experience will be gained. For it is precisely by contact with his superiors that a young man learns how to exercise leadership. Indeed, the more one considers the career prospects of a night-shift manager the more gloomy they appear. In large firms the difficulty can be overcome by *rotating* the junior team, each member taking a turn of shift-work as part of his training experience. But this is possible only if the team as a whole is large enough to be divisible.

The final difficulty with the 'junior-team' system is one which arises from the inherent character of management function. The essence of management, as against supervision, lies in the taking of *non-routine* decisions. Such decisions may be operational, i.e. may determine specific actions or they may be decisions which determine policy, i.e. determine the criteria applied to a particular class of subsidiary decisions. Policy decisions can be taken collectively, for example, by a Board of Directors; routine supervision can be delegated; but non-routine operational decisions are particularly difficult to delegate and must usually be taken by one man alone. That is to say, if a junior

† One firm, which employed a high proportion of middle-grade technicians, said they would lose all their staff if shift-work were required.

works manager is appointed to supervise the night-shift, however competent he is, he will eventually face some situation which he lacks the experience to resolve without reference to his supervisor. Typically, a piece of machinery breaks down and the deputy does not possess all the accumulated information and judgement necessary to decide whether it is best to close the factory and wait for the maintenance men to arrive in the morning or whether to attempt a running repair. If the deputy was a person who did possess the necessary experience, and he and his employers knew it, he would no longer be content with the salary of a junior. And if he were paid the salary of a principal, we are back to the problem we faced originally. In consequence, when machinery breaks down at night, either decisions are taken badly, or they are referred to the head manager. If the head manager is at home in bed, the outcome will be necessarily unhappy.† In short, shift-work creates considerable additional burdens on management, whose weight increases proportionately as the size of the firm reduces. In very small firms, where the managing director is also effectively the works manager, the cost is usually prohibitive. On the other hand it seems that this is an effect which disappears at lower levels of permitted output than does the effect of indivisibility in equipment; once a firm has reached a sufficient size economically to employ a good night foreman or deputy works manager, at least part of the problem is eliminated. We found that medium-sized establishments were in general able to solve the problem satisfactorily.‡

Management indivisibilities, then, are a further addition to the 'scale-effect', of particular importance at very low levels of planned output.

4.8. Fluctuations in Output

We have considered, so far, the position of a plant designer who is asked to provide for a given annual rate of planned final output in the most profitable way. We have assumed that the planned output is treated as certain. Obviously, the real-life designer will realise that actual output

† One works manager in a firm where 'economic' shift-working was necessary on a wide scale, graphically explained to us that the mere possibility, rather than the actual frequency, of nocturnal telephone calls considerably affected the nerves of managers faced with this problem.

‡ A passage from Mr MacLean's notes written after a series of interviews directed to this point is worth quoting verbatim: 'One point is clear, namely that it gives management a lot more work. The personnel manager needs to be something of a psychologist and to be on good terms with his labour force, but it is on the production side that the worst headaches may arise; for shift-work, even when it is not tied up with any re-equipment, means a tightening up of production—mistakes are magnified, probably not all the factory will be on shifts so that the problem of balancing the sections becomes acute, work must be left for the night-shift, and they in turn must complete their work if the day-shift is not to be idle for part at least of the day. These are not problems specific to shift-work, but they may require some complicated planning if the shift is to work smoothly, especially as supervision on the night-shift is normally inferior to that of the day-shift, the night-shift usually being in charge of a night foreman. Mass production, mechanical handling, all these things add to the strain on management and management may well consider that shift-work is not worth shedding either blood or tears and seeks its ulcers elsewhere.'

is going to fluctuate, but we might imagine that the output for which the plant is designed is based on some guess as to the *average* expected sales during its lifetime. However, if this assumption is investigated more carefully, we will find that it carries important implications for the design itself.

If demand is going to fluctuate, the firm will probably wish to be able to meet at least a reasonable proportion of the peak orders without unduly long delays in delivery. We might define the 'peak' output as the maximum annual† *rate* of demand the firm wished to be able to meet without abnormal delay: it is inherent in this definition that the plant must be so designed to be able to produce at an annual rate sufficient to meet the peak rate of demand whenever necessary, either by increasing the rate of utilisation or by activating machinery normally kept idle around the clock. Then we might imagine that a certain proportion of the total output of the plant over its whole life will be produced at the peak rate, while the remainder is produced at some rate we call 'normal'. In practice, the 'normal' rate of output will itself fluctuate, since normal is defined as any rate below the peak. This fact will present problems of indivisibility which must be evaluated in the light of the conditions of each particular case, but we can illuminate some more fundamental aspects of the matter by assuming that only the two rates of demand, 'normal' and 'peak' are ever experienced: 'normal' then becomes a single definite rate and we ignore conditions when demand is either below this rate or lies between it and the peak.

Suppose only two relative utilisation rates are considered, $h = 1$ and $h = 2$. Suppose the peak rate of output is at least double the normal rate. Then we have only to consider the most profitable rate of utilisation for the peak rate of output: if we are to meet the peak rate in the most economical way, the rate of utilisation occurring at the normal rate is academic; with a plant sufficient to meet peak demand at $h = 2$, normal demand must imply h is less than 1. What, then, is the best rate of utilisation for the peak rate, i.e. what rate of utilisation planned for the peak rate of output will maximise the average rate of profit earned by the plant over its whole life: shall we plan to meet peak demand by adding an extra shift, or by holding a reserve of machinery which is normally idle both night and day?

Consider the formula for the incentive to utilise, as originally developed in Chapter 2;

$$r^{\cdot} = h^{\cdot} - m^{\cdot} - h^{\cdot}m^{\cdot}. \qquad (2.5)$$

$r^{\cdot}$, it will be remembered, represented the proportionate change in the rate of profit earned over the plant as a whole due to an increase in utilisation, while $h^{\cdot}$ represented the proportionate difference between the two rates of utilisation and $m^{\cdot}$ the proportionate *decline* in the hourly rate of profit per unit of output associated with this increase. We need to modify the formula to read as follows: $r^{\cdot}$ must stand for the propor-

† Or, if the fluctuations are seasonal the peak would be defined as a monthly rate.

tionate change in the average rate of profit earned over the whole life of the plant, while $h^{\cdot}$ and $m^{\cdot}$ should relate only to alternative conditions in producing at the peak rate of output. Then it is not difficult to see that if p is the proportion of total output over the whole life of the plant which will be produced at the peak rate,

$$r^{\cdot} = h^{\cdot} - pm^{\cdot}(1+h^{\cdot}). \tag{4.11}$$

$h^{\cdot}$ and $m^{\cdot}$ are exactly the same as they would be if the formula were unmodified; therefore we can say for certain that the smaller p the *greater* the incentive to utilise at the peak rate of output. In other words if p is small, it is more likely, other things being equal, that a firm would plan to meet the peak output by adding an extra shift rather than by activating a daytime reserve of capacity. This is an important result, since it implies that a large proportion of observed multiple-shift working will be *occasioned* by short-run increases in demand. If a plant was originally designed to employ the potentialities of shift-work as a hidden reserve, when the reserve is brought into use, the increase in demand will seem the immediate cause and the original planning considerations are less likely to be remembered. This almost certainly is the explanation of the high proportion of replies to inquiries sent out by the Ministry of Labour (see Chapter 8) explaining shift-working in short-run terms. Such replies, from the point of view of economic theory, are 'superficial' since they cannot explain why other firms faced with the expectation of fluctuating demand chose instead to employ the method of holding a daytime reserve of idle capacity. Unfortunately, despite various attempts made in the course of the inquiry, it has proved almost impossible to obtain answers to questions asking firms why they do not do certain things in contrast to questions asking them why they do others.

Our result does not mean that if p is large, high rates of utilisation will never be planned for the peak output; it means merely that if p is large, high rates will be less likely. The effect, in fact, is to raise the critical value of $m^{\cdot}$, i.e., to raise the value of $m^{\cdot}$ at which the higher rate of utilisation becomes profitable. The critical-value formula originally given in Chapter 2 is modified therefore as follows:

$$m^{\cdot} < \frac{h^{\cdot}}{1+h^{\cdot}} \frac{1}{p}. \tag{4.12}$$

If p is unity, because all output is 'peak' output, the formula is the same as the original. If conditions are right, $m^{\cdot}$ may still be below the critical value nevertheless.

The foregoing may be generalised by dropping the assumption that the firm considers only two rates of output. Suppose, instead, a fairly wide range of possible levels of demand is envisaged and that to some or all of these levels the firm is able to attach a 'probability of occurrence'. The complete set of such estimates would represent a *probability-distribution* of expected demand and could be described by familiar statistical concepts: the most probable, or expected average level, is the 'mathematical expectation'; the variability, or spread around the average, can be measured by the *coefficient of variation*, i.e. by the standard deviation divided by the mean. A low coefficient of variation implies that demand is expected to be rather stable, and that only a relatively small proportion of total output is expected to occur under extreme conditions; a high coefficient implies unstable demand and relatively higher probabilities of experiencing extremes.

Faced with a probability-distribution of demand, the firm has a probability-distribution of profits, but, given the data, the probability-distribution of profits derived from a given probability-distribution of demand will depend on the character of the chosen investment plan. If the investment plan is to be chosen in such a way as to maximise the ratio of the mathematical expectation of profits to capital employed (i.e. to maximise the *most probable* rate of profit) the decision will be found to depend on the statistical characteristics or 'shape' of the probability-distribution of demand. If the distribution is symmetrical, we can show that the higher the coefficient of variation the more likely it is that the optimum investment plan should envisage meeting demand fluctuations mainly by variations in utilisation rather than by maintaining a reserve of instantaneous capacity. In other words, the more variable the expected future demand, the more likely it is to seem best to plan to meet periods of high demand by shift-work. If firms were following this principle we should expect to observe that, other things being equal, in industries where demand was known to be variable, the average occurrence of shift-work, taking one year with another, would be relatively frequent. Conversely, other things being equal, stability of demand should militate against shift-work. As will be seen in Part II, we were not able to test this prediction.

4.9. Summary and Glossary of Part I

The present chapter completes the theoretical part of our inquiry. In Chapter 5, the first chapter of Part II, we summarise our findings in a manner suited for empirical testing. In the meantime, however, because we have developed a number of new concepts, we recapitulate here the various definitions and the main theorems. The numbers and letters in square brackets indicate the page where a concept is first introduced and, where appropriate, its symbol.

GLOSSARY OF DEFINITIONS

Unit of equipment

A group of items of fixed capital whose members cannot be operated independently [27].

Rate of utilisation

The number of hours a unit of equipment is productively operated annually [3, h]. *Basic......*: rate of utilisation on a standard one-shift system [66, $\bar{h}$]. *Planned......*: rate of utilisation assumed in determining how many units of equipment are required to meet a given annual rate of output [7]. *Relative......*: ratio of the rate of utilisation on some given system to the basic rate of utilisation; thus, '*intensive utilisation*', to adopt a high planned relative rate of utilisation [64, h_i]. (See also 'optimum rate of utilisation' below.)

Instantaneous employment

The number of workers required to operate a given unit of equipment [13, l].

System of operation

A method of operating equipment (such as one-shift, double-day-shift, three-shift, etc.) implying a definite rate of utilisation and an associated average hourly wage rate for operative labour [30].

Basic wage rate

Hourly money wage rate payable on a standard one-shift system [36, $\bar{w}$]. *Real......*: basic wage rate divided by the assumed selling price of final product [54, $\bar{\bar{w}}$].

Utilisation differential

The proportionate increase in average hourly wage rate (or, more precisely, in hourly labour-cost, per unit of output) when comparing a system of high utilisation with some other system of lower utilisation [36, $w^{\cdot}$].

Activity

An industrial process capable of independent operation [61].

Plant

Collection of activities required to produce a given final product [61].

Technique of production

Specification of a type of equipment which can be used in some given activity. (In general, the specification of a technique of production implies unique values of output per unit of equipment per hour, output per man-hour, value of capital per unit of equipment and value of capital per unit of instantaneous employment.) [41]. *Inferior......*: a technique which, in the absence of restraints on the scale of output, will not be included in any optimum programme (see below) with any positive real basic wage rate [44]; (from which it follows that among a set of non-inferior techniques available for a particular activity, the ordering in terms of output per man-hour will be identical with the ordering in terms of capital per unit of instantaneous employment); thus '*mechanisation*', adoption from a given set of non-inferior techniques one involving relatively high output per man-hour [44]. *Degraded......*: a technique modified in such a way as to reduce the hourly rate of output per unit of equipment and also render it inferior [82].

Data

Specification of the characteristics of all systems and techniques (including relevant utilisation differentials) available for all activities in a given plant [43].

Incentive to utilise

The proportionate change in the rate of profit earned on fixed capital as a result of moving from a system of lower utilisation to a system of higher utilisation, in a single activity with a given technique [32, $r^{\cdot}$].

Elasticity of utilisation

The proportionate increase in rate of utilisation, divided by the corresponding utilisation differential, when moving from a system of lower to a system of higher utilisation, in a given activity with a given technique [45, E_u].

Elasticity of mechanisation

The proportionate increase in output per man-hour divided by the corresponding increase in capital per man (more strictly, in capital per unit of instantaneous employment) when changing from a technique of lower mechanisation to a technique of higher mechanisation, in a given activity on a given system [45, E_t].

Scale inversion

Condition where increased output per man, resulting from increased mechanisation, is associated with reduced output per unit of equipment [83].

Optimum rate of utilisation

The rate of utilisation associated with the system of operation yielding the maximum rate of profit in a single activity with a given technique [33].

Optimum programme

A statement of the system and technique of production to be used in each activity of a given plant, with given data and given real basic wage rate, in order to maximise the rate of profit on the fixed capital of the plant as a whole [43].

STATEMENT OF PROBLEM

The central concern of Chapters 2 to 4 has been the character of the factors determining the optimum programme under various conditions of data and real basic wage rate, and, in particular, the circumstances in which the optimum programme is likely to favour high rates of utilisation.

SUMMARY OF RESULTS

A. *Case with only one activity, one technique and no restraints on the scale of output*

The optimum rate of utilisation will tend to be higher, the higher the average level of the incentive to utilise as between the various available systems. The incentive to utilise tends in turn to vary with the following factors:

(i) Output per man-hour (directly);
(ii) Elasticity of utilisation (directly);
(iii) Real basic wage rate (inversely);
(iv) Other factors discussed in Chapter 2.

B. *Case where there may be several activities and a choice of techniques available to each activity, output still unrestrained*

Results depend on the elasticities of utilisation and of mechanisation, whose effects are interdependent. With given data, the higher the general level of either elasticity (given the other) the more likely is the optimum programme associated with any given real basic wage rate to involve relatively high rates of utilisation and/or relatively highly mechanised techniques of production, and vice versa. Thus the elasticity of mechanisation is itself a factor directly affecting utilisation.

C. *Case with restraints on output*

In the absence of scale inversion or degradation of techniques, restraints on the scale of output (e.g. due to limited markets) depress both utilisation and mechanisation in the optimum programme. Scale inversion or degradation of techniques permit the possibility that in some cases these effects might be reversed, but in all circumstances scale restraints depress the rate of profit.

D. *Other results*

(i) *Technical progress.* In the presence of technical progress, the firms most quick to employ new inventions are those most likely to find that their optimum programmes contain relatively high planned rates of utilisation.

(ii) *Indivisibility of management.* In small firms, management problems connected with shift-work are likely to operate in a manner similar to restraints on the scale of output.

(iii) *Fluctuations in output.* If demand is expected to be variable, the greater the expected degree of variation, the more likely will the investment plan associated with the optimum programme envisage meeting fluctuations by means of varying utilisation, rather than by maintaining a reserve of instantaneous capacity.

(iv) *Interdependent activities.* The effects of interdependence among activities, within one plant, cannot be summarised (see Chapter 3) but do not, in general, significantly modify conclusions derived from analysis of single-activity models.

ECONOMIC INTERPRETATIONS

(i) *Static*

Positive variations in planned capital utilisation generally involve reductions in capital cost at the expense of increased labour cost and are therefore opposite in effect to mechanisation. Mechanisation, for well-known reasons, is stimulated by positive variations in the real basic wage rate; utilisation, therefore, is discouraged. A very high real basic wage rate will yield an optimum programme involving the most mechanised of known techniques and the least intensive system of operation—e.g. single shifts—while a very low real basic wage rate will optimise a programme involving the least mechanised technique and the most intensive system of operation—e.g. continuous three shifts. (Any change involving an equal proportionate increase in output per man-hour on *all* known techniques of production has the same effect as a reduction in real basic wage rate.) Between the extreme positions there will lie a range of optimum programmes involving various combinations of system and technique, depending on the exact value of the wage rate. If, throughout the data, capital is generally a 'good' substitute for labour in the sense that the elasticities of mechanisation are generally high, the majority of the intermediate optimum programmes will tend to contain high rates of utilisation; if not, the majority will tend to display low rates of utilisation. Thus although 'mechanisation' and 'utilisation' represent in a sense opposite types of economic adjustment, technical conditions favouring the one also favour the other, and vice versa.

Imperfections of competition, international boundaries or any other factors limiting the size of markets will tend to depress the optimum rates of utilisation in any set of data, and thus contribute to the diseconomies of small-scale production.

(ii) *Dynamic*

In an economy considered as a whole, if (*a*) the rate of growth is closely dependent on the rate of profit (e.g. because profits are the most significant source of savings) and (*b*) manufacturing firms generally choose planned rates of utilisation in accordance with optimum programmes, there will be a direct association between the average (planned) rate of utilisation and the rate of economic growth. This tendency will be enhanced if the growth rate, though fast, is expected to be disturbed by cyclical fluctuations.

Where economic growth is wholly or partly the result of (or is closely associated with) technical progress, but the rate of innovation is distributed unequally among firms (in the sense that inventions are usually first adopted by a minority of firms, the majority following only after a significant time lag), even if the growth rate is modest, intensive capital utilisation will be profitable among the innovating minority, because for these firms, during the period of lag, the real basic wage will be lower and the rate of profit higher than in comparable firms in the economy at large. Thus utilisation is also associated with innovation.

MATHEMATICAL APPENDIX TO PART I†

A 1. NOTATION‡

1.1. In this appendix we write

$$\mathbf{t} = \begin{cases} v_1 \ldots v_i \ldots v_n \\ q_1 \ldots q_i \ldots q_n \end{cases}$$

to specify the technique used in each activity, and

$$\mathbf{h} = h_1 \ldots h_i \ldots h_n$$

to specify the corresponding rates of utilisation.

A 2. THEOREMS

2.1. We prove that if $\mathbf{h}^*, \mathbf{t}^*(\mathbf{k}, \varpi_1)$ is given by $\mathbf{t}$ and $\mathbf{h}$ and if $\mathbf{h}^*, \mathbf{t}^*(\mathbf{k}, \varpi_2)$ is given by $\mathbf{t}'$ and $\mathbf{h}'$, where $\varpi_1 > \varpi_2$ and, for example, $\mathbf{h}' = h'_1 \ldots h'_i \ldots h'_n$, then

$$\frac{q_j}{h_j v_j} \geqslant \frac{q'_j}{h'_j v'_j} \quad \text{for each} \quad j, \quad 1 \leqslant j \leqslant n. \qquad \text{(A. 1)}$$

Define
$$F(\mathbf{t}, \mathbf{h}) = \sum_{i=1}^{n} \frac{k_i f_{hi}}{v_i},$$

$$D(\mathbf{t}, \mathbf{h}) = \sum_{i=1}^{n} \frac{k_i q_i}{h_i v_i}.$$

Without loss of generality we may take $\bar{h} = 1$, we consider k fixed and independent of t, and write

$$R(\mathbf{t}, \mathbf{h}, \varpi) = R(\mathbf{k}, \mathbf{h}, \mathbf{t}, \varpi) = \frac{1 - \varpi F(\mathbf{t}, \mathbf{h})}{D(\mathbf{t}, \mathbf{h})}.$$

Lemma

If
$$R(\mathbf{t}, \mathbf{h}, \varpi_1) > R(\mathbf{t}', \mathbf{h}', \varpi_i)$$
and
$$D(\mathbf{t}, \mathbf{h}) \leqslant D(\mathbf{t}', \mathbf{h}'),$$
then
$$R(\mathbf{t}, \mathbf{h}, \varpi) > R(\mathbf{t}', \mathbf{h}', \varpi) \quad \text{for all} \quad \varpi < \varpi_i.$$

For
$$\frac{1 - \varpi_1 F(\mathbf{t}, \mathbf{h})}{D(\mathbf{t}, \mathbf{h})} > \frac{1 - \varpi_1 F(\mathbf{t}', \mathbf{h}')}{D(\mathbf{t}', \mathbf{h}')},$$
therefore

$$D(\mathbf{t}', \mathbf{h}')\, F(\mathbf{t}, \mathbf{h}) - D(\mathbf{t}, \mathbf{h})\, F(\mathbf{t}', \mathbf{h}') < \frac{1}{\overline{\varpi}}\{D(\mathbf{t}', \mathbf{h}') - D(\mathbf{t}, \mathbf{h})\}$$

$$\leqslant \frac{1}{\overline{\varpi}}\{D(\mathbf{t}', \mathbf{h}') - D(\mathbf{t}, \mathbf{h})\}.$$

Whence
$$\frac{1 - \varpi F(\mathbf{t}, \mathbf{h})}{D(\mathbf{t}, \mathbf{h})} > \frac{1 - \varpi F(\mathbf{t}', \mathbf{h}')}{D(\mathbf{t}', \mathbf{h}')}.$$

† As noted in the Introduction this Appendix is entirely the work of Mr Bernau.

‡ For a full description, see Chapter 3, §3.2.

Now suppose $\mathbf{h}^*, \mathbf{t}^*(\mathbf{k}, \bar{w}_1)$ is given by $\mathbf{t}, \mathbf{h}$ and that

$$R(\mathbf{t}', \mathbf{h}', \bar{w}_2) > R(\mathbf{t}, \mathbf{h}, \bar{w}_2) \qquad (*)$$

for some $\bar{w}_2 < \bar{w}_1$. We prove that if $(q'_j/h'_j\, v'_j) > (q_j/h_j\, v_j)$ for some j.

Then

$$R(\mathbf{t}'_j, \mathbf{h}'_j, \bar{w}_2) > R(\mathbf{t}', \mathbf{h}', \bar{w}_2).$$

Where
$$\mathbf{t}'_j = \begin{bmatrix} v'_1 \dots v'_{j-1}\, v_j\, v'_{j+1} \dots v'_n \\ q'_1 \dots q'_{j-1}\, q_j\, q'_{j+1} \dots q'_n \end{bmatrix},$$

$$\mathbf{h}'_j = [h'_1 \dots h'_{j-1}\, h_j\, h'_{j+1} \dots h'_n].$$

Write
$$\mathbf{t}_j = \begin{bmatrix} v_1 \dots v_{j-1}\, v'_j\, v_{j+1} \dots v_n \\ q_1 \dots q_{j-1}\, q'_j\, q_{j+1} \dots q_n \end{bmatrix},$$

$$\mathbf{h}_j = [h_1 \dots h_{j-1}\, h'_j\, h_{j+1} \dots h_n].$$

$R(\mathbf{t}, \mathbf{h}, \bar{w}) = R(\mathbf{t}', \mathbf{h}', \bar{w})$ when

$$\frac{1 - \bar{w}F(\mathbf{t}, \mathbf{h})}{D(\mathbf{t}, \mathbf{h})} = \frac{1 - \bar{w}F(\mathbf{t}', \mathbf{h}')}{D(\mathbf{t}', \mathbf{h}')},$$

$$\bar{w}^{-1} = \frac{D(\mathbf{t}, \mathbf{h})\, F(\mathbf{t}', \mathbf{h}') - D(\mathbf{t}', \mathbf{h}')\, F(\mathbf{t}, \mathbf{h})}{D(\mathbf{t}, \mathbf{h}) - D(\mathbf{t}', \mathbf{h}')}$$

$$= F(\mathbf{t}, \mathbf{h}) + D(\mathbf{t}, \mathbf{h}) \frac{F(\mathbf{t}', \mathbf{h}') - F(\mathbf{t}, \mathbf{h})}{D(\mathbf{t}, \mathbf{h}) - D(\mathbf{t}', \mathbf{h}')} \qquad (A.\ 2)$$

$$= F(\mathbf{t}', \mathbf{h}') + D(\mathbf{t}', \mathbf{h}') \frac{F(\mathbf{t}', \mathbf{h}') - F(\mathbf{t}, \mathbf{h})}{D(\mathbf{t}, \mathbf{h}) - D(\mathbf{t}', \mathbf{h}')} \qquad (A.\ 3)$$

From the Lemma and (*) we deduce that

$$D(\mathbf{t}, \mathbf{h}) > D(\mathbf{t}', \mathbf{h}'),$$

and hence that $\bar{w}_1 > \bar{w} > \bar{w}_2$.

Define $\bar{w}_j$ by
$$R(\mathbf{t}, \mathbf{h}, \bar{w}_j) = R(\mathbf{t}_j, \mathbf{h}_j, \bar{w}_j),$$

$$\bar{w}_j^{-1} = F(\mathbf{t}, \mathbf{h}) + D(\mathbf{t}, \mathbf{h}) \frac{F(\mathbf{t}, \mathbf{h}) - F(\mathbf{t}_j, \mathbf{h}_j)}{D(\mathbf{t}_j, \mathbf{h}_j) - D(\mathbf{t}, \mathbf{h})}, \qquad (A.\ 4)$$

and $\bar{w}'_j$ by
$$R(\mathbf{t}', \mathbf{h}', \bar{w}_j) = R(\mathbf{t}'_j, \mathbf{h}'_j, \bar{w}_j),$$

$$\bar{w}_j'^{-1} = F(\mathbf{t}', \mathbf{h}') + D(\mathbf{t}', \mathbf{h}') \frac{F(\mathbf{t}'_j, \mathbf{h}'_j) - F(\mathbf{t}', \mathbf{h}')}{D(\mathbf{t}', \mathbf{h}') - D(\mathbf{t}'_j, \mathbf{h}'_j)}. \qquad (A.\ 5)$$

As
$$R(\mathbf{t}, \mathbf{h}, \bar{w}_1) > R(\mathbf{t}_j, \mathbf{h}_j, \bar{w}_1),$$

and
$$D(\mathbf{t}_j, \mathbf{h}_j) - D(\mathbf{t}, \mathbf{h}) = \frac{k_j\, q'_j}{h'_j\, v'_j} - \frac{k_j\, q_j}{h_j\, v_j} > 0.$$

Therefore
$$\bar{w}_j > \bar{w}_1 > \bar{w},$$

therefore by (A. 2) and (A. 4)

$$\frac{F(\mathbf{t}',\mathbf{h}')-F(\mathbf{t},\mathbf{h})}{D(\mathbf{t},\mathbf{h})-D(\mathbf{t}',\mathbf{h}')} > \frac{F(\mathbf{t},\mathbf{h})-F(\mathbf{t}_j,\mathbf{h}_j)}{D(\mathbf{t}_j,\mathbf{h}_j)-D(\mathbf{t},\mathbf{h})}$$

$$= \frac{(k_j f_{h_j}/v_j)-(k_j f_{h'_j}/v'_j)}{(k_j\, q'_j/h'_j\, v'_j)\;(k_j\, q_j/h_j\, v_j)}$$

$$= \frac{F(\mathbf{t}'_j,\mathbf{h}'_j)-F(\mathbf{t}',\mathbf{h}')}{D(\mathbf{t}',\mathbf{h}')-D(\mathbf{t}'_j,\mathbf{h}'_j)}.$$

Therefore by (A. 3) and (A. 5)

$$\bar{\bar{w}}'_j > \bar{\bar{w}} > \bar{\bar{w}}_2,$$

and as $D(\mathbf{t}'_j,\mathbf{h}'_j) < D(\mathbf{t}',\mathbf{h}')$,

by Lemma $R(\mathbf{t}'_j,\mathbf{h}'_j,w_2) > R(\mathbf{t}',\mathbf{h}',w_2)$.

This shows that as the real basic wage rate, $\bar{\bar{w}}$, decreases then in each activity, the quantity $q_j/h_j\,v_j$, which is the ratio of effective capital per man-hour to output per man-hour, can never increase in the optimum programme, i.e. the statement of para. 2.1 is proved.

2.2. As corollaries we immediately deduce:

(i) If the technique in any activity is fixed, q_j and v_j are fixed. Thus as the basic real wage rate decreases, this activity will never be used less intensively in the optimum programme.

(ii) If the utilisation of any activity is held constant, h_j is fixed and under the same conditions as (i) this activity will never be used on a higher technique, i.e. a technique in which q_j and v_j both increase in such a way that q_j/v_j is also increased.

A 3. DETERMINATION OF THE OPTIMUM PROGRAMME

We now formulate rules for finding the optimum programme for any given wage rate.

3.1. Suppose at some wage rate $\mathbf{h}^*, \mathbf{t}^*$ is $\mathbf{t}\,\mathbf{h}$. By A. 2 above

$$R(\mathbf{t}',\mathbf{h}',\bar{\bar{w}}) = R(\mathbf{t},\mathbf{h},\bar{\bar{w}}),$$

when
$$\bar{\bar{w}}^{-1} = F(\mathbf{t},\mathbf{h}) + D(\mathbf{t},\mathbf{h})\,\frac{F(\mathbf{t}',\mathbf{h}')-F(\mathbf{t},\mathbf{h})}{D(\mathbf{t},\mathbf{h})-D(\mathbf{t}',\mathbf{h}')}. \tag{A. 6}$$

3.2. If we assume the wage rate to be reduced continuously then $\mathbf{t}, \mathbf{h}$ remain the optimum programme until the wage rate becomes smaller than the reciprocal of the right hand of (A. 6). The optimum programme will therefore change first to $\mathbf{t}', \mathbf{h}'$ if $\mathbf{t}', \mathbf{h}'$ make the right-hand side of (A. 6) as small as possible (and thus the corresponding wage rate as large as possible).

3.3. Thus we see that we must choose $\mathbf{t}', \mathbf{h}'$ so that

$$I = \frac{F(\mathbf{t}',\mathbf{h}')-F(\mathbf{t},\mathbf{h})}{D(\mathbf{t},\mathbf{h})-D(\mathbf{t}',\mathbf{h}')}$$

has its smallest possible value, subject to the restriction

$$(q_j/h_j v_j) \geqslant (q'_j/h'_j v'_j)$$

for all j.

Now

$$I = \frac{\sum_{i=1}^{n} \left[\frac{k_i f_{h'_i}}{v'_i} - \frac{k_i f_{hi}}{v_i} \right]}{\sum_{i=1}^{n} \left[\frac{k_i q_i}{h_i v_i} - \frac{k_i q'_i}{h'_i v'_i} \right]},$$

$$> \min_{i,\, q,\, v'_i,\, h'_i} \frac{\frac{k_i f_{h'i}}{v'_i} - \frac{k_i f_{hi}}{v_i}}{\frac{k_i q_i}{h_i v_i} - \frac{k_i q'_i}{h'_i v'_i}}$$

taken over all $q'_i h'_i v'_i$, such that

$$\frac{q_i}{h_i v_i} > \frac{q'_i}{h'_i v'_i}.$$

Thus the first change of optimum programme will in general be in one activity only and is independent of all other activities.

We define

$$e(v_i, q_i, h_i;\, v'_i, q'_i, h'_i) = \frac{\frac{k_i f_{hi}}{v'_i} - \frac{k_i f_{hi}}{v_i}}{\frac{k_i q_i}{h_i v_i} - \frac{k_i q'_i}{h'_i v'_i}}$$

$$= \frac{\frac{f_{h'i}}{v'_i} - \frac{f_{hi}}{v_i}}{\frac{k_i q_i}{h_i v_i} - \frac{k_i q'_i}{h'_i v'_i}} \qquad \text{(A. 7)}$$

and call e an indicator.

3.4. If $\bar{\bar{\varpi}}^{-1} < F(\mathbf{t}, \mathbf{h})\, R(\mathbf{t}, \mathbf{h}, \bar{\bar{\varpi}})$ is negative. Thus for a large enough wage rate the optimum programme has the slowest possible f/v, and hence the highest possible q/hv, value in each activity. Consider one activity and compute all indicators $e(v_i, q_i, h_i;\, v'_i, q'_i, h'_i)$ where v_i, q_i, h_i refer to this state and v'_i, q'_i, h'_i vary through all states of the activity for which $(q_i/h_i v_i) > (q'_i/h'_i v'_i)$. The v, q, h values corresponding to the smallest of these indicators are the next state of the activity in the optimum programme at some lower wage rate (but see paras. 4.1 and 4.2). We call this smallest indicator a CRITICAL INDICATOR.

3.5. Starting from this new state (set of v, q, h values) as base, calculate indicators for a further change of state to a lower q/hv value. Again the smallest such indicator is called a critical indicator and gives the next state of the activity in the optimum programme as the wage rate decreases. Continue until the lowest q/hv is reached. Similarly, compute all the critical indicators for all other activities.

3.6. Now arrange all the critical indicators in increasing order of magnitude. This order is the same as the order in which the corresponding changes of state in the optimum programme (to which the critical indicators refer) take place as the wage rate decreases. It remains to find the wage rate at which each such change occurs. We call each such wage rate a CRITICAL WAGE RATE corresponding to the appropriate critical indicator and change of state. Suppose e_{ij} is the ith critical indicator in the jth activity and $\bar{\varpi}_{ij}$ the corresponding critical wage rate. By (A. 2) above

$$\bar{\varpi}_{ij}^{-1} = F(\mathbf{t},\mathbf{h}) + e_{ij}D(\mathbf{t},\mathbf{h}), \tag{A. 8}$$

where $\mathbf{t},\mathbf{h}$ is the optimum programme immediately before the corresponding change of state. Starting from the state with the highest q/hv value in each activity, which we have shown above is optimal for a sufficiently high wage rate, compute in order the critical wage rates corresponding to each critical indicator. When all critical wage rates have been computed we find the optimum programme for any given wage rate $\bar{\varpi}$, by finding the two critical wage rates one larger and one smaller, nearest to it in magnitude.

The state between these two is the optimum programme for $\bar{\varpi}$.

3.7. We give an example of this calculation below with some detailed notes describing the calculations.

A 4. PROPERTIES OF CRITICAL INDICATORS AND WAGE RATES

4.1. We note first that if two or more indicators from different activities are equal the corresponding changes of state take place together at the same critical wage rate, for if

$$\frac{(f_{hj}'/v_j') - (f_{hj}/v_j)}{(q_j/h_j v_j) - (q_j'/h_j' v_j')} = \frac{(f_{hi}'/v_i') - (f_{hi}/v_i)}{(q_i/h_i v_i) - (q_i'/h_i' v_i')}$$

each is equal to

$$\frac{(k_j f_{hj}'/v_j') + (k_i f_{hi}'/v_i') - [(k_j f_{hj}/v_j) + (k_i f_{hi}/v_i)]}{(k_j q_j/h_j v_j) + (k_i q_i/h_i v_i) - [(k_j q_j'/h_j' v_j')\ (k_i q_i'/h_i' v_i')]},$$

so that (A. 2) shows that the combined change of state takes place at the same critical wage as any of the separate ones. As the combined state has the lowest $D(\mathbf{t}',\mathbf{h}')$ it is therefore the next optimum programme.

4.2. If two or more indicators from the same activity have the same value the change of state is to the lowest q/hv state; if these are also the same then the activity is indifferent between these states at every wage rate as they have the same value of f/v also.

4.3. The indicators defined by (A. 7) are independent of $\mathbf{k}$. Thus $\mathbf{k}$ does not affect the ordering of changes of state in the optimum programme.

However (A. 8) shows that as an increase of any k_i will increase F and D, all critical wage rates will accordingly be lowered. Thus at a fixed wage rate the effect of an increase or decrease in any k_i will be to raise or lower respectively the q/hv ratio in each activity.

4.4. Now consider the case of fixed techniques, i.e. q_i and v_i fixed for all i, any indicator is now

$$\frac{(f_{hi'}/v_i)-(f_{hi}/v_i)}{(q_i/h_i v_i)-(q_i/h'_i v_i)} = \frac{f_{hi'}-f_{hi}}{q_i[(1/h_i)-(1/h'_i)]}, \tag{A.9}$$

which is independent of v_i. Thus a change in any v_i will not affect the ordering of any changes of state in the optimum programme. (A.8) shows, however, that all critical wage rates will be raised if one v_i is raised. For fixed techniques at a fixed wage rate an increase or decrease in some v_i with no other changes made will tend respectively to raise or lower utilisation in each activity.

4.5. If q is increased in one activity and no other change made the effect is more complicated. Suppose q_j increases to q'_j. (A.9) shows that all indicators in activity j are reduced in the same ratio, and no other activities are affected. Thus the same changes in the jth activity take place in the same order as before, but may now precede changes in other activities which they previously followed. Let $\bar{\bar{w}}'_{1j}$ denote the new value of $\bar{\bar{w}}_{1j}$, the critical wage rate for the increase from h_j to h'_j.

In activity i $(i \neq j)$, let the utilisation before the increase from h_j to h'_j be h_i corresponding to q_j, ϕ and h_i corresponding to q_j $(h'_i \leqslant h^\phi_i)$. Let e'_{1j} be the new value of e_{ij}

$$e'_{1j} < e_{1j}, \quad q'_j e'_{1j} = q_j e_{1j}$$

and $$\bar{\bar{w}}'^{-1}_{ij} - \bar{\bar{w}}^{-1}_{1j} = \sum_{i \neq j} \frac{k_i f_{hi'}}{v_i} + \frac{k_j f_{hj}}{v_j} + e'_{1j}\left\{\sum_{i\neq j} \frac{k_i q_i}{h'_i v_i} + \frac{k_j q'_j}{h_j v_j}\right\}$$

$$-\left[\sum_{i\neq j} \frac{k_i f_{h_i}}{v_i} + \frac{k_j f_{h_j}}{v_j} + e_{1j}\left\{\sum_{i\neq j} \frac{k_i q_i}{h_i v_i} + \frac{k_j q_j}{h_j v_j}\right\}\right]$$

$$< \sum_{i\neq j} \frac{k_i(f_{hi'}-f_{hi})}{v_i} + e'_{1j} \sum_{i\neq j} \frac{k_i q_i}{v_i}\left(\frac{1}{h'_i}-\frac{1}{h_i}\right)$$

$$= \left[e'_{1j} - \frac{\sum_{i\neq j} \frac{k_i(f_{hi}-f_{hi'})}{v_i}}{\sum_{i\neq j} \frac{k_i q_i}{v_i}\left(\frac{1}{h'_i}-\frac{1}{h_i}\right)}\right] \sum_{i\neq j} \frac{k_i q_i}{v_i}\left(\frac{1}{h'_i}-\frac{1}{h_i}\right) < 0,$$

as $$\frac{\sum_{i\neq j} \frac{k_i(f_{hi}-f_{hi'})}{v_i}}{\sum_{i\neq j} \frac{k_i q_i}{v_i}\left(\frac{1}{h'_i}-\frac{1}{h_i}\right)} > \min_i \frac{\frac{k_i(f_{hi}-f_{hi'})}{v_i}}{\frac{k_i q_i}{v_i}\left(\frac{1}{h'_i}-\frac{1}{h_i}\right)} = e \quad \text{say}$$

and $$e > e'_{1j},$$

as e is the indicator for some increase from h'_i to h_i which now follows the increase from h_j to h'_j. Therefore

$$\bar{\bar{w}}'_{1j} > \bar{\bar{w}}_{1j}.$$

At the critical wage $\bar{\varpi}_{1m}(m \neq j)$, the only effect is that h_j may already have increased to h_{1j} say. No other activities are affected, therefore

$$\bar{\varpi}_{1m}'^{-1} - \bar{\varpi}_{1m}^{-1} = \frac{k_j f_{h_j'}}{v_j} + e_{1m}\frac{k_j q_j'}{v_j} - \frac{k_j f_{h_j}}{v_j} - e_{1m}\frac{k_j q_j}{h_j v_j}$$

$$\geqslant \frac{k_j q_j}{v_j}\left(\frac{1}{h_j} - \frac{1}{h_j'}\right)\left[\frac{f_{h_j'} - f_{h_j}}{q_j[(1/h_j) - (1/h_j')]} - e_{1m}\right],$$

$$> 0$$

as the change from h_j to h_j' previously followed the change corresponding to e_{1m}, therefore

$$\bar{\varpi}_{1m}' \leqslant \bar{\varpi}_{1m}.$$

Thus an increase in one q_j raises all critical wage rates in the corresponding activity and lowers them in all other activities. At a fixed wage rate then the effect will be to tend to increase utilisation in that activity and lower it in all others.

A 5. THE EFFECT OF A CONSTRAINT

5.1. Consider the effect of constraining the jth activity so that $h_j v_j$ must always be less than some fixed number. We assume that this affects the optimum programme by forbidding the use of what would otherwise be the best combination of technique and utilisation. We assume further that the only course is to use techniques and utilisations previously available; i.e. solutions such as reducing output by halving the length of a shift are not allowable.

5.2. We prove that however the constraint is met the effect will never be to use the activity more intensively than in the unconstrained optimum programme.

5.3. For economy of writing we drop suffixes. Suppose that v, q, h is the optimum programme in the activity at some stage and that the next change of state is to v_1, q_1, h_1. Assume that the constraint forbids this and the first change to an allowable state is to v_2, q_2, h_2, where v_2, q_2 is a lower technique and $h_2 > h_1$. Then $e(v, q, h; v_2, q_2, h_2) < e(v, q, h; v_2, q_2, h_i)$.

$$\frac{(f_{h_2}/v_2) - (f_h/v)}{(q/hv) - (q_2/h_2 v_2)} < \frac{(f_{h_i}/v_2) - (f_h/v)}{(q/hv) - (q_2/h_1 v_2)},$$

$$\left(\frac{q}{hv} - \frac{q_2}{h_1 v_2}\right)\left(\frac{f_{h_2}}{v_2} - \frac{f_h}{v}\right) < \left(\frac{q}{hv} - \frac{q_2}{h_2 v_2}\right)\left(\frac{f_{h_1}}{v_2} - \frac{f_h}{v}\right),$$

$$\frac{q}{hv}\left(\frac{f_{h_2}}{v_2} - \frac{f_{h_1}}{v_2}\right) + \frac{f_h}{v}\left(\frac{q_2}{h_1 v_2} - \frac{q_2}{h_2 v_2}\right)\frac{f_{h_1}}{v_2} - \frac{q_2}{h_2 v_2} - \frac{f_{h_2}}{v_2}\frac{q_2}{h_1 v_2} < 0,$$

$$\frac{q}{hv}(f_{h_2} - f_{h_1}) + \frac{f_h}{v}\left(\frac{q_2}{h_1} - \frac{q_2}{h_2}\right) + f_{h_1}\frac{q_2}{h_2 v_2} - f_{h_2}\frac{q_2}{h_1 v_2} < 0$$

$$\frac{q}{hv}(f_{h_2}-f_{h_1})+\frac{f_h}{v}\left(\frac{q_1}{h_1}-\frac{q_1}{h_2}\right)+f_{h_1}\frac{q_2}{h_2 v_2}-\frac{f_{h_2}}{v_2}\left[\frac{q_2}{h_2}+\frac{q_1}{h_1}-\frac{q_1}{h_2}\right]$$

$$<\frac{f_h}{v}(q_1-q_2)\left(\frac{1}{h_1}-\frac{1}{h_2}\right)+\frac{f_{h_2}}{v_2}\left[\frac{q_2}{h_1}-\left(\frac{q_2}{h_2}+\frac{q_1}{h_1}-\frac{q_1}{h_2}\right)\right]$$

$$=(q_1-q_2)\left(\frac{1}{h_1}-\frac{1}{h_2}\right)\left(\frac{f_h}{v}-\frac{f_{h_2}}{v_2}\right)$$

$$<0,$$

as $q, > q_2, h_2 > h_1$ and $(f_{h_2}/v_2) > (f_h/v)$ for if it were not the state $v_2, q_2; h_2$ would be reached before $v, q; h$ (see, for example, § A. 6.2). Hence rewriting the left-hand side

$$\left(\frac{q}{hv}-\frac{q_2}{h_2 v_2}\right)(f_{h_2}-f_{h_1})-\left(\frac{q_1}{h_1}-\frac{q_1}{h_2}\right)\left(\frac{f_{h_2}}{v_2}-\frac{f_h}{v}\right)<0,$$

therefore $\quad e(v_1, q_1, h_1; v_1, q_1, h_2) < e(v, q, h; v_2, q_2, h_2).$

Write

$$e(v_1, q_1, h_1; v_1, q_1, h_2) = e$$
$$e(v, q, h; v_2, q_2, h_2) = e'$$

and

$$v = v_j, q = q_j, h = h_j; v_1 = v_j', q_1 = q_j', h_1 = h_j'; v_2 = v_j'', q_2 = q_j'', h_2 = h_j''.$$

Let v_i, q_i, h_i be the states in the other activities before the change from v_j', q_j', h_j'; to v_j', q_j', h_i'';

v_i', q_i', h_i', the corresponding quantities for the change from v_j, q_j, h_j; to v_j'', q_j'', h_j'';

and w and w' the corresponding critical wage rates

As $\quad e' > e \dfrac{q_i'}{h_i' v_i'} \leqslant \dfrac{q_i}{h_i v_i} \quad (i = 1, 2 \ldots n),$

$$1/w'-1/w=\sum_{i\neq j}\frac{k_i f_{h_i'}}{v_i'}+\frac{k_j f_{h_j}}{v_j}+e'\left[\sum_{i\neq j}\frac{k_i q_i'}{h_i' v_i'}+\frac{k_j q_j}{h_j v_j}\right]$$

$$-\left\{\sum_{i\neq j}\frac{k_i f_{h_i}}{v_i}+\frac{k_j f_{h_j'}}{v_j'}+e\left[\sum_{i\neq j}\frac{k_i q_i}{h_i v_i}+\frac{k_j q_j'}{h_j' v_j'}\right]\right\}$$

$$>\left(\frac{k_j q_j}{h_j v_j}-\frac{k_j q_j'}{h_j' v_j'}\right)\left[e-\frac{k_j\left(\dfrac{f_{h_j'}}{v_j'}-\dfrac{f_{h_j}}{v_j}\right)}{k_j\left(\dfrac{q_j}{h_j v_j}-\dfrac{q_i'}{h_j' v_j'}\right)}\right]+$$

$$\sum_{i\neq j}k_i\left(\frac{q_i}{h_i v_i}-\frac{q_i'}{h_i' v_i'}\right)\left[\frac{\sum_{i\neq j}k_i\left(\dfrac{f_{h'}}{v_i'}-\dfrac{f_{h_i}}{v_i}\right)}{\sum_{i\neq j}k_i\left(\dfrac{q_i}{h_i v_i}-\dfrac{q}{h_i' v_i'}\right)}-e\right]$$

$$>0,$$

as the change v_j, q_j, h_j to v'_j, q'_j, h'_j precedes the change corresponding to e; and all the changes from v_i, q_i, h_i to $v'_i, q'_i, h'_i, i \neq j$, follow the change corresponding to e. Thus $w' < w$.

5.4. As the wage rate $\bar{\bar{w}}$ is such that v'_j, q'_j, h'_j should be the optimum programme in the jth activity we see that

$$\bar{\bar{w}} > w > w'.$$

5.5. Thus for an activity, such as this, in which the first change from v_j, q_j, h_j allowed by the constraint is to a lower technique at a higher utilisation, v''_j, q''_j, h''_j, then the critical wage rate for this change is less than $\bar{\bar{w}}$ and the activity stays in the state v_j, q_j, h_j. Thus the constraint cannot cause increased utilisation of the activity unless, possibly $h_j > h'_j$. This cannot happen in this case as a reduction of h_j in the optimum programme as the basic real wage rate is lowered requires a lowering of technique simultaneously. In this case $h'_j v'_j < h_j v_j$ and so contrary to hypothesis the change from v_j, q_j, h_j to v'_j, q'_j, h'_j is permitted by the constraint.

5.6. So far as the effect of this constraint on the other activities is concerned we prove: if in one activity certain states are proscribed and the optimum programme is found from among the remaining states then all critical wage rates are lowered in all other activities.

5.7. Let w and w' be critical wage rates in another state in the unconstrained and constrained cases and e, the same for each, the indicator for this change. Let v_j, q_j, h_j be the state of the jth activity when this change takes place in the unconstrained case and v'_j, q'_j, h'_j the corresponding state in the constrained case.

$$\begin{aligned} w'^{-1} - w^{-1} &= \sum_{i \neq j} \frac{k_i f_{hi}}{v_i} + \frac{k_j f_{h'j}}{v'_j} + e\left(\sum_{i \neq j} \frac{k_i q_i}{h_i v_i} + \frac{k_j q'_j}{h'_j v'_j}\right) \\ &\quad - \left[\sum_{i \neq j} \frac{k_i f_{hi}}{v_i} + \frac{k_j f_{hj}}{v_j} + e\left(\sum_{i \neq j} \frac{k_i q_i}{h_i v_i} + \frac{k_j q_j}{h_j v_j}\right)\right] \\ &= k_j \left(\frac{q_j}{h_j v_j} - \frac{q'_j}{h'_j v'_j}\right) \left[\frac{(f_{h'j}/v'_j) - (f_{h_j}/v_j)}{(q_j/h_j v_j)\,(q'_j/h'_j v'_j)} - e\right] \\ &> 0. \end{aligned} \tag{A. 10}$$

For write
$$\frac{(f_{h'j}/v'_j) - (f_{h_j}/v_j)}{(q_j/h_j v_j)\,(q'_j/h'_j v'_j)} = E.$$

Then if
$$\frac{q'_j}{h'_j v'_j} < \frac{q_j}{h_j v_j},$$

E is the indicator for a change which would in the unconstrained case follow that corresponding to e. Hence $E > e$ and (A. 10) holds.

If
$$\frac{q'_j}{h'_j v'_j} > \frac{q_j}{h_j v_j},$$

then E is the indicator for a change which in the unconstrained case would precede that corresponding to e. Hence $E < e$ and again (A. 10) holds.

5.8. This proves the result stated above. Thus if any constraint is applied in one activity, so as to proscribe certain of its states: then at a fixed basic real wage rate this tends to cause the optimum programme in all the other activities to use a state with a higher q/hv value.

A.6. EXAMPLE OF CALCULATION

6.1. The scheme used in Table 4.2 provides a convenient layout for the calculations required. We have labelled columns of indicators e_{ij} where e_{ij} is the critical indicator which appears in that column. The columns labelled D_{ij} and N_{ij} contain the denominators and numerators respectively of the entries in the e_{ij} column. The least entry in each e_{ij} column is shown in bold figures. This is the actual critical indicator e_{ij} for the ith change in the jth activity. Consider the critical indicator e_{22}, 0·0724 corresponding to $v = 9$, $q = 10, h = 3$; the preceding critical indicator e_{12} is 0·0400 corresponding to $v = 9$, $q = 10$, $h = 2$. The D_{22} entry corresponding to e_{22} is $0{\cdot}1852 = 0{\cdot}5556 - 0{\cdot}3704$ and the N_{22} entry $0{\cdot}0134 = 0{\cdot}1467 - 0{\cdot}1333$ where 0·5556 and 0·3704 are the q/hv values for (9, 10; 2) and (9, 10; 3) respectively and 0·1333 and 0·1467 are the corresponding f/v values. e_{22} corresponds to the change in optimum programme from (9, 10; 2) to (9, 10; 3). Indicators are only calculated to states with lower q/hv values than those of the state corresponding to the previous critical indicator.

6.2. The states marked * do not require calculation as in every case there is a smaller f/v value lower down the column and hence a smaller indicator.

6.3. In the second part of the calculation we have entered the critical indicators from all activities in increasing numerical order. In the line below each e_{ij} we enter the activity to which it refers and the state of that activity after the corresponding change has been made, with corresponding q/hv and f/v values. For convenience we enter these values for the initial state of each activity (highest q/hv) above these. The optimum programmes before and after the change corresponding to e_{ij} are entered in the lines above and below each e_{ij} and then the corresponding D and F values computed.

6.4. The $F + De$ entry gives the reciprocal of the critical wage rate $\bar{\bar{w}}_{ij}$ corresponding to each e_{ij}. (2) and (3) above show that this is the same using F and D from either immediately before or after the corresponding change.

6.5. For example, consider the line above $e_{ij} = 0{\cdot}0554$. This indicator refers to the change in activity 1 from (5, 13; 2) to (5, 13; 3). The changes corresponding to all smaller indicators have occurred so the optimum programme is found by using the last state of each activity entered above this line, i.e. (13, 16; 3) in activity 3 (9, 10; 2) in 2 and (5, 13; 2) in 1. This is entered in the optimum programme and the corresponding D and F values found.

6.6. If a constraint forbids any state in any activity remove all such states before starting the computation. The resulting set of optimum programmes will be the best using only the remaining allowable states.

Table 4.2. *Sample calculation of optimum programme with three activities*

PART I

Activity 1. $h = 1, 2, 3$. Techniques $(v, q) \equiv (2, 3), (4, 8), (5, 13)$. $f_1 = 1, f_2 = 1{\cdot}2, f_3 = 1{\cdot}32$															
(v, q)	h	$\frac{q}{hv}$	$\frac{f}{v}$	$\frac{q}{hv}-\frac{q^1}{hv^1} = D_{11}$	$\frac{f^1}{v^1}-\frac{f}{v} = N_{11}$	e_{11}	D_{21}	N_{21}	e_{21}	D_{31}	N_{31}	e_{31}	D_{41}	N_{41}	e_{41}
5, 13	1	2·6000	0·2000	—	—	—	—	—	—	—	—	—	—	—	—
4, 8	1*	2·0000	0·2500	0·6000	0·0500	0·0833	—	—	—	—	—	—	—	—	—
2, 3	1*	1·5000	0·5000	1·1000	0·3000	0·2727	—	—	—	—	—	—	—	—	—
5, 13	2	1·3000	0·2400	1·3000	0·0400	**0·0302**	—	—	—	—	—	—	—	—	—
4, 8	2*	1·0000	0·3000	1·6000	0·1000	0·0625	0·3000	0·0600	0·2000	—	—	—	—	—	—
5, 13	3	0·8667	0·2640	1·7335	0·0640	0·0369	0·4333	0·0240	**0·0554**	—	—	—	—	—	—
2, 3	2*	0·7500	0·6000	1·8500	0·4000	0·2162	0·5500	0·3600	0·6545	0·1167	0·3360	2·8792	—	—	—
4, 8	3	0·6667	0·3300	1·9333	0·1300	0·0672	0·6333	0·0900	0·1421	0·2000	0·0660	**0·3300**	—	—	—
2, 3	3	0·5000	0·6600	2·1000	0·4600	0·2190	0·8000	0·4200	0·5250	0·3667	0·3960	1·0799	0·1667	0·3300	**1·9796**

Activity 2. $h = 1, 2, 3$. Techniques $(v, q) \equiv (4, 2), (7, 5), (9, 10)$															
(v, q)	h	$\frac{q}{hv}$	$\frac{f}{v}$	D_{12}	N_{12}	e_{12}	D_{22}	N_{22}	e_{22}	D_{32}	N_{32}	e_{32}	D_{42}	N_{42}	e_{42}
9, 10	1	1·1111	0·1111	—	—	—	—	—	—	—	—	—	—	—	—
7, 5	1*	0·7143	0·1429	0·3968	0·0318	0·0801	—	—	—	—	—	—	—	—	—
9, 10	2	0·5556	0·1333	0·5555	0·0222	**0·0400**	—	—	—	—	—	—	—	—	—
4, 2	1*	0·5000	0·2500	0·6111	0·1389	0·2273	0·0556	0·1167	2·0989	—	—	—	—	—	—
9, 10	3	0·3704	0·1467	0·7407	0·0356	0·0481	0·1852	0·0134	**0·0724**	—	—	—	—	—	—
7, 3	2	0·3571	0·1714	0·7540	0·0603	0·0800	0·1985	0·0381	0·1919	0·0133	0·0247	1·8571	—	—	—
4, 2	2*	0·2500	0·3000	0·8611	0·1889	0·2194	0·3056	0·1667	0·5455	0·1204	0·1533	1·2733	—	—	—
7, 5	3	0·2381	0·1886	0·8730	0·0775	0·0888	0·3175	0·0553	0·1742	0·1323	0·0419	**0·3167**	—	—	—
4, 2	3	0·1667	0·3300	0·9444	0·2189	0·2318	0·3889	0·1967	0·5058	0·2037	0·1833	0·8999	0·0714	0·1414	**1·9804**

Activity 3. $h = 1, 2, 3$. Techniques $(v, q) \equiv (4, 3), (10, 9), (13, 16)$															
(v, q)	h	$\frac{q}{hv}$	$\frac{f}{v}$	D_{13}	N_{13}	e_{13}	D_{23}	N_{23}	e_{23}	D_{33}	N_{33}	e_{33}	D_{43}	N_{43}	e_{43}
13, 16	1	1·2308	0·0769	—	—	—	—	—	—	—	—	—	—	—	—
10, 9	1*	0·9000	0·1000	0·3308	0·0231	0·0698	—	—	—	—	—	—	—	—	—
4, 3	1*	0·7500	0·2500	0·4808	0·1731	0·3600	—	—	—	—	—	—	—	—	—
13, 16	2	0·6154	0·0923	0·6154	0·0154	**0·0250**	—	—	—	—	—	—	—	—	—
10, 9	2*	0·4500	0·1200	0·7808	0·0431	0·0552	0·1654	0·0277	0·1675	—	—	—	—	—	—
13, 16	3	0·4103	0·1015	0·8205	0·0246	0·0306	0·2051	0·0092	**0·0449**	—	—	—	—	—	—
4, 3	2*	0·3750	0·3000	0·8558	0·2231	0·2607	0·2404	0·2077	0·8640	0·0353	0·1985	5·6232	—	—	—
10, 9	3	0·3000	0·1320	0·9308	0·0551	0·0592	0·3154	0·0387	0·1259	0·1103	0·0305	**0·2765**	—	—	—
[illegible]	[illegible]	[illegible]	[illegible]	[illegible]	[illegible]	[illegible]	[illegible]	[illegible]	[illegible]	[illegible]	[illegible]	1·4205	0·0500	0·1080	**2·060**

e_{ij}	Activity	v, q	h	$\frac{q}{hv}$	$\frac{f}{v}$	Optimum programme: Activity 1 v, q, h	Optimum programme: Activity 2 v, q, h	Optimum programme: Activity 3 v, q, h	D	F	$(F+De)$	Critical wage rate $= w = \frac{1}{F+De}$
	1	5, 13	1	2·6000	0·2000							
	2	9, 10	1	1·1111	0·1111							
	3	13, 16	1	1·2308	0·0769							
						5, 13 1	9, 10 1	13, 16 1	4·9419	0·3880		
0·0250											0·5115	1·955
	3	13, 16	2	0·6154	0·0923	5, 13 1	9, 10 1	13, 16 2	4·3265	0·4034		
0·0308											0·5367	1·863
	1	5, 13	2	1·3000	0·2400	5, 13 2	9, 10 1	13, 16 2	3·0265	0·4434		
0·0400											0·5645	1·771
	2	9, 10	2	0·5556	0·1333	5, 13 2	9, 10 2	13, 16 2	2·4710	0·4656		
0·0449											0·5765	1·735
	3	13, 16	3	0·4103	0·1015	5, 13 2	9, 10 2	13, 16 3	2·2659	0·4748		
0·0554											0·6003	1·666
	1	5, 13	3	0·8667	0·2640	5, 13 3	9, 10 2	13, 16 3	1·8326	0·4988		
0·0724											0·6315	1·584
	2	9, 10	3	0·3704	0·1467	5, 13 3	9, 10 3	13, 16 3	1·6474	0·5122		
0·2765											0·9677	1·033
	3	10, 9	3	0·3000	0·1320	5, 13 3	9, 10 3	10, 9 3	1·5371	0·5427		
0·3167											1·0295	0·971
	2	7, 5	3	0·2381	0·1886	5, 13 3	7, 5 3	10, 9 3	1·4048	0·5846		
0·3300											1·0482	0·954
	1	4, 8	3	0·6667	0·3300	4, 8 3	7, 5 3	10, 9 3	1·2048	0·6506		
1·9796											3·0356	0·329
	1	2, 3	3	0·5000	0·6600	2, 3 3	7, 5 3	10, 9 3	1·0381	0·9806		
1·9804											3·0365	0·329
	2	4, 2	3	0·1667	0·3300	2, 3 3	4, 2 3	10, 9 3	0·9667	1·1220		
3·9600											4·9501	0·202
	3	4, 3	3	0·2500	0·3300	2, 3 3	4, 2 3	4, 3 3	0·9167	1·3200		

N.B. For explanation of this table, section A. 6 above.

PART II

TESTS AND APPLICATIONS

CHAPTER 5

SUMMARY OF THE THEORY AND ITS PREDICTIONS

5.1. Summary of the Theory

In the preceding chapters we developed a theory about the way firms plan to utilise their fixed capital. When designing a plant, a business man must not only choose between various alternative types of equipment, he must also decide how many hours the machinery is normally to be expected to operate annually. We cannot over-emphasise the significance of our interest in the factors determining the *planned* rate of utilisation rather than the actual rate which may be observed at any particular moment of time. Once a plant has been constructed, the rate at which it will actually be utilised at a particular time will depend largely on the contemporary level of demand. We treat our problem as an aspect of investment planning (plant design), rather than as an aspect of day-to-day management. The theory we developed commenced with the axiom that a business man faced with a given set of economic conditions will design his plant in such a way as to maximise the rate of profit earned on fixed capital employed subject to the limitations imposed by those conditions. The burden of our discussion has been an investigation of the effects of variations in conditions on the utilisation decision. We considered the position of an individual firm in some particular industry where there was sufficient competition (or sufficient restraint on his monopoly powers) that he could visualise a 'right' price for the products he was intending to sell, and that his power to vary this price effectively was not very great: if additional advertising would enhance the demand, the advertising expenditure would have to be deducted from our measurement of proceeds. We also assumed that the manufacturer faced 'given' conditions in his labour market, conditions which determined the price he must pay for labour of given efficiency. A particularly relevant aspect of these conditions was the collection of factors which determined the extent of the increase, if any, in unit labour costs when labour was demanded outside normal hours—overtime bonuses, shift-work premiums and restrictions on the employment of women and juveniles, etc. Finally, we implied that among the very relevant conditions were the state of technology in the industry, and the firm's particular comprehension of and ability to exploit this—of special importance was the firm's understanding of the latest developments, and, indeed, its ability to make such developments itself.

If in real life firms are not interested in the rate of profit earned on capital, or if they make the particular decisions in which we are interested entirely by some other criteria, the theory remains purely abstract. It would remain valid as an *a priori* construction, but could be tested only by logical analysis of the implications of the axioms. Thus if we attempt to test this theory against empirical evidence, we must remember that we are implicitly testing the assumptions as well as the theorems. It is worth pointing out, however, that the assumptions do not necessarily need to hold precisely as we have stated them for predictions implied in the theorems to be successful. Many business men, we know, tend to take decisions by minimising cost rather than maximising profit. In order to make these calculations, they must impute current 'costs' to their stock of capital: they must impute, in fact, a normal rate of profit and treat this as a cost. In our theoretical discussion, we have avoided this approach, because we believe that such a profit rate must often be chosen arbitrarily and in practice is often set too low. It is not difficult to show nevertheless that the decisions taken by the procedure for minimising costs will tend in the directions predicted by our theorems. However, unless the imputed rate of profit is as high as the maximum obtained in our solution, the incentive to utilise will be weakened.

A firm may be imagined to be designing a plant this year to be constructed next year and to remain in production for, say, the following ten years. It is desired that the plant shall have a capacity capable of meeting a certain peak annual rate of output. For this purpose it is necessary to order a certain number of units of equipment. The number of units required will depend on whether it is proposed that under peak conditions the plant will be operating on single shifts, single shifts with overtime, or on multiple shifts. Until this last question has been decided, the magnitude of the equipment requirement is not determined; and this is the decision with which our report is concerned. In order to arrive at a definite conclusion, we made certain additional assumptions which we believed to be empirically justified. We assumed that generally speaking, above-normal daily rates of utilisation involve the payment of above-normal efficiency wages: in the jargon we have developed, we believed that in general a positive 'utilisation differential' must be paid. We also assumed that firms were faced with limited markets for the products they were proposing to produce, and this had to be taken into account in their long-term planning. After a fairly extensive investigation, we came to the conclusion that firms would be more likely to decide in favour of high rates of utilisation, if any or all of the following conditions were present, provided they did not offset one another:

(1) If the utilisation differential were small relative to the proportionate increase in daily rate of utilisation with which it were associated, that is if the *elasticity of utilisation* were large.

(2) If the '*real basic wage*'—the ratio of the hourly money wage rate

normally paid on single shifts without overtime to the assumed price of the product—were small.

(3) If the *size of the market* were large.

(4) If the 'production function' implicit in the firm's technical knowledge were favourable in a sense which is summarised below.

(5) If the proportion of output produced at the peak rate were low.

(6) If shift-work would yield considerable economies in prime cost, as is the case, for example, in continuous-process industries.

By a 'favourable' production function we may mean one of two things. If the firm is faced with the situation in which there are virtually no non-inferior alternative types of equipment available we concluded that the higher the hourly rate of physical output per worker associated with this unique equipment the more likely it would be, given the real basic wage, that a relatively high rate of utilisation would be profitable in all processes in the plant. A high level of labour productivity in one process not only encourages high rates of utilisation in that process but in others also. Therefore we would expect the proportion of employees, in the plant as a whole, who are intended by the designer to be engaged on shift-work, to be relatively high where labour productivity is relatively high. We also found that the value of fixed capital employed per man had a significant effect on the profitability of shift-working in particular activities, but that its effect on the proportion of shift-working employees in the plant as a whole was uncertain: a high value of capital per man raised the incentive to utilise the activity concerned, but lowered the incentive in adjacent activities.

If the designer is faced with a certain number of alternative, non-inferior, techniques of production (types of equipment) the theorem is a little more complicated. We arrange the alternative techniques in an ascending hierarchy according to their characteristic hourly rate of output per man and we ignore 'inferior' techniques. Then we say that multiple shift-working will be more likely to be profitable if the 'production function' represented by the series of points in the hierarchy is possessed of a relatively high elasticity of mechanisation: when mechanisation is increased, the proportionate increase in output per man for a given proportionate increase in capital per man is relatively high.

5.2. Criteria for Testing

In order to test a theory, we must ask what it would seem to 'predict'. We must ask, that is, what types of empirical findings would tend to disprove the theory or at least cast serious doubts on its validity. What observations should we make, and how should we interpret them? Here we face a serious difficulty. The essence of our theory is related to a decision concerning the planned rate of utilisation. But, of its nature, this is a quantity which is difficult if not impossible to observe. We may observe actual rates of utilisation but it is not at all easy to discover original plans. If we could collaborate with a typical designer in the process of creation, we might be able to obtain some of the evidence we desire, but the traditional methods of economic research do not easily lend themselves to such procedures. We may interview business men who have already designed their plant, and attempt to elucidate their original motives; if we are lucky we may even succeed in interviewing business men in the process of decision-taking. But the interview method suffers inevitably from lack of generality; also, business men find retrospective explanation naturally difficult. Statistical data, by contrast, offer considerable opportunities for generalisation, but measure actual rather than planned events. For these reasons we have attempted in this inquiry to carry out qualitative and quantitative investigations in parallel. In both qualitative and quantitative analysis, however, we are forced to assume that there is some relationship, taking one firm with another, between planned and actual rates of utilisation, and therefore between planned rates and observed rates. If the validity of this assumption is denied, the position is hopeless.

It so happens that most of the available statistical data relate directly to the utilisation of labour rather than of machines. In other words, we have to employ statistics relating to the numbers of operatives engaged on shift-work, overtime, and short time as indirect indicators of capital utilisation. The statistic with which we shall mainly be concerned is the *shift-work ratio*, the proportion of operatives in a plant or industry reported as engaged on shifts. Clearly, the relation between this indicator and actual capital utilisation will not always be simple: for example, in a multi-process plant, only if capital and labour are equally divided between all processes will the shift-work ratio provide a direct measure of average capital utilisation. It will therefore be necessary to frame our predictions in such a way that although designed to test a theory about capital utilisation, they refer directly to the shift-work ratio. The problems involved in this transformation, and the method of their solution, are discussed later.

The summary given in the preceding section does not, of course, cover all the ramifications developed in Chapters 2 to 4. We cannot identify all the possible implicit predictions, some of which, in any case, would be untestable. The predictions below are selected as being the most significant of the testable propositions of the main theory and the important ramifications:

(1) The average hourly earnings of workers employed on shift-work systems should be higher than the earnings of comparable workers not so employed. Average earnings per worker in firms where the shift-work ratio is relatively high should be greater than those of other comparable firms where it is low: serious doubt would be cast on the validity of the theory if there was no tendency for firms within one industry to display this relationship. Serious doubts would also be cast if few of the official wage-agreements collectively negotiated between Trade Unions and employers' associations provided for shift-work premiums.

(2) Investigation of potential 'obstacles' to multiple-shift organisa-

tion—such as Trade Union restrictions, or transportation lacunae—should not show that these were so strong as virtually to dictate the observations.

(3) Within industries, those establishments employing superior techniques should tend to exhibit relatively high shift-work ratios and conversely those establishments showing relatively high shift-work ratios should be expected to be employing relatively superior techniques. As a corollary to this, the theorem relating to the 'incentive to utilise' would predict that the 'initial' or 'basic' ratio of profits to wages should, in these firms, be relatively high also.†

(4) Within individual industries the establishments displaying high shift-work ratios should represent *plants*‡ whose peak rate of output is on average higher than those of the others in the industry; and, subject to certain qualifications about the relationship between plants and establishments, this should imply that, among the establishments in each industry with high shift-work ratios, the average observed value of output per establishment should also be relatively high.

(5) In an industry as a whole, sharp historical changes in the average shift-work ratio should not be expected unless they can be explained either by short-term changes in demand, or by changes in the rate of technical progress relative to the rate of increase of the market rate of money wages (this is implied in the dynamic version of the theory developed at the end of Chapter 2).§

(6) Firms producing at their peak annual rate of output should be found to be more likely to be exhibiting high shift-work ratios if it is known that, taking one year with another, the coefficient of variation of output produced at the peak rate is relatively high.||

(7) The foregoing relate mainly to comparisons between firms within particular industries. In inter-industry comparisons, by contrast:

(i) We should not expect an association between the basic ratio of profits to wages and the observed shift-work ratio, because the theory of the incentive to utilise is not appropriate to such comparisons.¶

(ii) We should expect a significant correlation between the average size of establishments and the shift-work ratio and we should expect this relationship to be non-linear (because we saw that the effect of indivisibilities should become increasingly severe as the scale of permitted output is reduced).

† The 'initial' ratio of profits to wages is the ratio which the firm would experience if, faced with a given technique of production and real basic wage, it adopted single shifts. We shall use the expression 'basic' ratio to indicate an estimate of the initial ratio.

‡ For the distinction between our use of the word 'plant' and establishment see p. 61 above.

§ §2.14.

|| We have been unable to test this.

¶ The theory assumed that the firm can take the real basic wage as given and from this, and other appropriate data, set out to maximise the rate of profit. The real basic wage is the ratio of the money wage to the price of the product, and it is clearly absurd to regard this variable as 'given' *between* industries. More reasonably one would expect that prices and wages would find a competitive level such as to yield each industry a reasonable rate of profit. We found in fact that there was no significant inter-industry correlation between the distribution of the proceeds of output and the shift-work ratio.

(iii) We should expect that where evidence is available as to the character of the production function in an industry, a low elasticity of mechanisation would tend to depress the shift-work ratio.

It must be recognised, of course, that when these various tests are put into practice a negative result will not necessarily provide certain negation of the hypothesis tested; the variables we are able to observe will rarely be exactly those defined in the hypothesis, and failure may be due to the inadequacy of the estimates substituted. For example, an establishment with a high annual value of output may conceal a large number of small plants producing many different products. Conversely, if we do not obtain negative results, we have not 'proved' our theory, we have merely failed to disprove it. Were the theory trivial, absurd, or devoid of logical support, mere failure to disprove would mean nothing. If, however, the reader has found the reasoning leading to the theory convincing, then the fact that the theory is able to offer predictions which cannot be negated by observation becomes significant. In practice, of course, our results will rarely be so clear-cut as we should desire. The process of testing the original theory may suggest significant modifications. Furthermore, the process of testing may lead to new discoveries, for example to an assessment of the relative weights of the different factors in the planning decision. Thus, in the present case, we shall discover that restraints on output, due to market limitations, appear to be the dominant factors in the United Kingdom. This in turn has important implications for policy.

CHAPTER 6

SURVEY OF EMPIRICAL MATERIAL

6.1. Obstacles to Research in the United Kingdom

In the normal course of scientific research the investigator usually begins with phenomena he wishes to explain. He usually first sets up a tentative hypothesis or induction—a kind of primitive theory. The main part of his research will then consist of experiments aimed at testing and elaborating this theory and developing knowledge of the general behaviour of the phenomena. By this means a more comprehensive theory can be developed and in turn subjected to further, more precise tests. If the results of experiments which have been specifically designed to test a particular theory prove negative, the original theory may have to be completely abandoned. Alternatively, if the results are generally positive, they can be used not only to support the basic theory but also to fill in details. The essence of the procedure is the continuation of interplay between theorising and experimentation until a comprehensive, thoroughly tested theory has been established beyond reasonable doubt.

In the 'social' sciences, of which economics is clearly one, the equivalents of laboratory experiment are statistical inquiry, statistical analysis, industrial or domestic interviews, questionnaires and direct observation of behaviour. The organisation of these is inevitably cumbersome and time-consuming. In the case of statistics, although considerable advances have been made in the speed of computation, the process of collecting and preparing data remains painfully slow. For example, the first Census of Production to contain questions relating to shift-work was taken in 1951, but the reports of this census were not published until 1955. A special analysis of the primary returns begun at our request in the spring of 1954 was not completed until the spring of 1956. The results of the special tabulations inevitably threw up 'snags' of one kind and another, involving considerable further adjustment, rearrangement and estimation for their resolution. This took another year. Finally, therefore, six years after the Census was taken, the data became available in the form suitable for econometric analysis. About a dozen multiple regression equations (of which the results of only two were finally selected for presentation below) were then computed.

Not long ago a regression equation involving over 100 observations and several determining variables might have required the work of perhaps two comptometer operators for a week, per equation. Today, with the help of an electronic computer, the whole programme of twelve equations can be carried out in less than three days, and of these the greater part will still be spent in preparing the data for the machine rather than running the machine itself. It is clear therefore that if one is seeking the next major advance in the techniques of social measurement, one should look in the direction of data preparation and processing rather than of computation.

At the present time, given the form of one's data and given that one has access to a computer, one can usually exhaust the possibilities of statistical analysis fairly quickly. Given the form of the data, if they tell a story one can find it. But, unfortunately, more often than not, as a theory develops the required data-form changes also. The phase of data-preparation is therefore as much a part of the experimental process as the final work of computation. Clearly, experiments which have taken two years to carry out are extremely difficult to repeat. Yet a science in which experiments cannot be repeated is barely a science. If one's theoretical understanding of a problem is sufficiently sound from the outset that one is able to predict accurately the character of all the experiments one will wish to undertake, one is hardly faced with a scientific problem.

In the United Kingdom the difficulties are exacerbated by the fact that some of the most valuable data are collected by government departments, yet government departments are unable to give a high priority to work for outside research organisations. In the present case, the Census Office of the Board of Trade could hardly have been more helpful and co-operative. Nevertheless, the time taken to complete the work speaks for itself. Heterogeneous data, such as are recorded in a Census of Production, are particularly difficult to mechanise, and, even if staff could be detached on a large scale for special tabulations, the number of workers who can handle a particular collection of punched-cards at one time without getting in each other's way is inevitably limited. It is hardly surprising, therefore, that departments are always particularly reluctant to undertake a 'second round' of tabulations.

Where a problem requires the use of data from the Census of Production, the difficulties are particularly acute, owing to severe restrictions placed by Parliament on their access. 'Public opinion' favours protecting the investor by requiring companies to publish information relating to overall profits, assets and liabilities, but is hostile to suggestions for compulsory revelation of other information relating to economic efficiency, such as production, productivity, turnover, costs or profit margins. Business men believe that disclosure of these details might benefit competitors and, presumably, it is thought that if all businesses possessed all information about all others, competition in general might become uncomfortably intense, or, in the language of neo-classical economics, uncomfortably 'perfect'. In consequence, the rules laid down by the Statistics of Trade Act severely inhibit employment of the one type of experiment which might lead to a real break-through in the analysis of factors underlying industrial efficiency—that is, multiple-regression analysis based on cross-section data relating to individual firms. Restrictions on 'disclosure' also prevent the Census Office from issuing complete data, even in tabular form, wherever the material is of such a character that the number of firms in a cell is less than three. In the present case, the results of a major feature of the statistical operations originally planned eventually proved useless for this reason.

However, although the Census of Production was our major source of material, it was by no means the only one. Many industrial firms are prepared to give private inquirers information which they would never consent to include in a Census questionnaire. We made a considerable number of direct inquiries in industry and received widespread co-operation, although it must be admitted that it was difficult to obtain the information which would have provided a really rigid set of tests of the theory we have developed above. And here also we face the problem of experimental inflexibility. Ideally, we should have proceeded as follows; we should have undertaken pilot interviews with a small number of selected firms in order to suggest inductions; we should then have undertaken a pilot analysis of selected data from the Census; next a major Census tabulation and analysis, the result of which would probably have led us to reformulate our theory. Then, with the reformulated theory we could have undertaken more extensive interviews specifically designed to test it, and a similarly redesigned statistical programme. In the event, although the first two pilot stages were reasonably successful, it was impossible to wait the necessary period of years for the larger scale statistical tabulation to become available before conducting the larger scale interviews (also, as so often happens from inexperience, it was not at first realised how little could be done with partially complete data). The major interviewing programme and the major statistical programme were therefore carried on in parallel and it was only when the results of the first statistical analyses of the completed tabulations finally became available that we realised how many important lines of inquiry had been omitted from the interviews, as well, of course, as important tabulations omitted from the statistics. These are the characteristic tribulations of research in applied economics, and with experience one learns to anticipate them. But science is inevitably handicapped where experiments can only be successfully completed by the most experienced practitioners.

Fortunately, several factors helped to rescue us from some of the consequences of our own mistakes. With some difficulty we were able to rearrange the statistics in a satisfactory manner without further recourse to the Board of Trade and, in the case of the interviews, Mr MacLean, who conducted most of them, proved to have anticipated rudiments of the theory which was eventually developed and a good deal of appropriate material was available in his notes. Consequently, we believe that the empirical analyses we shall present below do, in fact, provide a not unreasonable set of tests of the theory. Roughly speaking, the interviews provided the main basis for the formulation of hypotheses, the statistics the main bases of testing them.† The value of the role of the interviews cannot be exaggerated. One may conduct nine interviews and learn nothing new; from the tenth springs the fertile seed of an idea. But this does not mean, of course, that the first nine interviews were valueless, because it would have been impossible to predict in advance which one would be germinal. In the present case the train of thought which led to the final theoretical formulation was started by an interview with one man.‡ We do not therefore need to apologise to those of our respondents who will not find in this report direct evidence of their contribution.§ The accidents of our requirements and the unpredictable development of our theory determined the selection of material, and no other factors.

The materials we shall deploy are as follows:

The results of the Census of Production of 1951.
The results of the Ministry of Labour Shift-Work Inquiry of 1954.
The results of the inquiry conducted by Employment Exchanges.
Statistics provided by the Factory Inspectorate.
The result of an inquiry into shift-workers' road transport problems.
The results of an inquiry into Trade Union policy.
Selected industrial case studies.

In addition, of course, information and ideas gained from industrial interviews are used, wherever appropriate, to back up or qualify observations based on the statistical results and other inquries generally. In the remainder of the present chapter we describe the character of each of the above in turn. The results and analyses are given in Chapters 7 to 9. Chapter 7 deals with the two main statistical sources, Chapter 8 with the three special inquiries and the Factory Inspectorate data, Chapter 9 comprises the industrial case studies. In the Statistical Appendix, Tables I, II and III give the results of the Board of Trade tabulations, adjusted by us in the manner described.

6.2. The Census of Production 1951

The Census form for 1951 included a special section (number 7) headed 'Shift-working' and worded as shown in Table 6.1. Wherever the replies to the sections indicated that some shift-work was occurring in the trade an appropriate table was presented in the published report. As already mentioned, this table gave the results in the form of broad aggregates only. We print below, as an example, the table in question for cotton spinning and doubling (Table 6.2).

† For an important qualification to this generalisation, see the account of the industrial case studies, §6.9, below, and the studies themselves, Chapter 9.

‡ Mr J. A. Scott, of Hayeshaw Ltd., Manchester, then assistant to the managing director, Col. Grierson.

§ For the list of acknowledgements see Introduction.

Table 6.1. *Shift-work questionnaire from the 1951 Census*

SECTION 7. Shift-working

(*a*) This section need only be completed by firms which worked shifts during the week ended 22 September 1951, and by firms which would have worked shifts during that week had it not been an abnormal week (see note (*c*)). Other firms should strike out the table; do not leave blank.

(*b*) The particulars returned in this table should relate to operatives only. Administrative, technical and clerical personnel should be excluded. See notes to Section 2 for definitions.

(*c*) Give figures for 22 September 1951, even if your business year ended earlier. If for any reason the week ended 22 September 1951 was not a normal week, give particulars for the nearest ordinary week and state here the week for which you have given particulars:

Week ended..195........

(See note (i) to Part A of Section 6)

Shift number	Description of shift (e.g. morning, afternoon, night)	Duration of shift*		Number of shifts worked in week ended 22 Sept. 1951	Average number of operatives employed on each shift during week ended 22 Sept. 1951
		From	To	No.	No.
1		......{a.m. p.m.	......{a.m. p.m.		
2		......{a.m. p.m.	......{a.m. p.m.		
3		......{a.m. p.m.	......{a.m. p.m.		
4		......{a.m. p.m.	......{a.m. p.m.		

* Cross out a.m. or p.m. as appropriate.

STATE HERE the average number of operatives who were employed on other than shift-work during the week ended 22 September 1951. No. ....

The reader will have little difficulty in seeing why these aggregates were insufficient for our requirements. Ideally, we needed to know how the frequency distribution of the shift-work ratios of the *establishments* was associated with their other characteristics at different ranges of the distribution. Unfortunately, for all the willingness of the Census Office to undertake appropriate tabulations, here we ran into a serious obstacle. In the Census of 1951, firms controlling more than one establishment were permitted to send in consolidated returns for large numbers of sections of the schedule and one of the sections affected, unfortunately, was the shift-work section. It is easy to show that a frequency distribution of shift-working characteristics by firms, rather than by establishments, would have little economic significance. Furthermore, the dispensation was voluntary; firms which preferred to send in separate returns were permitted to do so. Some of the shift-work returns, there-

Table 6.2. *Cotton spinning and doubling, shift-working, 1951*†

Larger establishments in Great Britain

	Total number of man-shifts worked in the week	Total number of shift-hours worked in the week	Number of returns showing the systems stated
Continuous 3 shift systems per 24 hours averaging 8 hours per shift	4308	34464	9
Continuous 4 shift systems per 24 hours averaging 6 hours per shift	—	—	—
All 2 shift systems	39274	318757	47
Other shift systems‡	14703	79595	70
Total	58285	432816	(§)

† Shift-working during week ended 22 September 1951.

‡ Evening shifts of approximately 4 hours' duration are included: 53 returns reported working such shifts, the total number of shift-hours worked in the week being 47201.

§ The number and percentage of returns showing shift-working and of operatives on shift-work were as follows:

	Returns		Operatives		
	Total in trade	Showing shift-work	Total in trade	Total on returns showing shift-work	Number employed on shift-work
Number	694	118	165125	45251	11481
Percentage of total in trade	100·0	17·0	100·0	27·4	7·0
Percentage of total on returns showing shift-work	—	—	—	100·0	25·4

fore, related to the single establishments of mono-factory firms, some to the many establishments of multi-factory firms, and some to the aggregate characteristics of all the establishments in multi-establishment firms.† We were driven, therefore, to the undesirable procedure of attempting to estimate the probable distribution by establishments of the data recorded on these so-called 'multi-establishment' returns. We were forced so to speak to attempt to reconstruct a picture of the egg before it had been scrambled: inevitably it was a picture which could not contain much detail.

All the data presented in the Statistical Appendix relate in principle to establishments and we have reason to believe that as far as they went our estimating procedures were not unsuccessful. The work of estimation took a number of months and was rendered particularly distressing by the reflection that most firms keep their primary records of this data on an establishment basis!

When we began the inquiries we had no well-developed theory for dealing with the distribution of utilisation rates between many activities

† This is an extremely good example of the dangers of instituting special inquiries without consideration of the hypotheses they are designed to test.

within one plant. We concentrated on a theoretical approach which treated each establishment as if it were engaged in a single activity. For this reason we decided to isolate for special study those establishments which seemed to have so high a proportion of shift-working employees as to suggest that the greater part of the fixed capital was being intensively utilised. We asked the Board of Trade to isolate all returns in which more than 35 % of the total operatives were recorded as employed on shift-work and to provide, for this selective group, comprehensive details of net output, of earnings and of the characteristics of the various shift-systems operated. In particular, we hoped to be able to deduce actual rates of utilisation, measured in machine-hours per week, and to group the establishments accordingly. Much of the work done for us by the Board of Trade was involved in this last part of the project, and it was therefore doubly unfortunate that we did not realise until the greater part of the results had been collated that the statutory prohibition on 'disclosure' had made mince-meat of them. Apart from these figures, however, all the rest of the special tabulations proved to be extremely valuable and, together with suitable comparative data from the main Census reports, are presented in the Statistical Appendix.

As our theoretical ideas developed, it became apparent that the idea of the existence of a discontinuity between establishments using their capital relatively intensively and 'the rest' was misconceived, but by this time, of course, it was too late to change the tabulation programme. Fortunately, the comparison of aggregate characteristics between the intensively studied group and the corresponding characteristics of the rest of each industry has proved generally suggestive and illuminating. But we must give warning of the dangers inherent in the estimating procedures we were forced to adopt in face of disclosure barriers and multi-establishment returns. Where for example the number of establishments in the intensively studied group was two or less, we were not allowed to have details of their net output and wages. The estimates shown in the tables for the industries affected were in some cases pure guesses and are included mainly for the purpose of obtaining aggregates. They should not be employed analytically. Similarly, where the proportion of net output accounted for by multi-establishment returns was high and where the intensively studied group represented a large proportion of the output of the industry, small errors in the estimated distribution of the multi-establishment output and wages could create large errors in the residuals obtained for the rest of the industry. For these reasons, although we have included such estimates in aggregates and in the summary data of Table I, we have suppressed all the dubious cases from the comparative ratios presented in Table II. This cost us about 20 % of our observations.†

† See Table II in the Statistical Appendix below. The ratios affected are 'relative size ratio', 'basic share of gross profits in net output', 'net output per operative differential ratio', 'earnings per operative differential ratio' and 'apparent utilisation differential'.

Table I, which gives a general survey of the results, and Table III, which analyses the average sizes of establishments according to different criteria, are relatively self-explanatory. Table II, which compares the salient characteristics of the over-35% shift-working group with the corresponding characteristics of the rest of each industry, requires some explanation. The relative *size-ratio* represents average net output per establishment in the 'over-35' group as a ratio of the corresponding average in the remaining establishments. The *net output per operative differential ratio* and the *annual earnings per operative differential ratio* represent corresponding comparisons for net output per operative and earnings per operative respectively. The 'apparent basic share of gross profits in net output' columns represent an attempt to compare the profit margins of the two groups of establishments on a comparable wage-rate basis. For the 'under-35' group the figure is an estimate of the profit margin as it actually was. For the 'over-35' group it is an estimate of what the margin would have been had these establishments been paying their operatives the same amount per head annually as the other establishments. The procedure for estimating profit margins was as follows:

(i) Compute the share of wages in net output in the two groups of establishments, but reduce the figure for the 'over-35' group in proportion to the net-earnings-per-operative differential ratio; the resulting pair of ratios are termed the 'basic' share of operatives' wages in net output in each group respectively.

(ii) Compute the proportion of the wages and salaries of other employees to net output for the industry as a whole from table 5 of the Report of the 1951 Census of Production; since these data could not be divided between the 'over-35's' and 'under 35's' it was necessary to assume that the salary burden was proportionately the same in both groups.

(iii) Compute the proportion of certain other variable costs, many representing items which, strictly, should not be included in net output, such as insurance and advertising expenditure; information about these details was given in the 1948 Census of Production and we assumed that for each industry they bore the same ratio to net output in 1951 as they had done in 1948, and, again, we assumed that the burden was proportionately the same in both groups of establishments.

(iv) The 'basic' share of wages, the share of salaries and the share of other variable costs, as computed above, were added together and subtracted from 100, thus yielding an estimate of the basic gross profit margin.

Column 13 in Table II, 'apparent utilisation differential', represents an attempt to estimate the average difference between the wages of shift-workers in each industry and the wages of day-workers in the same industry on the assumption that the whole of the difference in observed average annual net earnings between the two groups of establishments was attributable to the difference of average shift-work ratio. A further discussion of these estimates is given in the analysis of the data in Chapter 7, § 7.2.

This completes our preliminary account of the Census of Production data; we shall elaborate where necessary in the course of analysis.

6.3. Industrial Interviews

The main function of these interviews has already been described. Another function, of course, was to help us interpret individual Census of Production results. The interviews were conducted loosely with no precise list of questions. Firms were chosen because they happened to be in particular industries and because we had reason to believe that they would be able to give us information of interest. We might choose a firm on account of its location, on account of its activity, its size or because its name had been given us by a Trade Association. In retrospect, if we erred in selection it was in failing to visit a sufficient number of firms who were *not* operating a shift system in order to ask them why they were not. We found, not very surprisingly, that business men generally prefer to explain why they are doing one thing rather than why they are not doing something else.

In all, we interviewed representatives of some 120 firms and Trade Associations, and a high proportion of the people we contacted took a great deal of trouble on our behalf. Details have already been given in the introduction.

6.4. The Ministry of Labour Shift-Work Inquiry, 1954

In 1954 the Ministry of Labour included questions about shift-work in its routine half-yearly inquiry into earnings and hours. This episode represents a particularly unfortunate example of the consequences of the present administrative organisation of economic statistics in the United Kingdom. For reasons which will by now be obvious, almost no useful purpose could be served by a second inquiry into shift-work unless the data collected were comparable with the first. The Ministry of Labour figures, however, were obtained on a notably different basis from the Census of Production, and in such a way that direct reconciliation was impossible.

The Census of Production for 1951 records shift-workers and the corresponding number of 'day-workers' in larger establishments in Great Britain.† The Ministry of Labour Inquiry of 1954 records shift-workers, and the corresponding 'day' workers in a voluntary sample drawn from *all* establishments in the *United Kingdom*. The sample covered 75 % of all operatives in the United Kingdom, but is not random and must therefore possess an unknown element of bias. If, for example, small firms are under-represented, the shift-work ratios

† Larger establishments are those employing ten persons or over.

obtained from the Ministry of Labour will be overstated. On the other hand, the possible inclusion of some returns from very small firms employing less than ten people, where shift-work is normally non-existent, will tend in the opposite direction. The same goes for the inclusion of Northern Ireland where, we happened to discover, shift-work tends to be rather less prevalent than in Great Britain. On balance, it seems likely that the net effect, if any, of the bias would be upward rather than downward. Finally, the Ministry of Labour data relate to a week in April while the Board of Trade data relate to a week in September, and we have no way of knowing to what extent the comparison between them may be affected by seasonal factors.

However, if we are prepared to assume that despite the inclusion of Northern Ireland and small firms, the Ministry of Labour method never overstates the shift-work ratio as compared with the result which would have been obtained in the same year using the Board of Trade method, we may treat the Ministry of Labour ratios as estimates of the upper limit of the results which would have been obtained by Board of Trade methods in 1954. We may then ask what might be the lower limit of estimate for the same concept. This, fortunately, may be obtained with some precision. For it is difficult to suppose that the Ministry of Labour could have discovered in its voluntary sample more than the total numbers of actual shift workers in each industry at the time, and the required estimate may therefore be obtained by dividing the Ministry of Labour numbers by the known number of 'Board of Trade' operatives in 1954, the latter being available in the results of the 1954 Census of Production. Thus we present figures on two bases, the first assuming that the shift-work ratio obtained by the Ministry of Labour in 1954 was exactly that which would have been obtained using the methods and scope of the Census of Production of 1951. The second base represents the other limit of the possible bias in this concept. We are thus able to estimate within a range the change in the shift-work ratio for the major industrial orders between the two years; fortunately the largest and most significant change occurred in an industrial order (engineering) where the coverage of the Ministry of Labour sample appears to be good and the range of error therefore relatively small. We were quite unable to make any allowance for possible bias due to seasonality, but here again the significant industries seemed unlikely to be affected. The results of our analysis of the Ministry of Labour Census are given in Chapter 7, §7.5.

6.5. Inquiries by Employment Exchanges

The staff of a number of selected employment exchanges went to considerable trouble to help us by obtaining details about the main shift-working establishments in their jurisdiction. The object of this approach *inter alia* was to tackle such specific questions as whether shift-work was more prevalent in New Towns, and whether firms belonging to industries in which shift-working was not prevalent nevertheless tended to operate shifts if they had establishments located in areas close to other industries where shift-work was traditional. We also asked why the firm had started shifts and how long ago. Although the results proved inconclusive for some purposes, they were extremely illuminating in other directions. About 160 establishments were involved and we are very grateful to the Ministry of Labour officials who were responsible for this work. Analysis of this material is given in Chapter 8, §8.2.

6.6. Bus Services

With the kind and effective assistance of the Ministry of Transport a questionnaire was sent to a number of licensed omnibus undertakings in an endeavour to ascertain whether allegations that shift-work was prevented by transport difficulties were justified. The results were positive and useful, and are described in Chapter 8, § 8.4.

6.7. Trade Unions

We entered into a general correspondence with a number of trade union officers, and also interviewed local officials in order to ascertain policy. Here again the results were positive and will be discussed in Chapter 8, §8.5.

6.8. The Factory Inspectorate

It is illegal in this country, and in many others, to employ women and juveniles after 10 p.m. at night. Even in order to set up a double-day-shift system involving women and juveniles, it is necessary to obtain a statutory permit from the Ministry of Labour and this will not be given unless a secret ballot of all the employees has shown that a majority are in favour. The records of the Inspectorate in carrying out its duties under this legislation are a useful guide to the development of the double-day-shift system. We obtained data of authorisations granted in the years after 1941, together with the number outstanding in 1954. See Chapter 8, §8.3.

6.9. Industrial Case Studies

In the early stages of this work the main author was convinced that there must exist wide areas of United Kingdom industry where, in the absence of inertia, irrational obstacles or misunderstanding, shift-work would be considerably more widespread than it is. It was believed that if these areas could be identified and documented, and the causes of 'failure' explained, industrial leaders, Trade Associations and the government would be able to initiate policies designed to rectify such situations and thus improve the efficiency of the national economy.

The reader who has followed the argument of this final report up to the present point will have no difficulty in appreciating why we now regard our original ideas as naïve and oversimplified. There are certain *general* policy conclusions to be drawn (these are reserved for Chapter 10) and in one case (the cotton industry, see Chapter 8, p. 168) as everybody knows, a not unreasonable trade union policy has undoubtedly been an important factor in events. For the rest of the economy, however, we have now developed a theory—to be tested below—which places the greater emphasis on objective economic factors, rather than individual idiosyncrasy, in determining the shift-working practices of individual firms and industries. Therefore, the original purpose of a series of industrial case studies has lost much of its point.

The programme of writing the studies was conducted in parallel with the programme of general analysis. Industrial Orders were 'written up' in turn, as the results of the Census and the interviews became available, which meant, in effect, they were written in order of appearance in the Standard Industrial Classification. They were written by the main author, and the effect of the task was of great importance. As soon as one tried convincingly to explain the facts observed in a particular industry, and to interpret or validate the rationalisations suggested in interviews, one found oneself thrown back on the need for a basic theory. In effect, one had to work back and forth between theory and industrial case-history, and inevitably in the process each was modified. The *attempt* to write these case studies was just as important, in the development of theory, as the attempt to provide a satisfactory explanation of over-all statistics. Furthermore, as will be seen particularly in the case of the Chemicals Industry (see pp. 186 *et seq.*), the studies not infrequently threw up theoretical problems of considerable general importance which the more general approach was unable to notice. This part of the investigation, therefore, was as important as any.

Nevertheless, the going was found to be inordinately slow. By the time the more general investigation had been completed, only three Industrial Orders had been reported, and of these, only two and part of the third were sufficiently advanced to be publishable. It was realised that if the whole programme were to be completed, the delay in publishing the whole report would be substantially increased. However, there was every reason for publishing those studies which were finished. The reader may well feel that although considerable material from industrial interviews—in effect, from the embryo studies—has been or is about to be deployed in the exposition and validation of our theory, the theory itself has still to some extent the appearance of a set of 'empty economic boxes'. The studies in Chapter 9 are intended to remedy this defect. Thus we are able to give an example of 'process' economies and capital economies combining to yield a strong incentive to utilise an industry where commercial and technical developments have permitted one large company to produce on a very large scale, and thus engage in intensive utilisation (flat glass).

We are able to compare this with the conditions in an industry in which the production function is similar, but where commercial conditions impose severe scale restraints and therefore prevent intensive utilisation (non-flat glass). Another set of commercial considerations in an adjacent industry (glass containers) yields yet another result. In the case of domestic pottery we are able to produce a model, containing illustrative figures, of a complete programme-profitability matrix, including three systems and two techniques of production. In chemicals we are able to develop ideas about important phenomena of which the theory has said nothing. The predictions of the theory relate to the utilisation of capital; they do not discuss the relationship between capital utilisation and the average national shift-work ratio. Generally, the higher the level of capital utilisation the higher the shift-work ratio, but here we discover circumstances where this may not be so. We also discover factors (discussed more fully in Chapter 7) which seem to imply that in future increasingly intensive capital utilisation may become possible with a declining or constant national shift-work ratio. In chemicals, also, we are able to give an example of two plants, owned by the same company, producing the same product in different parts of the country. The shift-work ratio in one is considerably higher than in the other. We believe we are able to explain the difference in terms of the main theory. Finally, in vehicles, we are able to provide some interesting examples of the effects of fluctuating demand and of 'unplanned' changes in capital utilisation. The reader who has reached this point (or the reader who has found the theoretical sections too arid) is earnestly entreated, therefore, to look at these studies.

No apology is offered to other industries where we conducted interviews for the fact that, by the chance of coming later in the Standard Industrial Classification, they are not included in the published studies. Much of their material is included in other parts of the report (for example, the embryo cotton study is largely employed in the later sections of Chapter 2). Had we completed all the studies, the main theory would no doubt have become more refined, but we became convinced that we had already reached the point of diminishing returns: the same theoretical points were increasingly repeated.

Chapter 9, therefore, includes studies of Industrial Order III (Treatment of Non-Metalliferous Mining Products) and of its main subgroups, of Industrial Order IV (Chemicals and Allied Trades) and of its main subgroups, together with a short note on Industrial Order VII (Vehicles).

CHAPTER 7

STATISTICAL RESULTS, 1951 AND 1954

7.1. 1951 General†

Appendix Table I gives the main shift-working characteristics for the greater part of British manufacturing industry in 1951: the small number of trades which were for one reason or another excluded from the tabulations accounted for no more than 3 % of total manufacturing net output. A more synoptic view of the data may be obtained from Tables 7.1 and 7.2 below.

The Census, which related to firms in Great Britain employing more than ten persons, discovered in manufacturing about two and a quarter million shift-workers, representing under one-sixth of total operative employment. Probably less than one in eight, therefore, of all manufacturing employees were involved in any kind of shift system.

But 80 % of the shift-working operatives were concentrated in the small minority of establishments where the shift-work ratio was over 35 %. This proved to be a remarkable group of establishments. No more than 6 % of the total number, they were so much above average in size that they accounted for no less than 25 % of total net output. A quarter of the net output of British manufacturing, therefore, occurred in establishments where a considerable proportion of fixed capital was relatively intensively utilised. A typical shift-working operative may have behind his elbow two to three times as much fixed capital as a typical non-shift worker. On the other hand, capital which is operated on a shift system is used by two or three times as many workers daily as other capital. Therefore it is not improbable to assume that the proportion of fixed capital in manufacturing which is intensively utilised is not dissimilar from the over-all shift-work ratio measured in terms of operatives: if so we might suggest that taking one year with another between 10 and 20 % of British manufacturing capital is so utilised. And since it appears that capital operated on shifts is utilised on average two and a quarter times as intensively as the other capital, we might say that if shift-work were abolished altogether, British manufacturing would require perhaps 15 % more capital to produce 'normal' output and as much as 20 % more capital to produce peak output.

It appears that fluctuations in capital utilisation associated with fluctuations in the extent of shift-working are not inconsiderable. Anticipating the findings of our analysis of the Ministry of Labour data for 1954, we mention an apparent decline in the over-all shift-work ratio

† For the statistical sources and methods see Chapter 6, §6.2.

between 1951 and 1954 of no less than 5 percentage points; most of this was concentrated in the engineering industries and may well have reduced the proportion of total manufacturing net output produced on intensively utilised capital from 25 to 20 %. We shall revert to these broader questions in due course. We now discuss the Census of Production data in a more detailed manner with special reference to the theoretical predictions which have to be tested. We arrange the analysis into three subsections: (i) utilisation differential, (ii) utilisation incentive, (iii) influence of scale.

7.2. The Utilisation Differential

Table 7.1 shows that operatives in intensive shift-working establishments were estimated to have earned £390 per annum *per capita* in 1951, as against £326 *per capita* in the remaining establishments. This excess of approximately 21 % may be used to estimate the average difference, in manufacturing as a whole, between *per capita* earnings of shift-workers and of non-shift-workers and also to throw some light on the average incidence of the utilisation differential. Suppose we assume that the non-shift-working operatives in the intensive shift-working establishments were paid on average the same as non-shift-working operatives in other establishments; in other words that the whole of the difference in average *per capita* earnings between the two groups of *establishments* was entirely attributable to the difference in their average shift-work ratio. Then, since, as Table 7.1 shows, the shift-work ratio in the first group was 67 %, in the second group, 4 %, a simple calculation gives an apparent differential between the two groups of *operatives* of 32 %.

What biases are involved in the above calculation? Of the many possibilities, we may emphasise:

(i) The intensive shift-working establishments tended to be operated by large, growing firms who would be expected to pay above-average wages to *all* their workers.

(ii) Where it is impossible to offer all workers in a factory the opportunity to work shifts, contentment may require that non-shift-workers be paid almost as much as shift-workers.

(iii) Shift-workers often work shorter weekly hours than day workers, therefore the Census comparison based on annual earnings may understate the difference in hourly earnings.

The last factor works in the opposite direction to the other two, but is probably not very strong because some male shift-workers are known to work quite long hours. We may therefore say with some confidence that the difference between the hourly earnings of shift and non-shift-workers was probably rather less than 32 %; as a guess one might suggest 25 %.

When we consider the utilisation differential, the position is more complex. Strictly this differential is defined as the proportionate increase

Table 7.1. *Shift-work in manufacturing, 1951*

(Larger establishments† in Great Britain.)

Range of shift-work ratio	Establishments		Operatives		Net output		Average shift-work ratio (%)	Net output per establishment (£'000)	Earnings per operative (£)
	000's	%	Mil.	%	£'000 mil.	%			
Over 35 %	3·37	**6**	1·10	**19**	1·19	**25**	**67**	350	390
Less than 35 %	50·54	**94**	4·74	**81**	3·65	**75**	**4**	70	326
All establishments	53·91	**100**	5·84	**100**	4·83	**100**	**16**	90	338

† Employing more than ten persons.

Table 7.2. *Shift-working characteristics for all manufacturing establishments*

(Larger establishments† in Great Britain 1951.)

	Shift-work ratio											
	No shift-work		1–35 %		Over 35 %		All 1 % and over		All less than 35 %		All establishments	
	Nos.	%	Nos.	%	Nos.	%	Nos.	%	Nos.	%	Nos.	%
Establishments, no.	47450	**88·0**	3093	**5·75**	3372	**6·25**	6465	**12**	50543	**93·75**	53915	**100**
Operatives, 000's	3571	**61·7**	1171	**20·1**	1097	**18·8**	2268	**38·9**	4742	**81·2**	5839	**100**
Shift-workers, 000's	—	—	201	—	732	—	933	—	201	—	933	—
Net output, £ mil.	..	..	..	..	1186	**24·1**	..	..	3646	**75·9**	4833	**100**
Operatives earnings, £ mil.	..	..	..	..	428	**22**	..	..	1543	**78**	1971	—
Operatives per establishment	75	—	380	—	325	—	350	—	95	—	108	—
Net output per establishment, £000's	..	—	..	—	350	—	..	—	71	—	90	—
Net output per operative, £	..	—	..	—	1081	**141**	..	—	769	**100**	827	—
Earnings per operative, £	..	—	..	—	390	**120**	—	—	326	**100**	338	—
Average shift-work ratio	—	—	—	**17**	—	**67**	—	**41**	—	**4**	—	**16**
Ratio of operatives' earnings to net output	..	..	—	—	—	**36**	—	—	—	**42**	—	**41**

N.B. — indicates zero or void; .. indicates not available.

† Employing more than ten persons.

in hourly wage costs, per unit of output, to be expected to result from a one-step increase in the system of utilisation in a particular activity, technique of production remaining constant. Unfortunately, for reasons described earlier,† we were unable in general to distinguish between the different systems employed within the intensive shift-working group. We must therefore modify the definition of the differential to relate to a comparison of a typical one-shift system with a 'typical' multiple-shift system. If so, the second of the biases listed in the preceding paragraph becomes irrelevant: if shift-work in one activity causes an increase in wages in other activities, this is part of the cost of shift-work in the former. Thus it might seem that the figure of 32 % represents not a bad estimate of the average utilisation differential on the modified definition. Unfortunately, however, there is another cause of bias. To the extent that males are on average more productive than females, and the proportion of males among shift-workers being higher than among non-shift-workers, the observed differential will be biased upwards in relation to the measure defined.

We may obtain some indication of the order of magnitude of the problem by comparing the average earnings-per-operative differential ratio computed from Table 7.1 (120) with an unweighted average of the individual industry ratios given in Appendix Table II (110). Some of this difference will be due to the inclusion in the aggregate data of estimates for individual industries which are too unreliable for separate presentation but the greater part is due to the fact that the intensive shift-working establishments were to some extent concentrated in high-wage industries,‡ the latter, in turn, representing industries employing relatively small proportions of females. We do not know the average difference in productivity between men and women employed with the same equipment (often there is none); we do know that there is sufficient economic 'exploitation' of women to ensure that their efficiency wages *on average* are lower than men's. Taking all things into account one might surmise that a British management in 1951, and probably today, could typically expect to be able to double the rate of capital utilisation on a given activity at the expense of an increase in hourly labour costs which would be unlikely to be less than 20 % (cf. the biased estimate of the personal differential—32 %) or to exceed 30 %. This was the basis of our earlier suggestion that the elasticity of utilisation could be thought of as a number lying between three and five.

Appendix Table II gives the data for those individual industries where the estimates were considered sufficiently reliable. The column headed 'net earnings per operative differential ratio' represents the ratio of average earnings *per capita* among all operatives in the intensive shift-working establishments to the corresponding average among the

† Page 129.

‡ More precisely, the proportion of operatives employed in intensive shift-working establishments tended to be higher in industries where all operatives' earnings significantly exceeded the manufacturing average, and these in turn were industries in which the proportion of adult males was also above average. Cf. Tables 7.1, 7.2 and Appendix Tables I and II.

remaining establishments. The 'apparent mean utilisation differential' is an estimate of the average percentage difference between the earnings of shift-workers and of non-shift-workers, based on the assumption that the whole of the observed earnings differential was due to the difference, in the industry in question, between the two groups of establishments' shift-work ratios. We have discussed the bias in this type of ratio. Where the 'sex-efficiency bias' discussed in the previous paragraph is not a big factor, the ratio may be regarded as a reasonably approximate estimate of the relevant utilisation differential. The cases where sex-efficiency bias (an exaggeration of the utilisation differential) may be important are often indicated by unusually high apparent differentials, sometimes reaching to 100%: these tend to be industries such as drugs, bread and flour, cocoa and confectionery and rubber where it is known that the shift-workers are mainly men working at night, the non-shift-workers mainly women.

Of the seventy available individual observations of the earnings ratio, four-fifths exceeded 1·01. The unweighted average of all the observations, as already mentioned, was 110.† These results are highly significant: even if all shift-workers were paid more than all day workers in comparable occupations, one could not expect all the differentials to be positive, because the census-of-production industries are not sufficiently homogeneous. If one section of an industry is making a product to which female labour is particularly suited, there is no reason why a double-day-shift system might not be operated in this section while in another section, where male labour is required, conditions generally might happen to favour single shifts only. The intensive shift-working statistical group in the industry might then represent mainly the first section, leading to a negative statistical differential because women on double shifts were paid less than men on single shifts.

It is interesting to compare the foregoing results with direct information about officially negotiated premiums and hours. The data in Table 7.3 were gathered from a variety of sources, some of which cannot be disclosed, but they are believed to be reasonably accurate. They relate to the situation in England and Wales in 1955. However, it must be emphasised that they relate only to the double-day system, and that this system, owing to the relatively unattractive value of $h^{\cdot}$, is not very popular, and accounts for a relatively small proportion of the total number of shift-hours worked in industry as a whole.

It will be seen that the orders of magnitude of these figures are consistent with our general statistical findings and it will also be seen that double-day shifts are likely to be unattractive for employees as well as employers. In practice the system yields small or negligible increases in *weekly* earnings, because most of the gain in hourly earnings is swallowed up in reduced hours.

It cannot be too frequently emphasised that the officially negotiated shift premium is only one of the factors contributing to the effective

† See p. 139.

Table 7.3. *Weekly working hours and recognised premiums for shift-work*

Industry	Normal weekly working hours excluding recognised meal breaks: Single day shifts	Double day shifts	Average percentage wage-increase in double shift compared with single shift: Hourly	Weekly
Electric Cable Making	44	37½	22	3
Furniture Manufacture	45	41¼	18	9
Engineering	44	37½	17	0
Printing	43½	42	17	13
Rubber Manufacture	45	41¼	15	6
Paint, Varnish and Lacquer Manufacture	44	41¼	15	8
Rayon Yarn Production	44	41¼	12	6
Paper Making	48	46	12	7
Corn Trade	44	40½	12	1
Cement Manufacture	44	45½	12	15
Drugs and Fine Chemicals	44	41¼	11	5
Beet Sugar Manufacture	44	41½	11	3
Seed Crushing and Provender	44	41¼	10	3
Glass Container Manufacture	45	42	10	3
Cocoa, Chocolate, Sugar Confectionery, and Food Preserving	45	45	9	8
Flour Milling	44	42	8	2
Heavy Chemicals Manufacture	44	41¼	7	7
Unweighted average	44½	41¾	13	5½

utilisation differential: the double-day shift system is essentially designed for women; where, instead, men are substituted and a more attractive shift system is employed, the increase in labour costs is mainly determined by the difference in the efficiency wages of the two sexes. If women were paid the same as men for all work at which they were equally efficient, multiple shifts would be considerably more prevalent.† The traditional 'exploitation'‡ of female labour not only discourages mechanisation, but also, on account of the social objection to female night-work, intensive utilisation. It thus prevents the opposing effects of low wages on mechanisation and utilisation respectively from developing in the manner postulated in our basic theory.

7.3. The Utilisation Incentive

In the early sections of Chapter 2 we defined as the incentive to utilise the proportionate increase in profit rate associated with a one-step

† One firm gave as an explanation for working shifts that it did not like to see men and women doing the same work side by side being paid different wages. It therefore preferred to separate the sexes by means of a day-and-night shift system.

‡ Exploitation here means paying a person a low price for their services not because the services are of no great value to the buyer, but because the seller is willing, or is conventionally expected, to sell them cheap. In the present context 'exploitation' is therefore essentially a relative term.

increase in utilisation in a particular activity with given technique of production. Our data, however, relate not to activities but to establishments. We must therefore attempt in some way to modify the definition in order to abstract from the activity, at least to the 'plant'. We may think of a plant as an aggregation of activities, and we may consider the effects on the average rate of utilisation in the plant of a particular change in one activity. Clearly, if of a number of activities, only one is changed, the proportionate reduction in capital–output ratio in the plant as a whole will be considerably less than in the single activity. Nevertheless, we may take the shift-work ratio in a plant as a good indication of the average rate of utilisation of all capital in the plant because although, as we have seen in Chapter 3, we can expect capital per unit of instantaneous employment (q) to be higher in the intensively utilised activities, each unit of capital in these activities is utilised by two or three times as many individual workers annually, therefore capital per employee may be much the same throughout the plant. It follows that the very marked differences between the average shift-work ratios in the establishments where over 35 % of operatives were recorded as shift-workers and the remaining establishments usually indicate very considerable differences in average utilisation.

We wish to compare the indicated differences in utilisation with indicated values of the utilisation incentive. Where the analogy between the plant and the single activity is valid, the theory predicts that in the absence of scale restraint, intensive utilisation should be found wherever the apparent utilisation incentive is significantly positive. However, the ingredients of the utilisation incentive, it will be remembered, include not only the initial ratio of profits to wages, but also the ingredients of the elasticity of utilisation, i.e. $h^{\cdot}$ the proportionate utilisation difference, and $w^{\cdot}$ (in Chapter 3, $f^{\cdot}$) the utilisation differential. The latter can be estimated, the former, for reasons which should now be obvious, cannot. We can, however, put limits on $h^{\cdot}$, and we shall find that this method does, in fact, yield suggestive results. Appendix Table II, therefore, in columns 3 (*a*) and 3 (*b*) gives estimates of profit margins which are closely related to the initial profit–wage ratio.

In developing these estimates we have to take account of the fact that in practice higher rates of utilisation will tend to be associated with more mechanised techniques of production. Typically, the designer's choice will lie between high utilisation with mechanised techniques and low utilisation with more primitive techniques. Therefore, to measure the relevant value for the incentive to utilise we need to know what the ratio of profit to wages would be if the high techniques were operated at the low rate of utilisation. This value cannot be observed in data derived from actual firms operating low rates of utilisation because they, presumably, have chosen the lower technique. The best approximation we can obtain to the correct value will consist of the observed value of the ratio of profits to wages in the observed shift-working firms, adjusted in some way to allow for the utilisation differentials they are presumed to be paying. This is the basis of comparison adopted in Table II. It should be emphasised, however, that the comparison of 'basic' profit margins is not a comparison of one group of establishments working shifts with another working 'days'. It is a comparison of one group of establishments where shift-working is common with another in which it is less common. The adjustment factor applied to the wage-bill in order to estimate the basic profit margin in the 'over-35' group is therefore the earnings-per-operative differential ratio and not the apparent utilisation differential.

If the Census definition of net output comprised only the wages of operatives on the one hand, and gross profits on the other, the ratio of profits to wages would bear a unique relationship either to the share of wages in net output or to the share of profits. But because net output in fact includes not only salaries but also other items such as costs of advertising, postage, insurance premiums and local taxes, the position is a little more complicated. In our tables, for lack of better information, the burden of these costs in each industry was assumed to be the same in the 'over-35' group and the rest. Therefore the whole of the difference in the estimated basic share of gross profits in each industry is attributable to difference in the share of wages, from which it follows that we lose nothing in presenting the basic gross profit margins only. This argument does not hold, of course, for inter-industry comparisons, but as already explained, these particular ratios would have little theoretical significance for inter-industry comparisons.

If, within one industry, the average observed profit margin in the 'under 35 per cent' group of establishments is greater than the upper limit of the value which would render the incentive to utilise positive in one activity†, it is likely that the group contains a considerable proportion of establishments which could profitably raise their average utilisation rates by one-step changes in leading activities, were there no obstacles such as scale restraint. This does not mean, however, that the utilisation incentive has no influence in such cases. We have seen that scale restraint and the utilisation incentive are not alternative influences, but act together. This is true even in the most simple version of the theory of scale restraint, but is particularly the case when techniques can be degraded. Hence we are provided with a useful prediction: if a group of establishments in which capital is not utilised intensively displays basic profit data suggesting a high value of the incentive to utilise, there should be evidence of other obstacles to intensive utilisation; in general there should be evidence of scale restraint. We discuss the possible evidence in the following section, but we may note here that if the size of the establishment, measured in terms of net output, is a relevant indicator of scale, the prediction can be translated into statistical terms as follows: if, within one industry, there is a fairly clear division between the intensive shift-working establishments and the rest,

† This value is, of course, directly related to the critical wage.

and if, among the rest, the basic share of gross profits is sufficiently high to suggest that the incentive to utilise is nevertheless significantly positive, we would expect average output per establishment in this group to be significantly lower than in the intensive group. Also, as already suggested in Chapter 5,† since scale restraint is a general influence, we should expect intensive shift-working to be associated with large scale throughout the data, especially within single industries.

From here we are led to a second prediction. Suppose scale restraint is affecting a substantial proportion of firms in some industry. Then those firms which are less affected—as evidenced by their apparent ability to exploit higher utilisation rates—must be in a position not only to work shifts but also to adopt more mechanised techniques of production, for, the theory predicts, scale restraint reduces not only utilisation but also mechanisation. However, we also saw‡ that it is likely that in many industries we should find a dynamic minority of firms which were exploiting 'superior' techniques, that is techniques which gave increased output per man without increased capital per man. Superior techniques frequently display larger optimum scale than the techniques they have rendered inferior; that is to say the substitution of these techniques involves a reduction of the scale coefficient. In order to become a member of the dynamic minority, therefore, a firm will have to be in a position to sell, or to hope to sell, a larger than average scale of output. The firms which tend to be first to exploit newly invented superior techniques will therefore tend to be those which are already large or fast-growing. Therefore we expect to find, within many industries, two groups of establishments; the first relatively 'small', in some relevant sense, and displaying relatively low rates of utilisation; the second, by contrast, larger, tending to utilise their capital more intensively and tending to employ more mechanised and/or superior techniques. In general, the second group will be a minority. So long as the industry is reasonably homogeneous both as to labour market and to product market, firms employing either superior or more mechanised techniques must display a larger average 'basic' gross profit margin, except in the extreme case where the whole benefit of the superior technique is passed on in lower selling prices. But the extreme case is unlikely because, by reducing their rate of profit to the same level as that of the remaining firms, these potentially dynamic firms would be depriving themselves of the financial resources necessary to expand their share of the industry's capacity.§ Therefore, we should generally expect the profit margin to be higher in the large-size fast-expanding minority group of establishments. In what follows, we shall attempt to identify this group with the statistical group in which over 35 % of operatives were shift-workers. If the 'over-35's' do not generally exhibit larger basic profit margins than the rest, serious doubt will be thrown on the validity of our fundamental hypotheses.

† Page 121, prediction 4. ‡ Chapter 2, §2.14.

§ The reasoning here is closely dependent on the arguments of Chapter 2, §2.14.

One exception to test the rule. In some industries the predominant factor in shift-working decisions is not economy of capital but economy of prime or 'process' costs; for example, where the process is described as 'necessarily continuous' which means, in effect, that were it not run continuously prime costs would be prohibitive. It is often possible to manufacture so-called continuous process products by more primitive discontinuous techniques, i.e. by using types of equipment in which the relative economic disadvantage of discontinuous operation is less severe. Generally, such techniques exhibit larger scale-coefficients than the characteristic continuous techniques, and may therefore be employed by firms marketing a subvariety of the product for the benefit of a relatively small group of customers. The more primitive discontinuous technique would be formally inferior to the continuous-process technique and might well require, therefore, a larger gross profit margin in order to obtain the same rate of profit on capital. If the market for the product subvariety which is produced with these techniques is sufficiently specialised, the firms concerned may be able to stabilise their rate of profit at a reasonable level by charging higher prices than the firms producing the standard variety. If the two groups of firms are thus able to co-exist with more or less equal rates of profit on capital, the group producing the subvariety with the inferior technique will display a larger gross profit margin. Therefore, where this situation exists, the otherwise predicted relationship between shift-work ratio and gross profit margin may be reversed. It is to be noted that the required conditions involve not only a continuous process for the standard variety, but also a narrow, special market for the subvariety.

We now proceed to test two of the foregoing predictions. First, that in the absence of evidence of scale restraint, low shift-work ratios should be associated with gross profit margins which are less than the lower limit of the estimated critical value. Secondly, that irrespective of scale restraint, except in continuous process industries, the intensively shift-working establishments should display higher basic gross profit margins than the rest. We test the predictions directly relating to scale restraint in the next section. A cursory examination of Table II shows that even on the most conservative assumptions as to the values of the other ingredients, the incentive to utilise was almost certainly positive throughout the great majority of industries, including those where shift-work, in fact, was virtually non-existent. For example, only most improbable values of $h^{\cdot}$, $f^{\cdot}$, etc., would yield a critical initial profit margin smaller than 30 %. Yet Table II shows that of 117 observations of the average 'basic' share in establishments in the 'under-35' group only twenty-two are below this figure.† For this reason it seems likely that the incentive to utilise is probably significantly positive in a very large proportion of industrial activities which are not at present operated on a shift-work basis. One suspects that if the unadjusted value of the

† Of the seventy-eight observations in the 'over-35' group, only seven were below the figure.

incentive to utilise were the sole criterion of decision, rather than 16%, perhaps 70% of manufacturing operatives would today be working shifts.

In analysing the intra-industry comparisons of profit margins for the purpose of the second test we must first take note of the fact that the percentages recorded in Table II have been rounded to the nearest whole number and that in some cases, therefore, the difference between columns 3*a* and *b* is zero. In addition, looking at the matter subjectively, a measured difference of no more, say, than 1%, even if positive, could hardly be regarded as economically significant. Nevertheless, if we wish to test the 'null hypothesis'—to test, that is, the *anti*-prediction that the number of positive differences will not significantly differ from the number of negative differences—we must adopt a properly rigorous statistical procedure. We must treat every positive difference, however small, as positive, and vice versa, and we must assign the zeros *between the positive and negative groups in equal proportions.* On this basis the results are as follows: there are seventy-three observations, of which 52½, or 72%, are positive. This can validly be subjected to the 'Chi-squared' test and proves to be statistically highly significant. Roughly, one could say that the result would not arise by chance more than one time in six hundred.

As regards the exception discussed on p. 145 the two main groups of continuous-process industries are those in Industrial Order IV (Chemicals and Allied trades) and Industrial Order V (Metal Manufacturing). There are continuous-process industries elsewhere of course, but the concentration of cases is much higher in these Orders than in any of the others.† It is therefore of interest to note that although these two Orders provide less than a quarter of the total number of observations, they provide more than a third of the negative differences. Actually, the position is that in Chemicals there are eleven observations of which six are negative but in Metals six observations of which only two are negative. Thus out of seventeen observations in the two groups combined, almost a half are negative, a result which, unlike the result for manufacturing as a whole, is almost precisely consistent with the hypothesis that the distribution of signs is random with an equal chance, in any one industry, of finding a positive or a negative.‡ On a more sophisticated test for heterogeneity, the result for Chemicals may tentatively be estimated to differ significantly from that of all other Orders (excluding Metals) taken together, at least at the 10% probability level and possibly at a higher level.§

† For the reasons why we exclude Order III (Treatment of Non-Metalliferous Mining Products), see the case study of this group in Chapter 9.

‡ I am very much indebted to Mr John Longden of the Department of Applied Economics Cambridge, for these calculations. The ambiguity arises from alternative formulations of the precise hypothesis to be tested. There is a good logical case for a formulation yielding a considerably higher level of significance than the level quoted.

§ The reader who is familiar with the commercial structure of the Chemicals industry may suspect that the existence of one or two giant corporations may have led to unusual difficulties in estimating the distribution of 'multi-establishments' data. However, we have evidence

It would seem therefore that the prediction relating to intra-industry differences in profit margins has proved correct. But as far as the exception provided by Chemicals is concerned, the story does not end here. The industrial interviews of chemical firms, which are analysed in Chapter 9 below, throw up a set of considerations of far-reaching importance, especially for future developments, which the 'pure' theory entirely failed to predict. Suppose a plant consists of two activities in one of which capital per man is low, while in the other it is high. Perhaps, also, in this highly capital-intensive activity, shift-work provides considerable economy in process costs. Then suppose a superior technique of production is developed relating only to the second process, raising output per man-hour in that process while leaving unchanged, or even lowering, capital per man (q). Suppose this technique is adopted by one group of establishments in an industry but not, for some reason, by the rest. Previously, all firms have run the second activity on shifts but not the first, and all continued to follow this practice: the shift-work ratio in each establishment, therefore, reflects nothing more than the ratio of employment in the second activity to the first. But in those firms which adopt the superior technique, employment will decline in the second activity and therefore their over-all shift-work ratios will decline relatively to those of the other firms. Since their technique is superior, they will display a larger average gross profit margin and profit rate on capital. In other words, we have a further reason for reversing the 'normal' or predicted relationship between shift-work ratio and profit margin.

The conditions required for this perverse case are: (i) that the differences between capital per man in the two activities should be large; (ii) that the technical change should be concentrated in the high-capital activity; and (iii) that before the advent of the change, conditions already favoured shift-work in this activity. Obviously, other things being equal, these requirements are more likely to be met if the activity is one in which shift-work reduces prime as well as overhead costs.

An example would be found in an industry where one activity was a continuous process using considerable capital, while the other represented the task of maintaining this equipment. Maintenance is an activity which *serves* capital, but uses it little. Except where maintenance workers are required for emergency repairs, little is lost if they work in daytime only. Thus it is not unlikely that 'automation' leads to a state of affairs in which capital is utilised intensively but, the 'process worker' having disappeared, only a small fraction of the population is required for shift-work. This does not mean that the national shift-work ratio will necessarily decline. But it does imply that automation by no means necessarily requires the ratio to rise.

We have overwhelming evidence that such conditions already exist

(not from the Returns themselves!) that the largest giant sent in a separate reply for each establishment. In 'General Chemicals', the eighty-four establishments recorded on twenty-one multi-establishment returns accounted for only 14% of the total net output.

in many chemical trades. Indeed, it was in the course of our investigations among these trades that we first discovered and identified them. We call the phenomenon 'insufficient differentiation' because it produces statistical conditions where the division between the 'over-35's' and the 'under-35's' fails to distinguish genuine differences in the rate of capital utilisation. In Chemicals, almost all main processes have for some time been necessarily continuous, and a secular rise in output per man-hour in these processes has reduced the shift-work ratio. But automation in other industries may eventually produce the same effect, not so much because processes necessarily become continuous, but because of the increasing relative importance of maintenance work.

To sum up this phase of analysis, then, the results of the tests have not disproved our basic theory, and some additional inductions have been suggested. Most of the predictions of the basic theory related to the utilisation of capital. Tests have been applied to data relating to the shift-work ratio of employees, and, in interpreting them, we have discovered some interesting ways in which tendencies in the utilisation of capital can diverge from tendencies in the utilisation of workers. Our next step is to test the scale restraint hypothesis.

7.4. Scale Restraint

We again face a serious inconsistency between what we wish to observe and what we are able to observe. The theory predicts that if the peak scale of output per *plant*, i.e. per final product, is constrained, certain consequences will follow. We can observe output per *establishment* but we do not know how many different products are being produced at each establishment. We may hope that differences in mean net output per establishment as between two groups in one industry will at least to some extent reflect differences in mean net output per plant, but we cannot be sure that this will be so.

Over any group of establishments the average net output can be represented by a formula based on the statistical concepts of means and covariances.

Let m_i be the number of plants in establishment i.

Let y_i be the average output per plant in establishment i.

Then the total output of i is $y_i m_i$.

Let $\bar{m}$ be the unweighted average of m_i taken over all the establishments in the group.

Let $\bar{y}$ be the unweighted average of y_i taken over all the plants in all the establishments in the group.

Let $\bar{x}$ be weighted average net output per establishment in the industry.

Then, $\bar{x} = \bar{m}\,\bar{y} + \text{cov}\ m_i y_i$.

It follows that if we observe that $\bar{x}$ in one group of establishments—say the 'over-35's'—is greater than in another group—say the rest of the industry—the difference may be attributable to difference in $\bar{m}$, or in $\bar{y}$, or to a correlation between plants per establishment and output per plant. Positive correlation between m_i and y_i implies that those establishments which produce a relatively large number of products also tend to sell larger average amounts of each product. It is quite likely that such a tendency exists, but it is difficult to say how its strength will vary between any two specified groups of establishments. We are therefore forced to ignore this factor and to conduct the discussion entirely in terms of the behaviour of the averages, $\bar{m}$ and $\bar{y}$.

It would be possible for the whole of the difference between the average output per establishment in any two groups to be entirely explained by $\bar{m}$, that is, for $\bar{y}$ in both groups to be the same. Indeed, the difference in $\bar{y}$ might lie in the opposite direction to the difference in $\bar{m}$, the one being greater than the other. But it is of course only the difference in $\bar{y}$, if any, with which our theory is concerned. Faced with these rather deterring considerations we now recite the facts.

Table 7.2 shows that taking all the establishments covered by our data—nearly 54000 in all—the 3372 establishments in which shift-workers represented more than 35 % of all operatives averaged about five times the net output per establishment of the rest. To this general result, we may add the data for individual industries. Out of 128 industries covered by our statistics, there were thirty-eight in which no establishments operated any kind of shift-system at all: a cursory inspection shows that the average size of establishment in these industries was relatively very small. In the remaining industries, 90 % of the relative size ratios recorded in Table II were greater than 101, and the unweighted mean for all industries for which we have been able to give this ratio was 220. We have to consider whether this powerful statistical phenomenon, considered as a whole, could plausibly be explained mainly by differences in the average number of plants per establishment, rather than in the average output per plant.

Let us set up the hypothesis that the differences can be so explained. That is to say that the observed differences in $\bar{x}$ are largely due to differences in $\bar{m}$ rather than to $\bar{y}$. What would this imply? It would imply not only the failure of our prediction that intensity of capital utilisation should be closely associated with output per plant, but also that for some reason a tendency to produce many products in a single establishment was *positively* associated with shift-work. It is not impossible to think of reasons for such an association, but it is not easy. Not only the logic of our own theory, but also our industrial interviews (and also for that matter, a large part of existing economic theory generally) suggests that diversification discourages both mechanisation and utilisation.

Since we cannot measure the degree of diversification directly, our next best experimental procedure is to look for the most plausible hypothesis to explain the supposed association and try to test it. It could be argued that the problem of organising shift-work is largely a problem in labour management, and that so long as the number of *employees* attached to an establishment is large (in contrast to the net output of the establishment) the necessary arrangements for supervision can more easily and more economically be set up. This is no more than a particular extension of the theory of the indivisibility of management. However, if economies of personnel management were in fact the dominant causal factor at work in our data, we would expect to find a definite statistical association between shift-work and the size of establishments measured in terms of employment. Since there must be some association between size in terms of employment and size in terms of net output, a correlation in terms of net output would appear as well, but this would be irrelevant for our purposes.

Fortunately we are in a position to settle the point. Although, for purposes of comparisons of net output our data permit each industry to be divided into two groups only, for comparisons of operative employment we are able to add a third group. The published Census Tables, combined with our special data, enable us to subdivide the 'under-35's' into those establishments with no shift-workers at all and those with a shift-work ratio between 1 and 35 %. We call this last group the 'intermediate' establishments and can infer the mean shift-work ratio in the group in every industry. Thus we have a rudimentary frequency distribution of shift-work ratios which can be compared with the corresponding average sizes of establishment measured in terms of operatives.

The results, given in Table III, are extremely interesting. For they show that in general the 'intermediate' establishments—establishments with shift-work ratios between 1 and 35 %—are on average considerably larger in terms of operative employment than are the 'over-35's'. Thus in column 7 (Table III), where the operative size of the 'over-35's' is expressed as a ratio of that of the 'intermediates', out of eighty-five observations available, no less than three-quarters give percentages under 100. The weighted average of these ratios is 85; that is to say the average value of operatives per establishment in the group with more than 35 % of shift-workers is 15 % lower than the group where shift-work ratios lie between 1 and 35 %. This conclusively disproves our dummy hypothesis that the possession of a large number of employees encourages establishments to undertake large-scale shift-working. The average shift-work ratio in the 'over-35' group was no less than 67 %, while in the intermediate group it was no greater than 17 %. Thus in the comparison between these two groups taken as a whole, a quadrupling of the mean shift-work ratio is associated with a significant *reduction* in average operative size.

Have we, perhaps, proved too much? Is the fact that the intermediate establishments were consistently and significantly larger in terms of employment than the more intensive shift-working establishments a phenomenon that our theory fails to predict and therefore a cause for concern?† On the whole, the answer is negative. The results

† A failure to predict something that happens does not disprove a theory in the same sense as predicting something which does not happen. Nevertheless, where the unexpected

would be consistent with a plausible model which can be developed as a corollary to the basic theory, as follows. Large net output per establishment ($\bar{x}$) due to large net output per plant ($\bar{y}$) encourages high utilisation, but large net $\bar{x}$ due to diversification (according to the basic theory) has the opposite effect. The 'intermediate' establishments could be the relatively more diversified establishments, in which only a relatively small proportion of plants, and therefore processes, are producing an output adequate to be free of scale restraint. Therefore, over all the establishments in the group, the proportion of intensively utilised activities is small, and so, also, the average shift-work ratio. Scale restraint discourages not only intensive utilisation but also mechanisation: therefore a given net output would require a larger number of operatives. Most unfortunately, because of our original obsession with the special characteristics of the 'over-35's' we failed to ask for details of net output in the intermediate group.

We cannot prove that the above explanation is correct. But we accept the doctrine that, in principle, although theories of this kind can be disproved, they can never be proved beyond all doubt. We have shown that these statistical results are consistent with our theory, and we have tested some reasonably searching negative hypotheses. As a matter of fact, we may now reveal, there is considerable evidence from the industrial interviews to support the belief that the picture we have described is fairly accurate.† Not only did we come across numerous examples of large rambling factories employing not infrequently over a thousand operatives engaged on a wide variety of relatively labour-intensive activities operated on relatively low utilisation systems, but it was also suggested that some of the most outstanding examples of intensive capital utilisation were found in medium-sized factories producing no more than one, or perhaps two, final products.

Thus both of two famous confectionery manufacturers, Mars Ltd., and Cadburys Ltd., run shifts. Cadbury's, by any standard, is a very large enterprise, Mars is of middling size. In the Cadbury factory at Bournville the system involves only a relatively small all-male permanent night shift, whereas in the Mars factory at Slough all production has been based on a continuous three or four-shift system for a considerable number of years and the plant has been deliberately designed for

development occurs in a field with which the theory in question is particularly concerned, it is disturbing if some reasonable explanation, consistent with the theory, cannot be provided, *ex post*.

† Again, Mr Maclean at the time he conducted the interviews understood this group of problems rather better than the main author. He anticipated the significance of the large, diversified establishment with the relatively low shift-work ratio and directed specific inquiries to the point. Another explanation of the phenomenon, equally consistent with our basic theory, is that many of these establishments represent cases of vertical integration, i.e. the gathering into one factory of a number of processes related to a single end-product, which are otherwise carried out in separate specialist establishments. It seems to be the case that as processes are integrated, the chances of including activities whose production functions are unfavourable to shift-work increases. An interesting example was found in the ice-cream manufacturing industry.

this high rate of utilisation.† In other words the 'planned' rate of utilisation (which we are here able to observe directly as a result of collaboration by the two firms concerned) is clearly greater in Mars than in Cadbury's and it is significant therefore that the number of separate products made by Mars is very much less than the number made by Cadbury's. Total employment at Bournville is also, of course, much higher.

So much for the intra-industry comparisons; we now deploy our final series of tests of the scale hypothesis—the results of inter-industry regression analysis. Here we make no use of the division between 'over-35's' and other establishments, we simply correlate average net output per establishment in whole industries with the corresponding average shift-work ratios. In other words, the averages include many establishments with no shift-workers at all.

The theory predicts, it will be remembered, that the relationship between utilisation and the magnitude of maximum permissible output per plant should be non-linear. That is to say, as the scale of possible output increases, the strength of the effect on the chosen rate of utilisation should diminish. What sort of non-linear relationship should the theory predict between the average net output of the establishments of an industry and their average shift-work ratio? In a single-activity establishment, if the maximum permitted output is very large, and other conditions are suitable, maximum utilisation, according to the theory, can be achieved without difficulty. Then, if the maximum output is reduced, the situation will probably at first remain unchanged but as the restraint becomes increasingly severe the unit-requirement for the high-utilisation programmes will in due course fall below unity. These programmes, therefore, will first be degraded, then abandoned. Eventually, only the programme involving single-shifts and a low technique will be feasible.

The effect on the shift-work ratio is simple. There is only one activity; therefore any kind of shift system requires that all operatives be shift-workers: the shift-work ratio is either zero or 100%. The shift-work ratio for the industry, however, behaves rather differently. This we analyse in Fig. 7.1.

In Fig. 7.1, the single-establishment line embodies the jump in the shift-work ratio from zero to 100 when the scale of output passes a critical figure, which we here assume to be £200000 per annum. The other lines show the expected behaviour of the corresponding relationship between average net output per establishment and the average shift-work ratio of whole industries. The character of this relationship may be visualised by considering the position of an industry in which average net output is £200000 precisely: inevitably the industry will comprise some establishments with above-average output, all of whose

† For a short time, at the de-rationing of confectionery, Mars received permission, under a wartime Defence Regulation still in force then, to employ women production workers on the night shift and did in fact do so.

shift-work ratios will be 100, and some establishments with below-average output and shift-work ratios of zero. The average shift-work ratio in the two groups taken together will depend only on the distribution of employment between them. Such distributions are nearly always skewed to the right (i.e. there is usually a disproportionate amount of employment in the above-average sized firms), therefore the average shift-work ratio for an industry with average net output £200 000 is almost certain to be greater than 50 %. In an industry in which average net output is smaller, the proportion of firms with output exceeding £200 000 is smaller and so also their share in total employment. The average shift-work ratio will therefore decline in a smooth curve, as shown in the diagram. Conversely, as the average net output is raised, the proportion of employment in shift-working firms will rise, until at some very high figure of average net output, a position may be reached where there is no establishment which does not work shifts and the shift-work ratio of the industry becomes 100 %: in no circumstances, of course, can this figure be exceeded.

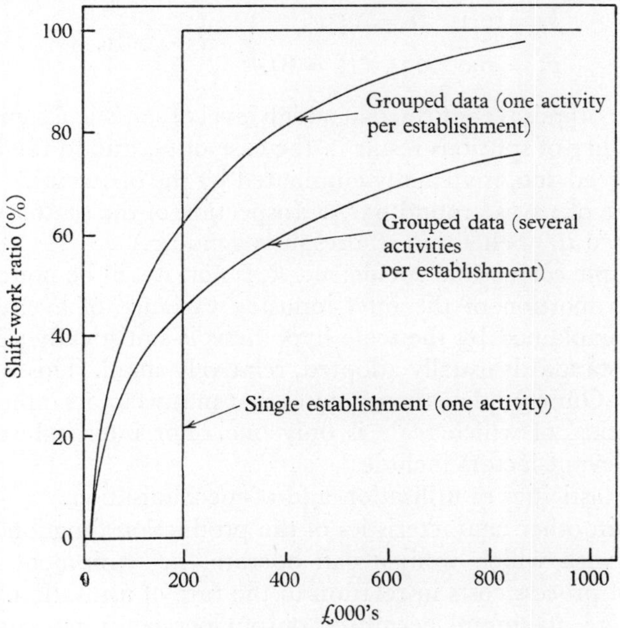

Fig. 7.1.

With more than one activity in each establishment, the picture remains essentially the same, but because shift-work ratios lying between zero and 100 % are now possible, the grouped-data curve will rise less rapidly.†

† It is not possible to generalise about the order in which activity programmes will be changed as the maximum scale of final output for each establishment is reduced, because this development, if it is carried out in the most profitable manner, must depend in a complicated way on the basic characteristics of the techniques of production, and of their susceptibility to degradation.

The hypothesis that the shift-work ratio will behave according to the lower curve in Fig. 7.1 may be tested by regression analysis, with the data from column 13 of Table I as the dependent variable and the data from column 10 of Table III as the determining variable, using a parabolic approximation to the curve predicted in the model. Writing r_{sw} for the industry shift-work ratio (col. 13, Table I) and x for average net output per establishment (col. 10, Table III), we fitted

$$r_{sw} = b_1 x - b_2 x^2 \qquad (7.1)$$

and obtained the following results:

$$\left.\begin{aligned} b_1 &= 0{\cdot}1 \quad (t = 14), \\ b_2 &= 0{\cdot}000034 \quad (t = 8). \end{aligned}\right\} \quad R = 0{\cdot}81.$$

Thus the hypothesis is confirmed at a high level of statistical significance. (The possibility of spurious result in the case of b_2, due to the fact that x cannot exceed **100**, is virtually eliminated by the observation that the highest value of x was around 65 %. Inspection of the scatter diagram also supported the belief that the result is genuine.)

The multiple correlation coefficient, R, is not, it will be noticed, very high: the proportion of the inter-industry variance of average shift-work ratios explained by the scale hypothesis is statistically significant but, by the standards usually adopted, relatively small. This is entirely satisfactory. Our complete theory states that many factors influence the observed ratios, of which scale is only one. For inter-industry comparisons, relevant factors include:

(1) The elasticities of utilisation and of mechanisation.

(2) Certain other characteristics of the production function, such as the facility with which women can operate the equipment and the behaviour of process costs in relation to the rate of utilisation.†

(3) Average maximum permitted output per plant as expressed in (i) average net output per establishment, and (ii) the average degree of diversification of production.

(4) The ratio of observed output to peak planned output.

Of the seven factors listed, only one, 3 (i), is included in the regression analysis: none of the others is susceptible to quantitative inter-industry comparison. If most of the variance in the shift-work ratio between industries were explained by factor 3 (i) one might be forced to infer that none of the others, in practice, was important.

Taking the evidence we have presented as a whole, one might venture to assert that while scale restraint is not by any means the only factor affecting capital utilisation, it may well be the most important one. This is a proposition which can neither be made precise nor proved; it is the expression of a subjective reaction to the evidence. It concludes our analysis of the Census of Production.

† This refers to the collection of factors discussed specifically in connection with the Chemical Industries discussed on p. 145 above.

7.5. The Ministry of Labour Inquiry

We have already explained† the problems involved in interpreting these figures. As compared with the Census of Production, they are probably biased, but we do not know for certain in which direction or to what extent. Two alternative assumptions have been described‡ and the results are given in Table 7.4. The 'range' in the Ministry of Labour column is our estimate of the limits within which the results would have fallen had they been obtained by applying the methods of the Census of Production of 1951 in the same set of industries in 1954.

It will be seen that the average shift-work ratio in manufacturing as a whole may have fallen by something of the order of five percentage points over the three years. However, during the same period average weekly working hours in manufacturing rose by about 1 %: therefore while the average relative rate of utilisation fell, the basic rate apparently rose. If we assume that capital used by the typical shift-worker is utilised two and a quarter times as intensively as capital used by other workers, the net effect of the two changes combined might be estimated to have reduced the average rate of fixed capital utilisation in manufacturing by perhaps two and one half per cent. If this development had represented a trend, the implications for the economy could be quite serious: for example, the rate of growth of manufacturing output corresponding to a given rate of growth of manufacturing capital might be as much as halved. We shall see in a moment that in fact the existence of a downward trend in capital utilisation is rather unlikely.

A glance at Table 7.4 will show that the main significant changes occurred in the industrial orders generically known as the metal-using—Industrial Orders VI, VII and VIII. It is common knowledge that these industries were operating at a very high level of activity in 1951 for a number of reasons associated directly or indirectly with the Korean war. However, this fact alone is not sufficient to explain the subsequent decline in shift-working and we should consider the theoretical implications of these results carefully. Our theory predicts that a decline in the *planned* peak-output rate of utilisation implies a decline in the incentive to utilise and/or a reduction in the average scale of peak-output per establishment. A decline in the incentive to utilise implies a rise in the real basic wage rate relative to output per man-hour and therefore a general decline in the rate of profit. A decline in average scale implies an increase in diversification relative to the secular trend of total output. Are we to believe that, due to such changes, the metal-using industries' shift-workers of 1951 were largely eliminated by means of an increase in capital stock sufficient to permit at least the same volume of output to be produced by day-work only?

The question is not quite so absurd as it sounds, because it is known that between 1951 and 1954 the stock of fixed capital in Order VI (Engineering), for example, rose by not much less than 20 %, while the

† Chapter 6, §6.4. ‡ P. 132 above.

Table 7.4. *Shift-work in manufacturing: larger establishments in Great Britain, 1951, and estimated range, 1954*

Percentages of operatives employed on shifts

	Industrial Order	September 1951†	April 1954‡	Change
III.	Bricks, glass, china, etc.	17	12 to 17	0 to −5
IV.	Chemicals, etc.	24	22 to 24	0 to −2
V.	Metal manufacture	40	36 to 42	+2 to −4
VI.	Engineering and electrical	23	5 to 6	−17 to −18
VII.	Vehicles	17	11 to 12§	−5 to −6
VIII.	Metal goods n.e.s.	12	6 to 8	−4 to −6
IX.	Precision instruments	2	3 to 4	+2 to +1
X.	Textiles	10	9 to 11	+1 to −1
XI.	Leather	1	1	0
XII.	Clothing	—	—	0
XIII.	Food, drink, tobacco	12	12 to 13	+1 to 0
XIV.	Wood and cork goods	2	½ to 1	−1 to −1½
XV.	Paper and printing	10	10 to 14	+4 to 0
XVI.	Other manufactures	23	16 to 22	−1 to −7
	All	16	10 to 12	−4 to −6

† Census of Production, 1951.

‡ Estimate of the comparable data based on figures published in the *Ministry of Labour Gazette*, October 1954. For method of estimation see text p. 132 above.

§ Adjusted to include an estimate for railway workshops, which are included by the Board of Trade, excluded by the Ministry of Labour.

volume of output rose by not much more than 10%. If we again make the assumption that shift-workers utilise capital 2¼ times as intensively as others, and if we take account of the small increase in average weekly hours which occurred in engineering, we can compute a decline in the average engineering capital-utilisation rate of about 12%—quite sufficient, therefore, to explain the gap between the change in output and the change in capital installed.†

Therefore we could also explain the observations by supposing that while output was at peak level in 1951, in 1954 demand was insufficient to support the peak output now enhanced by additions to capacity. When output is substantially below peak output, we have seen, the actual rate of utilisation must decline. If the changes observed were instead due to changes in planned utilisation, our theory would be confounded unless we could show that either the general level of profit margins in the engineering industry was exhibiting a declining secular

† For output and capital we use the same data as Reddaway and Smith, *Economic Journal* (March 1960). The method of estimating the decline in average utilisation is as follows:

Let h_t = utilisation rate in year t, in operating hours per annum and r_{swt} = shift-work ratio in year t.

Then $$h_t = [(2{\cdot}25 . r_{swt}) + (1 - r_{swt}) \times [\text{average hours per op. per year}].$$

The assumptions were:

$$h_{1951} = [(2{\cdot}25 \times 0{\cdot}17) + 0{\cdot}83] \times 2350 = 2850,$$
$$h_{1954} = [(2{\cdot}25 \times 0{\cdot}05) + 0{\cdot}95] \times 2375 = 2510.$$

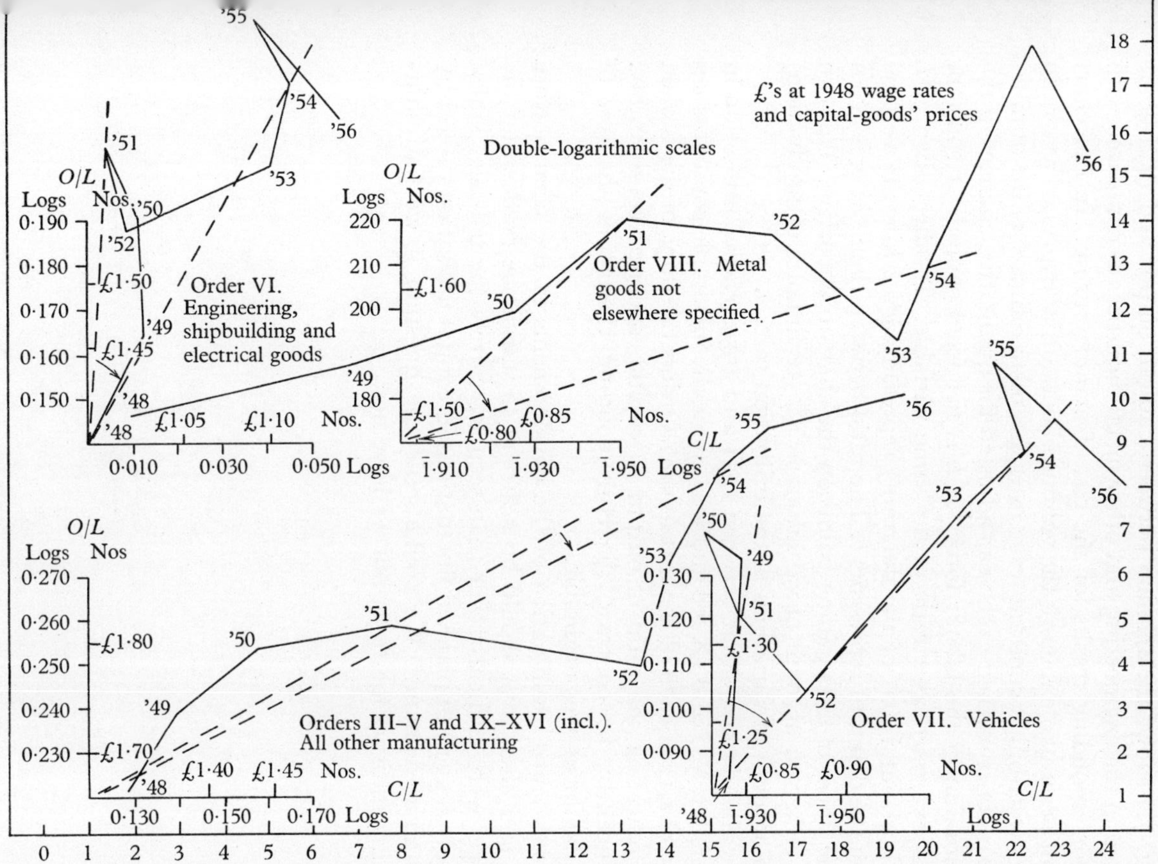

Fig. 7.2. Net output per unit of labour (O/L) and net fixed capital per unit of labour (C/L) in metal-using and other manufacturing industries, 1948 to 1956. *N.B.* (1) The same scale (1 cm = 0·010 log units = $2\frac{1}{2}$% change) has been used throughout, but, for convenience of comparison, origins vary, as indicated. The south and east edges of the base show a centimetre scale. (2) The broken lines indicate the effective capital–output ratios for 1951 and 1954 respectively. The arrows between them indicate the change in this ratio.

trend, or that the industry was becoming increasingly diversified relative to the volume of output. All the evidence in our possession tends to negate both suppositions. By contrast, there is considerable evidence that the phenomenon was, in fact, due to a recession in demand.

Fig. 7.2 shows the relation between capital, output and man-hours worked in the engineering and other metal industries as compared with the corresponding results for the rest of manufacturing. In this chart output per unit of labour is the volume of net output expressed as a ratio of the wage-bill at constant wage rates, i.e. of an estimate of the number of man-hours worked each year adjusted for qualitative changes in the composition of the labour force. C/L is net fixed capital, at constant prices, expressed as a ratio of the same variable. In effect then, C/L (the horizontal axis of the diagram) represents q/h while the vertical axis of the diagram represents v. The ratio between them, vh/q, is given by the slopes of lines joining points on the chart to the origin. This can vary either on account of variations in v/q (techniques of production) or on account of variations in the utilisation rate, h.

We already know that between 1951 and 1954 relative utilisation in Orders VI, VII and IX fell and we can see the inevitable consequences in the chart: in each of the metal-using Orders the slope of the broken line, reflecting the ratio of output to capital, declined considerably. Significantly, by contrast, the corresponding change in the rest of manufacturing was negligible.

A moment's examination of the developments in the Chart before 1951 and after 1954 should be sufficient to satisfy the reader that the changes were cyclical rather than secular. Surely the tell-tale 'kinks' strongly suggest unplanned fluctuations in capital utilisation caused by fluctuating demand? We could settle the question if we had shift-working statistics for 1955, but we have not.

CHAPTER 8

RESULTS OF SPECIAL INQUIRIES

8.1. Introduction

In this chapter we set out the results of various special inquiries which were instigated to test particular corollaries of the main theory. These inquiries, in order, were:

(i) An inquiry conducted by Employment Exchanges in order to investigate regional and geographical aspects.

(ii) Statistics provided by the Factory Inspectorate, concerning the double-day shift-system.

(iii) An inquiry of bus transport undertakings designed to find out to what extent difficulties in this field functioned as an independent obstacle to shift-work.

(iv) An inquiry of trade unions designed to discover general attitudes, methods of negotiating shift-work premiums and to assess the extent, if any, to which trade union policy constituted an independent obstacle.

8.2. Inquiries Conducted by Employment Exchanges

These inquiries were initiated for certain rather specific purposes. We wanted to see if we could discover tendencies for shift-work in one firm in an area to lead to a general spread of the practice: we knew, for example, that in Grays, Essex, shift-working, much under the influence of the cement industries, is a generally accepted practice, while by contrast in Luton, where the main employers, Vauxhall's, do not require shift-work from the majority of their operatives, other firms in the area find it difficult to obtain shift-work labour. We wanted to find, if we could, other examples of such patterns.

We also wished to see if there was a greater tendency to adopt shift-work in New Towns, where factories were still being built, than in towns where much of the industrial equipment is considerably depreciated. Finally, for general purposes, we posed the 'open-ended' question 'Why was shift-work instituted?' and addressed it to a widely spread, non-random sample of shift-working firms.

The answers on the first point proved inconclusive. It seems to be the case that, apart from steel towns and mining villages, whole communities where shift-work represents the general way of life are, in the United Kingdom, relatively rare. Many industrial interviews strongly suggested nevertheless that when one large employer in an area institutes shifts, or alternatively does not, the elasticities of utilisation facing other employers are affected, but the data we obtained here failed to prove or disprove this.

We found no evidence of an unusual amount of shift-work in New Towns, a result quite consistent with the final version of our theory (which implies that what happens in New Towns will depend mainly on the production functions and scale restraints in the industries which happen to settle in them), although until we had developed this theory, we definitely expected to find some difference. Indeed, this negative result was one of the clues which led us to the later ideas.

The replies to the final question were heterogeneous but illuminating. In principle it was put in the 'open-ended' manner, although, probably mistakenly, respondents were assisted by having a number of alternative possible types of answer suggested to them. However, internal evidence indicates that the bias thus imparted was not excessive.

One hundred and fifty firms answered the question and their replies can be divided into three broad categories, about an equal number falling into each. Thus, one-third of the replies clearly indicated that the primary cause of shift-work was economy of prime cost ('continuous process', 'to save process costs', 'necessary for production', and so on). One-third indicated, more or less directly, that long-run capital economies were involved ('maximum machine utilisation', 'to reduce overheads', or, in one case, the succinct reply 'economics'). The last third consisted of a wide variety of replies involving some kind of short-run consideration; according to these replies, shifts were started to 'meet an increase in demand', 'to overcome bottle-necks', 'to meet production requirements', 'to obtain maximum output from existing plant', or simply 'for maximum production'.

It is tempting to regard the answers in the second category as representing retrospective explanations of the considerations which led to the determination of the planned rate of utilisation at the time when plant was designed, and to regard the answers in the third category as representing explanations of circumstances which had led to 'unplanned' changes. But we have seen that even at the theoretical level, such interpretation is difficult, because the planned rate of utilisation must in the last analysis relate to peak demand conditions, and it is difficult to believe that all these firms had entirely failed to anticipate fluctuation. More likely, probably, it was implicit in the original plans that peak demand should be met by temporary increases in utilisation but that later, when faced with the question 'why did you institute shifts?', the respondent has described the occasion of the event rather than its deeper cause.

On further investigation the foregoing explanation does not appear entirely satisfactory. We asked the reason for *starting* shift-work. We were answered 'to meet increased demand'. Yet at least half of the firms giving this kind of answer reported in an adjacent column that they had first started shift-work more than ten years ago; not a few had commenced the practice more than fifty years ago! During the interval, much of their plant could therefore have been replaced several times over, which means that the interpretation of the replies is necessarily ambiguous. The fault lay in our wording of the question; we should have asked first why were shifts originally started and secondly why they were still going. For it seems that, not unsurprisingly, many firms discover the advantages of intensive capital utilisation from the initial stimulus of a short-run development. Demand increases unexpectedly, a second shift is introduced with the existing equipment, and when the time comes for the equipment to be replaced, almost unthinkingly the design of the new plant assumes that shift-work will be continued.

Moreover, it is in fact a corollary of our theory that an increase in demand will often cause both a short- and a long-term increase in utilisation. For the theory says that planned utilisation will be depressed by scale restraint. A short-run increase in the level of demand for the output of a particular firm implies, if it is maintained, a long-run easement of the scale restraint. Therefore it is natural that, when new plant is designed to meet the enhanced level of demand on a long-run basis, shift-working, which did not seem profitable when the old plant was built, now becomes feasible.

There is, however, another way of looking at the replies as a whole which would suggest they tended to contradict the fundamental propositions of our theoretical approach. As already indicated, the inquiry was designed at a time when the theory was relatively under-developed, and should not therefore be regarded as a precise experiment to test prediction. Nevertheless, it might well be argued that if a theory assumes that the motive for taking decisions in a particular field is the maximisation of the rate of return on capital, then replies to any open-ended questionnaire should, if they are to support this axiom, make specific reference to profit rates, or at least to profit. In other words, in reply to the question 'why were shifts started?' our theory could be said to predict that the reply should be 'to increase the rate of return on capital', or 'to increase profits'. This, however, is rather naïve. The habit of speaking of profit as a cost is so ingrained, so widely practised by accountants and so necessary to the political ethic of capitalism that business men rarely speak of maximising profit, although they often speak of minimising cost. If the rate of output from a given quantity of capital is doubled and the utilisation incentive is positive, the rate of profit is increased, or prices are reduced. But whether prices are actually reduced or no, the development will be referred to as 'reducing overheads' or 'making more economical use of expensive equipment'. We are not complaining of these euphemisms. We are merely pointing out that they are used. In a capitalist system profit is both a surplus and a cost. It is a surplus on current operations, a cost of growth. If profit, both short-run and long-run, is for ideological reasons nearly always referred to as cost, we should expect multiple shift-working to be generally referred to as a cost-reducing, rather than as a profit-increasing arrangement.

We conclude that while the inquiries described in this section did not constitute a strong test of our fundamental theoretical conceptions, they did little to discredit and much to illuminate them.

8.3. Statistics Provided by the Factory Inspectorate

We have explained the origin of these figures above.† They are displayed in Tables 8.1, 8.2 and 8.3, and require little further analysis. Our main interest in them is that they show that although the number of authorised two-shift systems for women and juveniles has been increasing, it is still relatively small. By far the great majority of shift-workers are adult males and the double-day shift, although much advocated by policy makers, probably affects less than 3 % of manufacturing capital.

Table 8.1. *Two-shift authorisations current at August 1954*

Industry	Permanent	Temporary	Totals
Engineering	271	3	274
Clothing	12	1	13
Wool	56	—	56
Cotton	163	1	164
Hosiery	94	2	96
Other textiles	165	1	166
Glass	48	—	48
Food and drink	148	1	149
Paper and cardboard	55	4	59
Brickmaking	13	—	13
Rubber	34	—	34
Woodworking	11	—	11
Miscellaneous	252	3	255
Totals	1322	16	1338

8.4. Bus Services

Shift-work means that employees will often be travelling to and from their place of work at unusual hours. This does not apply with all shift systems. It is a problem mainly facing the double-day shift and three-shift systems, where there is a turn-round of workers at 6 a.m. and 10 p.m. The day-and-night shift system is much less affected: the day shift arrive and depart during the normal working day, rarely starting before 7 a.m. or finishing after 9 p.m., while the night shift has usually started by 10 p.m. and rarely finishes before 6.30 a.m.

In order to discover whether or not capital utilisation is hindered by a lack of adequate transport facilities for shift-workers, a survey was made of thirty-seven cities and towns from all parts of the country and representing as many different urban types as possible.

† Chapter 6, §6.8.

Table 8.2. *Two-shift authorisations issued for years 1946 to August 1954*

Industry	1946			1947			1948			1949			1950			1951			1952			1953			1954			Total for period		
	Permanent	Temporary	Total	Permanent	Temporary	Total	Permanent	Temporary	Total	Permanent	Temporary	Total	Permanent	Temporary	Total	Permanent	Temporary	Total	Permanent	Temporary	Total	Permanent	Temporary	Total	Permanent	Temporary	Total	Permanent	Temporary	Total
Engineering	30	8	38	55	13	68	17	3	20	19	2	21	17	3	20	16	—	16	24	—	24	17	1	18	25	2	27	220	32	252
Clothing	—	—	—	—	—	—	1	1	2	2	—	2	3	—	3	3	—	3	—	—	—	1	—	1	2	—	2	12	1	13
Wool	12	1	13	13	7	20	6	—	6	11	—	11	12	—	12	1	—	1	7	8	15	7	3	10	4	—	4	73	19	92
Cotton	23	2	25	26	5	31	22	3	25	28	1	29	18	2	20	21	4	25	14	—	14	26	1	27	12	—	12	190	18	208
Hosiery	14	2	16	10	3	13	6	2	8	13	4	17	8	3	11	10	2	12	3	4	7	4	3	7	7	1	8	75	24	99
Other textiles	31	12	43	36	4	40	16	3	19	21	1	22	18	—	18	9	2	11	11	3	14	29	1	30	12	—	12	183	26	209
Glass	6	7	13	14	3	17	2	4	6	8	1	9	8	—	8	4	1	5	2	—	2	4	—	4	9	—	9	57	16	73
Food and drink	28	7	35	23	7	30	13	2	15	33	2	35	33	3	36	20	4	24	12	1	13	25	5	30	11	3	14	199	33	232
Paper and cardboard	13	5	18	13	6	19	6	1	7	6	2	8	4	3	7	6	1	7	6	1	7	7	3	10	5	3	8	66	25	91
Brickmaking	1	—	1	3	—	3	—	—	—	1	—	1	—	—	—	—	—	—	1	—	1	2	1	3	1	—	1	9	1	10
Rubber	5	—	5	5	—	5	3	—	3	5	—	5	4	—	4	4	—	4	1	—	1	7	—	7	4	—	4	38	—	38
Woodworking	4	1	5	1	1	2	1	—	1	1	—	1	—	—	—	2	—	2	—	—	—	1	—	1	2	—	2	12	2	14
Miscellaneous	58	13	71	78	16	94	36	3	39	37	1	38	39	1	40	25	5	30	25	4	29	33	8	41	34	3	37	365	54	419
	225	58	283	277	65	342	129	22	151	185	14	199	164	15	179	121	19	140	106	21	127	163	26	189	128	12	140	1499	251	1750

Table 8.3. *Permanent authorisations revoked 1946 to August 1954*

Industry	Year and cause																																							
	1946				1947				1948				1949				1950				1951				1952				1953				1954				Totals for period			
	Disuse	Factory closed down	Not stated	Total	Disuse	Factory closed down	Not stated	Total	Disuse	Factory closed down	Not stated	Total	Disuse	Factory closed down	Not stated	Total	Disuse	Factory closed down	Not stated	Total	Disuse	Factory closed down	Not stated	Total	Disuse	Factory closed down	Not stated	Total	Disuse	Factory closed down	Not stated	Total	Disuse	Factory closed down	Not stated	Total	Disuse	Factory closed down	Not stated	Total
Engineering	—	—	—	—	1	—	—	1	—	—	—	—	1	2	—	3	1	1	—	2	2	—	1	3	6	1	—	7	9	1	—	10	2	1	—	3	22	6	1	29
Clothing	—	—	—	—	—	—	—	—	—	—	—	—	—	—	—	—	—	—	—	—	—	—	—	—	—	—	—	—	—	—	—	—	1	—	—	1	1	—	—	1
Wool textiles	—	—	—	—	—	—	—	—	—	—	—	—	—	—	—	—	—	—	—	—	1	—	—	1	1	—	—	1	2	—	—	2	—	—	—	—	4	—	—	4
Cotton	—	—	—	—	—	—	—	—	—	—	—	—	1	—	1	2	—	—	—	—	—	—	—	—	10	—	—	10	7	1	—	8	1	—	—	1	19	1	1	21
Hosiery	—	—	—	—	—	—	—	—	—	—	—	—	1	—	—	1	1	—	—	1	1	1	—	2	2	—	—	2	1	1	—	2	1	—	—	1	7	2	—	9
Other textiles	—	—	1	1	—	—	—	—	—	—	—	—	—	—	—	—	1	—	—	1	—	—	—	—	2	1	—	3	3	1	—	4	3	1	—	4	9	3	1	13
Glass	—	—	—	—	—	—	—	—	—	—	—	—	—	—	—	—	1	—	—	1	2	—	1	3	—	—	—	—	1	—	—	1	1	—	—	1	5	—	1	6
Food and drink	—	—	—	—	—	—	—	—	—	—	—	—	1	1	1	3	3	3	—	6	2	4	1	7	4	5	—	9	5	1	—	6	1	—	1	2	16	14	3	33
Paper and cardboard	—	—	—	—	—	—	—	—	—	—	—	—	—	—	—	—	1	—	—	1	—	—	—	—	2	—	—	2	2	—	—	2	2	—	1	3	7	—	1	8
Brickmaking	—	—	—	—	—	—	—	—	—	—	—	—	—	—	—	—	—	—	—	—	—	—	—	—	—	—	—	—	—	—	—	—	—	—	—	—	—	—	—	—
Rubber	—	—	—	—	—	—	—	—	—	—	—	—	1	—	1	2	—	—	—	—	1	1	—	2	1	—	—	1	—	—	—	—	—	—	—	—	3	1	1	5
Woodworking	—	—	—	—	—	—	—	—	—	—	—	—	—	—	—	—	—	—	—	—	—	—	—	—	1	—	—	1	—	—	—	—	—	—	—	—	1	—	—	1
Miscellaneous	—	—	—	—	1	—	—	1	2	—	1	3	—	1	4	5	—	4	—	4	—	—	2	2	7	2	1	10	10	—	1	11	2	2	1	5	22	9	10	41
Yearly totals	—	—	1	1	2	—	—	2	2	—	1	3	5	4	7	16	8	8	—	16	9	6	5	20	36	9	1	46	40	5	1	46	14	4	3	21	116	36	19	171

Four questions were asked:

(1) How many scheduled routes are operated?

(2) How many services start before 6 a.m. and finish after 10 p.m.?

(3) Do you operate special services for shift-workers?

(4) Have you been approached since the end of the war by a firm in your area for special services for shift-workers, and what was the result?

The results are tabulated in Table 8.4.

The proportion of services which start early and finish late is approximately a third of all scheduled services. This, when taken with an estimated 500 special shift services and the apparent willingness of the bus companies to help in this matter, suggests that transport is not in fact a major obstacle. However, there may still be difficulties in individual cases especially in country districts. On the whole, services start later and finish earlier in the country and of course workers tend to be more scattered.

As to question (4), a substantial proportion of the forty-four replies indicated that the respondent had been approached, and had provided services. Eight volunteered the information that they would welcome an extension of shift-work in order to ease the peak load. Some of the statements are worth quoting. 'We would only be too pleased to provide services outside the normal peak times for any special requirements of shift-workers' (Luton).† 'It would help us considerably if more use was made of the shift system at factories, as we should be relieved of a certain amount of traffic at our heavy loading periods which would be spread more evenly through the day.' Bristol, Gloucester and Leeds were among the other towns that referred to the benefits of shift-work from the point of view of the transport companies.

The willingness of the transport companies to provide special shift services if the need for them is proved is underlined by some of the comments made in other replies. Leeds—'such requests are invariably conceded', while Barnsley stated that 'the number of special services for industrial workers has been greatly increased since the war'.

One licensing authority considered that 'the real obstacle to any extension of shift-working is not the inconvenient timing of public transport but rather a reluctance on the part of the workers to engage in shift-working because of the disturbance to family life. It is no new experience to find the real reason for resisting shift-working masked by an argument that public transport arrangements are unsuitable. The licensing authority holds the view that if shift-working could be arranged on a comprehensive basis it might solve some of the difficulties experienced at peak hours by operators of public transport systems.'

† Yet the Works Manager of a major employer in Luton whom we happened to interview stated emphatically that transport was his major headache in connection with shift-work! We believe he *thought* it was, but beyond that one cannot go.

Table 8.4. *Results of Transport Inquiry*

Area	No. of scheduled routes operated†	No. of routes on which normal services start before 6 a.m. and finish after 10 p.m.	No. of special services for shift-workers
North			
Tyneside and Sunderland	201	45	62
Teesside	279	60	10
North-west			
Preston	28	19	—‡
Manchester	77	16	—‡
Blackburn	38	6	—‡
Warrington	40	10	3
Accrington	45	5	—‡
Carlisle	39	4	1
Yorkshire			
Leeds	59	42	2
Hull	43	15	—
Sheffield	51	36	2
Rotherham	35	25	12
Barnsley	25	21	74
West Midlands			
Birmingham	64	52	—‡
Coventry	23	13	18
Nuneaton	55	13	—‡
Kidderminster	58	4	—‡
East Midlands			
Nottingham	193	143	18
Leicester	166	19	8
Derby	60	34	2
Lincoln	59	—	—
Oxford	65	—	5
Eastern			
Bedford	54	2	1
Norwich	64	4	1
Peterborough	31	2	—
Luton	29	12	8
Western and Southern			
Bristol	60	33	—‡
Plymouth	33	14	—
Swindon	9	—	—
Exeter	7	2	—
Gloucester	10	—	—
Portsmouth	58	16	—
S. Wales			
Newport	66	19	11
Swansea	74	37	13
Scotland			
Glasgow	81	53	—‡
Dundee	35	4	—
Kirkcaldy	19	6	—‡
Total	2333	786	

† Public stage carriage services.

‡ These companies operated special shift services but did not state the number.

8.5. Trade Unions†

The majority of workers engaged in manufacturing industry are either members of a trade union or work in factories covered by trade union agreements. The attitude of the trade unions to shift-work is thus obviously of great importance. Any discussion of this problem is complicated by the structure of the trade union movement in this country. The T.U.C. is the only organisation which can be said to represent the collective voice of the trade unions, and representatives of the T.U.C. did make a statement before the Committee of Inquiry into Double Day Shift-Working in 1947 to the effect that they were not opposed to shift-working should it prove to be in the national interest. The T.U.C. however is not a law-making body. At best it can only advise and exhort its members to follow a certain course of action and it has never initiated any policy or propaganda about shift-work. The question of shift-working is one on which some individual unions have formulated their own policy, by and large with very little publicity. This state of affairs is not surprising for the question varies greatly in importance between industries and on the whole its introduction tends to be gradual rather than sudden. Also the question of what to do about shift-working has arisen at different times in different industries. This does not mean that there is no room for a generally agreed policy among the unions, it means that shift-working has not aroused sufficiently widespread interest at any one time for the unions to get together and formulate an approach to it. In many unions the question is academic either because the industries they cover must of necessity work on shifts or because there is little likelihood of shift-working in the foreseeable future. Examples of the former are numerous, iron and steel, chemicals, glass, etc. Examples of the latter are clothing and brush manufacture. Where isolated cases of shift-work occur in an industry where it is rare, the usual procedure is for a special agreement to be made at the factory level.

In order to carry the inquiry further, we wrote directly to fifteen unions asking about their views on shift-working. Eight unions referred us to their national agreements. Sometimes these agreements have a general observation on shift-working but normally they merely set out the rates of pay, hours and conditions to be observed for shift-working. The 1945 agreement between the unions affiliated to the Engineering Joint Trades Movement and the Engineering and Allied Employers National Federation opened with the statement that 'The introduction of the system shall be for the purpose of absorbing unemployed'. This was part of one of the pre-war agreements and disappeared in later agreements which contained only the statements of wages, hours and conditions of work.

The national agreement for the Furniture trade states that 'when it is necessary to operate a furniture or bedding factory on a double-day

† For sources, see Chapter 6, §6.7.

or three-shift system in order to expedite products of national importance the following minimum working conditions should apply....'

The following unions commented on their attitude to shift-working:

Transport and General Workers. 'Broadly speaking, the attitude of our union is that where shift-work is necessary because of the nature of the industry or service, it should be worked. It is also necessary however to face the fact that shift-working imposes a considerable strain, not only on the worker but on his family. Social life and family life are alike disrupted. In addition, the provision of meals, etc., at special hours means an additional expense in the household budget, and in some cases this may be considerable. For all these reasons we require that some extra payment should be made to workers who are required to work on shifts.'

Amalgamated Engineering Union. 'The A.E.U. is not opposed to shift-work where it can be shown to be necessary.'

Amalgamated Union of Foundry Workers. 'The official attitude of our Unions to shift-working is that we realise that in our present industrial circumstances it is a necessity. We would prefer all work to be done in a normal day shift but this is not practical with the present structure of industry.'

Scottish Carpet Trade and Factory Workers Union. 'The official attitude of this Trade Union to shift-working is that we accept it as part of the effort which was made to put the industry back into competitive business after the war, during which the industry was almost completely closed down. Also we realised that the expensive machinery with which the industry was re-equipped after the war could not be profitably run for only 45 hours per week.'

Three unions, the Associated Society of Moulders and Foundry Workers, The National Society of Pottery Workers and the Power Loom Weavers and Textile Workers Association made no comment other than that they accepted the principle of shift-work.

There have not been many cases of outright opposition to shift-working, and the most important exception is found, needless to say, in Cotton. The Cotton unions were not faced with the question of shift-working until the years immediately following the end of World War II but they then reacted strongly against it. They felt that shift-work was alien to their whole conception of life. Thus the report of the Amalgamated Weavers Association for the year ending 31 March 1951 stated that 'The Lancashire Textile Operatives Union had been averse to the operation of double-day shifts and were most definitely opposed to any night shift-working. After numerous discussions, however, policy had later to be modified, and in order to encourage the installation of new machinery it was admitted that single shift-working would be uneconomic. This change in attitude was influenced by the stringency of the war years and the pressure exerted by the Government in conferences held in Manchester and Bolton.' Opposition to *night-work* was continued until the end of 1955. In the words of Mr Lewis Wright, the general secretary, this was 'the first time in the history of the union, going back more than 100 years, that the principle of treble shifts had been accepted' and the decision was finally reached after the issue had been 'very hotly debated'. Union approval of treble shift-working was however dependent on a closed shop for night shift-workers and on 'certain terms and conditions which only the most up to date and efficient companies will be able to meet'. This series of talks broke down in November 1955 over the question of the closed shop which the employers refused to accept, but at least the principle of treble shift-work had at last been established.

The fact that the unions and Employers Federation in the Cotton Industry had been unable to reach general agreement did not preclude the introduction of shift-work in particular cases. Forty-seven weaving mills were operating on a double-day shift before the 1950 agreement and one in the Wigan area introduced a three-shift system while the 1955 negotiations were still in progress. The operatives had voted unanimously in its favour and the local trade union had given its approval.

The other sections of the industry, spinning, carding, etc., followed a similar development, and the factors underlying the opposition of the cotton unions to shift-work are basically that the cotton areas are conservatively minded and there was no tradition for shift-work; that the introduction of shift-work threatened to be rapid and extensive; and that, a large proportion of the workers being female, the system would have to be the relatively unattractive double-day shift. Shift-work in the cotton industry would change the habits of life of whole societies and would not, as in engineering, be spread over the country in individual factories. The engineering industry works in close contact with industries which have traditionally worked shifts such as iron and steel and the metal-using industries. In cotton the concentration of the industry in particular areas meant that there was little or no experience of shift-work in those areas. The suddenness and possible extent of the change when compared with other industries must be stressed. It was not just a case of introducing a small night shift as in many other industries, but rather a change affecting the whole mill. Thus it is not entirely surprising that the cotton unions should have followed a different path from the rest of the trade union movement. The consequences have been discussed in Chapter 2.

Although there is no official trade union policy on shift-work in general, the various unions have much the same approach to shift-work. With the exception of cases such as cotton, the question has not led to any great controversy. Shift-work is a question that has been faced as and when it arose. The remark of the Amalgamated Union of Foundry Workers above that 'we would prefer all work to be done on the normal day shift' is a true reflection of the attitudes of most of the unions. The trade union movement does not welcome shift-work with open arms, but, with odd exceptions, neither does it act as a barrier;

rather it accepts shift-work as an unfortunate but necessary development of our modern industrial society. The position is summed up in the words of Mr J. Crawford, Chairman of the T.U.C. Production and Scientific Advisory Committee: 'Shift-work is a matter which solved itself by adjustment in the past and presumably will continue to do so.'

In order to understand fully the position of the trade union movement it is necessary to define the aims of the unions. The primary function of the union is to protect and further the interests of its members. If the shorter hours and/or bonus payments generally attendant on shift-work are regarded purely as a compensation for the inconvenience of shift-work then the worker is no better off as a result of the change. If wages are regarded as a payment for the disability of work, the shorter hours and bonus payments may be regarded as a payment for the greater disability of shift-work, in the same way as a less attractive type of work might have a higher wage rate. To the worker, the higher weekly wage on shifts is often sufficiently attractive to overcome any dislike of shift-work, but the trade unions do not define the interests of their members in purely monetary terms, as is shown by their attitude on overtime and piece rates. They are also concerned with the status of the worker in society and his development as an individual. But even in cotton, one suspects, had the technical characteristics† of the industry permitted the payment of higher premiums and had the change come more gradually, opposition would have been much reduced.

† See Chapter 2, §2.13.

CHAPTER 9

INDUSTRIAL CASE STUDIES†

9.1. Treatment of Non-Metalliferous Mining Products

The industries of this order have in common some form of heat treatment, which includes a chemical change, as a central feature of the manufacturing processes. On the output side, they are responsible for a wide variety of consumer and producer commodities, ranging from fine bone china at one extreme to Portland cement at the other: nevertheless, a large proportion of their total sales by value represents producers' goods, such as glass, building bricks or cement, which are capable in principle of considerable standardisation. There exists here, therefore, a permanent possibility of severe price-competition and a substantial probability that in the long run a small number of above-averagely efficient firms will drive out their rivals by competition or merger. Extensive mergers have already occurred in the case of cement and flat glass, and competitive growth of the Fletton industry is producing a similar effect in the case of building bricks; important implications from the point of view of our investigation will become apparent below.

There are two qualifications to the foregoing generalisations. First, there is a major technical distinction, with important economic consequences, between the industries making glass and glass products, and the rest. To make glass, a solid material, mainly sand, is slowly melted, chemically changed, fused, and then resolidified by cooling fairly rapidly. By contrast, in the 'kiln' industries, a semi-liquid mixture of clay and other products, having been won and prepared, is solidified and chemically changed by a long process of firing in the kiln. A kiln can be tended by a man and a boy, but a glass furnace yields a steady supply of molten glass which must be regularly taken off for moulding and cooling by a considerable team of workers who may themselves require the aid of additional machinery on a substantial scale. Hence, glass manufacture represents *par excellence* the case where extensive shift-working is favoured by the existence of major economies in prime cost (fuel); the 'kiln' industries do not.

The second qualification is that although many of the products of this group of industries are relatively homogeneous as to use, they are often heavy in weight relative to value and often require heavy raw materials. There will then be a tendency for the plants to be located *both*

† For an account of the nature and purpose of these studies, see Chapter 6, § 6.9.

near the source of the raw materials *and* near the market for the end product (an obvious exception lies in china and earthenware). This transport barrier has the effect of initially preventing nation-wide competition and inhibiting concentration until the stage of development is reached where new techniques sufficiently reduce production costs relative to transport costs; then, as we shall see, the transport barrier may rudely be broken and concentration proceed apace. But before this happens, the industry is faced with a large number of small local markets which militate against the exploitation of large scale, mechanised techniques of production and create a general condition of imperfect competition.

9.2. GLASS

As already indicated, glass manufacture is a case where considerable economies of prime cost—in this case fuel for the melting furnace—are to be obtained from continuous as against intermittent working. The economies in question may be so important that were they not exploited, the gross profits earned by a plant might be as much as halved. Nevertheless, glass making is also frequently a highly mechanised process and we shall find below that we can adequately explain the shift-working results for the industry in terms of capital theory alone, remembering merely that fuel-economy is yet another factor, albeit an important one, pulling in favour of shift-work.

About one-third of the output by value of flat glass is plate glass, i.e. flat glass finished by polishing.† There is a fairly wide range of qualities of plate glass, and the value per foot is greater for the larger sheets. However, at the present time, practically the whole of the nation's annual requirements of plate glass can be made on a single machine working continuous shifts. In the manufacture of sheet and rolled glass, on the other hand, the optimum scale of the production unit is not particularly great, but the commodity is relatively homogeneous as to use. Fairly highly mechanised methods of production of flat glass, particularly of the sheet and rolled varieties, began to be introduced in Europe at the end of the nineteenth century, and at one point the British domestic industry was nearly destroyed by intensive foreign competition: ultimately a mere handful of firms would be required to supply the whole west European area and it was touch and go whether any would be located in the United Kingdom. In the event, by 1900 only two important British firms were still in existence: Chance Brothers and Pilkington Brothers of St Helen's, Lancashire. Both firms controlled a number of large establishments. They struggled in intense technical and commercial rivalry over the next twenty-five years, but Pilkingtons' steadily established greater and greater ascendancy. Fairly soon after World War II, Chances' agreed to a merger; by the early 1950's they had been fully amalgamated with Pilkingtons', who are now

† The advent of float glass may have changed the picture described in this paragraph, since going to press.

the only producers of flat glass in this country. As already noted, it is not so much the case that with the latest machinery the technically most efficient size of the production unit for sheet and rolled glass is inordinately large as that, from the relatively undifferentiable nature of the product, any firm which for one reason or another develops an edge over the others can drive out competition; Pilkington Brothers' position today is almost entirely due to their superior technical efficiency and financial prowess in the past.†

The existence of the Pilkingtons' monopoly has embarrassing statistical consequences for this or any other similar inquiry employing data from the Census of Production, for it means that no data relating to flat glass production as such can legally be published. The industry is therefore statistically 'scrambled' with the whole of the Census Trade 'Glass other than Containers', which includes, in addition to flat glass, a host of non-flat miscellaneous products, the gross value of whose sales is as great as that of flat glass itself (for further details, see below). The inquiry is therefore much indebted to Messrs Pilkingtons' for providing certain information which proved of critical value in building up the interpretation which follows.

In 1951, the Census trade 'Glass other than Containers' covered some 300 industrial establishments in Great Britain. Of these, only fifty are shown in Table I as doing any shift-work at all. But these fifty establishments were responsible for as much as three-quarters of the total net output of the trade and for some 70 % of the operative employment; on average they employed about 500 operatives per establishment, compared with the mere forty or fifty or so which was typical in the remainder of the trade. (Employment in some of the Pilkingtons' plants runs into the thousands.) It is clear that the group of fifty shift-working establishments in the 1951 Census was largely dominated by the group of eight factories which constituted the nation's flat glass industry—i.e. the establishments now controlled by Pilkingtons'—together with the single plant in which the national supply of electric light bulbs is produced on the notorious 'ribbon machine', and a handful of others. Now it happens that in the production of flat glass a considerable proportion of the total labour force will normally be employed not in the actual process of glass-making but in various ancillary processes such as cutting, sorting, packing, transport and maintenance. Hence, although 95 % of the operatives employed in the central process must work in shifts (see above), as many as half the *total* operatives are able to work on 'days'. As we shall see this is a not uncharacteristic situation in a number of industries—in effect, the data favour shift-work in the central process but not, in the existing state of machinery design and technical knowledge, in the ancillary processes. In consequence, in this

† This passage results from conversations with Miss Leslie Cook, whose work in The Cambridge University Industrial Research Group resulted in the publication of *The Effects of Mergers*, by Ruth Cohen and Leslie Cook (London, 1958). Neither Miss Cook nor Messrs Pilkington (who considerably assisted the inquiry), however, can be held responsible for it.

case the distinction in our statistics of the 'over-35 %' shift-working plants fails to be helpful, since shift-working establishments organised in the characteristic manner just described will tend to be found in significant numbers lying rather closely on either side of the dividing line, and moderate differences in their observed shift-working ratios will not reflect real differences in the intensity of utilisation of the central plant; this might well have been working 24 hours a day in all the cases. Thus in the present example, the mean shift-work ratio in the shift-working establishments with shift-work ratios between zero and 35 % was 26 %, which indicates a modal or 'typical' figure of perhaps as high as 30 %. Conversely, had the over 35 % group been dominated statistically by a significant number of firms in which the ancillary processes as well as the central process had in fact been put on to shifts (as was the case at the electric light bulb plant) we would have expected to observe a mean shift-work ratio for the whole group of the order of 75 %; the actual figure was no higher than 53 %, indicating a mode of say 40 %. The over 35 % group and the 'intermediate' group are therefore much better considered as a single statistical unit, and for this reason a special attempt has been made in Table 9.1 to estimate net output and wages in the intermediate group in this trade despite the absence of the relevant data in the primary tables.†

It will be seen that the table suggests that not only is the difference between the mean shift-working ratio in the intensive and intermediate groups relatively modest, but also that net output and earnings per man were in fact higher on average in the latter group than in the former. If, however, the first two rows of the table are amalgamated, we observe what is shown in Table 9.2. Thus the shift-working group as a whole, mainly producers of flat glass, were clearly more capitalistic in their methods of production than the rest of the trade; they paid higher wages, they obtained more net output from each worker and, had they not been paying higher wages, gross profits would have taken as much as two-fifths of the value of their net output in contrast to the rest's one-quarter.‡ What then was the real economic difference between this group and the rest? In truth, as we have already hinted, the 250 establishments, mainly small, which recorded no shift-working at all represented virtually another industry, a non-competing group. They made what is described in the Census as 'Domestic and Fancy Glassware', scientific and optical glass and a wide variety of miscellaneous (non-flat) glass products. Their characteristic wares, from the point of

† The estimates are based on consideration of the information given in Table 4 of the 1951 Census, 'Analysis by Size'. They are considered to be sufficiently reliable to support the argument in the text above with some confidence, because, according to the Census, small firms in this industry demonstrate a very marked difference in characteristic net output and wages per man as compared with the larger firms.

‡ The published Census tables for 1948 and 1951 suggest that in order to derive gross profits from net output it is necessary in this trade to deduct (in addition to operatives' wages) about a further 20 % of net output on account of the wages and salaries of other employees, repairs and maintenance of buildings, costs of research, costs of advertising, employers' contributions to National Insurance, rates, etc. (See Table 7 in the 1948 Census.)

Table 9.1. *Shift-working in the Census trade 'Glass, other than Containers'*

(Great Britain, 1951.)

	Total establishments		Total operatives		Total net output		Average no. of operatives per establishment		Average net output per operative		Average wage per operative		Proportion of operatives on shifts	Share of operatives' wages in net output
	No.	%	No.	%	£ mil.	%	No.	%	£	%	£	%	(%)	(%)
Establishments with														
Over 35% of ops. on shifts	30	10	14200	40	11·7	43	473		825		359		53	44
Less than 35% but more than zero	20	7	10400	30	(9·2)	(34)	520		(885)		(390)		26	(44)
} combined									750		354			47
No shift-work whatsoever	250	83	10400	30	(6·3)	(23)	42		(605)		(320)		—	(53)
All establishments	300	100	35000	100	27·2	100	117		776		356		29	46

Table 9.2. *Synopsis of Table 9.1*

(Source: Table 9.1)

	All shift-working establishments	All non-shift-working establishments
Average number of operatives per establishment	490	42
Estimated average earnings per operative (£)	370	320
Estimated average net output per operative (£)	850	605
Apparent basic share of gross profits in net output (%)	42	28
Observed wages differential	15%	
Observed net output differential	40%	

view of the lay observer, were such as the domestic drinking glass, the heat-proof glass cooking utensil, the decorative fruit bowl, the glass vase, the salt cellar, the ash tray, the spectacle glass, the lens. But although these firms were so very different from the flat glass producers from the point of view of the consumer, this does not mean that the comparison between the two groups is not of considerable interest for our inquiry. For domestic and fancy glass is still glass, and although the *technical* factors determining conditions in the industry, in contrast to the commercial factors, are no doubt different, they are not so greatly different from those of the flat glass industry: automatic moulding machines could be designed to manufacture salt cellars, and they have been designed and are in use to produce 'pyrex'-type ovenware, just as automatic rolling machines have been designed and are indeed in use to produce flat glass. Further, it appears that the pull of the heat-economy factor in favour of shift-working is by and large no less strong in non-flat glass factories than in flat, so that in factories where only day shifts are worked, for example, the furnaces nevertheless have to be kept burning all night. Further still, it was found that a significant minority of the firms making domestic glassware did in fact operate shift systems of one kind or another and must have been included in the fifty firms so recorded in the Census (the 'handful of others' referred to above).† Yet despite all it is abundantly clear that the predominant technique of production in the non-flat section of this Census trade, taken as a whole, was considerably less mechanised than in the flat section and for that reason did not favour shift-working: the basic share of profits, Table 9.2 shows, was one of the few to lie below the 30% criterion suggested in Chapter 7.‡

The explanation lies, of course, in the highly differentiated (i.e. heterogeneous) nature of the non-flat products. They are products whose sale depends on consumer taste and fashion, or at least on the interpretation of consumer taste provided by the buyers of the retail

† They may have been responsible for as much as 20% of the industry's net output.

‡ See p. 145. We are advised that since 1951 there has been a considerable increase in the use of automatic techniques in all sections of the industry, including the non-flat section.

stores. Competition between rival firms' wares is therefore as much based on design as on price. Frequent changes of design are essential to survival and long runs of a single product are difficult or impossible. But it so happens that for technical reasons the automatic moulding machines which are available to the trade operate efficiently only at a very high rate of output; thus an automatic salt-cellar-producing machine might comfortably turn out the whole of one year's national requirements of salt cellars in 3 weeks of continuous working. If automatic machines are used, therefore, they must often be stopped for changes of mould; but the moulds themselves are expensive and form a significant proportion of the total capital cost of the process.

As a consequence of these facts it is not easy to achieve the technically most efficient scale of output using automatic machinery: in a country the size of the United Kingdom therefore, if automatic machines are in fact installed the problem is often to find enough work to keep them occupied during the normal working day, let alone on shifts.† Thus this breaking up of the market has the effect of permitting the survival of a large number of small firms of widely varying technical efficiency (in marked contrast, it will be remembered, to the case of flat glass) and preventing economic use of the more highly mechanised of known techniques. This, we have seen (Chapter 4), must discourage utilisation.‡ It will also be remembered that if the size of the firm is small, the entrepreneur himself, as much as his capital, may perforce become the 'indivisible factor' on which decisions as to operating technique will be based. This again, we saw, is likely in practice to militate against shift-work: it is not irrelevant to note, therefore, that the Census reported the existence of no less than sixty 'Working Proprietors' in this trade, that is to say owner-managers of non-incorporated businesses, let alone the large number of working directors of small private companies of the family type which must abound in any branch of industry where the average number of operatives per establishment is as low as is the case here. Thus in the comparison of the two distinct groups which we have identified in Census trade 'Glass other than Containers', we find an almost perfect example of the way in which 'imperfect competition' influences the incidence of shift-working, an example which is particularly valuable because, despite the difference in the market conditions for their products, the technological factors in the two groups of firms are relatively similar. If every household in the country were prepared to drink from a standard drinking glass, pour salt from a standard salt cellar and make use of a standard ash tray, as they are in fact prepared to bake in a standard pyrex oven-dish,§ and if the effective size of the market could be enlarged sufficiently so that the total annual demand for

† Two such machines whose existence was mentioned were known to be used only a few months in the year.

‡ In the language of Chapter 4, scale restraint has reduced both mechanisation and utilisation leading to a low adjusted 'initial' profit margin.

§ No suggestion is intended that such a situation would necessarily be desirable.

each standardised product was no less than the capacity of the relevant automatic machine, then shift-working would be as prevalent over the Census trade as a whole as it is now in its present shift-working section. Alternatively, the development could come about from the discovery of cheaper and more versatile automatic moulding machines.

The other Census trade involved in glass manufacture is 'Glass Containers'. Glass containers in ordinary language are mainly glass bottles and jars. They are made with highly automatic machinery operating at considerable speeds. These capitalistic methods of production drove out the older hand-blowing (or more strictly, mouth blowing) methods over the period 1900 to 1914.

Essentially the economic position is very similar to that in the flat glass industry, and to what would be the position in the non-flat section of 'Glass other than Containers' if the section's products were standardised. Glass bottles, which are essentially a producers' good, appear to compete mainly on their price and their technical utility for the purpose in hand, rather than on 'fancy' variations of shape or colour. This state of affairs arises from the nature of the economic need which a glass bottle or jar is intended to satisfy. The great bulk of the value of the output of the trade consists of beer bottles, milk bottles and jam jars. It appears that in the course of time a process of trial and error has evolved 'ideal' shapes for these containers which best reconcile the conflicting requirements of manufacturer, distributor and final consumer. There is therefore much less scope for the development of imperfect competition in this trade. The technically optimum methods of production can be used, and the technique is one which favours shift-working. Indeed, Table II suggests that over this trade *as a whole* the basic share of profits was of the order of 43 %, i.e. about the same as in the shift-working establishments in 'Glass, other than Containers' and quite high enough therefore to ensure the general profitability of shift-working. Hence it is hardly surprising to find that out of sixty or so establishments which make up the trade as a whole, fifty or so displayed shift-work ratios over 35 % and that this group employed no less than 97 % of the labour force of the trade. Little more need be said.

The remaining Census trades in the industrial order are Brick and Fireclay, China and Earthenware, Cement, Abrasives, Building Materials, Roofing Felts and Manufactured Fuel. Of these, we select the three remaining 'kiln' industries—Brick and Fireclay, China and Earthenware and Cement—for a detailed discussion in these notes:† basic shift-working data concerning the others are available in Appendix Tables.

† The Building Materials Trade (20 % of the net output of the order) is omitted because its products, and more important, its processes, are so heterogeneous as to make investigation peculiarly difficult. The other trades are omitted because they are small, together accounting for little over 5 % of the net output. The trades discussed in these notes account, therefore, for about 75 % of the net output of the order.

9.3. The 'Kiln' Industries

Taken together these three industries (see above), and in particular their subsections manufacturing domestic pottery, building bricks and Portland cement respectively, provide almost as good an example as could be wished of the application of the basic theory. In pottery, the shape of the known production function at the time when most of the plant in even the largest and most go-ahead concerns was installed was such that the most profitable programme was one which did not favour shift-work at all: more recently invented highly mechanised or 'automated' techniques have not yet had time to penetrate significantly and also are held up by the influence of product variation. In addition the potteries demonstrate admirably the way in which a production function which offers a low-mechanised technique using a high proportion of female labour can militate powerfully against shift-work in the manner suggested in Chapter 2. In cement, by extreme contrast, a production function was discovered in the early part of the present century which is highly profitable and strongly favourable to shift-work over a wide range of effective real wage rates. Finally, with building bricks we have in the expansion of the Fletton brick industry an excellent example of intensive shift-work spreading through the trade from the dynamic effects of a more recently discovered technique.

In the 'kiln' industries the size of the kiln uniquely determines the maximum rate of output. But a kiln can usually be kept burning, day and night, with the direct involvement of at most 12 % of the total labour force, and this fact, coupled with the fact that unless mechanised techniques are also employed in the ancillary processes, the cost of the kiln is likely to form a high proportion of the total fixed capital, means that little economy in the over-all ratio of capital to output is likely to be achieved by putting the ancillary processes themselves on to shifts: in other words, even in the absence of any positive utilisation differential, a change in an establishment's shift-work ratio from 10 % to, say, 50 % might raise the rate of gross profit on capital by no more than one percentage point in ten.† Hence the study of shift-work in these industries is essentially a study in the techniques of production used in winning, preparing and shaping clay before it enters a kiln.

† This is based on likely conditions in an old-fashioned brick works employing adult male operatives only. With the kiln fired continuously (including Sundays, Christmas Day and all other holidays) and the remaining processes run on a 50-hour week, stepping up the working week on these processes to 168 hours would reduce the overall capital–output ratio by no more than a tenth, e.g. raise the rate of gross profit on capital from 10 to 11 %, or from 20 to 22 %. Even a quite small effective wage cost differential therefore would be sufficient to rule shift-work out altogether.

9.4. CEMENT

Cement is made by mixing clay with chalk or lime into a liquid slurry. This is then dripped into a rather complicated and expensive type of metal kiln burning powdered coal, solidified into a clinker, removed and ground into a powder in large ball mills. The main features of this basic equipment of machinery reached their modern form as early as the 1920's and the outfit is evidently expensive. The clay is won with mechanical excavators, mixed into slurry in mixers as near the quarry as possible, and the slurry sent to the kilns in pipes. As is well known, the industry is considerably monopolised, the mergers having occurred in the 1930's mainly, apparently for commercial rather than technical reasons. In the earlier history of cement making (the product was effectively invented around the 1880's), there were at one time as many as sixty separate firms, in contrast to the present nine; the clay was won by hand, the kilns were much cruder and the whole technique of production less capital-intensive. With contemporary techniques of production, net output per operative in 1951 was very high (about £1800 per annum, compared with the £825 average for all industries covered in the study) but although 97 % of the labour force consisted of adult males, weekly earnings were on average about £8. 10*s*. 0*d*. a week—little higher than the £8 to £8. 10*s*. 0*d*. recorded in the *Ministry of Labour Gazette* as the national average for adult males in 1951. Hence, the basic share of profits when employing these techniques at the 1951 level of effective real wage rate appears to have been extremely high: Table II indicates 62 %. This has subsequently been found, by the Restrictive Practices Court,† to be consistent with a net return on capital around 10 %; in other words, the capital–output ratio in the industry is unusually high. Consequently, the incentive to utilise is overwhelming, a fact which was recognised in other evidence suggesting a remarkable sensitivity of profits to small variations in utilisation rates.‡ One would expect to find, therefore, that shift working was *de rigeur*.

In fact, the Appendix Tables show that thirty-one out of the forty-eight cement plants in Great Britain, employing 80 % of the operatives, were in the group with shift-work ratios of over 35 %, and that practically all the remaining establishments were in the intermediate group, i.e. all did some shift-work. The separation between the intermediate and the 'intensive' group in this case, however, is subject to an unusually wide margin of error, as (no doubt owing to the distinctive commercial structure of the industry) 'multi-establishment' returns not only accounted for nearly 65 % of the total net output of the trade but also displayed the peculiarly enigmatic characteristic that the total number

† See Restrictive Practices Court, in re Cement Makers' Federation Agreement, 1961, *Law Reports*, 2 R.P., p. 282. The calculation, however, related to a period which began after 1951, and its basis was also questioned by the Registrar on other grounds (*op cit.* p. 264).

‡ *Op cit.* p. 246.

of shift-working operatives recorded on them was just 40 % of the total number of all operatives recorded on them; this made reliable estimation of the distribution of the establishments according to shift-work ratio almost impossible without special knowledge. But what is a hard fact is that over 99 % of the total operatives in this industry as a whole were on returns showing some shift-work, and that no less than 38 % of all the operatives in the trade were shift-workers. This could only indicate an industry where intensive shift-working of the main machinery is an extensive and probably almost a universal practice, together probably with a high degree of shift-working of ancillary machinery. The figure of 38 % compares with a corresponding figure of 17 % for the industrial order taken as a whole.

We have in fact obtained direct information that the foregoing interpretation of the statistics is correct. The greater part of the machinery of a typical cement plant is indeed kept working night and day, including weekends and, in addition, the men take staggered holidays. Little more therefore need be said of this case, except perhaps to note and emphasise that cement is a homogeneous product (a fact of course which is no doubt much responsible for the monopolistic tendencies). There is no barrier therefore to realising the technical optimum in scale of output and the Census showed that over 70 % of the net output in 1951 was produced in establishments with turnover (gross output) of £1 million per annum or over, a figure which compares with one of little over 45 % for manufacturing industry as a whole (1951).

9.5. China and Fireclay

The basic processes involved in the manufacture of domestic pottery are generally familiar; many readers will have seen them in operation. The important variations in the methods of commercial production, of course, lie mainly in the degree to which the familiar processes are mechanised; whether the wheel is turned by hand or machinery, how much the potter is aided by other mechanical devices, whether the movement through the ovens is mechanical or not, and so on. As in the case of non-flat domestic glassware this is also an industry where some highly automatic techniques largely eliminating manual labour in the moulding process ('potting') are known but they are not widely used on account of the need for a wide degree of product variation to satisfy consumer tastes. In addition, the extensive demand for decorated pottery powerfully militates in the same direction.

Actually, only about half the gross value of the output in this Census trade represents domestic pottery, the rest consists of a wide range of products, mostly producers' goods or near producers' goods, such as tiles, sanitary earthenware, electrical ware and slabbed work which are capable in principle of a rather greater degree of standardisation. Nevertheless, the predominant condition as regards shift-working in domestic pottery (i.e. almost nil) seems to prevail over the greater part of the rest of the trade. In the trade as a whole, intensive shift-work is non-existent and even moderate shift-working is rare: there were no establishments with shift-working ratios of over 35 %, and less than 10 % of the total of 240 establishments in the trade reported any shift-work whatsoever. In these notes therefore we concentrate the discussion on the conditions prevailing in a large pottery.

We have been very considerably aided by information kindly provided by Messrs Josiah Wedgwood and Sons Ltd. of Barlaston, Staffs., whose main factory employs no less than 1500 people. Messrs Wedgwoods provided us with rough estimates of the amounts of fixed capital of various types which they were using, of their labour force, its composition and distribution, and of their operatives' earnings. From these data it was possible to obtain an indication of the typical ratio of labour cost to capital cost involved in the manufacture of pottery on this scale (a scale which is of course much larger than is typical in the industry). In addition, from examination of the published Census of Production tables it was possible to estimate the probable ratio of operatives' wages to net output prevailing in the larger potteries in the U.K., and hence by combining the information from these two sources we obtained an idea of the typical ratio of gross capital to net output. Hence, with the addition of estimates of staff salaries and other production expenses we were able to construct a more or less complete model of the relevant economic conditions likely to be found in a large pottery. The results are given in Table 9.3. We must emphasise that the table in no way purports to describe precisely conditions in Messrs Wedgwoods' or any other particular pottery; it merely attempts to indicate the orders of magnitude which are thought to be likely to obtain in any typical large-scale plant in this industry. In particular, the figure for gross profits is entirely hypothetical and the main concern of the model, of course, is not with the absolute figure of the rate of gross profit, but with the differences in the rate depicted at the bottom of the various columns.

35–40 % of the labour force in a pottery is employed on actual potting, i.e. in operating one version or another of the potter's wheel; at least half the 'potters' are women or girls. Another 25 % of the labour force is engaged in decorating and an efficient female sex ratio for this stage of the work may be anything from 75 to 100 %. Hence potteries as a whole employ much female and juvenile labour, paying them hourly wage rates on average some 40 % below that of the men: the result is an efficient and profitable technique of production involving a relatively low level of mechanisation. Using this technique, if men were employed, their productivity would be very much less than the necessary 65 % greater than that of the women which would be necessary to offset the difference in wage rate.

First consider that part of the table which depicts the alternatives available under 'Technique A', which is thought to embody the

Table 9.3. *A model of economic conditions in a large pottery*

(Resources required and profits with net output £1 million p.a.)

Resources required and profits obtainable	Technique A (typical 1955) Single-shift (men 1 × 10 × 5 = 50, others 1 × 8½ × 5 = 42½, average = 45½) £000's	Two-shift (men 2 × 8 × 5 = 80, others 2 × 8 × 5 = 80) £000's	Three-shift (men only, 3 × 8 × 5 = 120) £000's
Capital			
Kilns	220	220	220
Other plant	330	190	125
Buildings	550	380	300
Working, say	500	400	355
Total, say	1600	1190	1000
Labour			
Adult male ops.	300	375	760
Other ops.	220	235	—
Staff	130	140	140
Total, say	650	750	900
Other expenses, say	100	100	100
Gross profits			
Amount	250	150	—
Percentage on total capital	15½	12½	—

Resources required and profits obtainable	Technique B (highly automatic) Single-shift (men only, 1 × 10 × 5 = 50) £000's	Two-shift (men only, 1 × 10 × 5 + 1 × 8 × 5 = 90) £000's	Three-shift (men only, 3 × 8 × 5 = 120) £000's
Capital			
Kilns	220	220	220
Other plant	880	500	365
Buildings	500	370	335
Working, say	500	400	350
Total, say	2100	1490	1270
Labour			
Adult male ops.	280	315	350
Other ops.	—	—	—
Staff	150	160	160
Total, say	430	475	510
Other expenses, say	100	100	100
Gross profits			
Amount	470	425	400
Percentage on total capital	22	28½	31

capital and labour requirements for £1 million of net output at 1955 prices involved in the actual techniques largely prevailing at the time of writing. Single shifts, with a normally balanced labour force, 40 % adult male, 60 % women and juveniles (the percentages relate to numbers of operatives) show a realisable gross profit on gross capital of 15 %. Double shifts, which legally would have to be double day shifts on account of the large number of females, with a shift-work premium of 6 % for women and juveniles and 25 % for men, would be less profitable than single shifts; a continuous system using an all male labour fource would be quite out of the question even if, as has been assumed, the all male labour force was on average no more than 10 % more productive than the normally balanced force. Nor, it can be shown, would a 'mixed' shift system with permanent day work (average $45\frac{1}{2}$ hours per week) for the normally balanced force plus the addition of a permanent 8-hour night shift of men, be profitable either—the men's wage rates are altogether too high. Part of the difficulty, it will be seen, is the 'kiln effect'; the reduction of over-all capital–output ratio under the various shift systems is only moderate, i.e. single-shift, 1·6; double-shift, 1·2; treble-shift, 1·0.

As already mentioned, there does exist automatic machinery for moulding pottery, and some firms employ some. A rough idea of the potentialities of such machinery is indicated under Technique B, but it is essential to remember that the figures are drawn up on the assumption that the machines suffer no loss of output on account of market limitations for individual products. Technique B, being highly mechanised, would definitely favour shift-work at current wage rates with an all male labour force. It would also probably show a considerably higher profit rate even on single shifts (although the figures for profits given in the table are pure guesses as we have no indications, direct or indirect, to guide us). Why then is not this technique widely used in the industry, with shift-work and a male labour force? There are two answers to this question. In the first place, Technique B has only been developed since the war, while the large, relatively modern factory of the leading firm in the industry, i.e. Wedgwoods, was built just before the war. Much the same is true of other potteries. In other words, the new technique has not yet had time to penetrate: we have seen that the mere existence of a technique will by no means ensure its immediate adoption even in a progressive industry. As the middle-aged potteries depreciate and the effective real wage rate rises, the new automatic techniques may be expected to begin their penetration. If they do so fast enough, *relatively* to the speed of the rise in real wage rate, then we may begin to see shift-working practices develop in this industry.

The other reason why Technique B is not more widely used is one with which we are now familiar, and one which must qualify the arguments at the end of the preceding paragraph. Automatic machines for moulding ceramics, as for glass, have a very high rate of economic output. For them to be operated at these high rates, long runs of production on individual products are necessary; it is an open question whether consumers would be persuaded to accept the aesthetic consequences.

We have already noted that potteries on the scale assumed in the table are abnormal: the average net output per establishment among specialist producers of 'other' earthenware (which was largely domestic earthenware) was given by the Census in 1951 as about £100 000, in contrast to the £1 000 000 in our model. But we chose to depict conditions in a plant which was much larger than average, partly because it was from such a plant that our illustrative information was derived, but also to demonstrate the point that a large scale of total output does not necessarily lead to high mechanisation and shift-work.

9.6. Chemicals and Allied Trades

No less than seventeen trades are covered by this heading, but one, General Chemicals, accounts for as much as a quarter of the total net output. Both products and processes are considerably more heterogeneous than in the order discussed in the previous section. The central processes are inevitably mechanical—and hence a large part of the labour force in a typical plant is engaged on either maintenance, or on what must strictly be defined as 'ancillary' processes such as receiving and preparing the raw materials, bagging and dispatching the finished product. This applies to most of the trades in the group, including paint, varnish, ink and soap; the only major exceptions appear to be the manufacture of drugs and pharmaceutical preparations, and ladies' perfumes.

Evidently, in the production and sale of such a heterogeneous group of commodities, there is much scope for the play of imperfect competition by means of product variation; many small and medium-size firms are able to survive for this reason. In those branches where the products are perforce more homogeneous—the trades in basic standard, or so-called 'heavy' chemicals—it is common for one large combine to swallow the whole or a large part of the market; but in contrast to the case of building materials, the large firms have not been content to specialise in single products; thus ICI and the Distillers' Company have moved into market after market. The explanation of this pattern of development should not be hard to find, but is outside the scope of the present inquiry. The *consequence* is that each combine has a greater resilience to competition than had, say, Chance Brothers, so that the complete absorption of the market for a single product by one combine, though not unusual, is by no means inevitable.

9.7. Characteristics of Shift-Working in the Chemical Trades

We expect, of course, an unusual amount of shift-working dictated by the need for economies in prime costs and we have already examined the statistical evidence of this.† Chemical processes tend to be by nature continuous and usually involve heat treatment; one would expect that if such processes were interrupted, losses both in labour time (workers idle while the process is restarted) and in fuel and raw materials, would be substantial. But the point should not be exaggerated. Managers of several plants stated that the increases in prime costs which would be experienced if the process over which they had charge were run discontinuously, though significant, would not necessarily be prohibitive: these managers overwhelmingly emphasised capital economies as the justification for shift-working. Wherever the truth may lie, it is certain that, as in the case of glass, the known production function in a wide range of chemicals is such as substantially to favour shift-working on the grounds of capital economy as well.

In a large number of chemicals trades, the operatives' shift-working ratio forms an unusually poor indicator of the average intensity of capital utilisation. Indeed, the shift-working ratio may even vary perversely, i.e. may be lower in some establishments which employ their capital intensively than in others which do not. It is certainly not uncommon to find two establishments producing an identical product by a process which is run continuously for 168 hours every week in both, yet employing their workers in ways so different as to yield notably different shift-work ratios. The general reasons were discussed in Chapter 7. Typically, in the production of 'main line' chemicals, a central process involves the greater part of the fixed capital of the establishment and the production function relevant to this process will be such as to favour shift-work at the going effective real wage rate and wage cost differential. But in the ancillary processes, consisting mainly of raw material preparation and bagging and despatch of the finished product, the known production function is much less favourable to shift-work under the same wage condition. Further, there are a number of examples of trades, or establishments within trades, where conditions tend towards those postulated in the robot-factory discussed on p. 147. Thus in mineral oil refining (which is classified in the chemicals group but not included in the summary statistics presented in this chapter‡) a great modern refinery may show a labour return in which 90 % of the total weekly paid staff are classified as maintenance workers; these workers are overwhelmingly employed on ordinary day work, hence the over-all shift-working ratio of the refinery is likely to be quite low. Nevertheless, the refineries are of course operated for 168 hours per week. Outside oil refining few examples of completely automated factories exist in the United Kingdom at the time of writing, in the

† See Chapter 7, p. 146. ‡ Owing to idiosyncratic statistical practices.

chemicals or in other industry, but the *tendency* exists and as we have seen it is a tendency which may in certain circumstances pull down the overall shift-working ratio in an establishment in which capital is in fact being used very intensively.† A more typical example in chemicals, which is in fact based on information kindly supplied by the central labour department of I.C.I., might appear as shown in Table 9.4. It will be seen that the plant shift-work ratio of the imaginary establishment depicted in the Table is made up from three components: (i) the shift-work ratio of the tradesmen, 15 %; (ii) the shift-work ratio of the general workers, 40 %; and (iii) the proportion of tradesmen in total employment, 20 %. The establishment is, in fact, depicted as being on the borderline between inclusion in the statistical category of 'intensive' shift-work working and inclusion in the intermediate group (four of the twelve chemicals divisions of I.C.I. showed in 1955 over-all shift-work ratios within plus or minus three points of 35 %, two more were within 6 points) so that small and probably insignificant changes in the component ratios would affect the classification of the establishment in our Statistical Appendix. Any of the component ratios might vary independently of the intensity of operation of the central process. Thus, if the central process were operated continuously, but the work of the bagging department were not, a slight increase in the relative productivity of the 'process' workers to the bagging workers would *reduce* the shift-work ratio of the general workers as a whole and this in turn would reduce the plant shift-work ratio to below 35 %. Alternatively, changes in conditions might lead to the introduction of mechanical handling equipment for the bagging operations, and the plant ratio would be driven in the opposite direction. Similarly, as already noted, an increase in the proportion of tradesmen (tending to the 'robot factory') will reduce the plant ratio unless the change is offset by an increase in the shift-work ratio of the tradesmen themselves, and so on.

On the whole, variations in the shift-work ratio among the tradesmen or among the general workers seemed in practice to dominate the variations in plant shift-work ratios both in the separate divisions of Imperial Chemicals and the separate establishments of the Distillers

† There is a major qualification when conditions fall short of complete automation. It is by no means certain that if new machinery is installed which yields a higher rate of output per process worker, the relative amount of maintenance required will necessarily increase: indeed the new machinery may be so designed that it is easier to maintain than the old. To put the point more precisely, as final output per process worker increases, so also may final output per maintenance worker; hence the proportion of maintenance workers to total workers required may remain more or less constant. An excellent example was found in a seed crushing mill, for which Unilevers Ltd. kindly supplied data relating to conditions both before and after a substantial accession of new equipment. The technical changes involved led not only to a doubling of the productivity of the process workers (both in mill and refinery) but also apparently to a comparable increase in the productivity of the maintenance and service departments. Before re-equipment, the over-all shift-work ratio of the establishment was a little under 40 %, a ratio of over 80 % among mill and refinery workers being offset by a ratio of no more than 5–10 % among maintenance workers. After re-equipment both ratios and the two relative weights in total employment remained virtually unchanged; so also, therefore, the plant ratio. Continuous operation of the main machinery was essential, of course, both before and after the change.

Table 9.4. *Model distribution of labour force*

	Proportion of total labour force (%)	Shift-work ratio (%)
Tradesmen and engineers	20	15
General workers	80	40
Total	100	35

Company.† The lesser factor—variation in the proportion of maintenance workers in the total labour force—was only significant in a sense special to this inquiry: that is the factor was not infrequently seen to be responsible for carrying the plant shift-work ratio just over the 35 % borderline.

Thus, in the lime division of I.C.I. the proportion of tradesmen to total workers was 20 %, a figure only a little above the average for Distillers and I.C.I. chemicals taken together. The average shift-work ratio of the general workers was not very high (40 %—the other 60 % being engaged mainly on daytime bagging operations) so that it would have been expected that, given that a lime works requires a substantial number of maintenance workers, the plant shift-work ratio would have been a little below the borderline. However, it so happens that in this plant it was technically desirable that as high a proportion of the tradesmen worked shifts as of the general workers and, in the event, the plant ratio in fact worked out at 38 %. In the Distillers Company, of two plants manufacturing an identical product—carbon dioxide—one exhibited a shift-work ratio of 45 %, the other 70 %: both, needless to say, were operating their central process continuously. The explanation proved to be simply that in the more modern plant of the two, all the tradesmen (17 % of the total labour force) were employed on shifts while in the other none were. The further explanation given by the management deserves quoting: 'Plant *A* has engineers on shift in charge of the process, and these men are able not only to supervise the whole of the process, but also deal with any breakdown which may occur to the compressors and other parts of the plant. Plant *A* is a modern factory and it is expected that the future pattern of Plant *B* will be towards following that pattern.'

Distillers also provided us with an excellent example of the effect of varying practices in the packing department. In two factories producing an identical product the central process was running 168 hours per week, but in one factory the packing was done on a double-day

† The information given by I.C.I. was summarised by divisions, that given by Distillers related to individual plants, although in some cases the I.C.I. Division was in fact concentrated in a single establishment. The Distillers data was particularly valuable in demonstrating sharp differences in shift-work ratio among different plants producing almost identical products. The authors are grateful to both these firms for exceptional collaboration.

shift system, in the other a single shift only was operated. In consequence, in the first factory the plant shift-work ratio was nearly 60 %, while in the second it was just below the 35 % borderline. The explanation provided a nice confirmation of our main theory. The technical data for the two processes moderately but not overwhelmingly favoured the programme in which both activities went on shifts. The selling price of the final products was the same for both plants, so also apparently the basic money wage rate, from which it would appear that the difference between the decision taken at the two plants must have been due to a difference in the elasticity of utilisation. At first sight the explanation given by the management supported this deduction. They reported that the two plants were located in different geographical areas, in one of which female labour suitable for the packing process was scarcer than in the other. Single shifts were worked in the labour-scarce area in order to encourage recruitment. Thus differences in the supply of labour relative to the stock of capital in the two areas led to differences in the scarcity of labour. In certain 'ideal' models of the functioning of the economic system this should lead to a reduction of the basic real wage in the labour-surplus area until the enhanced profitability of investment there had evened things out. In practice, because the basic wage is not flexible, this does not happen. Instead, concealed differences in the wage bargain appear, such as the labour-scarce area offering the same terms for non-shift work as offered for multiple shift-work in the labour-surplus area. More fundamentally, the workers in the labour-surplus area were prepared to accept these terms because they preferred shift-work and the income associated therewith, to staying at home. We could not ask the Distillers' Company whether they were conscious of a difference in the rate of profit earned at the two plants, but it would be interesting to know if, in discussing plans for new plants, they would tend to favour, other things being equal, areas where packing shift-workers could be obtained cheaply. Unfortunately, of course, other things are never equal.

Thus, taken as a whole, the information provided by individual organisations such as I.C.I. and Distillers qualifies the statement with which this section opened, that in the chemicals industry the operatives' shift-working ratio is a bad indicator of the intensity of capital utilisation. Nevertheless, the statement remains broadly correct and it is supported by an analysis of the statistics for the order as a whole which now follows.

Table 9.5 analyses the data relating to all chemicals trades in which the shift-work ratio in the 'intermediate' group was known to be over 20 %. There were nine such trades and they accounted for over half the output and employment of the order. The table tends to confirm the hypothesis that the 'intermediate' establishments were weakly differentiated from the 'intensives'. For if the establishments in the two groups in a given trade were using the same or similar techniques of production they would be expected to differ little in average net output

Table 9.5. *Data relating to chemicals trades in which the average shift-work ratio in the 'intermediate' establishment was 20 % or over*

Trade	Percentage of total ops. Establishments with shift-work ratio of			Av. percentage shift-work ratio. Establishments with shift-work ratio of			Net output per head. Establishments with shift-work ratio of			Basic share of wages. Establishments with shift-work ratio of	
	Zero	1–35 %	35 %	1–35 %	> 35 %	1–100 %	< 35 %	> 35 %	0–100 %	< 35 %	> 35 %
Coke ovens	1	9	90	26	52	50	874	1065	1046	44	36
Dyes	13	73	14	30	42	32	1771	1705	1762	25	24
Fertilisers	30	9	61	21	42	39	1361	1311	1331	27	26
Coal tar	3	67	30	22	35	26	1186	1449	1265	33	27
General chemicals	10	59	31	27	49	34	1517	1494	1510	27	27
Oils and greases	80	14	6	28	48	34	1988	1165	1936	17	28
Seed crushing	6	14	80	24	51	47	1278	1058	1102	46	..
Glue	30	37	33	28	49	38	1425	1217	1356	25	29
Plastic	4	8	88	25	58	55	1501	1603	1591	24	26
Total	14	40	46	26	50	39	1540	1353	1455		

Note: For comparison

	Net output		Employment		Net output per op. (£)
	£ mil.	%	000's	%	
In the above group	208	56½	143	54	1455
Rest of the order	160	43½	122	46	1310
Total	368	100	265	100	1390

per head, and this is exactly what materialises in the third column of the table. Although the statistics of net output per head perforce amalgamate establishments in the 'intermediate' group with those in which no shift-work took place at all, net output per head in the 'intensive' group was if anything lower than in the others, a result which if more than a coincidence might be taken as a manifestation of 'robot factory' tendency. That is to say, the 'intermediate' establishments may on average have been employing *more* mechanised techniques than the 'intensive' establishments, but have been showing lower over-all shift-work ratios for the reasons discussed earlier. In these nine trades, therefore, it seems legitimate to discuss all the shift-working establishments as a single group, without emphasising the distinction between the so-called 'intensive' group and the rest. Considered in this way, the data convey an overwhelming impression of an industry in which intensive use of capital was to be expected, and was found. It was to be expected because average net output per head was nearly twice the manufacturing average, the basic share of wages low, and that of profits high. Further, as may be seen in Table III, with only one exception large establishments were of dominating importance. Indeed it might be estimated that as much as 60 % of the manpower and a considerably larger proportion of the total capital was accounted for by establishments whose fixed capital in 1951 would have cost at least a quarter of a million pounds to replace. It is therefore unlikely that shift-working in these trades would have been inhibited by scale-restraint.

The evidence for intensive capital utilisation throughout the group consists in the fact that at least 70 % of the operatives were employed in establishments which did some shift-work and in six trades this ratio was as high as 85 %. In the nine trades as a whole, 45 % of the operatives were employed in establishments with over 35 % of operatives on shifts (the so-called 'intensives') compared with an average for all manufacturing of 19 %; 40 % were employed in the remaining shift-working establishments, compared with a manufacturing average of 50 %. Appendix Table I shows that the average shift-work ratio in the 'intensive' establishments in Chemicals as a whole was just under 49 %, while in the intermediate group it was 21 %. The difference between the two ratios is not only considerably less than the corresponding difference for the rest of manufacturing industry but also suggests that a significant proportion of the establishments classified in the 'intermediate' group must have been close to the borderline. Table 9.6 sets out the position more clearly. Thus the difference of 28 percentage points between the shift-working ratios in the two groups in chemicals contrasts with a difference of 52 points in the rest of manufacturing. The 'intermediate' establishments in many chemicals trades are evidently weakly differentiated from the corresponding 'intensive' establishments, and hence, in any trade in the industry in which the shift-work ratio in the intermediate establishments is over, say, 20 %, there is no ground

Table 9.6. *Summary of shift-working statistics for chemicals and the rest of manufacturing industry*

	Total operatives		Shift operatives		Shift-work ratio	
Shift-work ratio:	> 35 % 000's	1–35 % 000's	> 35 % 000's	1–35 % 000's	> 35 % 000's	1–35 % 000's
Chemicals	83	97	41	25	**49**	**21**
Rest of manufacturing	1014	1074	691	176	**68**	**16**
Total	1097	1074	732	201	**67**	**19**

for thinking that the average intensity of capital utilisation in these establishments is much less than in the establishments actually classified as 'intensive' by virtue of their shift-work ratio.

As already indicated, the inquiry was led towards the above conclusions by invaluable information provided by I.C.I. and the Distillers Company and confirmed in other interviews. It is therefore unnecessary to discuss the nine trades of Table 9.5 in separate detail. The remaining eight trades in the chemicals order include drugs, toilet preparations, explosives, paint, soap, polishes, ink and oil refining. The last represents a special case. The shift-working ratio in 'intermediate' refineries averaged 22 %, but the trade could not be included in the table because abnormal statistical practices by the oil companies prevent the computation of meaningful estimates of net output per head and basic share of wages. However, thanks to kind assistance from the Esso Petroleum Co., the position in the trade is not difficult to analyse. Oil refineries are of course operated day and night, but the industry does not display a high average over-all shift-work ratio: although there was no refinery which employed no shift-workers, at least half were 'intermediate' and the average shift-work ratio among the 'intensives' was under 50 %. This, as has already been suggested, is an excellent example of robot factory tendency, with a large team of day-working maintenance workers dominating the total employment picture.

In the seven trades left after the exclusion of oil refining, shift-working was not very common. They are compared with the other chemicals trades and with the rest of manufacturing industry in Table 9.7. Since there is no evidence against using the shift-work ratio as an indicator of the intensity of capital utilisation, the figures may reasonably be interpreted as implying a propensity to utilise capital much less intensively than in the trades listed in Table 9.5, less, even, than in the rest of manufacturing. Indeed so rare is intensive shift-working in the group that the Board of Trade was usually forced to apply the Disclosure provisions of the Statistics of Trade Act, with the result that many of the relevant figures included in the Appendix Tables are perforce estimates—estimates sufficiently accurate it is thought, to justify inclusion in statistical totals, but almost certainly too inaccurate to be capable of

Table 9.7. *Shift-working tendencies in chemicals compared with other manufacturing industries*

	Percentages of total operatives employed		
Shift-work ratio:	Zero	1–35 %	Over 35 %
Trades in Table 9.5	14	40	46
Rest of chemicals†	58	30	12
Rest of manufacturing‡	**63**	**19**	**18**
All manufacturing	62	20	19

† Excluding Mineral Oil Refining.
‡ Including Mineral Oil Refining.

supporting close reasoning in relation to the individual trades. Nevertheless, a detailed, if impressionistic study of three cases—paint, soap and drugs—was undertaken, and proved illuminating.

For there is no simple general explanation of the low level of capital utilisation in the group. Net output per head is about the same as in Table 9.5, wages costs are considerably lower, and the basic share of profits in net output is actually higher than in those trades. It is true that the lower wages are partly due to greater exploitation of female labour—the median trades in Table 9.5 employed 90 % adult males compared with 55 % in the present group—but a rough calculation is sufficient to show that even were adult males substituted for all the females in every establishment in the group, the rise in average wages, though considerable, would still leave the basic share of profits higher than on average in Table 9.5. We clearly cannot, therefore, use the sex-efficiency explanation. Finally, a glance at Appendix Table III suggests that the average size of plants measured in terms of employment is little different from that of the plants included in Table 9.5: more precisely, it may be computed from the Appendix that in terms of net output average size of plants is some 20 % lower, but a difference of this magnitude, as such, would seem insufficient to support an explanation based on the theory of scale restraint entirely. However, when we come to detailed examination we shall find that scale restraints do indeed figure strongly in the picture, because although plants in the two groups are of much the same average size, the products of a typical establishment in the second group tend to be more diversified, and product diversification, rather than establishment size, is, as we have seen, a most powerful enemy of scale.

9.8. Paint and Varnish

In 1951, paint and varnish establishments in Great Britain numbered some 340, and they produced nearly £40 millions of net output (gross output was the best part of three times this figure, owing to high material costs). The trade is of interest in appearing to provide an excellent example of low capital utilisation due to product variety. Essentially the process of production consists in grinding pigments into the 'vehicle' (the latter typically linseed oil) in a mechanically operated ball mill. The labour required to operate the mills is negligible and most of the manual work in a paint factory consists of preparing the vehicle (by heating), handling the liquids between processes, canning, labelling, storage and despatch. A ball mill can grind continuously without difficulty, but must be stopped for a rather lengthy process of cleaning if it is to be changed from one colour to another. Given that paint firms like to market a 'full' line of colours under their brand name, it seems inevitable that unless the sales of each colour are large enough to keep a single mill grinding continuously all the year round, the loss of time in changing from one colour to another will provide a clear example of scale restraint. Some of the difficulty can be avoided by undertaking longer runs of production for stock, but with fluctuating raw material prices and varying demands for colours, stock holding is inevitably risky and in consequence there seems to be a definite minimum size for the battery of mills required by any firm marketing a full range of products. If this is so, a firm will be unable to obtain much benefit from shift-working unless it can achieve total sales, of all colours, considerably larger than implied by summing the maximum single-shift output of all the mills included in the minimum battery or 'outfit'. Thus suppose the minimum outfit of mills, including their ancillary equipment and buildings, had a replacement value of a quarter of a million pounds, and suppose that with this outfit on single shift and no overtime one could produce a full range of colours to the wholesale value of half a million pounds per annum; then, even if the utilisation differential were zero, no advantage whatsoever could accrue from shift-working until a turnover of half a million pounds had in fact been achieved. One could not dispense with half the equipment and work the other half on shifts because a quarter of a million pounds' worth of equipment represents the minimum outfit necessary to produce a full range of colours whatever method of employment of capital and labour is adopted. In practice, on these figures, if a two-shift system were to be considered, it would not appear really profitable unless the turnover reached one million pounds, a figure which in 1951 was achieved by no more than 5 % of the establishments in the industry.

It may be asked why, in such circumstances, do not a few aggressive firms drive out the others by competition and so expand to the optimum size? The answer appears to be that owing to the nature of the product, the consumer is badly placed to judge its quality, and therefore tends to believe that a low priced brand must be inferior. Price cutting is therefore unusual and competition instead takes the form of advertising, secret rebates and the employment of highly paid commercial travellers to an even greater extent than in most trades. (Research carried out by the Cambridge University Department of Estate Management has shown that although paints vary considerably in their power of lasting as well as in their power of covering, the price per gallon of given covering power differs little from brand to brand.) It is well known that such conditions are ideal for breaking up a market into a large number of small, relatively uneconomic, units, since potentially aggressive firms are inhibited from using their natural weapon of expansion, i.e. price competition.

In some industries the conditions described might lead to the preservation of a high proportion of firms using less mechanised or degraded techniques. But in the case of paint, the advantages of the ball mill are so great—given the prevailing relation of wage rates to selling prices—that they overweigh all other considerations. Therefore the ball mill is used, not degraded, at a low rate of utilisation. Thus we seem to have a classic example of scale-restraint effects. This conclusion is confirmed both by rule and exception in the facts relating to the industry. As a rule, shift-work is rare; many managements said they had never considered it, some said it was immoral. Despite a high basic profit margin, no more than two establishments in the whole 340 had more than 35 % of the operatives on shifts and 85 % of the total operative employment was accounted for by establishments doing no shift-work whatsoever. The exception (or one of them) lay in the Paint Division of I.C.I. at Slough, makers of 'Dulux' paints, who gave considerable assistance to the inquiry. Here, shift-working was general (mostly 168 machine-hours a week) and the equipment used, though basically similar to that of the rest of the industry, was more highly mechanised in a number of secondary ways (notably in the methods of handling materials between processes) and thus represented a more mechanised level generally. Significantly, the turnover was very much greater than the one million pounds suggested above as the minimum necessary for profitable shift-working. I.C.I. and one or two other similar firms (not all of whom work shifts, however) have achieved sales of this magnitude by means of their national reputation, discreet advertising and effectively convincing the public that the product is superior. In consequence they are able to employ techniques which if operated on single shifts would require more capital per worker than the techniques used in the rest of the industry but, on account of the consequent increase in output per worker, would probably yield much the same rate of profit. With multiple shifts they can obtain profit rates substantially higher. Shift-working would be highly profitable, even with the less mechanised, 'normal' technique, but is not practised because the turnover of the firms concerned is too small. Only if the minimum outfit of equipment for the normal technique were divisible could higher rates of profit be obtained with low turnover.

9.9. Soap, Candles and Glycerine

Nearly three-quarters of the output of this trade consists of bar and tablet soap, soap flakes, soap powder and soapless detergents, the last named, of course, having expanded considerably at the expense of the rest since the end of the war. The trade is of interest because although soap is a consumer good capable of considerable diversification, and susceptible, evidently, to aggressive advertising, production has become heavily concentrated. (Perhaps the explanation is that although a consumer good, the product is basically more like glass, say, than like paint.) The two largest producers, Hedley and Unilever, are said to control 90% of the market.† Both firms, of course, operate a number of establishments, since if the total soap and detergent requirements of the nation were met by only two factories, each would have to be a mammoth of some seven thousand employees, considerably beyond optimum size. By the same token, it is unlikely that either of the two firms mentioned would normally operate establishments below optimum size, since the huge turnovers—running to over £35 millions per annum per firm—enable head offices to organise the distribution of production more or less at will. Consequently it is hardly surprising to find the Census of Production statistics showing a quite extraordinary degree of concentration in the industry: in 1954, out of 115 establishments in the United Kingdom (including producers of glycerine, candles and all the other minor products of the trade) the ten largest were responsible for 80% of the total net output. None of these top ten establishments employed less than 500 persons or, say, 350 operatives, and on *average* each employed nearly 1000 operatives, produced a gross output of £7 millions and a net output of £2 millions per annum. Their net output per operative was over double the average for the rest of the industry and it seems almost certain that the great majority belonged to either the Hedley or the Unilever organisations.

By contrast, in 1954, the 105 establishments making up the rest of the trade were on average abnormally small. Despite the fact that the statistical group in question permits inclusion of establishments employing up to 500 persons (350 operatives), on average they employed only fifty operatives, and their average net output was no more than £60 000. These firms were largely specialist producers of fancy toilet soap and other minor products of the trade such as candles. Since their average size in terms of operatives was considerably less than that of all non-shift-working firms in manufacturing industry as a whole (80), for reasons by now familiar we should not expect to find much shift-working among them. But at the other end of the spectrum, among the 'top ten' large-scale soap producers, the opposite argument applies; so long as financial conditions were favourable, intensive use of capital could be expected to be general. The production process here is apparently highly capitalistic, with perhaps £3 of fixed capital (at replacement cost) required for every £1 of net output (or say £3 of gross output). The apparent basic share of gross profits in net output for

† Since soap and detergents constitute nearly three-quarters of the gross output of the Census trade, this would imply that at least 65% of the gross output originates with the firms mentioned.

the trade as a whole, given in Table II as 40 %, would, therefore, if earned in soap manufacture, provide a modest return of rather under 15 % on total capital. In practice the share of profits in the net output of the top ten soap producers is probably above average for the trade, because, as may be seen from the Census, the share of wages and salaries is below average. In fact so low is the share of operatives' wages in this group (it is under 20 %) that shift-working would in theory be profitable even if the utilisation differential were 100 %. In short, we should expect to find the statistics showing a small number of large establishments with high shift-work ratios, while in the rest of the trade shift-work would be practically non-existent.

Unfortunately it is not easy in practice to test this prediction because it appears that either one or both of the two great soap combines sent in 'scrambled' shift-working returns covering several establishments. 'Multi-establishment' shift-work returns account for nearly a third of the net output of the whole trade and it is quite impossible to carry out the usual analysis. There are however certain clues to the situation. Shift-working operatives in the whole trade in 1951 are known to have numbered no more than 2220. If these were entirely concentrated among establishments employing more than 500 persons† (an extreme but, from other evidence,‡ not unreasonable assumption) the average shift-work ratio in the group may be estimated at the surprisingly low figure of just over 20 %. This average no doubt concealed considerable variations on either side (indeed we know from interviews of at least one plant where the ratio was nearer 70 %) but nevertheless in a high proportion of the establishments in the group the shift-work ratio must have been quite low, probably in some cases as low as 10 %. If this deduction is correct, we have a result which at least appears to contradict the hypothesis that shift-working would be general and extensive among the large-scale soap manufacturers.

The probable explanation lies in Chemicals. The basic processes of soap and detergent manufacture (hydrolysation-distillation-saponification and sulphonation-neutralisation-crutching, respectively) benefit technically from continuous operation and, as we have seen, are capital intensive. But in many cases these processes do not involve more than 40 % of the operative labour force: the rest are employed on packing, warehousing and shipping. For the latter activities, on account of low capital per worker (q), the advantages of shift-work are more marginal. Furthermore, these activities can conveniently employ female labour;

† In 1951 there were fourteen of these in contrast to ten in 1954. Between 1951 and 1954 the total number of establishments in the trade in the United Kingdom fell from 134 to 115; the over-500 group, somewhat surprisingly, contributing disproportionately to this decline.

‡ Total operatives employed in the 'top ten' in 1954 totalled about 9000. The total in the 'top fourteen' in 1951 may be estimated to have been about 10000. Total operative employment shown on all returns indicating some shift-work was given as 11 200, so, providing every establishment in the top fourteen in 1951 had at least a few shift-workers, the total employment in establishments outside the top group cannot have exceeded about 1000 in 1951, of whom, say, 200 may have been shift-workers: if more were shift-workers, the estimate of the shift-work ratio in the top fourteen must be correspondingly reduced.

in fact only just over half of the operatives employed in the whole Census trade are adult males.

None of these considerations imply that the packing and shipping workers in the soap industry would never be put on shifts—in several cases they already are—but they do imply that the advantages of shift-work are sufficiently modest that management will not go to great lengths to obtain them. If the factory is located in an area where shift-work is unfamiliar or unpopular (the two usually go together), i.e. where the utilisation differential is likely to be high, management will be content with the small amount of shift-working necessary to support continuous working of the basic chemical processes only. If, on the other hand, shift-working can be obtained at a reasonable cost in wages and employee morale, it will be practised on a much wider scale. Most managements in the industry seem to favour shift-work in principle, and it remains surprising that, given the intensity of competition, the large turnovers and the philosophy of management, the over-all shift-work ratio in the soap industry is so low. Even among the top ten, 'intensive' shift-working establishments are almost certainly in the minority. On the whole, this industry must be regarded as a 'prediction failure' for our theory.

9.10. Drugs and Pharmaceutical Preparations

Self-evidently, the products of this trade are varied; the total demand for many individual drugs is too small to permit large-scale production. (The biggest single item is penicillin, output of which in 1951 was valued at £7 millions.) However, this is not a trade of small establishments. Average net output per plant in 1951 was double the average for all Chemicals and allied trades: several pharmaceutical plants were very large indeed, the four largest in 1951 employing an average of 3000 persons and producing gross output worth £12 millions.

Shift-working was practised, but not extensively. A summary of the position in 1951 is given in Table 9.8. The 'intensive' shift-working establishments were a tiny minority, and accounted for only one-half of 1 % of total operative employment. (They conformed to the rules, however, in having higher net output per head and paying higher wages than the rest of the trade.) Intermediate establishments were statistically important, accounting for over 40 % of the employment, but the shift-working ratio among them was low. Female efficiency, diversification and special difficulties in supervision appeared to be the main factors, together with the fact that many of the 'process workers' are semi-professional salaried persons, among whom, we have already noted, dislike of shift-work is especially strong.

One firm in the industry, when interviewed, gave suggestive support to the dynamic model outlined at the end of Chapter 2. They said they had used to work shifts, but had given them up in face of an increasing shortage of labour, particularly of technically qualified supervisory

Table 9.8. *Shift-working in drugs and pharmaceuticals trade, Great Britain, 1951*

<table>
<tr><th>Shift-work ratio</th><th>Zero</th><th>1–35 %</th><th>> 35 %</th><th>Total</th></tr>
<tr><td>Establishments, no.</td><td>246</td><td>35</td><td>5</td><td>286</td></tr>
<tr><td>Operatives, %</td><td>58</td><td>41½</td><td>½</td><td>100</td></tr>
<tr><td>Shift-work ratio, %</td><td>—</td><td>15</td><td>49</td><td>6</td></tr>
<tr><td>Ops per establishment, no.</td><td>85</td><td>429</td><td>41</td><td>126</td></tr>
<tr><td>Net output per op.</td><td colspan="2">£1373</td><td>£1510</td><td>£1374</td></tr>
<tr><td>Wages per op.</td><td colspan="2">£267</td><td>£363</td><td>£268</td></tr>
</table>

labour. 'A shortage of labour' is another name for a state of affairs where very high wages would have to be paid if more labour were to be obtained; the basic wage rate at the margin is much higher than the wage rate actually being paid. It will be remembered that the theory postulated that a jump in technical progress in a particular branch of industry would tend to encourage shift-working (or more precisely encourage the construction of plants designed to be worked on shifts) in the establishments where the new technique was adopted. But then, as real wages rose, so also would the wages it would be necessary to pay to actual and prospective workers in the branch of industry in question; $\bar{\bar{w}}$ would rise and shift-work would cease to be profitable until the fruits of another jump in technique were embodied in new capital equipment. This might well happen in a different group of firms, so that the identity of the shift-working firms in the industry would historically be changing.

9.11. Vehicles

This industrial order comprises the motor trade, the aircraft industry and the trades producing railway rolling stock and locomotives. The motor trade is responsible for over half the operative employment (i.e. for 300 000 out of 560 000 operatives in 1951) and in our statistics has been divided into two groups of establishments, the first comprising those with output consisting mainly of complete vehicles and chassis, the second comprising those which make only parts. The final output of the trade as a whole consists of private cars, commercial vehicles, chassis and bicycles. In the railway vehicle trades, there is a major distinction between the establishments owned and operated by British Railways and those owned by 'private' companies. On the one hand the railway shops produced almost exclusively for their own corporation and 70 % of their gross output consisted of repair work; they also produced a large proportion of the new locomotives, carriages and wagons required for use on British main lines. The companies, on the other hand, undertook little repair work and were perforce strongly export oriented, particularly in the case of locomotives. For both the locomotives trade and the carriages and wagons trade, the Census of Production distinguishes between the railway shops and the company establishments in nearly all the main tables (excluding the shift-working tables), but in the special shift-working tabulations made for this inquiry the two groups were in both cases amalgamated. This procedure, originally followed at our request, then seemed desirable but now appears to have been mistaken.

Establishments engaged mainly on motor repairs were excluded from the scope of this inquiry, therefore the motor trade here consists of a larger number of specialised producers of parts (including such fundamental components as bodies and wheels) supplying a much smaller number of what are essentially assembly plants. In the latter, however, manufacture of many major components such as engine blocks and even bodies is also undertaken on a large scale but to a varying extent in the different enterprises. The average size of the 125 assembly plants is considerable: in terms of operatives it is five times greater than in manufacturing industry as a whole and two and a half times greater than among the specialised producers of motor parts. One tends to think of the 'big five' motor car assembly plants as outstanding examples of large-scale mechanised modern industry, and indeed the layman's image of 'modern times' is closely associated with the picture of a motor car assembly line in a plant employing several thousands of workers; each worker passes the day performing a single operation on the line, or tending the needs of a voracious but highly productive, highly automatic, fabricating machine. In truth, however, any kind of assembly line, at least until recently, was not a highly mechanised activity; despite the conveyor-belt, the greater part of the critical operations were performed by hand. The highly mechanised operations in motor manufacture come earlier, in body shops, in machine shops generally and in some of the specialised establishments. In the assembly plants, therefore, the over-all utilisation incentive is not as strong as might be expected, a fact which is borne out in Table I. Furthermore, although the plants are large, it is well known that in the United Kingdom they tend to fall well short of the size required for maximum economy of scale: more precisely, the total number of different automobile models produced in this country each year is substantially greater than the number which could most efficiently employ the largest indivisible items of mechanised equipment in the industry, such as body presses. Scale restraint is therefore important. It is significant, therefore, that the over-all shift-work ratio in the United States automobile industry is apparently nearly double the ratio in the United Kingdom and that the ratio in both sections of the British trade is surprisingly low. In the 'parts' section in Great Britain in 1951 only 8 % of the operatives were employed in intensive shift-working establishments and only just over half were in 'intermediates'. In the assembly plants, the proportion of operatives employed in the 'over-35's' was rather greater, indeed nearly as high as 30 %, but in the rest of the industry still nearly half the operatives were employed in establishments where there was no shift-work whatsoever. The interpretation of the position in the assembly plants is difficult. The thirty-seven estimated intensive shift-working establishments comprise statistically a group of three fairly large plants operated on a two-shift system (average shift-work ratio 66 %) together with a considerably larger group of thirty-four establishments reported on multi-establishment returns in which the shift-work ratio averaged no less than 80 %. By contrast, the over-all shift-work ratio in the fourteen establishments in the intermediate group was no more than 17 %. These latter establishments were on average very large indeed (nearly 3000 operatives per establishment) whereas the average size of the 'over-35's' was little greater than for the trade as a whole. In the fourteen intermediate establishments we appear to have a clear case of the integration-effect first discussed in Chapter 7:† the group probably corresponded fairly closely with the plants controlled by the 'big five' motor manufacturers. The statistical picture presented by the group certainly corresponded well with the impression gained in interviews. Vauxhall, for example, told us that it was the policy of General Motors to keep shift-working to the minimum because the Company believed the practice to be anti-social. But although this firm like many others decides the question of multiple versus single shifts on the merits of the case in each department (and largely by rule of thumb) one suspects that the over-all result is as much based on economic as on social policy—a suggestion which is borne out by the fact that the shift-work ratio in General Motors' establishments in other countries tends to be higher than in the United Kingdom. Unfortunately, however, no interview was obtained with a firm operating an establishment in the intensive shift-working group and it is still not clear exactly who these firms were or what were the main factors (other than the reverse operation of integration-effect) governing their shift-working decision. It seems likely that a disproportionate number among them were specialists in the production of commercial vehicles in contrast to private cars, and it is known that at least two leading commercial vehicle manufacturers engaged in extensive shift-work.‡ Another famous commercial vehicle firm, A.E.C., who gave valuable assistance to the inquiry, never have more than about 20 % of their operatives on shifts and most of these are in the machine shops (but even there the shift-work ratio rarely reaches 30 %): shift-working on the assembly line is negligible. The firm gave a number of reasons for not undertaking more shift-work, all of which seemed ultimately to resolve into one aspect or another of scale restraint. For example, a new, highly mechanised transfer machine which was installed a few years ago was not at first worked on shifts because its minimum efficient output on single shifts was sufficient for the firm's needs at the time. It was explained, however, that shifts would be worked as demand grew.

† Pp. 150–2.

‡ Another possibility is that they were producing military vehicles for the Korean War.

There was also a small minority of intensive shift-working establishments in the parts and components section of the trade, but their identity could not be determined. They also were smaller than the intermediate establishments of this section, but the comparison of size was not so striking as in the case of the assembly plants. Otherwise they fitted quite well with our general theory: net output per head among them was nearly 15 % higher than in the rest of the trade and the basic profit margin probably considerably higher also (we were unable to estimate this reliably).

In September 1951, when the shift-work census was taken, the private car manufacturers were operating at some 15–25 % below peak capacity: in the earlier part of the year they suffered a shortage of steel and in the latter part they were beginning to feel the effects of a sharp decline in export demand. In Fig. 7.2, where we analysed the cyclical behaviour of capital utilisation in the metal-using industries, it will be noticed that, unlike the Engineering group, the Vehicles group had passed their peak by 1951, and were running at a utilisation rate little higher, apparently, than that of the subsequent low year 1954. In fact, if we were able to separate the road from the rail vehicles we should almost certainly find that in September 1951 activity in road vehicles was higher than 1954. For by contrast with road vehicles, the most important discovery we made in the *railway vehicles* industry was that private locomotive shops experienced a major secular decline in demand between 1951 and 1954. They considerably reduced total employment, and therefore, of course, shift-work. The industry had been declining since 1948; the short-lived boom of 1951 was recognised as such and met by shift-work rather than by capacity expansion. By 1955, when we conducted our interviews, most people in this industry seemed to have forgotten that there had ever been much shift-work and assured us that it was a trade to which the system was particularly ill-suited! We estimate that taking the railway shops and companies combined, the 6000 shift-workers found by the Census of Production in 1951 had been reduced to about 1500 by 1954, and that most of these were in the railway shops where a certain amount of shift-work is always required in connection with urgent repairs. Since the capital–output analysis of Fig. 7.2 related to 'Vehicles' as a whole, these findings in connection with railway vehicles must qualify the suggestion made in Chapter 7 that the behaviour in the chart was largely cyclical. In the case of railway vehicles, a declining industry with excess capacity demonstrated a classic example of a secular 'unplanned' decline in capital utilisation.

This concludes our empirical chapters. The points we believe to have been established are summarised in the final chapter, which follows immediately.

CHAPTER 10

IMPLICATIONS FOR POLICY

10.1. Shift-work and Efficiency

Our theoretical and empirical inquiries completed, we conclude with a brief discussion of implications for economic policy. When we began this research, the main author was much attracted by the possibility that a widespread extension of shift-work could significantly improve economic efficiency and help promote growth. The results of the completed inquiry, however, suggest that the policy implications are much less clear-cut than was originally supposed. For example, we may reinterpret the arguments of Chapters 1 and 2 as follows: it is probably true that a reduction of resistance to shift-work will, by increasing the elasticity of utilisation, raise the relative profitability of high-intensive systems of operation at any given point in the history of wages and productivity. This will tend to raise the average level of utilisation and also, by increasing the rate of profit associated with any given real wage level, permit a faster rate of capital replacement (and/or of accumulation) and hence probably induce faster technical progress and growth. In other words, if the economic system were a single person, it could 'trade off' between growth and shift-work. But the economic system is not a single person, and we could find no logical method of arbitrating between those individuals who would prefer fast growth with inconvenient hours and those preferring slower growth with day-work only.

We also saw that if 'irrational' factors were tending to depress the elasticity of utilisation—i.e. factors which all would be happy to eliminate—an unambiguous gain should result if they were reduced. To the extent that transport barriers, trade union policies or managerial inertia could be counted as such (which means ignoring the feelings of drivers, trade unionists and managers' doctors), the inquiries described in Chapter 8 seem to have shown that the first two, at least, are not of great importance. As to managerial inertia, we certainly found many managements who gave unconvincing explanations of decisions not to work shifts. But we also found that many such explanations could well represent intuitive rationalisations of valid economic arguments. For example, few managers told us explicitly of 'scale restraint' or 'indivisibilities', even in other words. Many, however, told us that demand was inadequate (to permit shift-work). Were they then confusing the short run with the long run, confusing 'planned' and 'unplanned' utilisation? Probably they were. And if asked 'why did you not construct a factory half the size, designed to be run on shifts, and thus produce the same output for half the capital cost?' they were at loss for reply. But in many of these cases there was considerable evidence that the scale of output was in fact significantly restrained.

We may put our point another way. We have developed a theory of how the shift-work decision would be made in the absence of inertia. We suggest the theory has not unsuccessfully explained observed facts. This does not prove that inertia was absent, but it does show that the hypothesis of widespread inertia is not essential to explain the facts. It is true, of course, that the facts would have been difficult to explain without a theory of scale restraint. And it is also true that the observations we employed to test the existence of widespread scale restraint might have been interpreted as implying no more than that there is less inertia in large factories than small. But here our more detailed results may help. We found that shift-work was associated with size in terms of output, but not in terms of employment. This was consistent with the theory of scale restraint, but would not so easily be consistent with a theory based on inertia. In short, as a result of five years' research and reflection the author no longer believes that a miraculous acceleration of economic growth could (or should) be achieved by knocking together the heads of managers and trade unionists in order to persuade them rapidly to convert us into a universal double-shift society.

What, then, *are* the implications of our findings? It is for the reader to judge the extent to which the empirical tests in Part II have validated the theory suggested in Part I. However, in order to draw conclusions, we must indicate the points we ourselves believe to have been established. These are listed in § 10.2.

10.2. The Points Established

We believe we have established the following propositions:

(i) Partly because of the position of women, and partly because even men usually require compensation for shift-work, there is a significant increase in labour costs associated with all shift systems as against 'normal' systems.

(ii) The effect of this 'utilisation differential' is to create a state of affairs where shift-work is by no means always profitable. Shift-work will tend to be profitable, given the *elasticity of utilisation*, where the *elasticity of mechanisation* is high, where money wages are relatively low or the price of the product relatively high. In a dynamic analysis, shift-work in an industry will tend to be most prevalent among the minority of firms which is the first to adopt newly invented techniques. As an extension of this theorem, we can say that the stimulus (as measured by the difference in profit rates) to adopt newly invented techniques rapidly will be greater, the greater the elasticity of utilisation, thus confirming the suggestion made in Chapter 1 that the greater the elasticity of utilisation the greater will tend to be the average national rates of capital replacement and technical progress.

(iii) There is strong evidence for the existence of widespread scale restraint in British industry. Since scale restraint reduces not only utilisation but mechanisation, we may infer that this factor is not only causing us to utilise our capital less intensively than would otherwise be the case, but also to adopt less mechanised techniques of production.

(iv) Our society regards women primarily as actual or potential domestic mates, but nevertheless admits them to industrial employment. It treats them, however, as marginal members of the labour force, and pays them wages which, after adjustment for differences in productivity, are on average substantially below the males'. Also, because they are members of a weaker and fairer sex they are chivalrously protected from excessive physical exertion or unusual temptations to debauchery. Therefore, they are legally prohibited from employment at night. In consequence, an especially cheap form of labour is associated with an especially low elasticity of utilisation.

(v) There is some evidence that the spread of the industrial techniques collectively known as 'automation' may permit more intensive capital utilisation with constant or declining proportions of human shift-work.

10.3. Implications of the Incentive to Utilise

Clearly, if conclusion (ii) were our main one, policy recommendations, except on the basis of value judgement, would be impossible. An increase in the elasticity of utilisation, brought about for example by government *fiat*, would accelerate economic growth, but one could not assert that this would necessarily improve long-run social welfare. However, an elected government which decided so to act would, on any reasonable interpretation of democracy, be quite within its rights. (Our own views on the matter are somewhat coloured by the discovery—proposition (v)—that the question is possibly becoming academic.)

Perhaps a more useful conclusion from proposition (ii) is behaviouristic. We implied in Chapter 1, and we have confirmed in Chapters 2 and 7, that the relationship between shift-work and economic growth must run in both directions. If an economic system for any reason is growing fast, either because the distribution of income favours profits or because business men are quick to adopt new inventions, the 'incentive to utilise' will tend generally to be high, at any given level of the utilisation elasticity. This can be shown either in terms of the 'macro' model of Chapter 1, or in terms of the individual-industry dynamic model of Chapter 2. In the first case, the high incentive to utilise appears as a result of the (relatively) low initial wage–profit ratio; in the second case, the dynamic shift-working minority of firms in the typical industry will tend to be relatively important: both cases, as we have already emphasised, would represent different aspects of the same coin. In other words, suppose we regard the elasticity of utilisation as 'given'; then, given also the level of scale restraint, the amount of shift-work displayed by an economy will merely *reflect* that economy's rate of growth. On these assumptions then, if we observed extensive shift-work associated with rapid growth, we could not properly include the shift-work among the causes of the rapid growth; rather we should describe it as a by-product of real causes such as distribution of income or business dynamism. If therefore it is thought that our findings concerning the general intensity of capital utilisation in the United Kingdom (pp. 136–7) display an 'unsatisfactory' position, this can be regarded as a reflection of the deeper causes which have led to the country's slow rate of economic growth. Although we have not been able to obtain precise information, we have the strong impression that shift-work and intensive capital utilisation are considerably more prevalent in more rapidly growing (capitalist) economies. Certainly there is definite evidence that this was true in respect of the United States before that country fell into economic stagnation. In other words, if we wish to make the British economy grow faster, we should look for the deeper causes, rather than attempt artificially to stimulate shift-work.

10.4. Implications of Scale Restraint

The above conclusions, however, are those deriving from proposition (ii) only. With propositions (iii) and (iv) the position is rather different. It has long been recognised that scale restraint, through indivisibilities, may depress the level of mechanisation; it has also been recognised that scale restraint may generally raise production costs by preventing plants from expanding to 'optimum size'. The definition of 'size', however, has usually ignored the problem of capital utilisation. When utilisation can be varied, size in terms of output is not the same as size in terms of units of capital. Our findings show that restraints on size in terms of output may have considerably more far reaching effects than has sometimes been supposed. By causing under-utilisation as well as under-mechanisation, they extend the 'misallocation' of resources; in particular they deny the economic system the use of what is sometimes a cheap method of saving capital. And it is to be noted that the effect relates directly to the level of utilisation, not to the amount of human shift-work. Thus even if, under automation, high levels of utilisation could be achieved with relatively small shift-work ratios (i.e. were virtually 'costless'), the effects of restraint on the maximum output of individual plants would still operate. Only if (and this, fortunately, seems not unlikely) automation also reduces the output rates of minimum divisible units of equipment, 'miniaturising' our production system, so to speak, can this point be blunted.

Scale restraint arises from the competitive practices of private enterprise. These practices can cause markets to be stably divided between large numbers of moderately sized firms where, in many cases, from a technical point of view, a smaller number of larger firms could serve more efficiently. In consequence the consumer is offered a variety of brands where he would otherwise have less choice. We cannot tell whether the consumer prefers this state of affairs because, in the nature of things, he is never offered a choice between standardisation and cheapness on the one hand, and higher cost variety on the other. In effect, he is presented with a *fait accompli*. It is also known that, generally speaking, of any list of ten varieties of a product, some three, say, will on any objective test be of considerably better value than the others, while among the 'rump' themselves, differences will be rather insignificant. However, modern manufacturing corporations are highly diversified, and sometimes, but not always, a firm which is high on the value-for-money list in one line is not so high in others. Variety and consequential scale restraint, flowing from this relatively low degree of specialisation, may be a necessary feature of the process by which individual firms search for lines where by skill and fortune they can find a comparative advantage. In short, an increase in specialisation would almost certainly increase the short-run technical efficiency of the economy, but, even were there only one consumer, would not necessarily increase efficiency and/or welfare in the long run. The present author believes that it would in fact be possible to carry out a considerable industrial rationalisation in such a way as to preserve most of the forms of variety which (to him, at least) are of value, and at the same time relieve the economy of much of its present burden of scale restraint. This, however, is an opinion, or at least a considered judgement, rather than a scientific observation. The degree of re-organisation required would be radical, and would not be consistent with the maintenance of the present autonomy of corporate capitalism.

There are some ways of lifting scale restraint without reducing variety. The most obvious is a substantial increase in the size of the national market. Since the population of the United Kingdom is growing very slowly, the moral of this particular conclusion need hardly be spelled out.

10.5. Implications of Unequal Pay

Finally, we reach the second sex. If the social arrangements summarised in proposition (iv) are considered 'rational' it could be presumed that the economic consequences are 'rational' also. If, however, the social arrangements, taken as a whole, are considered illogical, then the resulting allocation of economic resources is very irrational indeed. It is not for the economist to say how society should treat women. He can, however, discuss the consistency, and hence the rationality, of the economic arrangements associated with a given collection of social attitudes. It is perfectly logical to admit women to the industrial community on special terms, for example imposing the condition that they shall not work at night (the same condition is imposed on juveniles, is widely practised in the western world and embodied in one of the Conventions of the International Labour Office). It may seem less logical to couple these conditions with unequal efficiency wages. There is considerable controversy as to the economic cause of the lower wages paid to females. Even where short-run productivity is equivalent, many employers argue that the shorter industrial life of women implies an unrewarding investment in their training which must necessarily be offset by lower wages. It seems most unlikely, however, that this factor is predominant. There is no evidence that the efficiency-wage sex-differential varies between industries in association with the degree of training required, nor are women who do not get married paid more than others. An elderly, reliable and experienced married woman who returns to the cotton industry after raising her family is still paid much less than a man would expect to earn if he operated the same machinery. And there is considerable evidence that the differentials are fixed as much by convention as by any other factor. There is overwhelming evidence that the different 'supply' position, or bargaining position, of women is the major factor. One reason for this is that the majority of women are not breadwinners and are therefore prepared to work for less. Another is simply that once society has established a convention, strongly supported by other workers, that a certain class of worker should be paid less than other classes, it is extremely difficult for the 'depressed' class to escape from the situation. This applies as much to women workers in the United Kingdom as to negro workers in the United States. As Baroness Wootton has so effectively established,† the determination of wage differentials in society is as much based on hierarchical considerations as it is on the laws of supply and demand. In effect, hierarchical attitudes constrain the economic structure within which supplies and demands for labour operate. It is as much a social as an economic collective choice, therefore, that determines the differential wages of the sexes.

If the foregoing argument is accepted we can definitely accuse society of logical inconsistency in admitting women to industry on special terms at reduced wages. A society, of course, has as much right to behave inconsistently as an individual, and, being a collective, is often likely to be inconsistent. In the present instance, however, government has frequently indicated that it recognises a responsibility in the matter,‡ and it is not denied that government, working in association with trade unions and employers could, if desired, bring about considerable changes. It is therefore useful to underline certain consequences of this particular social inconsistency. In the past the case for equal pay for women has mainly been argued on moral grounds, although the distortion of the price mechanism has not gone unnoticed. In the present study we believe we have discovered a particularly important aspect of this distortion. We have shown that the association of an especially low elasticity of utilisation with an especially low basic wage for women must tend, throughout the economy, to encourage the adoption of

† *The Social Foundations of Wages Policy*, by Barbara Wootton (London, 1954).

‡ See the Report of the Royal Commission on Equal Pay (London, 1946).

investment plans involving a significantly lower level of both utilisation and of mechanisation than would otherwise be the case.

Unfortunately, however, we cannot leap to the conclusion that if Equal Pay were decreed tomorrow by government *fiat* the results would be either easily predictable or unambiguously 'desirable'. There seems little doubt that if the *fiat* also lifted the ban on night work, provided the economy were able to accumulate the new capital appropriate to the newly optimised programmes, the adjustments would represent an improvement in the rationality of resource allocation. But if, as would be much more likely, the disability were retained while the wage was raised, the results would be more complex. We investigate them at the end of the chapter in a 'postscript on Equal Pay'.

10.6. The Effects of Reductions in Basic Hours

As the standard of living rises, an industrial society may be expected to reduce the length of the normal or average working week. This represents a reduction in the length of the basic shift, in effect a reduction in the basic rate of utilisation, $\bar{h}$. During the twentieth century a secular decline in the weekly hours of the average worker has in fact occurred, and this was accelerated in the nineteen-thirties. After World War II, however, the decline halted, or at least paused. In the early post-war period, average weekly individual hours in United Kingdom manufacturing steadily rose, reaching a peak in the middle nineteen-fifties. But they then began an irregular decline, suggesting that the old trend might well be re-asserting itself. By 1960, for example, almost the whole of the post-war increase had been eliminated.

This new tendency caused concern in some government circles, because they recognised that a decline in the basic rate of utilisation, even if real hourly wages were unchanged, could cause a decline in the rate of profit through increase in capital–output ratio. This, in turn, might adversely affect economic growth. Interest was directed, therefore, to the question of whether the situation might not be eased by an offsetting tendency in the relative rate of utilisation. Was it possible that the decline in basic rate of utilisation would cause an increase in the incentive to utilise? If so, the decline in basic rate would be associated with an increase in the *chosen* relative rate, leading possibly to a restoration of the absolute rate.

In order to analyse the question, it is necessary to put the problem in perspective. For this purpose we may use the technical-progress model of §1.5 in Chapter 7. Suppose, in the context of that model, an economic system is growing at a steady rate. Wages are rising with productivity, the share of wages in the product, the profit margin and the profit rate are all constant, and the profit rate is consistent with a rate of capital replacement (obsolescence) which, given the inventiveness of the economy, is just sufficient to generate the postulated rate of technical progress (productivity growth). (It is unlikely that any real economy, at any actual period of history, would be observed in this condition, but these are assumptions necessary to isolate the question at issue.) We may also assume that the average rate of capital utilisation is constant. Were it not, the rate of profit would not be steady unless wages were rising at a different speed from productivity, the difference being just sufficient to offset the trend in capital–output ratio. If, therefore, there was in fact a downward trend in the basic rate of utilisation, the preservation of steady growth would require less rapid growth of real wages.

Even if utilisation were declining, the rate of growth of real wages could remain substantial. Given the values of the variables, including the trend in basic utilisation, the 'permissible' trend in real wages depends on the invention function. If the invention function is 'favourable', indicating buoyant technical dynamism, the absolute loss involved in the reduction of hours might not seem serious, particularly when it is recognised that the reduction of hours represents an increase in leisure, which may be regarded as an economic commodity itself contributing to rising living standards.

In practice, reductions of hours are closely associated with increases in hourly wages. (The 'basic' real wage rate to which we refer above is, of course, the hourly rate throughout.) Usually the same weekly wage is paid for a shorter working week. But it is usually assumed that provided the rise in hourly real wage does not exceed the trend of productivity, profits will be protected. This, however, ignores the additional depression of the profit rate caused by the decline in basic rate of utilisation. If the profit rate is to be fully protected it is necessary that, however the negotiations are conducted, hourly earnings rise a little less than productivity. How much earnings may be permitted to rise, if a decline in profit rate is to be avoided, depends, as already indicated, on the productivity trend itself, which is in turn, in our conception, associated with the rate of profit (were this not the case, we should be less concerned). If the technical dynamism of the system were adequate it might be possible to permit hours to be reduced yet real *weekly* wages to rise, because the permissible rate of hourly-earnings growth was so rapid. Alternatively, if technical dynamism were low, it might be necessary to insist that weekly real earnings be reduced, or that the working-week decline be retarded. In the United Kingdom output per man-hour in manufacturing, in the late nineteen-fifties, was rising at about 3 % per annum. Had manufacturing represented the whole economic system, in the absence of a trend in utilisation, weekly real wages could have been permitted to rise at the same speed without endangering the profit rate or rate of growth. If, however, basic hours were to decline by 1 % annually, with no change in relative utilisation, the permissible growth of weekly real wages would have been reduced to 1 % per annum:† the 'rate of exchange' between changes in hours

† If relative utilisation is constant, and the annual change in basic hours is small, we can obtain an approximation for the permitted growth rate (proportionate increase per annum)

and changes in consumption was thus 2:1.† In an economy where productivity is rising only slowly, therefore, the effect is severe. Two opposing factors modify this application in the United Kingdom. In practice, hours have been declining more slowly than assumed; since 1956, when it appears to have begun, the trend of decline seems to have been nearer to one-half of 1 % per annum than to 1 %. On the other hand, manufacturing by no means represents the whole economy; its rate of progress is considerably faster than elsewhere, and it is expected to 'carry' a considerable proportion of the fixed-productivity occupations. The spreading of the benefits of manufacturing productivity growth is achieved by a declining trend in the prices of manufactured goods *relative* to other goods. This implies that only part of the manufacturing productivity increase is available to support rising wages or falling hours in manufacturing itself. Therefore one could calculate very roughly that if *weekly* real wages were to rise at the same speed in manufacturing as elsewhere, an annual 0·5 % decline in hours would again permit weekly wages to rise by no more than 1 % annually. It is clear therefore that the problem is by no means insignificant and that the questions posed at the beginning of the section well deserve consideration.

If we continue to assume that by some means or other the rate of profit is held constant, we see that the 'model' of events outlined in the preceding paragraphs implies that the initial wage–profit ratio in the economy at large must be declining: if basic utilisation were constant, the ratio would be constant, but with basic utilisation declining it is necessary to contrive a decline in relative wage costs in order to offset the effect of the rising capital–output ratio.‡ Since the wage–profit ratio is an essential ingredient in the general incentive to utilise, we might expect managers in consequence gradually to raise the chosen relative rate of utilisation (provided, of course, there was no downward trend in the elasticity of utilisation, a tendency which might well, in fact, be associated with a downward trend in basic hours). This, by tending to restore the capital–output ratio, would act as a general offset to the effects we have been describing. There is no way of assessing the strength of the effect; in general it would seem likely to be secondary. All we can

in weekly real wage rate per worker (weekly money wage divided by average product prices) by the formula

$$w_W^{\cdot} = o^{\cdot} - \frac{\bar{h}^{\cdot}}{w}, \qquad (10.1)$$

where $w_W^{\cdot}$ is growth rate of weekly wage rate, $o^{\cdot}$ growth rate of productivity, $\bar{h}^{\cdot}$ annual proportionate decline in basic utilisation, w initial proportion of wages and salaries in the value of net output (so defined in the present section *only*). This formula takes account both of the direct effect of utilisation change (the need to keep the hourly wage share at least constant) and the indirect effect (the need to reduce hourly wage cost by an amount sufficient to offset the effect of reduced utilisation on the capital–output ratio). It is reasonably accurate provided the trend of basic utilisation does not exceed about 5 %.

† The rate of exchange is $1/w$. We have taken w as roughly 0·5. w of course is itself associated with the rate of growth, so the position is quite complex.

‡ This means, unfortunately, that the permissible growth rate of weekly wages associated with a constant growth rate of productivity and leisure is itself gradually changing.

say is that it is one among the several factors determining the permissible rate of weekly wage increase, but probably not a strong one. To the extent that it exists, however, the rate of exchange between growth of leisure and growth of consumption is improved.

It is doubtful if we have described the problem as it appears to the government. The government probably fears that the decline in basic hours will not be compensated for by reduced wage growth, and wonders whether the position may not be restored by increased relative utilisation. To this question, there are two answers. One may always accelerate (or prevent a deceleration of) economic growth by 'artificially'† raising the rate of utilisation. Where this, however, involves longer working hours or increased use of the shift system, the welfare consequences are ambiguous, since both longer or less convenient hours may depress subjective welfare. Alternatively, if one is asking whether the relative utilisation rate will not in these circumstances rise naturally (assuming a given utilisation elasticity), the answer depends on what in fact happens to the rate of profit. In order to illuminate the point more sharply we may usefully clear the ground by dropping our supposedly realistic model, and reverting to one in which technical progress is absent, for example the model of § 1.4. Here, the rate of growth of output and employment depends uniquely on the rate of profit; this depends in turn on the wage rate and the (fixed) level of productivity. If then utilisation is reduced, the rates of growth and of profit will also be reduced unless the wage rate is varied by a compensating amount. If a compensating change in wage rate does not occur, what will be the outcome? In the theory expounded in Chapters 2 and 3 we saw that the basic rate of utilisation could not affect the choice of optimum programme in an individual activity, and we find that on the present assumptions this is true for the whole economy. A change in the basic rate of utilisation affects *all* the profit rates in a programme matrix in the same proportion; therefore it cannot affect the ordering of programme profit rates; therefore it cannot change the optimum programme. Neither the optimum level of mechanisation nor that of relative utilisation will be changed. The optimum programme, given the data (and given absence of progress), can change only through a change in basic wage rate. If basic wage rate is lowered to compensate a decline in profit rate, *then* the optimum programme may change, but not otherwise. If the government wishes to avoid 'undesirable' effects on economic growth from a declining working week, it must act more directly: either the growth of weekly real wages must be retarded (this, of course, may well happen through inflation as companies protect their profit margins by price increases), or the economic growth rate associated with a given rate of profit must be improved. For example, the proportion of profits saved must be increased, or the technical dynamism of the economy stimulated by structural intervention. However, since

† By an artificial action we mean an interference with decisions of private companies in a capitalist economy. The adjective has little meaning in a socialist economy.

declining working hours are an aspect of economic welfare, these 'musts' represent particular value judgements. The rate of exchange between the growth rates of leisure and consumption is to some extent a fact of life. It can be changed deliberately only by measures acting on the relation between economic growth and the profit rate, two examples of which have just been mentioned. But both would seem to require rather radical changes in the economic philosophy followed by British governments since 1955.

10.7. Effects of Taxation

Economic policy is sometimes implemented by means of special fiscal devices and, more generally, informed opinion is always concerned with the effects of different types of taxation on particular economic decisions. In the present case, the circumstances surrounding the imposition or withdrawal of a tax must be specified rather carefully if anything definite is to be said about the qualitative effect on capital utilisation. As a general rule, however, we can say that if firms are taking investment decisions on the basis of optimum programmes, the average planned rate of utilisation will be affected only if the tax alters the relation between the general level of wage costs and the general level of wholesale prices, that is, alters the effective real basic wage rate and the average rate of profit. Direct taxes are not usually thought of as having such an effect, except perhaps in senses which would not be relevant here. Indirect taxes, and especially payroll taxes, are another matter. For example, a mere transfer of taxation between income taxes and excise taxes, leaving total proceeds and government expenditure unchanged, would probably have little result, but a payroll tax, however spent, must raise wage costs and alter the basic real wage rate unless conditions are such that the whole burden can be passed on to consumers. If the whole burden cannot be passed on (i.e. if, with given programmes, manufacturers would be bound to suffer some reduction of profits), there will be a tendency for optimum programmes to change in the direction of either increased mechanisation or reduced utilisation. The actual result will depend on the average levels of the elasticities of mechanisation and of utilisation in industry at large. Very loosely, if in industry generally the 'marginal productivity of capital' is relatively high and/or resistance to shift-work relatively slight, it is more likely that the tax will stimulate increased mechanisation rather than reduced utilisation. But, conversely, in an economy where technical conditions are such that the marginal productivity of capital is low, the tax, instead of producing increased mechanisation, may merely produce reduced utilisation, or we might say, at least part of the effect may be 'wasted' in this way. The effect on economic growth, of course, will depend on the way the tax is spent. If total investment, government and private, is not increased but, say, remains constant, and if the main effect of the tax is reduced utilisation, the rate of growth will be unambiguously reduced, because the same savings ratio will be applied to a higher capital–output ratio. If mechanisation is increased, a once-and-for-all increase in output per man might be followed by a decline in the rate of capital accumulation or replacement. On the assumptions of the model described in Chapter 1, § 1.5, for example, the lower rate of replacement, due to lower utilisation, would involve lower technical progress and hence a lower growth-rate of productivity. In the long run, therefore, the effects might not be beneficial at all. This does not mean there may not be other good arguments for the tax.

10.8. Postscript: Possible Consequences of Equal Pay

Analysis of the possible consequences of a government *fiat* which ensured 'equal pay for equal work' but did not remove the prohibition on female (and juvenile) night work requires a moderately complicated deployment of our basic theoretical apparatus; therefore, in order to avoid dislocation of the narrative of this concluding chapter, we have reserved it for a postscript. We present no new empirical material, we merely apply the formal theory whose validity we claim to have reasonably established. In effect, having tested the predictions of the theory in various fields, we now develop certain specific predictions which could not be tested unless the government were in fact to act in the manner postulated.

We have to decide which of two very different macro-models of the current situation in respect of female employment best represents reality. Suppose we visualise the economy as producing only one commodity, facing a choice of only two techniques and two systems of utilisation. In principle, therefore, we face a two-by-two programme matrix. But we complicate the position by assuming that rather than absorb the consequences of the female-employment situation into a definition of the utilisation differential, we regard programmes employing women as variants or additions to the basic matrix. System 1, then, is a single-shift system employing men. System 1F is the same system employing women. System 2 is a multiple-shift system employing men. System 2F would be the same system employing women, but is illegal (we ignore the double-day shift). For simplicity women are supposed to be as efficient as men on both techniques of production: we are concerned with the problems posed by differences in efficiency wages only. We have then a total programme matrix (Table 10.1). In order to compute the corresponding profitability matrix we need, in addition to the data, the basic real wage of men (for programmes 1, 1, 1, 2, 2, 1 and 2, 2) and of women (for programmes 1, 1F and 2, 1F). Suppose we take the data from the matrices whose profit rates are given in Table 2.2. Let us assume that men's wages are as in matrix 2 in that table, and let us identify the bottom left-hand segment of matrix 2 with the 'male' portion of our present matrix. Let us assume

Table 10.1. *Male and female programme matrix*

System ...		1	1F	2
Technique	1	1, 1	1, 1F	1, 2
	2	2, 1	2, 1F	2, 2

that women's wages are $18\frac{1}{2}\%$ lower than men's and take the female profit rates from the corresponding section of Table 2.2, matrix 3. We thus obtain a male and female programme profit matrix as shown in Table 10.2. On these assumptions, then, the feminine 'handicap' of being prohibited from shift-work is precisely offset by the difference in real wage. Women will be employed indifferently in techniques 1 and 2 and these programmes earn the same rates as the men's. However, given the reasons so far advanced for the difference between male and female wages, such a result would seem to appear only as a coincidence. Is this really the case?

Table 10.2. *Male and female profit-rate matrix*

4	8	1
6	8	8

Suppose female wages happened to be lower. Then the rate of profit in programmes 1, 1F and 2, 1F would be higher, and the former now higher than the latter. Can we consider such a situation stable? If it is possible to produce a given commodity at a higher rate of profit, why would programmes such as 2, 2 be adopted? Why would there not be a tendency, when capital was due for replacement, to plan more female programmes, fewer male programmes? Assuming a system in which total output is somehow held constant, why would not the relative demand for women employees tend to rise, improve the female bargaining position and tend to adjust the wage differential?

The answers are that we know our economy does not necessarily possess so much flexibility. It is possible for wage rigidities to permit persistent differences in rates of profit, persistent excess demand for females and persistent deficiency in the demand for males, all concealed perhaps in a general excess of demand for labour as a whole. Firms which happened to be in a position to tap the female labour supply and use the female programme could consistently earn higher profits, or charge lower prices.

In other words, we may either assume that the analysis begins from a model of 'initial equilibrium' in which the female wage rate has been adjusted so as to equalise profit rates, or we may assume 'initial disequilibrium', in which case the analysis commences from a position in which the optimum female profit rate, such as 1, 1 F, is significantly below the male, such as 2, 2.

This is not the only difficulty. Suppose the government decrees that female money wages shall be raised to equal males'. It is not at all clear how the *real* wages of the two sexes will then subsequently develop. If employers cannot pass on the cost increases to the public, female real wages rise by the full amount of their money wages. But if, after a process of inflation, employers succeed in passing on some increases, the effect may be to *lower* male real wages, so that male and female real and money wages come to equality at a position somewhere between their original levels. The characteristics of this position are difficult to determine, but, since initial male employment greatly exceeds female, one might intuitively suppose that the decline in male real wages would in some sense be substantially smaller than the increases in females'.

We call the first assumption about wages the 'no-inflation' assumption, the second the 'with-inflation' assumption. In the first case the average rate of profit in the economy as a whole is reduced, in the second case it need not be, and we shall assume that it is not.

We are unable to offer evidence as to whether the initial equilibrium or the initial disequilibrium is the more realistic, and the choice between the two assumptions about the course of real wages depends on anticipated government policy. We are therefore compelled to treat the problem taxonomically, that is to investigate separately the consequences of each of the four combinations of pairs of assumptions.

Table 10.3. *Profit-rate matrix from initial equilibrium, no inflation*

4 6	4 6	11 8

Starting from an initial-equilibrium model, if female real wages rise the whole distance, males remaining constant, we obtain the matrix shown in Table 10.3. In other words, initial equilibrium leads to disequilibrium. If we assume that the initial equilibrium was not a coincidence, but the result of systematic adjustment of female wages, and if this flexibility is maintained, the new situation cannot persist. New investment will increasingly be directed toward programme 2, 2, employing males, and the relative demand for females will decline, thus, presumably, driving female wages back to where they came from. However, if it is now *illegal* to 'discriminate' against females, we have created conditions preventing flexibility and the situation can persist and must. There will now be chronic excess relative demand for males, and companies able to obtain males will be able to earn above-average profits. Alternatively the products of these companies become cheaper. The average rate of profit in the economy is reduced, with possible consequences for growth. We have somehow to assume that the private sector nevertheless attempts to reconstruct the capital stock in the manner required for the new pattern of programmes. If not, female employment may decline.

Table 10.4. *Profit-rate matrix of initial disequilibrium*

4	12	1
6	10	8

Table 10.5. *Profit-rate matrix from initial disequilibrium, no inflation*

4	4	1
6	6	8

The matrix for an initial disequilibrium situation might appear as shown in Table 10.4. With no-inflation this, after the *fiat*, would become as shown in Table 10.5. We still have a disequilibrium situation, but the character of the disequilibrium is reversed; in the long run, an excess demand for *males* should develop. (This is not an accidental result of the figures chosen, but is inevitable from the assumptions.) However, it is by no means certain that conditions permitting a persistent disequilibrium in one direction will necessarily permit a persistent disequilibrium in the other. It would be by no means impossible that as a result both of the decline in average profit rate and the decline in the relative profitability of female programmes, female employment might decline in this case also. The government could avoid the disequilibrium, but not the decline in average national profit rate, if by some means female wages were raised only to the extent necessary to create the conditions first described in Table 10.2. In other words, we have here a model in which initially female wages are about $33\frac{1}{2}$ % below men's. If the differential is reduced to $18\frac{1}{2}$ %, we obtain the 'equilibrium' position in which both male and female optimum programmes earn 8 %. But if wages are equalised, we obtain the 'disequilibrium' position depicted in Table 10.3.

'With-inflation' results must necessarily be less determinate. Suppose, starting from an initial differential of $18\frac{1}{2}$ % in an initial-equilibrium model, real wages are equalised after a male decline of just under 5 %, combined with a female rise just under 20 %.† (More drastic changes would raise the average rate of profit.) The new matrix would appear somewhat as shown in Table 10.6. We again face disequilibrium and the

Table 10.6. *Profit-rate matrix from initial equilibrium, with inflation*

5	5	4
7	7	9

† Since women's wages are initially $18\frac{1}{2}$% below men's, they must rise $22\frac{1}{2}$% to close the gap if men's do not fall.

attendant paradoxes. The conclusions are similar to those flowing from Table 10.3.

Alteration of the initial assumptions has little effect on the conclusions of the with-inflation combinations. So long as the end result is constrained by the assumption that wages are equalised at a level which leaves the general rate of profit more or less unchanged, some disequilibrium is inevitable.

We are therefore ready to conclude. Women are paid lower efficiency wages than men in the sense that their average money wages are lower than can be explained by a difference between average output-per-woman-hour and average output-per-man-hour using comparable equipment. It has sometimes been argued that other feminine disabilities, such as their relatively short industrial life (which increases the burden of training costs) are sufficient to explain the phenomenon. But there can be little doubt in practice that at least a part is due to bargaining position and convention. However, it is possible that in the prohibition on night work we have found a further and explanatory disability. If the various possible disabilities taken together are in fact a sufficient explanation of the whole of the existing difference in average wages, there may exist an equilibrium situation in which the average long-run rate of profit in programmes employing females is much the same as in programmes employing males. This should be associated with less mechanisation in the female programmes, a phenomenon which is, in fact, observed. If the 'initial equilibrium' hypothesis is correct, 'artificial'† government action to equalise efficiency wages would provoke either a chronic imbalance in the relative demand for males and females, a reduction in female employment, or both. Alternatively, if in fact the existing situation is not an equilibrium one (as seems by no means unlikely), and female wages are lower than can be explained by the disabilities, government action could produce a precise equilibrium result (see Table 10.2), unless the *fiat* specified that rather than efficiency wages be equalised, female wages be raised by no more than necessary to produce a state of affairs in which it was possible for a single-shift programme with women to earn as much as a multiple-shift programme with men. In short, if society places industrial disabilities on women, it cannot expect them to be employed at equal pay, even though, during any hour of operation they are, after training, fully efficient. Since society benefits from the production of the women workers, socio-economic justice would seem to require that they be in some way compensated for being deprived of the right to decide their own price for shift-work.

In practice there are considerable difficulties in devising legislation enforcing equal efficiency wages. The problem is even greater when a theoretically determinate, empirically vague, relativity, rather than equality, is desired. If we believe that the present situation is a disequilibrium one, and that a corrective policy is desirable, we can suggest

† See p. 212 (n.).

that a payroll tax should differentiate against female employment, i.e. be levied at a higher rate on the female payroll than the male. This would raise the *cost* of female employment, and induce mechanisation. The differential should not, in principle, be greater than necessary to yield an 'equilibrium' situation; otherwise a reduced relative demand for women might depress female relative wages in part compensation for the tax. Then, in justice, the male portion of the working force should pay for society's gallantry by a transfer of purchasing power: the proceeds of the excess payroll tax on women should be devoted to income tax concessions for unmarried female workers, additional family allowances for *employed* married women, and the like.

This is the type of proposal which has met with almost no response ever since welfare economics was invented. Also, since it would not affect the rate of utilisation, it could be said to be outside our terms of reference. Let us, however, interpret our terms of reference broadly by saying no more than that they are concerned with problems of economic policy which arise from an investigation of the theory and practice of utilisation. Economic policy is concerned exclusively with economic welfare. If this is denied, the concept of policy is meaningless. If governments are concerned with economic growth other than because growth means welfare, their actions—except in a purely belligerent sense—are pointless. Unfortunately, government and public opinion in western countries display highly conventional views as to legitimate scope of policy. Means are confused with ends, production with utility, travel with arrival. Simple measures to increase production, such as persuading workers to abandon demands for shorter hours, are welcomed. Measures which might improve the welfare associated with a given level of production are regarded as academic. True, the 'academic' measures are often complex in theoretical origin and uncertain in quantitative effect. But innocent are they who believe that no uncertainty is involved in assessing the effects on welfare of a particular exchange between leisure and consumption, or of conventional laws relating to the employment of women.

STATISTICAL APPENDIX TO PART II

NOTE. Throughout this Appendix, — signifies zero or small and .. signifies 'not available'. For further explanation of the tables see p. 130 above. Owing to rounding, columns or rows do not necessarily add to totals, and indicated ratios, which are in all cases derived from unrounded data, may differ substantially from the figures implied by their rounded components where printed.

Table 1. *Primary data relating to shift-work, Great Britain, 1951*

Industrial order	Number of establishments: Estabs. with shift-work ratio of Zero (1)	1–35 % (2)	> 35 % (3)	All estabs. (4)	Total number of operatives: Estabs. with shift-work ratio of Zero (000) (5)	1–35 % (000) (6)	> 35 % (000) (7)	All estabs. (000) (8)	Of which adult males (%) (9) M	Average shift-work ratios: Estabs. with ratios of 1–100% (%) (10) R	1–35 % (%) (11)	> 35 % (%) (12)	All estabs. (%) (13)
III. *Treatment of non-metalliferous mining products other than coal*													
1. Brick and fireclay	869	67	97	1 033	48·55	10·70	9·68	68·94	87	46	13	83	14
2. China and earthware	310	32	—	342	61·41	5·64	—	67·05	38	17	17	—	1
3. Glass containers	10	—	54	64	0·73	—	21·52	22·25	76	56	—	56	55
4. Glass (other than containers)	252	21	30	303	10·49	10·36	14·17	35·02	72	42	26	53	29
5. Cement	7	10	31	48	0·06	1·88	8·08	10·01	97	38	26	41	33
6. Abrasives	35	3	2	40	2·15	2·91	0·84	5·91	79	18	10	48	12
7. Building materials	867	16	49	932	33·28	3·03	7·95	44·26	92	47	18	59	12
8. Roofing felts	18	—	3	21	0·90	—	0·48	1·38	88	44	—	39	15
Total	2 368	149	266	2 783	157·57	34·53	62·72	254·81	72	44	18	58	17

Industrial order	Net output. Estabs. with shift-work ratios of			Operatives' earnings. Estabs. with shift-work ratios of			Net output per operative. Estabs. with shift-work ratios of			Earnings per operative. Estabs. with shift-work ratios of		
	> 35 % (£000) (14)	All other (£000) (15)	All (£000) (16)	> 35 % (£000) (17)	All other (£000) (18)	All (£000) (19)	> 35 % (£) (20)	All other (£) (21)	All (£) (22)	> 35 % (£) (23)	All other (£) (24)	All (£) (25)
III. *Treatment of non-metalliferous mining products other than coal*												
1. Brick and fireclay	7 000	39 100	46 100	3 800	22 500	26 300	726	659	669	398	379	382
2. China and earthware	—	33 700	33 700	—	18 200	18 200	—	503	503	—	271	271
3. Glass containers	15 500	900	16 400	8 400	450	8 850	721	1 284	739	389	..	398
4. Glass (other than containers)	11 700	15 500	27 200	5 100	7 400	12 500	825	742	776	359	354	356
5. Cement	14 500	3 600	18 200	3 700	900	4 500	1 801	1 880	1 816	452	461	454
6. Abrasives	1 100	6 800	8 000	300	1 900	2 300	1 357	1 348	1 349	391	381	383
7. Building materials	8 900	27 800	36 700	3 300	13 800	17 100	1 120	767	830	416	379	386
8. Roofing felts	600	1 800	2 400	100	500	600	1 141	2 042	1 728	224	502	405
Total	59 400	129 300	188 700	24 700	65 650	90 350	947	673	741	394	342	355

Table I (*continued*)

Industrial order	Number of establishments: Estabs. with shift-work ratio of: Zero (1)	1–35% (2)	> 35% (3)	All estabs. (4)	Total number of operatives: Estabs. with shift-work ratio of: Zero (000) (5)	1–35% (000) (6)	> 35% (000) (7)	All estabs. (000) (8)	Of which adult males (%) (9) M	Average shift-work ratios: Estabs. with ratios of: 1–100% (%) (10) R	1–35% (%) (11)	> 35% (%) (12)	All estabs. (%) (13)
IV. *Chemicals and allied trades*													
1. Coke ovens and by-products	8	—	77	85	0·09	1·49	14·51	16·09	98	50	26	52	50
2. Dyes and dyestuffs	20	10	6	36	1·66	9·65	1·85	13·16	88	32	30	42	28
3. Fertiliser, disinfectant, insecticide, etc.	120	23	31	174	4·47	1·28	8·99	14·74	87	39	21	42	27
4. Coal-tar products	12	44	17	73	0·13	3·07	1·38	4·58	94	26	22	35	24
5. Chemicals (general)	209	159	120	488	6·42	37·68	19·46	63·56	90	34	27	49	31
6. Drugs and pharmaceutical preps.	246	35	5	286	20·86	15·03	0·20	36·10	43	15	15	49	6
7. Toilet preps. and perfumery	78	3	—	81	6·43	0·79	—	7·22	24	8	8	—	1
8. Explosives and fireworks	43	14	2	59	9·62	6·30	10·30	26·22	65	32	10	45	20
9. Paint and varnish	340	18	2	360	17·57	2·28	0·70	20·54	74	19	10	50	3
10. Soap, candles and glycerine	111	14	9	134	4·84	8·83	2·42	16·09	56	20	9	58	14
11. Polishes	73	—	—	73	3·72	—	—	3·72	39	—	—	—	—
12. Ink	42	10	2	54	1·61	0·91	0·16	2·69	84	21	13	63	8
13. Mineral oil refining	0	8	7	15	—	5·74	3·53	9·28	96	32	22	47	32
14. Oils and greases	161	10	7	178	4·83	0·82	0·38	6·04	79	34	28	48	7
15. Seed crushing and oil refining	12	11	24	47	0·48	0·99	5·88	7·35	92	47	24	51	44
16. Glue, gum, paste and allied trades	39	13	12	64	1·18	1·50	1·33	4·01	78	38	28	49	27
17. Plastics materials	22	6	40	68	0·62	1·07	12·07	13·75	90	55	25	58	53
Total	1 536	378	361	2 275	84·53	97·43	83·17	265·13	75	34	21	49	24

Industrial order	Net output. Estabs. with shift-work ratios of			Operatives' earnings. Estabs. with shift-work ratios of			Net output per operative. Estabs. with shift-work ratios of			Earnings per operative. Estabs. with shift-work ratios of		
	> 35% (£000) (14)	All other (£000) (15)	All (£000) (16)	> 35% (£000) (17)	All other (£000) (18)	All (£000) (19)	> 35% (£) (20)	All other (£) (21)	All (£) (22)	> 35% (£) (23)	All other (£) (24)	All (£) (25)
IV. *Chemicals and allied trades*												
1. Coke ovens and by-products	15 500	1 400	16 800	6 000	600	6 600	1 065	874	1 046	414	385	411
2. Dyes and dyestuffs	3 200	20 000	23 200	900	4 900	5 700	1 705	1 771	1 762	461	431	435
3. Fertiliser, disinfectant, insecticide, etc.	11 800	7 800	19 600	3 800	2 000	5 800	1 311	1 361	1 331	418	351	392
4. Coal-tar products	2 000	3 800	5 800	500	1 300	1 700	1 449	1 186	1 265	352	393	381
5. Chemicals (general)	29 100	66 900	96 000	8 100	17 900	26 000	1 494	1 517	1 510	419	405	409
6. Drugs and pharmaceutical preps.	300	49 300	49 600	100	9 600	9 700	1 510	1 373	1 374	363	267	268
7. Toilet preps. and perfumery	—	12 000	12 000	—	1 600	1 600	—	1 659	1 659	—	222	222
8. Explosives and fireworks	6 200	8 500	14 700	3 600	5 200	8 800	601	535	561	349	327	335
9. Paint and varnish	1 600	37 600	39 100	300	6 500	6 800	2 269	1 892	1 905	376	328	330
10. Soap, candles and glycerine	2 900	17 100	19 900	900	4 400	5 300	1 187	1 248	1 239	374	320	328
11. Polishes	—	5 300	5 300	—	1 000	1 000	—	1 426	1 426	—	263	263
12. Ink	300	4 600	4 800	100	1 000	1 000	1 813	1 800	1 803	381	391	391
13. Mineral oil refining	(5 400)	(8 600)	(14 000)	1 500	2 600	4 000	..	..	..	414	444	433
14. Oils and greases	400	11 200	11 700	100	1 900	2 000	1 165	1 988	1 936	355	336	338
15. Seed crushing and oil refining	6 200	1 900	8 100	2 100	900	2 900	1 058	1 278	1 102	350	586	398
16. Glue, gum, paste and allied trades	1 600	3 800	5 400	500	900	1 400	1 217	1 425	1 356	376	353	360
17. Plastics materials	19 300	2 500	21 900	4 900	600	5 500	1 603	1 501	1 591	406	385	403
Total	105 800	262 200	368 000	33 200	62 800	96 000	1 272	1 450	1 335	399	345	362

Table I (*continued*)

Industrial order	Number of establishments: Estabs. with shift-work ratio of Zero (1)	1–35% (2)	> 35% (3)	All estabs. (4)	Total number of operatives: Estabs. with shift-work ratio of Zero (000) (5)	1–35% (000) (6)	> 35% (000) (7)	All estabs. (000) (8)	Of which adult males (%) (9) M	Average shift-work ratios: Estabs. with ratios of 1–100% (%) (10) R	1–35% (%) (11)	> 35% (%) (12)	All estabs. (%) (13)
V. *Metal manufacture*													
1. Blast furnaces	1	4	41	46	0·01	1·38	22·74	24·13	97	56	34	58	56
2. Iron and steel (matting and rolling)	148	74	176	398	12·76	27·18	131·91	171·85	92	57	15	65	53
3. Iron foundries	828	41	33	902	70·09	20·70	12·78	103·56	87	39	12	83	13
4. Steel sheets	2	3	26	31	0·23	0·99	15·76	16·98	92	68	30	71	67
5. Tinplate	2	2	40	44	0·12	0·20	15·03	15·35	81	57	32	57	56
6. Wrought iron and steel tubes	105	19	32	156	6·03	8·95	18·66	33·64	85	52	17	69	43
7. Non-ferrous metals (smelting, rolling, etc.)	308	96	89	493	22·46	30·45	34·22	87·13	82	48	20	73	36
Total	1 394	239	437	2 070	111·70	89·85	251·09	452·64	88	54	17	67	40

Industrial order	Net output. Estabs. with shift-work ratios of			Operatives' earnings. Estabs. with shift-work ratios of			Net output per operative. Estabs. with shift-work ratios of			Earnings per operative. Estabs. with shift-work ratios of		
	> 35 % (£000) (14)	All other (£000) (15)	All (£000) (16)	> 35 % (£000) (17)	All other (£000) (18)	All (£000) (19)	> 35 % (£) (20)	All other (£) (21)	All (£) (22)	> 35 % (£) (23)	All other (£) (24)	All (£) (25)
V. *Metal manufacture*												
1. Blast furnaces	19 700	1 400	21 100	10 000	600	10 500	864	1 040	874	438	413	437
2. Iron and steel (matting and rolling)	131 200	41 900	173 100	59 400	16 500	75 800	995	1 049	1 007	450	412	441
3. Iron foundries	11 500	68 100	79 600	5 600	36 400	41 900	899	750	769	436	400	405
4. Steel sheets	17 100	1 200	18 200	7 300	500	7 800	1 082	959	1 073	462	436	460
5. Tinplate	15 500	400	16 000	6 300	200	6 400	1 034	1 303	1 039	416	587	419
6. Wrought iron and steel tubes	20 400	13 300	33 700	7 800	5 600	13 400	1 092	886	1 000	416	375	397
7. Non-ferrous metals (smelting, rolling, etc.)	39 600	59 100	98 700	14 300	20 600	34 900	1 156	1 117	1 133	418	390	401
Total	254 900	185 400	440 300	110 500	80 300	190 800	1 015	920	973	440	399	422

Table I (*continued*)

Industrial order	Number of establishments: Estabs. with shift-work ratio of Zero (1)	1–35 % (2)	> 35 % (3)	All estabs. (4)	Total number of operatives: Estabs. with shift-work ratio of Zero (000) (5)	1–35 % (000) (6)	> 35 % (000) (7)	All estabs. (000) (8)	Of which adult males (%) (9) M	Average shift-work ratios: Estabs. with ratios of 1–100% (%) (10) R	1–35 % (%) (11)	> 35 % (%) (12)	All estabs. (%) (13)
VI. *Engineering, shipbuilding, and electrical goods*													
1. Shipbuilding and repairing	672	—	14	686	154·06	—	17·98	172·04	94	100	—	100	10
2. Marine engineering	72	10	14	96	17·67	9·10	14·74	41·50	91	68	17	100	39
3. Machine tools	570	14	97	681	42·89	5·64	21·29	69·81	81	78	10	96	30
4. Textile machinery and accessories	429	17	14	460	37·39	15·79	4·83	58·00	84	33	13	99	12
5. Small arms	20	—	—	20	4·40	—	—	4·40	70	—	—	—	—
6. Mechanical handling equipment	176	7	3	186	18·64	3·81	1·04	23·49	89	36	19	98	7
7. Printing and bookbinding machinery	102	3	14	119	10·29	1·74	2·63	14·66	87	52	6	82	4
8. Mechanical engineering (general)	2 445	169	341	2 955	229·50	70·90	111·32	411·72	84	59	11	89	26
9. Electrical engineering (general)	846	51	127	1 024	108·98	32·45	77·24	218·68	64	55	20	69	28
10. Electrical wires and cables	22	33	22	77	3·83	23·43	9·78	37·04	64	36	20	74	32
11. Radio and telecommunications	377	5	81	463	116·39	1·98	66·66	185·04	62	56	11	57	20
12. Batteries	38	15	—	53	3·28	10·19	—	13·48	48	15	15	—	12
13. Electric lighting accessories and fittings	138	10	—	148	10·44	1·37	—	11·82	44	13	13	—	2
Total	5 907	334	727	6 968	757·75	176·41	327·51	1261·67	78	57	15	79	23

Industrial order	Net output. Estabs. with shift-work ratios of			Operatives' earnings. Estabs. with shift-work ratios of			Net output per operative. Estabs. with shift-work ratios of			Earnings per operative. Estabs. with shift-work ratios of		
	> 35 % (£000) (14)	All other (£000) (15)	All (£000) (16)	> 35 % (£000) (17)	All other (£000) (18)	All (£000) (19)	> 35 % (£) (20)	All other (£) (21)	All (£) (22)	> 35 % (£) (23)	All other (£) (24)	All (£) (25)
VI. *Engineering, shipbuilding, and electrical goods*												
1. Shipbuilding and repairing	10 700	92 600	103 200	7 100	60 600	67 800	593	601	600	397	394	394
2. Marine engineering	11 200	17 000	28 100	5 600	9 300	15 000	757	635	678	382	349	361
3. Machine tools	19 900	43 800	63 700	8 800	18 200	26 900	936	903	913	411	375	386
4. Textile machinery and accessories	3 700	38 400	42 200	1 900	19 400	21 300	774	723	727	394	365	368
5. Small arms	—	2 900	2 900	—	1 700	1 700	—	667	667	—	380	380
6. Mechanical handling equipment	800	20 800	21 700	400	8 700	9 100	806	928	923	401	387	388
7. Printing and bookbinding machinery	2 900	11 000	13 800	1 000	4 400	5 500	1 083	912	943	398	368	373
8. Mechanical engineering (general)	104 600	263 100	367 700	43 600	114 200	157 800	940	876	893	392	380	383
9. Electrical engineering (general)	71 900	112 500	184 400	27 800	44 700	72 400	931	795	843	359	316	331
10. Electrical wires and cables	9 900	26 400	36 300	3 400	9 200	12 700	1 014	967	979	352	338	342
11. Radio and telecommunications	47 600	73 800	121 400	20 300	37 000	57 300	715	624	656	305	313	310
12. Batteries	—	11 100	11 100	—	4 300	4 300	—	826	826	—	316	316
13. Electric lighting accessories and fittings	—	8 700	8 700	—	3 300	3 300	—	739	739	—	282	282
Total	283 300	722 200	1 005 500	120 200	336 000	456 100	865	773	797	367	360	362

Table I (*continued*)

Industrial order	Number of establishments: Estabs. with shift-work ratio of: Zero (1)	1–35 % (2)	> 35 % (3)	All estabs. (4)	Total number of operatives: Estabs. with shift-work ratio of: Zero (000) (5)	1–35 % (000) (6)	> 35 % (000) (7)	All estabs. (000) (8)	Of which adult males (%) (9) M	Average shift-work ratios: Estabs. with ratios of: 1–100% (%) (10) R	1–35 % (%) (11)	> 35 % (%) (12)	All estabs. (%) (13)
VII. *Vehicles*													
1. Motor vehicles and cycles (parts)	804	62	26	892	85·20	98·16	16·51	199·86	83	27	17	82	15
2. Motor vehicles and cycles (complete)	125	14	37	176	32·56	39·45	29·28	101·28		42	17	77	29
3. Aircraft manufacture and repair	165	44	6	215	51·27	53·39	4·88	109·54	87	26	21	78	14
4. Railway locomotive shops and locomotive manufacturing	282	23	34	339	9·88	54·58	8·05	72·51	93	25	17	81	22
5. Railway carriages, wagons and trams	559	28	—	587	24·64	54·38	—	79·02	94	12	12	—	9
Total	1 935	171	103	2 209	203·54	299·95	58·71	562·21	86	27	17	79	17

Industrial order	Net output. Estabs. with shift-work ratios of			Operatives' earnings. Estabs. with shift-work ratios of			Net output per operative. Estabs. with shift-work ratios of			Earnings per operative. Estabs. with shift-work ratios of		
	> 35 % (£000) (14)	All other (£000) (15)	All (£000) (16)	> 35 % (£000) (17)	All other (£000) (18)	All (£000) (19)	> 35 % (£) (20)	All other (£) (21)	All (£) (22)	> 35 % (£) (23)	All other (£) (24)	All (£) (25)
VII. *Vehicles*												
1. Motor vehicles and cycles (parts)	16 300	157 400	173 700	7 400	76 300	83 700	985	858	869	448	416	419
2. Motor vehicles and cycles (complete)	25 800	66 900	92 800	14 100	30 000	44 100	882	930	916	481	417	435
3. Aircraft manufacture and repair	4 100	94 200	98 300	1 200	43 100	44 300	849	900	897	249	411	404
4. Railway locomotive shops and locomotive manufacturing	4 600	33 700	38 300	3 100	25 400	28 400	575	523	529	379	394	392
5. Railway carriages, wagons and trams	—	44 200	44 200	—	31 100	31 100	—	559	559	—	393	394
Total	50 800	396 400	447 200	25 700	205 900	231 600	866	787	796	438	409	412

Table I (*continued*)

Industrial order	Number of establishments: Estabs. with shift-work ratio of: Zero (1)	1–35 % (2)	> 35 % (3)	All estabs. (4)	Total number of operatives: Estabs. with shift-work ratio of: Zero (000) (5)	1–35 % (000) (6)	> 35 % (000) (7)	All estabs. (000) (8)	Of which adult males (%) (9) M	Average shift-work ratios: Estabs. with ratios of: 1–100 % (%) (10) R	1–35 % (%) (11)	> 35 % (%) (12)	All estabs. (%) (13)
VIII. *Metal goods not elsewhere specified*													
1. Tool and implement	299	15	5	319	18·23	5·68	1·65	25·56	65	29	15	79	8
2. Cutlery	159	6	—	165	9·47	2·61	—	12·08	43	21	21	—	5
3. Chain, nail, screw and misc. forgings	614	39	34	687	46·39	14·09	10·06	71·44	62	46	14	86	16
4. Wire and wire manufacture	198	32	63	293	9·35	6·45	13·26	29·06	75	49	26	60	33
5. Hardware, holloware, metal furniture, etc.	1 896	88	75	2 059	109·03	24·89	14·40	148·32	58	40	16	83	11
6. Brass manufacture	560	13	5	578	33·57	4·82	0·64	39·03	61	21	13	85	3
7. Needles, pins, fish hooks and metal smallwares	171	18	1	190	14·94	5·12	0·20	20·27	32	7	5	50	2
Total	3 897	211	183	4 291	240·99	63·67	41·10	345·76	59	39	15	76	12

Industrial order	Net output. Estabs. with shift-work ratios of			Operatives' earnings. Estabs. with shift-work ratios of			Net output per operative. Estabs. with shift-work ratios of			Earnings per operative. Estabs. with shift-work ratios of		
	> 35 % (£000) (14)	All other (£000) (15)	All (£000) (16)	> 35 % (£000) (17)	All other (£000) (18)	All (£000) (19)	> 35 % (£) (20)	All other (£) (21)	All (£) (22)	> 35 % (£) (23)	All other (£) (24)	All (£) (25)
VIII. *Metal goods not elsewhere specified*												
1. Tool and implement	1 100	16 800	17 900	600	7 500	8 100	645	704	700	374	315	319
2. Cutlery	—	12 500	12 500	—	3 600	3 600	—	1 034	1 034	—	297	297
3. Chain, nail, screw and misc. forgings	10 300	45 800	56 100	4 400	19 100	23 500	944	757	786	405	315	329
4. Wire and wire manufacture	13 800	14 500	28 300	5 100	5 400	10 500	1 043	915	973	385	343	362
5. Hardware, holloware, metal furniture, etc.	11 400	97 800	109 200	4 800	41 800	46 500	793	730	737	330	312	314
6. Brass manufacture	600	31 900	32 500	300	12 400	12 600	903	831	832	395	323	324
7. Needles, pins, fish hooks and metal smallwares	100	12 100	12 200	100	5 100	5 100	600	601	601	255	253	253
Total	37 300	231 400	268 700	15 100	94 900	110 100	908	759	777	368	312	318

Table I (*continued*)

Industrial order	Number of establishments: Estabs. with shift-work ratio of: Zero (1)	1–35 % (2)	> 35 % (3)	All estabs. (4)	Total number of operatives: Estabs. with shift-work ratio of: Zero (000) (5)	1–35 % (000) (6)	> 35 % (000) (7)	All estabs. (000) (8)	Of which adult males (%) (9) M	Average shift-work ratios: Estabs. with ratios of: 1–100% (%) (10) R	1–35 % (%) (11)	> 35 % (%) (12)	All estabs. (%) (13)
IX. *Precision instruments, jewellery, etc., scientific, surgical and photographic instruments, etc.*													
1. Scientific, surgical and photographic instruments	724	13	—	737	49·14	9·42	—	58·56	61	19	19	—	3
2. Watch and clock	76	6	—	82	5·49	3·68	—	9·17	46	6	6	—	2
3. Jewellery and plate	356	—	—	356	5·90	—	—	5·90	48	—	—	—	—
4. Musical instruments	108	—	—	108	16·12	—	—	16·12	70	—	—	—	—
5. Precious metals refining	20	7	2	29	3·19	0·89	0·08	4·16	72	28	24	75	7
Total	1 284	26	2	1 312	79·84	14·00	0·08	93·91	58	16	16	75	2

Industrial order	Net output. Estabs. with shift-work ratios of > 35 % (£000) (14)	All other (£000) (15)	All (£000) (16)	Operatives' earnings. Estabs. with shift-work ratios of > 35 % (£000) (17)	All other (£000) (18)	All (£000) (19)	Net output per operative. Estabs. with shift-work ratios of > 35 % (£) (20)	All other (£) (21)	All (£) (22)	Earnings per operative. Estabs. with shift-work ratios of > 35 % (£) (23)	All other (£) (24)	All (£) (25)
IX. *Precision instruments, jewellery, etc., scientific, surgical and photographic instruments, etc.*												
1. Scientific, surgical and photographic instruments	45 400	—	45 400	19 400	—	19 400	—	775	775	—	332	332
2. Watch and clock	6 400	—	6 400	2 900	—	2 900	—	698	698	—	312	312
3. Jewellery and plate	11 200	—	11 200	4 800	—	4 800	—	1 895	1 895	—	808	808
4. Musical instruments	4 800	—	4 800	2 100	—	2 100	—	298	298	—	130	130
5. Precious metals refining	7 900	—	7 900	1 500	—	1 500	—	1 926	1 889	—	379	372
Total	75 600	—	75 600	30 700	—	30 700	—	806	805	—	327	327

Table I (*continued*)

Industrial order	Number of establishments: Estabs. with shift-work ratio of: Zero (1)	1–35 % (2)	> 35 % (3)	All estabs. (4)	Total number of operatives: Estabs. with shift-work ratio of: Zero (000) (5)	1–35 % (000) (6)	> 35 % (000) (7)	All estabs. (000) (8)	Of which adult males (%) (9) M	Average shift-work ratios: Estabs. with ratios of: 1–100 % (%) (10) R	1–35 % (%) (11)	> 35 % (%) (12)	All estabs. (%) (13)
X. *Textiles*													
1. Cotton spinning and doubling	623	84	36	743	120·52	30·99	10·35	161·86	32	25	12	66	7
2. Cotton weaving	715	65	39	819	87·08	16·34	8·57	111·99	31	30	14	61	7
3. Woollen and worsted	1 248	176	64	1 488	118·84	43·43	10·45	172·71	41	22	13	62	7
4. Rayon, nylon, etc., and silk production	—	4	16	20	—	2·07	30·75	32·82	52	52	15	55	52
5. Rayon, nylon, etc., and silk weaving	261	48	57	366	26·06	10·74	11·45	48·24		40	16	62	18
6. Linen and soft hemp	69	8	—	77	7·32	3·90	—	11·22	23	19	19	—	7
7. Jute	55	13	5	73	8·12	7·36	1·11	16·60	39	25	14	97	13
8. Hosiery and other knitted goods	795	246	40	1 081	52·58	44·42	6·79	103·79	24	20	16	48	10
9. Lace	185	50	5	240	6·98	3·31	0·30	10·59	37	20	17	50	7
10. Carpets	105	18	3	126	15·18	8·35	0·75	24·28	42	16	13	50	6
11. Narrow fabrics	188	13	7	208	14·43	2·28	0·89	17·60	25	34	21	66	6
12. Canvas goods and sacks	280	—	—	280	11·62	—	—	11·62	26	—	—	—	—
13. Made-up household textiles	134	—	—	134	4·89	—	—	4·89	8	—	—	—	—
14. Textile finishing	582	87	28	697	41·95	19·70	7·82	69·47	68	26	17	50	11
15. Asbestos	51	13	2	66	5·63	6·74	0·29	12·66	70	27	25	69	15
16. Flock and rag	165	22	5	192	5·09	1·48	0·17	6·74	48	27	21	72	7
Total	5 456	847	307	6 610	526·29	201·11	89·68	817·08	38	28	15	58	10

Industrial order	Net output. Estabs. with shift-work ratios of > 35 % (£000) (14)	All other (£000) (15)	All (£000) (16)	Operatives' earnings. Estabs. with shift-work ratios of > 35 % (£000) (17)	All other (£000) (18)	All (£000) (19)	Net output per operative. Estabs. with shift-work ratios of > 35 % (£) (20)	All other (£) (21)	All (£) (22)	Earnings per operative. Estabs. with shift-work ratios of > 35 % (£) (23)	All other (£) (24)	All (£) (25)
X. *Textiles*												
1. Cotton spinning and doubling	5 700	103 200	109 000	2 800	42 300	45 000	556	681	673	266	279	278
2. Cotton weaving	6 100	67 500	73 600	2 600	29 100	31 800	708	653	657	309	281	284
3. Woollen and worsted	7 800	113 500	121 300	3 000	45 300	48 300	747	699	702	292	279	280
4. Rayon, nylon, etc., and silk production	45 900	1 800	47 700	11 700	700	12 400	1 492	865	1 492	380	359	378
5. Rayon, nylon, etc., and silk weaving	7 900	24 300	32 200	3 600	10 700	14 300	689	662	668	316	290	297
6. Linen and soft hemp	—	5 900	5 900	—	2 500	2 500	—	528	528	—	222	222
7. Jute	600	7 700	8 300	300	3 900	4 200	507	500	500	244	253	253
8. Hosiery and other knitted goods	7 700	56 500	64 200	1 900	24 300	26 200	1 140	582	619	280	251	253
9. Lace	300	8 800	9 100	100	2 600	2 700	1 149	851	859	284	257	258
10. Carpets	500	14 200	14 700	200	6 600	6 900	607	605	605	281	283	283
11. Narrow fabrics	400	10 800	11 300	200	3 800	4 000	497	648	641	236	226	226
12. Canvas goods and sacks	—	7 500	7 500	—	2 600	2 600	—	642	642	—	226	226
13. Made-up household textiles	—	3 400	3 400	—	1 000	1 000	—	691	691	—	214	214
14. Textile finishing	6 600	47 300	53 900	2 700	21 100	23 800	846	767	776	345	342	343
15. Asbestos	400	15 500	15 900	100	4 500	4 600	1 254	1 252	1 253	361	362	362
16. Flock and rag	200	7 000	7 200	100	1 900	2 000	960	1 068	1 065	322	293	293
Total	90 100	494 900	585 000	29 300	203 100	232 400	1 004	680	716	326	279	284

Table I (*continued*)

Industrial order	Number of establishments: Estabs. with shift-work ratio of: Zero (1)	1–35 % (2)	> 35 % (3)	All estabs. (4)	Total number of operatives: Estabs. with shift-work ratio of: Zero (000) (5)	1–35 % (000) (6)	> 35 % (000) (7)	All estabs. (000) (8)	Of which adult males (%) (9) M	Average shift-work ratios: Estabs. with ratios of: 1–100% (%) (10) R	1–35 % (%) (11)	> 35 % (%) (12)	All estabs. (%) (13)
XI. *Leather, leather goods and fur*													
1. Leather (tanning and dressing)	434	19	—	453	26·00	2·64	—	28·64	80	14	14	—	1
2. Fellmongery	43	—	—	43	1·44	—	—	1·44	89	—	—	—	—
3. Leather goods	349	—	—	349	14·92	—	—	14·92	27	—	—	—	—
4. Fur	193	3	—	196	6·08	0·38	—	6·46	47	12	12	—	1
Total	1 019	22	—	1 041	48·45	3·01	—	51·46	61	13	13	—	1

Industrial order	Net output. Estabs. with shift-work ratios of			Operatives' earnings. Estabs. with shift-work ratios of			Net output per operative. Estabs. with shift-work ratios of			Earnings per operative. Estabs. with shift-work ratios of		
	> 35 % (£000) (14)	All other (£000) (15)	All (£000) (16)	> 35 % (£000) (17)	All other (£000) (18)	All (£000) (19)	> 35 % (£) (20)	All other (£) (21)	All (£) (22)	> 35 % (£) (23)	All other (£) (24)	All (£) (25)
XI. *Leather, leather goods and fur*												
1. Leather (tanning and dressing)	—	25 500	25 500	—	9 900	9 900	—	892	892	—	345	345
2. Fellmongery	—	..	..	—	..	..	—	286	286	—	329	329
3. Leather goods	—	7 200	7 200	—	3 400	3 400	—	482	482	—	228	228
4. Fur	—	4 500	4 500	—	2 100	2 100	—	700	700	—	326	326
Total	—	37 700	37 700	—	15 900	15 900	—	732	732	—	308	308

Table I (*continued*)

Industrial order	Number of establishments: Estabs. with shift-work ratio of: Zero (1)	1–35 % (2)	> 35 % (3)	All estabs. (4)	Total number of operatives: Estabs. with shift-work ratio of: Zero (000) (5)	1–35 % (000) (6)	> 35 % (000) (7)	All estabs. (000) (8)	Of which adult males (%) (9) M	Average shift-work ratios: Estabs. with ratios of: 1–100% (%) (10) R	1–35 % (%) (11)	> 35 % (%) (12)	All estabs. (%) (13)
XII. *Clothing*													
1. Tailoring, dressmaking, etc.	5 775	—	—	5 775	349·16	—	—	349·16	14	—	—	—	—
2. Hats, caps and millinery	297	—	—	297	14·63	—	—	14·63	35	—	—	—	—
3. Glove	206	—	—	206	9·86	—	—	9·86	25	—	—	—	—
4. Umbrella and walking stick	55	2	—	57	1·86	0·61	—	2·47	30	33	33	—	—
5. Boot and shoe	1 022	4	—	1 026	100·92	1·88	—	102·80	48	6	6	—	—
Total	7 355	6	—	7 361	476·43	2·49	—	478·91	22	13	13	—	—

Industrial order	Net output. Estabs. with shift-work ratios of			Operatives' earnings. Estabs. with shift-work ratios of			Net output per operative. Estabs. with shift-work ratios of			Earnings per operative. Estabs. with shift-work ratios of		
	> 35 % (£000) (14)	All other (£000) (15)	All (£000) (16)	> 35 % (£000) (17)	All other (£000) (18)	All (£000) (19)	> 35 % (£) (20)	All other (£) (21)	All (£) (22)	> 35 % (£) (23)	All other (£) (24)	All (£) (25)
XII. *Clothing*												
1. Tailoring, dressmaking, etc.	—	152 800	152 800	—	78 800	78 800	—	438	438	—	226	226
2. Hats, caps and millinery	—	7 400	7 400	—	3 900	3 900	—	502	502	—	265	265
3. Glove	—	4 600	4 600	—	2 200	2 200	—	467	467	—	219	219
4. Umbrella and walking stick	—	1 000	1 000	—	500	500	—	420	420	—	199	199
5. Boot and shoe	—	59 100	59 100	—	29 800	29 800	—	575	575	—	290	290
Total	—	224 900	224 900	—	115 100	115 100	—	470	470	—	240	240

Table I (*continued*)

Industrial order	Number of establishments: Estabs. with shift-work ratio of: Zero (1)	1–35 % (2)	> 35 % (3)	All estabs. (4)	Total number of operatives: Estabs. with shift-work ratio of: Zero (000) (5)	1–35 % (000) (6)	> 35 % (000) (7)	All estabs. (000) (8)	Of which adult males (%) (9) M	Average shift-work ratios: Estabs. with ratios of: 1–100 % (%) (10) R	1–35 % (%) (11)	> 35 % (%) (12)	All estabs. (%) (13)
XIII. *Food, drink and tobacco*													
1. Grain milling	77	83	167	327	1·78	7·62	13·29	22·70	84	39	25	47	36
2. Bread and flour confectionery	1 419	119	322	1 860	54·61	17·09	29·30	100·99	67	40	19	52	25
3. Biscuit	106	3	18	127	27·53	1·50	5·86	34·89	30	48	6	58	10
4. Bacon curing and sausage	379	2	—	381	18·55	0·51	—	19·06	59	28	28	—	1
5. Preserved meat	24	—	—	24	4·77	—	—	4·77	31	—	—	—	—
6. Milk products	581	11	28	620	35·74	2·15	3·71	41·61	76	57	26	75	8
7. Ice cream	68	—	3	71	3·92	—	1·43	5·36	61	51	—	51	14
8. Sugar and glucose	16	5	29	50	0·95	0·94	16·06	17·94	78	57	14	59	54
9. Cocoa, chocolate and sugar confectionery	342	17	4	363	40·79	18·71	1·20	60·69	33	31	29	67	10
10. Preserved fruit and vegetables	354	5	6	365	37·23	3·86	1·29	42·38	28	16	4	50	2
11. Margarine	24	2	4	30	1·09	0·47	2·78	4·34	62	47	5	54	35
12. Fish curing	164	2	—	166	4·09	0·68	—	4·77	47	10	10	—	2
13. Cattle, dog and poultry foods	163	12	31	206	4·99	0·46	6·58	12·03	87	50	26	52	29
14. Vinegar and other condiments	30	—	—	30	1·39	—	—	1·39	59	—	—	—	—
15. Starch	8	3	8	19	0·60	0·49	0·95	2·04	65	42	15	56	30
16. Ice	4	7	5	16	0·17	0·29	0·07	0·53	98	20	13	48	14
17. Misc. preserved foods	197	8	1	206	11·98	1·98	0·14	14·10	32	17	15	50	3
18. Tea blending and coffee roasting	102	2	—	104	4·64	0·34	—	4·98	56	10	10	—	1
19. Brewing and malting	532	87	4	623	37·24	18·76	0·11	56·10	82	11	10	67	4
20. Wholesale bottling	477	1	2	480	19·43	0·96	2·02	22·41	47	40	21	50	5
21. Spirit distilling	24	27	49	100	0·40	1·29	2·54	4·23	90	41	33	46	37
22. Spirit rectifying and compounding	12	2	—	14	0·92	0·15	—	1·07	60	10	10	—	1
23. Soft drinks, British wines and cider	545	2	—	547	10·73	0·99	—	11·71	54	9	9	—	—
24. Tobacco	102	—	—	102	37·15	—	—	37·15	37	—	—	—	—
Total	5 750	400	681	6 831	360·67	79·24	87·32	527·22	56	37	19	54	12

Industrial order	Net output. Estabs. with shift-work ratios of > 35% (£000) (14)	All other (£000) (15)	All (£000) (16)	Operatives' earnings. Estabs. with shift-work ratios of > 35% (£000) (17)	All other (£000) (18)	All (£000) (19)	Net output per operative. Estabs. with shift-work ratios of > 35% (£) (20)	All other (£) (21)	All (£) (22)	Earnings per operative. Estabs. with shift-work ratios of > 35% (£) (23)	All other (£) (24)	All (£) (25)
XIII. *Food, drink and tobacco*												
1. Grain milling	17 500	10 600	28 100	5 100	3 200	8 300	1 319	1 128	1 240	381	343	365
2. Bread and flour confectionery	27 300	41 600	68 800	12 600	21 600	34 200	931	580	682	431	301	339
3. Biscuit	4 600	19 100	23 800	1 500	6 400	7 900	792	659	681	263	220	227
4. Bacon curing and sausage	—	14 500	14 500	—	5 200	5 200	—	759	759	—	273	273
5. Preserved meat	—	4 500	4 500	—	1 100	1 100	—	951	951	—	235	235
6. Milk products	3 000	30 100	33 100	1 600	12 600	14 200	816	793	795	423	332	340
7. Ice cream	1 700	4 800	6 500	500	1 200	1 600	1 198	1 212	1 208	318	302	306
8. Sugar and glucose	15 700	2 900	18 500	5 300	600	5 900	975	1 521	1 032	332	309	330
9. Cocoa, chocolate and sugar confectionery	1 800	45 100	46 900	500	15 100	15 600	1 506	758	773	402	254	257
10. Preserved fruit and vegetables	1 000	29 200	30 200	300	9 100	9 400	752	710	712	224	222	222
11. Margarine	4 000	1 400	5 400	1 000	500	1 500	1 445	885	1 244	354	300	335
12. Fish curing	—	2 700	2 700	—	1 300	1 300	—	561	561	—	265	265
13. Cattle, dog and poultry foods	9 200	6 000	15 300	2 400	1 800	4 200	1 403	1 106	1 268	368	322	347
14. Vinegar and other condiments	—	2 200	2 200	—	400	400	—	1 605	1 605	—	300	300
15. Starch	900	1 400	2 300	400	300	700	965	1 254	1 119	387	312	347
16. Ice	—	500	500	—	200	200	—	1 175	1 017	—	404	349
17. Misc. preserved foods	—	14 300	14 300	—	3 400	3 400	—	1 028	1 017	—	247	245
18. Tea blending and coffee roasting	—	5 900	5 900	—	1 400	1 400	—	1 184	1 184	—	271	271
19. Brewing and malting	100	85 000	85 100	—	18 200	18 300	991	1 517	1 517	362	325	326
20. Wholesale bottling	3 300	33 200	36 500	500	5 400	5 900	1 630	1 630	1 630	264	264	264
21. Spirit distilling	3 100	4 000	7 100	900	700	1 600	1 217	2 346	1 669	372	391	380
22. Spirit rectifying and compounding	—	4 000	4 000	—	300	300	—	3 703	3 703	—	309	309
23. Soft drinks, British wines and cider	—	17 900	17 900	—	5 200	5 200	—	1 528	1 528	—	445	445
24. Tobacco	—	63 300	63 300	—	10 600	10 600	—	1 704	1 704	—	287	287
Total	93 200	444 000	537 300	32 600	125 800	158 400	1 079	1 009	1 019	374	286	301

Table I (*continued*)

Industrial order	Number of establishments: Estabs. with shift-work ratio of: Zero (1)	1–35% (2)	> 35% (3)	All estabs. (4)	Total number of operatives: Estabs. with shift-work ratio of: Zero (000) (5)	1–35% (000) (6)	> 35% (000) (7)	All estabs. (000) (8)	Of which adult males (%) (9) M	Average shift-work ratios: Estabs. with ratios of: 1–100% (%) (10) R	1–35% (%) (11)	> 35% (%) (12)	All estabs. (%) (13)
XIV. *Manufacture of wood and cork*													
1. Timber	1 743	15	16	1 774	69·91	3·22	2·19	75·31	80	38	20	66	3
2. Furniture and upholstery	1 398	5	2	1 405	78·52	2·34	0·82	81·68	76	32	26	51	1
3. Soft furnishings	301	—	—	301	14·33	—	—	14·33	40	—	—	—	—
4. Shop and office fittings	278	3	1	282	13·45	0·50	0·14	14·09	86	26	13	71	1
5. Wooden containers and baskets	540	1	4	545	24·17	0·04	0·60	24·81	67	78	26	82	2
Total	4 260	24	23	4 307	200·37	6·10	3·75	210·22	74	38	22	65	2

Industrial order	Net output. Estabs. with shift-work ratios of			Operatives' earnings. Estabs. with shift-work ratios of			Net output per operative. Estabs. with shift-work ratios of			Earnings per operative. Estabs. with shift-work ratios of		
	> 35 % (£000) (14)	All other (£000) (15)	All (£000) (16)	> 35 % (£000) (17)	All other (£000) (18)	All (£000) (19)	> 35 % (£) (20)	All other (£) (21)	All (£) (22)	> 35 % (£) (23)	All other (£) (24)	All (£) (25)
XIV. *Manufacture of wood and cork*												
1. Timber	2 200	47 800	50 000	700	23 600	24 400	1 004	654	664	337	323	324
2. Furniture and upholstery	500	52 800	53 400	300	30 300	30 600	654	653	653	375	375	375
3. Soft furnishings	—	8 600	8 600	—	3 900	3 900	—	602	602	—	275	275
4. Shop and office fittings	100	10 600	10 700	100	5 500	5 500	759	761	761	390	393	393
5. Wooden containers and baskets	300	14 100	14 500	200	7 200	7 400	575	583	583	300	298	298
Total	3 200	134 000	137 200	1 300	70 600	71 900	850	649	652	342	342	342

Table I (*continued*)

Industrial order	Number of establishments: Estabs. with shift-work ratio of: Zero (1)	1–35% (2)	> 35% (3)	All estabs. (4)	Total number of operatives: Estabs. with shift-work ratio of: Zero (000) (5)	1–35% (000) (6)	> 35% (000) (7)	All estabs. (000) (8)	Of which adult males (%) (9) M	Average shift-work ratios: Estabs. with ratios of: 1–100% (%) (10) R	1–35% (%) (11)	> 35% (%) (12)	All estabs. (%) (13)
XV. *Paper and printing*													
1. Paper and board	78	25	179	282	4·92	5·75	54·10	64·77	75	48	29	50	44
2. Wallpaper	32	—	—	32	4·63	—	—	4·63	62	—	—	—	—
3. Cardboard box, carton and fibre-board packing case	438	12	6	456	37·72	4·92	1·55	44·18	32	23	15	47	3
4. Manufactured stationery, paper bag, etc.	370	12	9	391	31·42	7·14	2·22	40·78	35	21	8	63	5
5. Newspaper and periodical printing and publishing	517	54	—	571	39·97	19·07	—	59·03	88	21	21	—	7
6. Printing, publishing, bookbinding, engraving, etc.	2 742	4	—	2 746	143·36	5·03	—	148·39	54	20	20	—	1
Total	4 177	107	194	4 478	262·02	41·91	57·87	361·78	59	37	19	50	10

Industrial order	Net output. Estabs. with shift-work ratios of			Operatives' earnings. Estabs. with shift-work ratios of			Net output per operative. Estabs. with shift-work ratios of			Earnings per operative. Estabs. with shift-work ratios of		
	> 35% (£000) (14)	All other (£000) (15)	All (£000) (16)	> 35% (£000) (17)	All other (£000) (18)	All (£000) (19)	> 35% (£) (20)	All other (£) (21)	All (£) (22)	> 35% (£) (23)	All other (£) (24)	All (£) (25)
XV. *Paper and printing*												
1. Paper and board	91 500	13 000	104 500	20 900	3 400	24 300	1 692	1 216	1 613	386	319	375
2. Wallpaper	—	3 700	3 700	—	1 400	1 400	—	805	805	—	303	303
3. Cardboard box, carton and fibre-board packing case	2 200	35 200	37 400	500	10 900	11 400	1 437	825	846	339	256	259
4. Manufactured stationery, paper bag, etc.	3 400	36 800	40 200	700	10 300	11 000	1 544	954	986	322	266	269
5. Newspaper and periodical printing and publishing	—	91 100	91 100	—	26 200	26 200	—	1 544	1 544	—	444	444
6. Printing, publishing, bookbinding, engraving, etc.	—	107 600	107 600	—	49 300	49 300	—	725	725	—	332	332
Total	97 100	287 400	384 500	22 100	101 500	123 600	1 679	946	1 063	382	334	342

Table I (*continued*)

Industrial order	Number of establishments				Total number of operatives					Average shift-work ratios			
	Estabs. with shift-work ratio of				Estabs. with shift-work ratio of					Estabs. with ratios of			
	Zero (1)	1–35% (2)	> 35% (3)	All estabs. (4)	Zero (000) (5)	1–35% (000) (6)	> 35% (000) (7)	All estabs. (000) (8)	Of which adult males (%) (9) M	1–100% (%) (10) R	1–35% (%) (11)	> 35% (%) (12)	All estabs. (%) (13)
XVI. *Other manufacturing industries*													
1. Rubber	190	87	51	328	13·69	41·98	27·12	82·79	65	39	25	60	32
2. Linoleum, leather-cloth and allied trades	19	12	2	33	1·24	7·67	2·28	11·19	86	31	29	38	28
3. Brushes and brooms	218	1	—	219	11·47	0·31	—	11·77	39	13	13	—	—
4. Toys and games	184	9	1	194	17·93	2·00	0·15	20·08	27	18	15	64	2
5. Plastic goods and fancy articles	380	70	34	484	15·26	9·60	4·13	28·99	39	33	22	60	16
Total	991	179	88	1 258	59·60	61·55	33·67	154·82	54	37	25	59	23

Industrial order	Net output. Estabs. with shift-work ratios of > 35% (£000) (14)	All other (£000) (15)	All (£000) (16)	Operatives' earnings. Estabs. with shift-work ratios of > 35% (£000) (17)	All other (£000) (18)	All (£000) (19)	Net output per operative. Estabs. with shift-work ratios of > 35% (£) (20)	All other (£) (21)	All (£) (22)	Earnings per operative. Estabs. with shift-work ratios of > 35% (£) (23)	All other (£) (24)	All (£) (25)
XVI. *Other manufacturing industries*												
1. Rubber	30 900	45 300	76 300	11 300	17 300	28 500	1 141	815	922	416	310	345
2. Linoleum, leather-cloth and allied trades	2 000	9 600	11 600	700	3 400	4 200	859	1 078	1 033	327	384	372
3. Brushes and brooms	—	7 500	7 500	—	2 800	2 800	—	636	637	—	240	240
4. Toys and games	100	10 700	10 800	—	4 900	4 900	551	537	537	252	244	244
5. Plastic goods and fancy articles	2 600	14 300	16 900	1 200	6 600	7 800	629	575	582	295	265	269
Total	35 600	87 400	123 000	13 300	34 900	48 200	1 057	722	795	394	288	312

Table II. *Characteristics of establishments with over 35 % of operatives on shift-work, Great Britain, 1951*

Industrial order	Proportion of total operative employment (%) (1)	Relative size ratio (%) (2)	Apparent basic share of gross profits in net output: In these establishments (%) (3a)	Apparent basic share of gross profits in net output: In remaining establishments (%) (3b)	Net output per operative differential ratio (%) (4)	Annual earnings per operative differential ratio (%) (5)	Apparent mean utilisation differential (%) (6)
III. *Treatment of non-metalliferous mining products other than coal*							
1. Brick and fireclay	14	171	30	24	110	105	6
2. China and earthware	—	—	—	27	—	—	—
3. Glass containers	97	..	30	..	..	..	..
4. Glass (other than containers)	40	684	38	33	111	101	3
5. Cement	81	..	62	..	..	..	..
6. Abrasives	14	..	..	52	..	..	..
7. Building materials	18	587	45	30	146	110	17
8. Roofing felts	35	..	..	59	..	..	..
Total	25	437	46	32	141	117	—
IV. *Chemicals and allied trades*							
1. Coke ovens and by-products	90	115	51	43	122	108	29
2. Dyes and dyestuffs	14	80	46	47	96	107	48
3. Fertiliser, disinfectant, insecticide, etc.	61	693	47	48	96	119	52
4. Coal-tar products	30	174	48	42	122	90	—
5. Chemicals (general)	31	134	50	50	98	104	14
6. Drugs and pharmaceutical preps.	1	34	49	48	110	136	89
7. Toilet preps. and perfumery	—	—	—	52	—	—	—
8. Explosives and fireworks	39	..	..	14	..	..	—
9. Paint and varnish	3	..	..	53	..	..	—
10. Soap, candles and glycerine	15	235	41	42	95	117	33
11. Polishes	—	—	—	47	—	—	—
12. Ink	6	..	..	51	..	..	—
13. Mineral oil refining	38	72	52	52	..	93	..
14. Oils and greases	6	88	36	47	59	105	12
15. Seed crushing and oil refining	80	311	..	33	..	..	—
16. Glue, gum, paste and allied trades	33	182	43	47	85	107	21
17. Plastics materials	88	543	50	48	107	106	15
Total	31	214	44	48	88	116	—

V. *Metal manufacture*							
1. Blast furnaces	94	171	35	44	83	103	15
2. Iron and steel (melting and rolling)	77	394	44	46	95	109	17
3. Iron foundries	12	446	40	31	120	109	11
4. Steel sheets	93	274	48	44	113	106	13
5. Tinplate	98	..	37	..	..	..	—
6. Wrought iron and steel tubes	55	596	47	39	123	111	20
7. Non-ferrous metals (smelting, rolling, etc.)	39	305	49	48	104	107	12
Total	61	511	45	41	110	110	—
VI. *Engineering, shipbuilding and electrical goods*							
1. Shipbuilding and repairing	10	554	18	18	99	101	1
2. Marine engineering	36	386	33	24	119	109	10
3. Machine tools	30	273	40	38	104	110	10
4. Textile machinery and accessories	8	307	37	34	107	108	8
5. Small arms	—	—	—	24	—	—	—
6. Mechanical handling equipment	4	234	29	35	87	104	4
7. Printing and bookbinding machinery	18	197	43	37	119	108	10
8. Mechanical engineering (general)	27	304	37	35	107	103	4
9. Electrical engineering (general)	35	453	40	34	117	114	21
10. Electrical wires and cables	26	94	44	43	105	104	7
11. Radio and telecommunications	36	305	29	23	115	98	..
12. Batteries	—	—	—	38	—	—	—
13. Electric lighting, accessories and fittings	—	—	—	37	—	—	—
Total	26	336	37	31	112	102	—
VII. *Vehicles*							
1. Motor vehicles and cycles (parts)	8	345	..	..	115	108	10
2. Motor vehicles and cycles (complete)	29	145	..	..	95	116	24
3. Aircraft manufacture and repair	4	151	23	25	94	61	..
4. Railway locomotive shops and locomotive manufacturing	11	123	16	10	110	96	..
5. Railway carriages, wagons and trams	—	—	—	16	—	—	—
Total	10	262	32	28	110	107	—

Table II (*continued*)

Industrial order	Proportion of total operative employment (%) (1)	Relative size ratio (%) (2)	Apparent basic share of gross profits in net output: In these establishments (%) (3a)	Apparent basic share of gross profits in net output: In remaining establishments (%) (3b)	Net output per operative differential ratio (%) (4)	Annual earnings per operative differential ratio (%) (5)	Apparent mean utilisation differential (%) (6)
VIII. *Metal goods not elsewhere specified*							
1. Tools	6	407	29	33	92	119	25
2. Cutlery	—	—	—	50	—	—	—
3. Chain, nail, screw and misc. forgings	15	433	48	40	125	128	35
4. Wire and wire manufacture	46	348	47	43	114	113	26
5. Hardware, hollow-ware, metal furniture, etc.	10	310	39	36	109	106	7
6. Brass manufacture	2	214	47	44	109	122	27
7. Needles, pins, fish-hooks and metal smallwares	1	156	37	38	100	101	2
Total	12	364	46	40	120	118	—
IX. *Precision instruments, jewellery, etc., scientific, surgical and photographic instruments, etc.*							
1. Scientific, surgical and photographic instruments	—	—	—	33	—	—	—
2. Watch and clock	—	—	—	32	—	—	—
3. Jewellery and plate	—	—	—	35	—	—	—
4. Musical instruments	—	—	—	36	—	—	—
5. Precious metals refining	2	..	..	62	..	..	—
Total	—	—	—	36	—	—	—

X. *Textiles*							
1. Cotton spinning and doubling	6	108	35	44	82	95	..
2. Cotton weaving	8	179	46	43	108	110	16
3. Woollen and worsted	6	153	44	41	107	105	8
4. Rayon, nylon, etc., and silk production	94	638	..	..	173	109	23
5. Rayon, nylon, etc., and silk weaving	24	176	..	..	104	109	15
6. Linen and soft hemp	—	—	—	43	—	—	—
7. Jute	7	106	35	34	101	96	..
8. Hosiery and other knitted goods	7	357	60	39	196	112	29
9. Lace	3	162	57	50	135	110	24
10. Carpets	3	145	35	34	100	99	..
11. Narrow fabrics	5	106	35	45	77	105	7
12. Canvas goods and sacks	—	—	—	43	—	—	—
13. Made-up household textiles	—	—	—	53	—	—	—
14. Textile finishing	11	332	37	33	110	101	2
15. Asbestos	2	..	..	52	..	..	..
16. Flock and rag	3	108	45	49	90	110	15
Total	11	371	56	42	148	117	—
XI. *Leather, leather goods and fur*							
1. Leather (tanning and dressing)	—	—	—	41	—	—	—
2. Fellmongery	—	—	—	—	—	—	—
3. Leather goods	—	—	—	28	—	—	—
4. Fur	—	—	—	29	—	—	—
Total	—	—	—	36	—	—	—
XII. *Clothing*							
1. Tailoring, dressmaking, etc.	—	—	—	27	—	—	—
2. Hats, caps and millinery	—	—	—	20	—	—	—
3. Glove	—	—	—	24	—	—	—
4. Umbrella and walking stick	—	—	—	30	—	—	—
5. Boot and shoe	—	—	—	30	—	—	—
Total	—	—	—	27	—	—	—

Table II (*continued*)

Industrial order	Proportion of total operative employment (%) (1)	Relative size ratio (%) (2)	Apparent basic share of gross profits in net output: In these establishments (%) (3a)	In remaining establishments (%) (3b)	Net output per operative differential ratio (%) (4)	Annual earnings per operative differential ratio (%) (5)	Apparent mean utilisation differential (%) (6)
XIII. *Food, drink and tobacco*							
1. Grain milling	59	159	50	46	117	112	47
2. Bread and flour confectionery	29	315	48	28	161	143	94
3. Biscuit	17	146	48	42	120	120	34
4. Bacon curing and sausage	—	—	—	43	—	—	—
5. Preserved meat	—	—	—	47	—	—	—
6. Milk products	9	210	33	32	103	128	38
7. Ice cream	27	799	60	61	99	105	11
8. Sugar and glucose	89	..	50	..	..	..	..
9. Cocoa, chocolate and sugar confectionery	2	357	58	41	199	158	111
10. Preserved fruit and vegetables	3	206	47	46	106	101	2
11. Margarine	64	1852	67	53	163	118	34
12. Fish curing	—	—	75	28	—	—	—
13. Cattle, dog and poultry foods	55	874	49	43	127	115	30
14. Vinegar and other condiments	—	—	75	56	—	—	—
15. Starch	47	89	37	44	77	124	51
16. Ice	13	—	80	46	—	—	—
17. Misc. preserved foods	1	—	70	46	—	—	—
18. Tea blending and coffee roasting	—	—	—	..	—	—	—
19. Brewing and malting	1	18	48	60	65	111	18
20. Wholesale bottling	9	..	..	64	..	..	..
21. Spirit distilling	60	81	52	68	52	95	..
22. Spirit rectifying and compounding	—	—	79	71	—	—	—
23. Soft drinks, British wines and cider	—	—	73	44	—	—	—
24. Tobacco	—	—	85	68	—	—	—
Total	17	190	52	51	107	131	—

XIV. *Manufacture of wood and cork*							
1. Timber	3	511	44	28	154	104	6
2. Furniture and upholstery	1	..	..	24	..	..	—
3. Soft furnishings	—	—	—	29	—	—	—
4. Shop and office fittings	1	..	..	27	..	..	—
5. Wooden containers and baskets	2	288	28	29	99	101	1
Total	2	448	39	26	131	100	—
XV. *Paper and printing*							
1. Paper and board	84	..	65	..	..	..	—
2. Wallpaper	—	—	—	42	—	—	—
3. Cardboard box, carton and fibreboard packing case	4	471	64	51	174	133	73
4. Manufactured stationery, paper bag, etc.	5	394	60	49	162	121	34
5. Newspaper and periodical printing and publishing	—	—	—	40	—	—	—
6. Printing, publishing, bookbinding, engraving, etc.	—	—	—	33	—	—	—
Total	16	748	58	44	173	114	—
XVI. *Other manufacturing industries*							
1. Rubber	33	370	54	43	140	134	99
2. Linoleum, leathercloth and allied trades	20	323	..	41	..	..	..
3. Brushes and brooms	—	—	—	38	—	—	—
4. Toys and games	1	..	..	33	..	..	..
5. Plastic goods and fancy articles	14	238	34	30	109	112	23
Total	22	540	49	36	146	136	—

Table III. *Average size of shift-working and other establishments, Great Britain, 1951*

Industrial order	Average number of operatives per establishment: Shift-work ratio: Zero (1)	1–35 % (2)	Over 35 % (3)	All estabs. (4)	Comparative ratios: Zero/Rest (%) (5)	> 35 %/Zero (%) (6)	> 35 %/1–35 % (%) (7)	Average net output per establishment. Shift-work ratio: 0–35 % (£000) (8)	> 35 % (£000) (9)	All (£000) (10)
III. *Treatment of non-metalliferous mining products other than coal*										
1. Brick and fireclay	56	160	100	67	33	179	63	42	72	45
2. China and earthware	198	176	—	196	113	—	—	99	—	99
3. Glass containers	73	—	399	348	18	547	—	90	287	256
4. Glass (other than containers)	42	493	472	116	9	1 124	96	57	390	90
5. Cement	9	188	260	209	4	2 889	138	212	468	379
6. Abrasives	61	971	420	148	8	689	43	179	550	200
7. Building materials	38	190	162	47	22	426	85	31	182	39
8. Roofing felts	50	—	161	66	31	322	—	100	200	114
Total	67	232	236	92	29	352	102	51	223	68
IV. *Chemicals and allied trades*										
1. Coke ovens and by-products	11	180	188	189	5	1 709	—	175	201	198
2. Dyes and dyestuffs	83	965	308	366	12	371	32	667	533	644
3. Fertiliser, disinfectant, insecticide, etc.	37	56	290	85	19	784	518	55	381	113
4. Coal-tar products	11	70	81	63	15	736	116	68	118	79
5. Chemicals (general)	31	237	162	130	15	523	68	182	243	197
6. Drugs and pharmaceutical preps.	85	429	41	126	22	48	10	175	60	173
7. Toilet preps. and perfumery	82	262	—	89	31	—	—	148	—	148
8. Explosives and fireworks	224	450	5 149	444	22	2 299	1 144	149	3 100	249
9. Paint and varnish	52	126	350	57	35	673	278	105	800	109
10. Soap, candles and glycerine	44	631	269	120	9	611	43	137	322	149
11. Polishes	51	—	—	51	—	—	—	73	—	73
12. Ink	38	91	80	50	42	211	88	88	150	89
13. Mineral oil refining	—	718	505	618	—	—	70	1 075	771	933
14. Oils and greases	30	82	55	34	42	183	67	65	57	66
15. Seed crushing and oil refining	40	90	245	156	20	613	272	83	258	172
16. Glue, gum, paste and allied trades	30	115	111	63	27	370	97	73	133	84
17. Plastics materials	28	178	302	202	10	1 079	170	89	483	322
Total	55	258	230	117	23	418	89	137	293	162

V. *Metal manufacture*										
1. Blast furnaces	9	345	555	524	2	6 167	161	280	480	459
2. Iron and steel (melting and rolling)	86	367	749	432	14	871	204	189	745	435
3. Iron foundries	85	505	387	115	19	455	77	78	348	88
4. Steel sheets	114	330	606	548	20	532	184	240	658	587
5. Tinplate	58	101	376	349	16	648	372	100	388	364
6. Wrought iron and steel tubes	57	471	583	216	11	1 023	124	107	638	216
7. Non-ferrous metals (smelting, rolling, etc.)	73	317	384	177	21	526	121	146	445	200
Total	80	376	575	219	16	719	153	114	583	213
VI. *Engineering, shipbuilding and electrical goods*										
1. Shipbuilding and repairing	229	—	1 284	251	18	561	—	138	764	150
2. Marine engineering	245	910	1 053	432	25	430	116	207	800	293
3. Machine tools	75	403	219	103	31	292	54	75	205	94
4. Textile machinery and accessories	87	929	345	126	13	397	37	86	264	92
5. Small arms	220	—	—	220	—	—	—	145	—	145
6. Mechanical handling equipment	106	545	348	126	22	328	64	114	267	117
7. Printing and bookbinding machinery	101	581	188	123	39	186	32	105	207	116
8. Mechanical engineering (general)	94	420	326	139	26	347	78	101	307	124
9. Electrical engineering (general)	129	636	608	214	21	471	96	125	566	180
10. Electrical wires and cables	174	710	445	481	29	256	63	480	450	471
11. Radio and telecommunications	309	396	823	400	39	266	208	193	588	262
12. Batteries	86	679	—	254	13	—	—	209	—	209
13. Electric lighting, accessories and fittings	76	137	—	80	55	—	—	59	—	59
Total	128	528	450	181	27	352	85	116	390	144
VII. *Vehicles*										
1. Motor vehicles and cycles (parts)	106	1 583	635	224	8	599	40	182	627	195
2. Motor vehicles and cycles (complete)	260	2 818	791	575	19	304	28	481	697	527
3. Aircraft manufacture and repair	311	1 213	813	509	27	261	67	451	683	457
4. Railway locomotive shops and locomotive manufacturing	35	2 373	237	214	3	677	10	110	135	113
5. Railway carriages, wagons and trams	44	1 942	—	135	2	—	—	75	—	75
Total	105	1 754	570	255	8	543	32	188	493	202

Table III (*continued*)

Industrial order	Average number of operatives per establishment: Shift-work ratio: Zero (1)	1–35 % (2)	Over 35 % (3)	All estabs. (4)	Comparative ratios: Zero/Rest (%) (5)	> 35 %/Zero (%) (6)	> 35 %/1–35 % (%) (7)	Average net output per establishment. Shift-work ratio: 0–35 % (£000) (8)	> 35 % (£000) (9)	All (£000) (10)
VIII. *Metals goods not elsewhere specified*										
1. Tools	61	379	330	80	17	541	87	54	220	56
2. Cutlery	60	435	—	73	14	—	—	76	—	76
3. Chain, nail, screw and misc. forgings	76	361	322	104	22	424	89	70	303	82
4. Wire and wire manufacture	47	202	210	99	23	447	104	63	219	97
5. Hardware, hollow-ware, metal furniture, etc.	58	283	192	72	24	331	68	49	152	53
6. Brass manufacture	60	371	127	68	20	212	34	56	120	56
7. Needles, pins, fish-hooks and metal smallwares	87	285	200	107	31	230	70	64	100	64
Total	62	302	225	81	23	363	75	56	204	63
IX. *Precision instruments, jewellery, etc., scientific, surgical and photographic instruments, etc.*										
1. Scientific, surgical and photographic instruments	68	725	—	79	9	—	—	—	—	62
2. Watch and clock	72	613	—	112	12	—	—	—	—	78
3. Jewellery and plate	17	—	—	17	—	—	—	—	—	31
4. Musical instruments	149	—	—	149	—	—	—	—	—	44
5. Precious metals refining	159	128	40	143	15	25	31	—	3950	272
Total	62	538	40	72	12	65	7	—	37800	58

X. *Textiles*										
1. Cotton spinning and doubling	193	369	287	218	56	149	78	146	158	147
2. Cotton weaving	122	251	220	137	51	180	88	87	156	90
3. Woollen and worsted	95	247	163	116	42	172	66	80	122	82
4. Rayon, nylon, etc., and silk production	—	519	1922	1641	—	—	370	450	2869	2385
5. Rayon, nylon, etc., and silk weaving	100	224	201	132	47	201	90	79	139	88
6. Linen and soft hemp	106	488	—	146	22	—	—	77	—	77
7. Jute	148	566	222	227	31	150	39	113	120	114
8. Hosiery and other knitted goods	66	181	170	96	37	258	94	54	193	59
9. Lace	38	66	59	44	58	155	89	37	60	38
10. Carpets	145	464	250	193	33	172	54	115	167	117
11. Narrow fabrics	77	176	127	85	48	165	72	54	57	54
12. Canvas goods and sacks	41	—	—	41	—	—	—	27	—	27
13. Made-up household textiles	36	—	—	36	—	—	—	25	—	25
14. Textile finishing	72	226	279	100	30	388	123	71	236	77
15. Asbestos	110	518	146	192	24	133	28	242	200	241
16. Flock and rag	31	67	35	35	51	113	52	37	40	38
Total	96	237	292	124	38	304	123	79	293	89
XI. *Leather, leather goods*										
1. Leather (tanning and dressing)	60	139	—	63	43	—	—	56	—	56
2. Fellmongery	34	—	—	34	—	—	—	—	—	—
3. Leather goods	43	—	—	43	—	—	—	21	—	21
4. Fur	32	125	—	33	26	—	—	23	—	23
Total	48	137	—	49	35	—	—	36	—	36
XII. *Clothing*										
1. Tailoring, dressmaking, etc.	60	—	—	60	—	—	—	26	—	26
2. Hats, caps and millinery	49	—	—	49	—	—	—	25	—	25
3. Glove	48	—	—	48	—	—	—	22	—	22
4. Umbrella and walking stick	34	305	—	43	11	—	—	22	—	22
5. Boot and shoe	98	469	—	100	21	—	—	18	—	18
Total	65	415	—	65	16	—	—	58	—	58
								31	—	31

Table III (*continued*)

Industrial order	Average number of operatives per establishment: Shift-work ratio: Zero (1)	1–35 % (2)	Over 35 % (3)	All estabs. (4)	Comparative ratios: Zero/Rest (%) (5)	> 35 %/Zero (%) (6)	> 35 %/1–35 % (%) (7)	Average net output per establishment. Shift-work ratio: 0–35 % (£000) (8)	> 35 % (£000) (9)	All (£000) (10)
XIII. *Food, drink and tobacco*										
1. Grain milling	23	92	80	69	27	348	87	66	105	86
2. Bread and flour confectionery	38	144	91	54	36	239	63	27	85	37
3. Biscuit	260	501	326	275	74	125	65	175	256	187
4. Bacon curing and sausage	49	255	—	50	19	—	—	38	—	38
5. Preserved meat	199	—	—	199	—	—	—	188	—	188
6. Milk products	62	196	133	67	41	215	68	51	107	53
7. Ice cream	58	—	477	75	12	822	—	71	567	92
8. Sugar and glucose	59	188	554	359	12	939	295	138	541	370
9. Cocoa, chocolate and sugar confectionery	119	1 101	299	167	13	251	27	126	450	129
10. Preserved fruit and vegetables	105	772	216	116	22	206	28	81	167	83
11. Margarine	45	237	696	145	8	1 547	294	54	1 000	180
12. Fish curing	25	341	—	29	7	—	—	16	—	16
13. Cattle, dog and poultry foods	31	39	212	58	19	684	544	34	297	74
14. Vinegar and other condiments	46	—	—	46	—	—	—	73	—	73
15. Starch	75	164	119	108	57	159	73	127	113	121
16. Ice	41	42	14	33	137	34	33	45	—	31
17. Misc. preserved foods	61	247	140	68	36	230	57	70	—	69
18. Tea blending and coffee roasting	45	172	—	48	26	—	—	57	—	57
19. Brewing and malting	70	216	26	90	34	37	12	137	25	137
20. Wholesale bottling	41	959	1 008	47	4	2 459	105	69	1 650	76
21. Spirit distilling	17	48	52	42	34	306	108	78	63	71
22. Spirit rectifying and compounding	75	75	—	77	100	—	—	286	—	286
23. Soft drinks, British wines and cider	20	493	—	21	4	—	—	33	—	33
24. Tobacco	364	—	—	364	—	—	—	621	—	621
Total	63	198	128	77	41	203	65	72	137	79

XIV. *Manufacture of wood and cork*										
1. Timber	40	214	137	42	23	343	64	27	138	28
2. Furniture and upholstery	56	468	408	58	12	729	87	38	250	38
3. Soft furnishings	48	—	—	48	—	—	—	29	—	29
4. Shop and office fittings	48	167	141	50	30	294	84	38	100	38
5. Wooden containers and baskets	45	38	150	46	35	333	395	26	75	27
Total	47	254	163	49	22	347	64	31	139	32
XV. *Paper and printing*										
1. Paper and board	63	230	302	230	22	479	131	126	511	371
2. Wallpaper	145	—	—	145	—	—	—	116	—	116
3. Cardboard box, carton and fibrewood packing case	86	410	259	97	24	301	63	78	367	82
4. Manufactured stationery, paper bag, etc.	85	595	247	104	19	291	42	96	378	103
5. Newspaper and periodical printing and publishing	70	353	—	103	20	—	—	160	—	160
6. Printing, publishing, bookbinding, engraving, etc.	52	1 256	—	54	4	—	—	39	—	39
Total	61	391	298	79	18	489	76	67	501	86
XVI. *Other manufacturing industries*										
1. Rubber	72	483	532	252	14	739	110	164	606	233
2. Linoleum, leathercloth and allied trades	65	639	1 142	339	9	1 757	179	310	1 000	352
3. Brushes and brooms	53	305	—	54	17	—	—	34	—	34
4. Toys and games	97	222	147	104	45	152	66	55	100	56
5. Plastic goods and fancy articles	40	137	121	60	30	303	88	32	76	35
Total	60	344	383	123	17	638	111	75	405	98

INDEX